D1564251

# ❧ MARK'S OTHER GOSPEL ❧

Rethinking Morton Smith's
Controversial Discovery

Studies in Christianity and Judaism /
Études sur le christianisme et le judaïsme : 15

Studies in Christianity and Judaism / Études sur le christianisme et le judaïsme
publishes monographs on Christianity and Judaism in the last two centuries before
the common era and the first six centuries of the common era, with a special interest in studies of their interrelationship or the cultural and social context in which
they developed.

Studies in Christianity and Judaism /
Études sur le christianisme et le judaïsme : 15

# ⊰ MARK'S OTHER GOSPEL ⊱

## Rethinking Morton Smith's
## Controversial Discovery

### Scott G. Brown

Published for the Canadian Corporation for Studies in Religion/
Corporation Canadienne des Sciences Religieuses
by Wilfrid Laurier University Press
2005

This book has been published with the help of a grant from the Canadian Federation for the Humanities and Social Sciences, through the Aid to Scholarly Publications Programme, using funds provided by the Social Sciences and Humanities Research Council of Canada. We acknowledge the financial support of the Government of Canada through the Book Publishing Industry Development Program for our publishing activities. We acknowledge the Government of Ontario through the Ontario Media Development Corporation's Ontario Book Initiative.

Library and Archives Canada Cataloguing in Publication

Brown, Scott G. (Scott Gregory), 1966–
    Mark's other gospel : rethinking Morton Smith's controversial discovery / Scott G. Brown.

(Studies in Christianity and Judaism = Études sur le christianisme et le judaïsm ESCJ ; 15).
Includes bibliographical references and indexes.
ISBN 0-88920-461-6

1. Secret Gospel according to Mark.  I. Canadian Corporation for Studies in Religion
II. Title.  III. Series: Studies in Christianity and Judaism ; 15.

BS2860.S42B76 2005                     229´.8                     C2005-901621-3

Cover design by Leslie Macredie. Cover image: St. Mark at his desk, from the Gospel of St. Mark (vellum) by French School (9th century), Ebbo Gospels (816–35) Ms 1 fol. 60v. Courtesy of Bibliotheque Municipale, Epernay, France/Giraudon/Bridgeman Art Library.

Text design by Catharine Bonas-Taylor.

Excerpts from *Clement of Alexandria and a Secret Gospel of Mark* by Morton Smith reprinted by permission of the publisher from CLEMENT OF ALEXANDRIA AND A SECRET GOSPEL OF MARK by Morton Smith, pp. 446–48, 450, 452. Cambridge, MA: Harvard University Press, Copyright ©1973 by the President and Fellows of Harvard College.

Printed in Canada

Order from:
Wilfrid Laurier University Press
Wilfrid Laurier University
Waterloo, Ontario, Canada  N2L 3C5
www.wlupress.wlu.ca

For my parents,
Judy and Doug, Eric and Claire

# ⇥ Contents ⇤

# ⊰ Acknowledgments ⊱

A number of people contributed in important ways to the production of this book. Above all, I want to thank my family for all the encouragement and support they gave me. Without their patience and generosity, this book would never have come about.

I am also indebted to numerous scholars and friends. When this book was still a dissertation, my supervisor, Leif Vaage, read through the manuscript three times, offering insightful feedback on practically every page; his thoroughness and high standards made this a much better work. Michel Desjardins read the dissertation manuscript twice and corrected more scribal errors than I care to admit. Schuyler Brown and John Kloppenborg took turns supervising me during the period before my general exams. I want to thank the former for directing me to a form of biblical scholarship that is theoretically intelligible; the latter, for directing me away from thesis topics that would never have been as interesting as this one.

I am likewise indebted to the series editor, Peter Richardson, under whose guidance this book lost most of the trappings of a dissertation. Peter and the staff at Wilfrid Laurier University Press were easy to work with and very accommodating of my concerns. My work has also benefited greatly from my ongoing correspondence with Charles W. Hedrick and from the insightful comments of the two anonymous appraisers for the Aid to Scholarly Publications Programme.

Other scholars whom I have not yet had the pleasure to meet took the time to reflect on my work or answer my inquiries and send me materials. I will mention them in roughly the order in which I corresponded with them. Quentin Quesnell amiably and generously assisted my investigation by clarifying issues pertaining to his article on longer Mark and offering feedback on the finished dissertation. Shawn Eyer provided me with copies of some materials I could not locate. Andrew Criddle offered me detailed information about the methodology he employed in his article. And Marvin Meyer took on the role of external reviewer for my dissertation late in 1998. Many more scholars offered me their insights after I defended my dissertation in February 1999, and their assistance helped shape this revised and updated version. Edward C. Hobbs thoughtfully replied to numerous inquiries and gave me a different perspective on various scholarly and unscholarly exchanges. Shaye Cohen, Hershel Shanks, Thomas Talley, Annewies van den Hoek, Glenn Bowman, and Charles E. Murgia likewise shed light on matters that were inaccessible to me. And it has been my pleasure to correspond with William M. Calder III and John Dart, from whom I learned some interesting facts about Morton Smith. Although reconstructing the past from scraps of evidence is the standard method of the historian, it is no substitute for asking people direct questions.

My interest in the longer Gospel of Mark began about a year after Dr. Smith's death. But I still wish to acknowledge the enormous contribution that his commentary on the *Letter to Theodore* made to my research.

# ⊰ Preface ⊱

Afew of my conventions require explanation. Most readers are struck by my aversion to the title the Secret Gospel of Mark. This title is a translation of the words *mystikon euangelion*, which Clement of Alexandria used in his *Letter to Theodore* to describe a longer version of Mark's gospel that was used only in Alexandria (II.6, 12). I deliberately avoid using that translation as a title because I consider it not only incorrect but also misleading. A "mystic gospel" is not a concealed gospel but a gospel that contains concealed meanings. Unfortunately, the English word *mystic* does not have the same connotations as the Greek word upon which it is based, and I could not think of a better term. So I settled on the bland expression "the longer Gospel of Mark," which is a description that was often used by Morton Smith, the man who discovered the letter. Clement's expression *mystikon euangelion* is actually not the title for this gospel but only one of two descriptive phrases he used to distinguish this edition of Mark from the more familiar, canonical gospel. I likewise use a variety of phrases to denote the longer gospel, such as longer Mark, the longer text, the mystic gospel, and the amplified gospel. Perhaps the best description is Clement's own expression "a more spiritual gospel," by which he meant a gospel that concentrates on the interior, symbolic significance ("spirit") of the external narrative ("body"). When relating the positions of scholars who think of this text as a secret gospel, I sometimes put *secret* in quotation marks in order to indicate my rejection of this characterization. I also use the phrase "the Markan gospel" as a way of referring to the contents that canonical Mark and longer Mark have in common, that is, to the literary context in which the distinctive longer text materials existed.

Although I intend to demonstrate that Mark wrote both gospels, I use the cumbersome phrase "the author of the longer gospel" in order not to

---

Notes to preface start on page 239

prejudice my argument. When I wrote my dissertation, I did not consider the question of authorship to be important to my literary-critical analysis. When I started rewriting my dissertation for publication as a book, I decided to investigate this question, motivated by the reality that the matter of authorship would preoccupy my readers. I was surprised to discover that my literary-critical observations could answer this historical question.

Readers unfamiliar with Clement of Alexandria may be confused by my references to his gnosis. When I use the terms *gnosis* and *gnostic* in connection with Clement's Alexandrian theology, I am referring to something other than speculative theories about the origins of the universe and dualistic myths of descent into matter. For Clement, gnosis determines one's spiritual progression toward God, but not in the sense of the return of a divine being to the realm from which it had fallen. Clement subscribed to the gnostic mythology that Jesus (the Word) descended to impart to a select few a saving gnosis that would permit their eventual deification and perfect, mystic contemplation of God, through education and instruction in secret traditions. He also thought that this progressive self-deification would be completed after death. But in contrast to most gnostics, Clement did not perceive any *innate* differences among Christians, only acquired differences in their stages of perfection, which he hoped would not be permanent.[1]

The Greek transcription of the *Letter to Theodore* used in this book is from Morton Smith's scholarly book on longer Mark but follows the corrections made in the commentary section.[2] The Roman numerals refer to the page of the manuscript. Numeral "I" refers to folio 1 recto, "II" to folio 1 verso, and "III" to folio 2 recto. The numbers following these Roman numerals refer to the line number. The line divisions given are not exactly those of the manuscript, for it proved simpler not to split up individual words at the line divisions, particularly in English translation. References to Clement's other writings use Roman numerals in the conventional way, to refer to book divisions within a larger book. For example, *Strom.* I.11.50.1 refers to *Stromateis* Book One, chapter 11, paragraph 50 (counted from the beginning of a book, not from the beginning of that chapter), section ("verse") 1. Likewise, *Prot.* 12.120.1–2 refers to *Protrepticus* chapter 12 (it is in one book), paragraph 120 (from the very beginning), sections 1 and 2. And *Qds* 5.1 refers to *Quis dives salvetur?* paragraph 5, section 1. (In the standard text of Clement's works by Otto Stählin, the paragraph and section numbers are given on the right side of the page. The line numbers on the left side are for his index volume, where he referred to the volume, page, and line of his books; Smith adopted that convention.)

The English translation of the letter is from the same book; I revised Smith's wording in a few places where I dispute the sense and consider the difference to be important.[3] The gospel citations are my literal translations, intended to preserve the idiosyncrasies of their Markan phraseology. When referring to particular sentences within these two quotations from the longer gospel, I use the versification contained in the Scholars Version,[4] along with its division of these verses into SGM 1 and 2 (Secret Gospel of Mark 1 and 2), which I have changed to LGM 1 and 2 (longer Gospel of Mark). LGM 1 denotes the story about the raising and instruction of the dead man in Bethany, whereas LGM 2 denotes the two sentences describing Jesus' refusal to receive the man's sister, his mother, and Salome in Jericho. I further subdivided LGM 1 into 1a and 1b so that the raising of the young man can be referred to as 1a and the scene of the young man's instruction in the mystery of the kingdom of God can be referred to as 1b. The partition at 1:10 is not intended to be precise (LGM 1:9 is transitional, so really belongs to both parts) and is used merely as a convenient shorthand. The author of longer Mark might have considered the division in LGM 1 to come at 1:11 since, in Markan usage, the historical present that occurs there usually signifies a shift to new material.

Biblical quotations in this book are based on the RSV translation, which I occasionally revised in order to give a more literal rendering. Unless otherwise indicated, quotations from Clement's undisputed writings are from Wilson's translation in ANCL 4, 12, 22, and 24, except for quotations from Books One to Three of the *Stromateis*, which are from the recent translation by John Ferguson, and quotations from *Quis dives salvetur?* which are from the translation by G.W. Butterworth.

Some of the changes I made in the process of converting my dissertation into a book are worth noting. Following my editor's advice, I eliminated most peripheral footnote discussions and half-page notes documenting every work that expressed the same idea over the last century. Where many others have expressed the same idea before me, I now note only discussions that are worth looking up. Also gone is the separate chapter on the history of scholarship, which was not essential to this undertaking. In its place is a general overview of the standard ways in which scholars responded to the new evidence. Various sections, particularly in the second chapter, have been rewritten in order to address research published between the fall of 1998 (when my dissertation was completed) and the middle of 2003. The third chapter is mostly new and is directed against the most popular conservative and liberal conceptions of the longer gospel. The remaining chapters are still close to their original formats, except the concluding chapter, which now provides a more thorough summary of my conclusions, an argument for Mark's authorship, and a discussion of longer Mark's relevance to the study of Christian origins.

The bibliography has been restructured so that academic opinions on the longer Gospel of Mark are easier to locate. Most of the secondary literature has been produced by people who have not conducted original research on this subject, so I certainly do not commend all of these discussions. The quality and accuracy of these discussions can vary considerably according to the author's research and expertise, so it is best to seek out the most knowledgeable opinions on the relevant subjects: Alexandrian Christianity (Annewies van den Hoek, Birger A. Pearson, A.F.J. Klijn, C. Wilfred Griggs, Attila Jakab); Clement (Claude Mondésert, R.P.C. Hanson, André Méhat, Salvatore Lilla, John Ferguson, Jean-Daniel Kaestli, Alain Le Boulluec, Guy G. Stroumsa, Annewies van den Hoek, Arkadi Choufrine); patristic traditions about the evangelist Mark (Terence Y. Mullins, John J. Gunther, C. Clifton Black); traditions about Salome (Richard Bauckham); statistical analysis (Andrew Criddle); Clement's style (Morton Smith); Mark's style (David Peabody); syntax criticism (Raymond A. Martin); form and tradition criticism (Morton Smith, Reginald Fuller, Helmut Koester); the manuscript tradition in the second century (Helmut Koester, Frederik Wisse, Eldon Jay Epp, Larry Hurtado, David C. Parker). Most articles, chapters, and books on longer Mark are worth reading (critically). I recommend those by Richard Bauckham, F.F. Bruce, Shawn Eyer, Robert H. Gundry (the excursus in his commentary on Mark), Charles W. Hedrick, Theodore W. Jennings, Jr., Frank Kermode, Marvin W. Meyer, Winsome Munro, Frans Neirynck, Eckhard Rau, Hans-Martin Schenke, Philip Sellew, Morton Smith, Guy G. Stroumsa, Walter Wink, and Wilhelm H. Wuellner (ed.). Bear in mind that when scholars form opinions on non-canonical gospels they rarely stray from their religious commitments. Nowhere is this more obvious than in the assessments of longer Mark that appear in book reviews, surveys of extracanonical gospel evidence (esp. books on the historical Jesus), and commentaries on the Gospel of Mark. The opinions that scholars express in these forums often reveal little more than the religious and philosophical predilections of the authors and tend to be as predictable and presumptuous as the opinions expressed by political pundits. In my opinion, the most productive approach to the secondary literature is to read the most carefully researched scholarship written on *other* subjects related to longer Mark. I myself learned the most about the *Letter to Theodore* and the longer Gospel of Mark indirectly from books and articles on Clement and canonical Mark.

# ⊰ List of Abbreviations ⊱

This list supplements the abbreviations in Patrick H. Alexander et al., *The SBL Handbook of Style*, 121–52.

| | |
|---|---|
| AAR-SBL | American Academy of Religion-Society of Biblical Literature |
| AARSR | American Academy of Religion Studies in Religion |
| ANCL | Ante-Nicene Christian Library |
| *CA* | *Clement of Alexandria and a Secret Gospel of Mark* (Cambridge: Harvard University Press, 1973) |
| *CSR* | *Christian Scholar's Review* |
| *CT* | *Christianity Today* |
| *CTSR* | *Chicago Theological Seminary Register* |
| *Ecl.* | *Eclogae propheticae* |
| *Exc. ex Theod.* | *Excerpta ex Theodoto* |
| *FORUM* | *Foundations & Facets Forum* |
| JBLMS | Journal of Biblical Literature Monograph Series |
| *JHC* | *Journal of Higher Criticism* |
| KJV | King James Version |
| L | Special Luke |
| LGM 1 | Longer Gospel of Mark 1 (= Clement's *Letter to Theodore* II.23–III.11) |
| LGM 2 | Longer Gospel of Mark 2 (= Clement's *Letter to Theodore* III.14–16) |
| *LM* | *Longer Mark: Forgery, Interpolation, or Old Tradition?* Protocol of the Eighteenth Colloquy: 7 December 1975, |

|  | ed. by Wilhelm H. Wuellner (Berkeley: Center for Hermeneutical Studies in Hellenistic and Modern Culture, 1976) |
|---|---|
| M | Special Matthew |
| NEB | New English Bible |
| NRSV | New Revised Standard Version |
| *Paed.* | *Paedagogus* |
| *Prot.* | *Protrepticus* |
| Q | Q (the Sayings Gospel or the synoptic sayings source) |
| *Qds* | *Quis dives salvetur?* |
| RSV | Revised Standard Version |
| SFSHJ | South Florida Studies in the History of Judaism |
| *SG* | *The Secret Gospel: The Discovery and Interpretation of the Secret Gospel According to Mark* (New York: Harper and Row, 1973) |
| SGM | Secret Gospel of Mark |
| *Strom.* | *Stromateis* |
| TWAS | Twayne's World Authors Series |

# ⇥ The *Letter to Theodore* ⇤

**I.1** From the letters of the most holy Clement, the author of the *Stromateis*. To Theodore.

**I.2** You did well in silencing the unspeakable teachings of the Carpocratians.

**I.3** For these are the "wandering stars" referred to in the prophecy, who wander from the

**I.4** narrow road of the commandments into a boundless abyss of the carnal and bodily sins.

**I.5** For, priding themselves in knowledge, as they say, "of the deep things of Satan," they do not know that they are casting themselves away into

**I.6** "the nether world of the darkness" of falsity, and, boasting

**I.7** that they are free, they have become slaves of servile desires. Such men

**I.8** are to be opposed in all ways and altogether. For, even if they should say something true, one who

**I.9** loves the truth should not, even so, agree with them. For not all true things are the truth, nor

**I.1** + ἐκ τῶν ἐπιστολῶν τοῦ ἁγιωτά–του Κλήμεντος τοῦ στρωματέως· Θεοδώρῳ.

**I.2** καλῶς ἐποίησας ἐπιστομίσας τὰς ἀρρήτους διδασκαλίας τῶν Καρποκρατιανῶν.

**I.3** οὗτοι γὰρ οἱ προφητευθέντες "ἀστέρες πλανῆται," οἱ ἀπὸ τῆς στενῆς τῶν ἐντολῶν

**I.4** ὁδοῦ εἰς ἀπέρατον ἄβυσσον πλανώμενοι τῶν σαρκικῶν καὶ ἐνσωμάτων ἁμαρτιῶν.

**I.5** πεφυσιωμένοι γὰρ εἰς γνῶσιν, ὡς λέγουσιν, "τῶν βαθέων τοῦ Σατανᾶ," λανθάνουσιν εἰς

**I.6** "τὸν ζόφον τοῦ σκότους," τοῦ ψεύδους, ἑαυτοὺς ἀπορρίπτοντες· καὶ καυχώμενοι

**I.7** ἐλευθέρους εἶναι, δοῦλοι γεγόνασιν ἀνδραποδώδων ἐπιθυμιῶν. τούτοις οὖν

**I.8** ἀντιστατέον πάντη τε καὶ πάντως, εἰ γὰρ καί τι ἀληθὲς λέγοιεν οὐδ' οὕτω

**I.9** συμφωνοίη ἂν αὐτοῖς ὁ τῆς ἀληθείας ἐραστής. οὐδὲ γὰρ πάντα τἀληθῆ ἀλήθεια. οὐδὲ

I.10 should that truth which merely seems true according to human opinions be preferred to the

I.11 true truth, that according to the faith. Now of the things they keep saying about the divinely inspired

I.12 Gospel according to Mark, some are altogether falsifications, and others, even if they do contain some true

I.13 elements, nevertheless are not reported truly. For the true things being mixed

I.14 with inventions, are falsified, so that, as the saying goes, even the

I.15 salt loses its savor. As for Mark, then, during Peter's stay in Rome

I.16 he wrote an account of the Lord's doings, not, however, declaring all of them, nor yet hinting at the

I.17 mystic[1] ones, but selecting what he thought most useful for increasing the

I.18 faith of those who were being instructed. But when Peter died a martyr, Mark came

I.19 over to Alexandria, bringing both his own notes and those of Peter,

I.20 from which he transferred to his former book the things suitable to those studies which make for[2] progress

I.21 toward knowledge. Thus he composed a more spiritual

I.10 τὴν κατὰ τὰς ἀνθρωπίνας δόξας φαινομένην ἀλήθειαν προκριτέον τῆς

I.11 ἀληθοῦς ἀληθείας τῆς κατὰ τὴν πίστιν. τῶν τοίνυν θρυλουμένων περὶ τοῦ θεοπνεύστου

I.12 κατὰ Μᾶρκον εὐαγγελίου, τὰ μὲν ψεύδεται παντελῶς, τὰ δέ, εἰ καὶ ἀληθῆ τινα

I.13 περιέχει, οὐδ᾽ οὕτως ἀληθῶς παραδίδοται, συγκεκραμένα γὰρ τἀληθῆ

I.14 τοῖς πλάσμασι παραχαράσσεται ὥστε—τοῦτο δὴ τὸ λεγόμενον—"καὶ τὸ

I.15 ἅλας μωρανθῆναι." ὁ γοῦν Μᾶρκος, κατὰ τὴν τοῦ Πέτρου ἐν Ῥώμῃ διατριβήν,

I.16 ἀνέγραψε τὰς πράξεις τοῦ Κυρίου, οὐ μέντοι πάσας ἐξαγγέλλων, οὐδὲ μὴν τὰς

I.17 μυστικὰς ὑποσημαίνων ἀλλ᾽ ἐκλεγόμενος ἃς χρησιμωτάτας ἐνόμισε πρὸς

I.18 αὔξησιν τῆς τῶν κατηχουμένων πίστεως. τοῦ δὲ Πέτρου μαρτυρήσαντος, παρῆλθεν

I.19 εἰς Ἀλεξάνδρειαν ὁ Μᾶρκος, κομίζων καὶ τὰ [τ] αὐτοῦ καὶ τὰ τοῦ Πέτρου

I.20 ὑπομνήματα ἐξ ὧν μεταφέρων εἰς τὸ πρῶτον αὐτοῦ βιβλίον τὰ τοῖς προκόπτουσι

I.21 περὶ τὴν γνῶσιν κατάλληλα συνέταξε πνευματικώτερον

---

1 Smith: "secret."

2 Smith's translation has "to whatever makes for progress toward knowledge." I replaced that phrase with the rendition Smith gave in *CA*, 91.

I.22 Gospel for the use of those who were being perfected. Nevertheless, he yet did not divulge the things not to be uttered,

I.23 nor did he write down the hierophantic teaching of

I.24 the Lord, but to the stories already written he added yet others and, moreover,

**I.25** brought in certain traditions[3] of which he knew the interpretation would, as a mystagogue, lead the hearers into the

I.26 innermost sanctuary of that truth hidden by seven veils. Thus, in sum,

I.27 he prepared matters, neither grudgingly nor incautiously, in my opinion, and,

I.28 dying, he left his composition to the church

**II.1** in Alexandria, where it even yet is very securely kept,[4] being read

II.2 only to those who are being initiated into the great mysteries. But since the

II.3 foul demons are always devising destruction for the race of men,

II.4 Carpocrates, instructed by them and using deceitful arts, so enslaved

**II.5** a certain presbyter of the church in Alexandria

I.22 εὐαγγέλιον εἰς τὴν τῶν τελειου–μένων χρῆσιν οὐδέπω ὅμως αὐτὰ τὰ ἀπόρρητα

I.23 ἐξωρχήσατο, οὐδὲ κατέγραψε τὴν ἱεροφαντικὴν διδασκαλίαν τοῦ

I.24 Κυρίου, ἀλλὰ ταῖς προγεγραμ–μέναις πράξεσιν ἐπιθεὶς καὶ ἄλλας, ἔτι

I.25 προσεπήγαγε λόγιά τινα ὧν ἠπίστατο τὴν ἐξήγησιν μυστα–γωγήσειν τοὺς ἀκροατὰς

I.26 εἰς τὸ ἄδυτον τῆς ἑπτάκις κεκαλυμμένης ἀληθείας. οὕτως οὖν

I.27 προπαρεσκεύασεν, οὐ φθονερῶς οὐδ' ἀπροφυλάκτως, ὡς ἐγὼ οἶμαι. καὶ

I.28 ἀποθήσκων κατέλιπε τὸ αὐτοῦ σύγγραμμα τῇ ἐκκλησίᾳ τῇ

**II.1** ἐν Ἀλεξανδρείᾳ ὅπου εἰσέτι νῦν ἀσφαλῶς εὖ μάλα τηρεῖται, ἀναγινωσκόμενον

II.2 πρὸς αὐτοὺς μόνους τοὺς μυ–ουμένους τὰ μεγάλα μυστήρια. τῶν δὲ

II.3 μιαρῶν δαιμόνων ὄλεθρον τῷ τῶν ἀνθρώπων γένει πάντοτε μηχανώντων, ὁ

II.4 Καρποκράτης ὑπ' αὐτῶν διδαχ–θεὶς καὶ ἀπατηλοῖς τέχναις χρησάμενος,

**II.5** οὕτω πρεσβύτερόν τινα τῆς ἐν Ἀλεξανδρείᾳ ἐκκλησίας κατε–δούλωσεν

---

3 Smith: "sayings."

4 Or "most perfectly honoured," or perhaps "unerringly appropriated." Smith: "most carefully guarded."

II.6 that he got from him a copy of the mystic[5] Gospel, which he

II.7 both interpreted according to his blasphemous and carnal doctrine and,

II.8 moreover, polluted, mixing with the spotless and holy words utterly shameless

II.9 lies. From this mixture is drawn off the teaching of the Carpocratians.

II.10 To them, therefore, as I said above, one must never give way;

II.11 nor, when they put forward their falsifications, should one concede that it is Mark's

II.12 mystic Gospel,[6] but should even deny it on oath. For, "Not all

II.13 true things are to be said to all men." For this reason the Wisdom of God, through Solomon,

II.14 advises, "Answer the fool from his folly," teaching that

II.15 the light of the truth should be hidden from those who are mentally blind. Again

II.16 it says, "From him who has not shall be taken away," and, "Let the fool walk in darkness." But we

II.17 are "children of light," having been illuminated by "the day-spring" of the spirit

II.18 of the Lord "from on high," and "Where the Spirit of the Lord is," it says, "there is liberty," for "All

II.6 ὥστε παρ' αὐτοῦ ἐκόμισεν ἀπόγραφον τοῦ μυστικοῦ εὐαγγελίου, ὅ καὶ

II.7 ἐξηγήσατο κατὰ τὴν βλάσφη-μον καὶ σαρκικὴν αὐτοῦ δόξαν, ἔτι

II.8 δὲ καὶ ἐμίανε, ταῖς ἀχράντοις καὶ ἁγίαις λέξεσιν ἀναμιγνὺς ἀναιδέστατα

II.9 ψεύσματα. τοῦ δὲ κράματος τούτου ἐξαντλεῖται τὸ τῶν Καρποκρατιανῶν

II.10 δόγμα. τούτοις οὖν, καθὼς καὶ προείρηκα, οὐδέποτε εἰκτέον,

II.11 οὐδὲ προτείνουσιν αὐτοῖς τὰ κατεψευσμένα συγχωρητέον τοῦ Μάρκου

II.12 εἶναι τὸ μυστικὸν εὐαγγέλιον, ἀλλὰ καὶ μεθ' ὅρκου ἀρνητέον. "οὐ γὰρ ἅπασι πάντα

II.13 ἀληθῆ λεκτέον." διὰ τοῦτο ἡ σοφία τοῦ Θεοῦ διὰ Σολομῶν-τος

II.14 παραγγέλλει, "ἀποκρίνου τῷ μωρῷ ἐκ τῆς μωρίας αὐτοῦ," πρὸς τοὺς τυφλοὺς τὸν

II.15 νοῦν τὸ φῶς τῆς ἀληθείας δεῖν ἐπικρύπτεσθαι διδάσκουσα, αὐτίκα

II.16 φησί, "τοῦ δὲ μὴ ἔχοντος ἀρθήσεται," καὶ "ὁ μωρὸς ἐν σκότει πορευέσθω." ἡμεῖς

II.17 δὲ "υἱοὶ φωτός" ἐσμεν, πεφωτισ-μένοι τῇ ἐξ ὕψους ἀνατολῇ τοῦ πνεύματος

II.18 τοῦ Κυρίου. "οὗ δὲ τὸ πνεῦμα τοῦ Κυρίου," φησίν, "ἐκεῖ ἐλευ-θερία," "πάντα" γὰρ

---

5   Smith: "secret."
6   Smith: "that the secret Gospel is by Mark" Adapting C. Mondésert's translation (*CA*, 52: "c'est là l' 'Evangile mystique' de Marc").

II.19 things are pure to the pure." To you, therefore, I shall not hesitate to answer the questions you have asked,

II.20 refuting the falsifications by the very words of the Gospel.

II.21 For example, after "And they were in the road going up to Jerusalem," and what

II.22 follows, until "After three days he shall arise," the text[7] brings the following material word for word:

II.23 "And they come to Bethany. And there was there a certain woman whose brother of hers [*sic*]

II.24 had died. And coming, she prostrated before Jesus and says to him, 'Son

II.25 of David have mercy on me.' But the disciples rebuked her. And having become angry

II.26 Jesus went away with her into the garden where the tomb was. And

III.1 immediately was heard from the tomb a great cry. And approaching, Jesus

III.2 rolled the stone from the door of the tomb, and going in immediately where

III.3 the young man was, he stretched out the hand and raised him, having grasped

III.4 the hand. But the young man, having looked upon him, loved him and

III.5 began to beg him that he might be with him. And going out from

II.19 "καθαρὰ τοῖς καθαροῖς." σοὶ τοίνυν οὐκ ὀκνήσω τὰ ἠρωτη-μένα ἀποκρίνασθαι,

II.20 δι' αὐτῶν <τῶν> τοῦ εὐαγγελίου λέξεων τὰ κατεψευσμένα ἐλέγ-χων.

II.21 ἀμέλει μετὰ τὸ, "ἦσαν δὲ ἐν τῇ ὁδῷ ἀναβαίνοντες εἰς Ἱερο-σόλυμα," καὶ τὰ

II.22 ἑξῆς ἕως, "μετὰ τρεῖς ἡμέρας ἀναστήσεται," ὧδε ἐπιφέρει κατὰ λέξιν,

II.23 "καὶ ἔρχονται εἰς Βηθανίαν, καὶ ἦν ἐκεῖ μία γυνὴ ἧς ὁ ἀδελφὸς αὐτῆς

II.24 ἀπέθανεν· καὶ ἐλθοῦσα προσ-εκύνησε τὸν Ἰησοῦν καὶ λέγει αὐτῷ, υἱὲ

II.25 Δαβὶδ ἐλέησόν με. οἱ δὲ μαθη-ταὶ ἐπετίμησαν αὐτῇ· καὶ ὀργισθεὶς ὁ

II.26 Ἰησοῦς ἀπῆλθεν μετ' αὐτῆς εἰς τὸν κῆπον ὅπου ἦν τὸ μνη-μεῖον. καὶ

III.1 εὐθὺς ἠκούσθη ἐκ τοῦ μνη-μείου φωνὴ μεγάλη. καὶ προσ-ελθὼν ὁ Ἰησοῦς

III.2 ἀπεκύλισε τὸν λίθον ἀπὸ τῆς θύρας τοῦ μνημείου, καὶ εἰσελθὼν εὐθὺς ὅπου

III.3 ἦν ὁ νεανίσκος ἐξέτεινεν τὴν χεῖρα καὶ ἤγειρεν αὐτόν, κρατήσας

III.4 τῆς χειρός. ὁ δὲ νεανίσκος ἐμβλέψας αὐτῷ ἠγάπησεν αὐτὸν καὶ

III.5 ἤρξατο παρακαλεῖν αὐτὸν ἵνα μετ' αὐτοῦ ᾖ. καὶ ἐξελθόντες ἐκ

---

7  Smith: "secret Gospel."

III.6 the tomb they went into the house of the young man; for he was rich. And after

III.7 six days Jesus gave charge to him; and when it was evening the

III.8 young man comes to him donning a linen sheet upon his naked body, and

III.9 he remained with him that night; for Jesus was teaching him

III.10 the mystery of the kingdom of God. Now rising,

III.11 he returned from there to the other side of the Jordan." After these words follows the text, "And

III.12 James and John come to him," and all that

III.13 section. But "naked man with naked man," and the other things about which you wrote, are not

III.14 found. And after the words, "And he comes into Jericho," the text[8] adds only, "And

III.15 there were there the sister of the young man whom Jesus loved him [*sic*] and

III.16 his mother and Salome, and Jesus did not receive them."

III.17 But the many other things about which you wrote both seem to be and are falsifications.

III.18 Now the true explanation and that which accords with the true philosophy...

III.6 τοῦ μνημείου ἦλθον εἰς τὴν οἰκίαν τοῦ νεανίσκου· ἦν γὰρ πλούσιος. καὶ μεθ'

III.7 ἡμέρας ἓξ ἐπέταξεν αὐτῷ ὁ Ἰησοῦς· καὶ ὀψίας γενομένης ἔρχεται ὁ

III.8 νεανίσκος πρὸς αὐτὸν περι- βεβλημένος σινδόνα ἐπὶ γυμ- νοῦ καὶ

III.9 ἔμεινε σὺν αὐτῷ τὴν νύκτα ἐκείνην. ἐδίδασκε γὰρ αὐτὸν ὁ

III.10 Ἰησοῦς τὸ μυστήριον τῆς βασιλείας τοῦ Θεοῦ. ἐκεῖθεν δὲ ἀναστὰς

III.11 ἐπέστρεψεν εἰς τὸ πέραν τοῦ Ἰορδάνου." ἐπὶ μὲν τούτοις ἕπεται τὸ, "καὶ

III.12 προσπορεύονται αὐτῷ Ἰάκω- βος καὶ Ἰωάννης," καὶ πᾶσα ἡ

III.13 περικοπή. τὸ δὲ "γυμνὸς γυμνῷ" καὶ τἆλλα περὶ ὧν ἔγραψας οὐχ

III.14 εὑρίσκεται. μετὰ δὲ τό, "καὶ ἔρχεται εἰς Ἰεριχώ," ἐπάγει μόνον, "καὶ

III.15 ἦσαν ἐκεῖ ἡ ἀδελφὴ τοῦ νεανίσκου ὃν ἠγάπα αὐτὸν ὁ Ἰησοῦς καὶ

III.16 ἡ μήτηρ αὐτοῦ καὶ Σαλώμη, καὶ οὐκ ἀπεδέξατο αὐτὰς ὁ Ἰησοῦς."

III.17 τὰ δὲ ἄλλα τὰ πολλὰ ἃ ἔγραψας ψεύσματα καὶ φαίν- εται καὶ ἔστιν.

III.18 ἡ μὲν οὖν ἀληθὴς καὶ κατὰ τὴν ἀληθῆ φιλοσοφίαν ἐξή- γησις

---

8 Smith: "secret Gospel."

# Clement's Citations from the Longer Gospel

[**LGM 1a**: after Mark 10:32–34] [1] And they come to Bethany. And there was there a certain woman whose brother of hers had died. [2] And coming, she prostrated before Jesus and says to him, "Son of David have mercy on me." [3] But the disciples rebuked her. [4] And having become angry Jesus went away with her into the garden where the tomb was. [5] And immediately was heard from the tomb a great cry. [6] And approaching, Jesus rolled the stone from the door of the tomb, [7] and going in immediately where the young man was, he stretched out the hand and raised him, having grasped the hand. [8] But the young man, having looked upon him, loved him and began to beg him that he might be with him. [9] And going out from the tomb they went into the house of the young man; for he was rich. [**LGM 1b**] [10] And after six days Jesus gave charge to him; [11] and when it was evening the young man comes to him donning a linen sheet upon his naked body, [12] and he remained with him that night; for Jesus was teaching him the mystery of the kingdom of God.

[13] Now rising, he returned from there to the other side of the Jordan. (then Mark 10:35–45)

[**LGM 2**: expansion of Mark 10:46] [1] (And he comes to Jericho.) And there were there the sister of the young man whom Jesus loved him and his mother and Salome, [2] and Jesus did not receive them. (And as he was leaving Jericho, with his disciples and a great multitude, the son of Timaeus, Bartimaeus…)

[**LGM 1a**: after Mark 10:32–34] [1] καὶ ἔρχονται εἰς Βηθανίαν, καὶ ἦν ἐκεῖ μία γυνὴ ἧς ὁ ἀδελφὸς αὐτῆς ἀπέθανεν· [2] καὶ ἐλθοῦσα προσεκύνησε τὸν Ἰησοῦν καὶ λέγει αὐτῷ, υἱὲ Δαβὶδ ἐλέησόν με. [3] οἱ δὲ μαθηταὶ ἐπετίμησαν αὐτῇ· [4] καὶ ὀργισθεὶς ὁ Ἰησοῦς ἀπῆλθεν μετ' αὐτῆς εἰς τὸν κῆπον ὅπου ἦν τὸ μνημεῖον. [5] καὶ εὐθὺς ἠκούσθη ἐκ τοῦ μνημείου φωνὴ μεγάλη. [6] καὶ προσελθὼν ὁ Ἰησοῦς ἀπεκύλισε τὸν λίθον ἀπὸ τῆς θύρας τοῦ μνημείου, [7] καὶ εἰσελθὼν εὐθὺς ὅπου ἦν ὁ νεανίσκος ἐξέτεινεν τὴν χεῖρα καὶ ἤγειρεν αὐτόν, κρατήσας τῆς χειρός. [8] ὁ δὲ νεανίσκος ἐμβλέψας αὐτῷ ἠγάπησεν αὐτὸν καὶ ἤρξατο παρακαλεῖν αὐτὸν ἵνα μετ' αὐτοῦ ᾖ. [9] καὶ ἐξελθόντες ἐκ τοῦ μνημείου ἦλθον εἰς τὴν οἰκίαν τοῦ νεανίσκου· ἦν γὰρ πλούσιος. [10] [**LGM 1b**] [10] καὶ μεθ' ἡμέρας ἓξ ἐπέταξεν αὐτῷ ὁ Ἰησοῦς· [11] καὶ ὀψίας γενομένης ἔρχεται ὁ νεανίσκος πρὸς αὐτὸν περιβεβλημένος σινδόνα ἐπὶ γυμνοῦ [12] καὶ ἔμεινε σὺν αὐτῷ τὴν νύκτα ἐκείνην. ἐδίδασκε γὰρ αὐτὸν ὁ Ἰησοῦς τὸ μυστήριον τῆς βασιλείας τοῦ Θεοῦ.

[13] ἐκεῖθεν δὲ ἀναστὰς ἐπέστρεψεν εἰς τὸ πέραν τοῦ Ἰορδάνου. (then Mark 10:35–45)

[**LGM 2**: expansion of Mark 10:46] [1] (καὶ ἔρχεται εἰς Ἰεριχώ,) καὶ ἦσαν ἐκεῖ ἡ ἀδελφὴ τοῦ νεανίσκου ὃν ἠγάπα αὐτὸν ὁ Ἰησοῦς καὶ ἡ μήτηρ αὐτοῦ καὶ Σαλώμη, [2] καὶ οὐκ ἀπεδέξατο αὐτὰς ὁ Ἰησοῦς.

# ✄ PART I ✄

## Rethinking the Dominant Paradigms

# ⚛ 1 ⚛

# A Longer, Esoteric Version
# of Mark's Gospel

High up in the tower of the ancient desert monastery of Mar Saba, about twenty kilometres southeast of Jerusalem, is a small, dilapidated library where books and manuscripts centuries-old lie in various configurations under ever-deepening layers of dust. More like an attic than a library, it houses reading materials that long ago ceased to be of interest to the monks. Yet as we all know, one monk's junk is an historian's treasure, so it happened that in the summer of 1958, the late Professor Morton Smith of Columbia University arrived at the monastery with permission to catalogue the manuscripts. What he found in that little room changed the course of his career and opened one of the most opprobrious chapters in the history of New Testament scholarship.

Near the end of his three-week visit, Smith came across a copy of the 1646 edition of Isaac Voss's *Ignatius of Antioch: Genuine Letters of Saint Ignatius the Martyr*. On the blank end pages, scrawled in an eighteenth-century hand, was a Greek manuscript sporting the title "From the letters of the most holy Clement, the author of the *Stromateis*. To Theodore."[1] This previously unknown letter by a late-second-century church father relates a tradition about the apostle Mark's production of a second, expanded version of his gospel for the church in Alexandria. According to Clement, Mark wrote his first gospel in Rome for catechumens. But when he ventured to Alexandria following Peter's death, Mark brought with him "his own and Peter's notes" and from these transferred into his former writing "things suitable to those studies which make for progress toward knowledge" (*Letter to Theodore* I.15–21).[2] The additional passages consisted of mystic materials (I.17, 25–26) as well as other, ordinary stories like those in the first version (I.24). He thus created "a more spiritual gospel for the use of those who were being perfected"

Notes to chapter 1 start on page 239

(I.21–22). Upon his death, this gospel became the possession of the church in Alexandria, where even in Clement's day it was still "very securely kept" and was "being read only to those persons who were being initiated into the great mysteries" (II.1–2).

Clement of Alexandria's descriptions of the nature of the longer Gospel of Mark and of the manner of its composition are quite detailed. Since Clement was replying to a letter that has not been preserved (III.13, 17), his reasons for disclosing this information must be educed from his *Letter to Theodore*. The sequence of events leading up to Clement's reply is not easy to trace, but it appears that Theodore was involved in theological debates with followers of Carpocrates, a heterodox teacher of the early second century, and that these opponents supported their positions by quoting passages from this longer gospel. The fact that Theodore had already censured their teachings (I.2) suggests that he had some authority within his own church and that his theological opponents had either joined this congregation or were evangelizing there. Since Theodore was not acquainted with the longer text of Mark yet knew where to ask about it, we can suppose that they directed him to inquire in Alexandria for proof of this text's legitimacy or at least mentioned that it originated there. Thus Theodore wrote to Clement, reporting what he had heard about this gospel's contents and asking if there was any truth to what the Carpocratians were saying about the Gospel of Mark.

Clement opened his response by assuring Theodore that he was right to censure the Carpocratians, explaining that the things they had told him were at best half truths (I.2–15). Mark really did produce a longer version of his gospel, but it contained nothing that should not be set out in writing and certainly none of the unsavoury things that the Carpocratians had told him about (I.15–27). What happened was that Carpocrates used magic to coerce an elder of the Alexandrian church into making him a copy of this text, "which he both interpreted according to his blasphemous and carnal doctrine and, moreover, polluted, mixing with the spotless and holy words utterly shameless lies." Carpocrates based his teachings on this adulterated version of the expanded text (II.2–9). Because the Carpocratian gospel is a distortion of the truth, Theodore should respond to them in kind and assure them with an oath (presumably an oath declaring that this is what he learned from the church in Alexandria) that they do not possess "Mark's mystic gospel" (II.10–16).

In order to prove that none of the troubling phrases about which Theodore was concerned are found in the true mystic Gospel of Mark, Clement quoted "word for word" two of the passages that Theodore had asked him about, stating where they appear relative to the common text of

Mark. Following these citations, Clement ventured to offer "the true explanation and that which accords with the true philosophy…" (III.18). Here the manuscript ends, and we do not learn Clement's understanding of the theological truths conveyed by these passages.

The first passage Clement cited (II.23–III.11) is another version of the raising of Lazarus, which is inserted immediately before the request for positions of honour by James and John (II.21–22; III.11–13), which is to say, after Mark 10:34. This thirteen-verse story, which I call LGM 1 (longer Gospel of Mark 1), is written in Mark's style and contains none of the theological discourse found in the Johannine story, in fact, no direct speech by Jesus at all. The storyline is also different from the Johannine version in many obvious respects: In John, Jesus interacts with Lazarus, Mary, and Martha—three siblings whom Jesus knows and loves. In longer Mark, the dead man is not named; he is simply described as a young man, which likely means a man in his early twenties.[3] Neither he nor his sister are known to Jesus, and only one sister appears in the story—again, unnamed. Both accounts begin in a location called Bethany (John 10:40; 1:28; LGM 1:1). But whereas in John's gospel Jesus hears about the illness from messengers, tarries for two days in Peraea waiting for Lazarus to die, and then journeys for four more days to *another* place called Bethany in order to perform the miracle, in longer Mark Jesus encounters the sister in Bethany and the miracle occurs immediately, without any trip to another location. The miracle is very different, too. In John, Jesus orders others to remove the stone and then shouts from a distance "Lazarus, come out!"; in longer Mark, the loud cry comes from the dead man while Jesus is still walking to the garden, and Jesus removes the stone himself, raising the man by the hand. Where John has the dead man walk out wrapped in grave clothes, longer Mark has the dead man look at Jesus, love him, and plead to be "with him." Finally, the story in longer Mark has an addendum not found in John. We are told that Jesus and the young man left the tomb and went into the man's house; after six days Jesus taught him the mystery of the kingdom of God. Surprisingly, this instruction occurs at night, and the young man wears nothing but a linen sheet over his naked body. Stranger still, this is apparently the same young man who appears in canonical Mark at the moment of Jesus' arrest, again wearing only the linen sheet (14:51–52).[4]

The second quotation (III.14–16), which I call LGM 2, consists of two sentences inserted between the two clauses of Mark 10:46. In context, the passage reads, "And he comes into Jericho. And there were there the sister of the young man whom Jesus loved him [*sic*] and his mother and Salome, and Jesus did not receive them. And as he was leaving Jericho…." The reader is left to wonder what *did not* transpire between Jesus and these women in Jericho.

# Scholarly Assessments of the Longer Gospel

The manuscripts that Smith catalogued were the property of the Greek Patriarchate, so Smith left the book in the tower library and took with him a set of black and white photographs of the letter.[5] His first impulse was to show these photographs to experts in Greek handwriting, who concurred that the style was typical of the eighteenth century.[6] Once back in the United States, Smith resolved to determine whether the attribution of the letter to Clement was correct. He therefore spent the next two years comparing the *Letter to Theodore* with the thought, style, and vocabulary of Clement of Alexandria's undisputed works. The conformity was impressive, so at the annual meeting of the Society of Biblical Literature in 1960 he announced that he had discovered a letter of Clement. At that meeting, Pierson Parker, an expert in the Gospels of Matthew and Mark, offered a preliminary report on the relationship between the gospel fragments and the canonical gospels.[7] Parker's illogical arguments to the effect that the quotations are "not noticeably 'Markan'" were eventually discarded by Smith in the course of his subsequent research, which took six years to complete.[8] During this time he consulted with numerous experts in relevant fields. This work culminated in his monumental commentary *Clement of Alexandria and a Secret Gospel of Mark*, which was essentially complete in 1966 but took another seven years in the production stage to attain its published form.

In the early phase of his research on the two gospel quotations, Smith determined that the vocabulary, phrasing, and grammatical constructions are typical of the Gospel of Mark. That much has seemed obvious to nearly everyone, although scholars have explained this congruence in varying ways. Smith recognized that Markan vocabulary and sentence construction could point either to Mark's authorship or to imitation of Mark by another author. Smith noted three features that suggest imitation: the text contains more Markan phrases than is typical of stories in the canonical gospel; some of these verbal parallels are rather lengthy and include "main narrative elements" in addition to the stereotyped phrases that frequently appear at the beginnings and endings of Mark's stories; and LGM 1 and 2 have "less of the peculiar details which individualize the canonical [text's] stories." More generally, he noted that "The text was more like Mark than a section of Mark should be."[9]

Though Smith perceived these signs of imitation, the text did not seem to him to be a cento or pastiche (a patchwork of phrases from other works) or to show knowledge of any gospels other than Mark. As he put it, "the text is too well constructed and economical to be a cento: there are no irrelevant details, every word comes naturally in its place, the narration moves without delays or jumps."[10] And though the author's knowledge of Mark is obvious from the fact that this text is a longer version of that gospel, the almost complete lack of Johannine characteristics in LGM 1 speaks strongly against knowledge of John. Likewise, Smith deemed the contacts with Matthew and Luke to be too tenuous to suggest that the author of LGM 1 and 2 used those gospels.[11] For these reasons, Smith viewed the gospel excerpts as free imitations of Mark that were composed without knowledge of Matthew, Luke, and John. Smith further demonstrated that LGM 1a does not contain any of the secondary traits found in the parallel story in John 11. He concluded that LGM 1 provides an older, independent, and more reliable witness to the oral tradition upon which John based his more theologically developed drama of the raising of Lazarus.[12]

Parker's report brought to Smith's attention the fact that the placement of LGM 1 within the section of Mark leading up to the passion narrative corresponds to the placement of the raising of Lazarus within the Gospel of John. Smith carried this observation further and noted extensive parallels between the materials within Mark 10:1–34 plus LGM 1 and John 10:40–11:54, indeed, between the whole of Mark 6:32–15:47 and John 6:1–19:42.[13] The pervasive differences between the two gospels even where these parallels exist, however, led Smith to conclude that neither John nor longer Mark was directly dependent upon the other as a source but, rather, that both authors had recourse to very different Greek editions of an earlier Aramaic gospel. The authors of canonical Mark and longer Mark both knew and used the same Greek version of this proto-gospel as a source, but the former author, writing around 75 CE, chose not to include the raising and initiation of the young man (LGM 1) and the reprise of this story (LGM 2). The latter author, writing around 95 CE, placed these and other unused passages in their appropriate places, and in the process reworked them into Markan style.[14]

Smith also conjectured that Clement's copy of the longer text contained a few errors and revisions. The scribal tendency to harmonize Mark's phrases with the more familiar wording found in Matthew and Luke led to the replacement of the Markan phrase "for he was having many possessions" (10:22) in LGM 1:9 with Luke's more familiar "for he was (very) rich" (18:23), a recollection that was possibly triggered by the repetition of a phrase from Mark's version of that story in LGM 1:8 ("looking upon him loved him").[15] Since LGM 2:2 uses a non-Markan verb when it states that Jesus did not "receive" the three women, Smith conjectured that that whole sentence is a second-century gloss made by a redactor who cut something out, most likely a dialogue between Jesus and Salome.[16] And Smith decided that the reference to Jesus *teaching* the young man the mystery of the kingdom of God must be a scribal error, because the young man is dressed for an initiation, and initiations are not taught but performed. Considering that the reference to the mystery of the kingdom of God in Mark 4:11 uses the verb "to give" rather than the verb "to teach," LGM 1:12 probably read "for Jesus *gave* him the mystery of the kingdom of God."[17]

It is Smith's theories about the subject matter and historical background of LGM 1b that are most remarkable. Building upon a suggestion sent to him by Cyril C. Richardson in a letter dated 13 January 1961, Smith interpreted the linen sheet worn by the resuscitated young man as the garment worn for the rite of baptism.[18] Drawing upon diverse sources, Smith read this private instruction as evidence that Jesus offered his closest disciples a mystery rite that involved union with his spirit and a mystical (hypnotically induced) ascent to the heavens; through this "mystery" the initiate would enter God's heavenly kingdom and be freed from the Mosaic laws that apply in the lower world; this is what is meant by the phrase "for Jesus [gave] him the mystery [rite] of the kingdom of God." Smith speculated that after Jesus' death the mystery was offered to all converts and became a rite of initiation into the church, but as the number of followers increased, time constraints and the complexity of the procedure led to the elimination of the libertine and magical aspects, and the ceremony became a simple baptism that bestowed the gift of the spirit. The unorthodox elements continued only in libertine sects, including the Carpocratians, and in the orthodox Alexandrian church of Clement's day (though in a truncated form). In Smith's view, the great mysteries mentioned in Clement's letter refer to a second baptism of advanced Christians into an elite, esoteric clique in that church; on the night of the Paschal vigil, a baptismal lection consisting of Mark 10:13–45 and LGM 1 and 2 was read to Christians entering this inner circle.[19]

The publication in 1973 of the letter together with Smith's commentary and analysis generated a sensation among New Testament scholars, whose more outlandish and visceral responses have been summarized by Shawn Eyer in an eminently readable account.[20] The commentary that Smith produced on the letter and gospel quotations was widely praised for its thoroughness and erudition, but his reconstruction of Christian origins based on the hypothesis that Jesus was a libertine who performed a hypnotic rite of ascent struck most reviewers as utterly fantastic and wholly unsupported—even by the quotations from the "secret" gospel.[21] Scholars with a conservative disposition were thoroughly annoyed with Smith's presumption that a non-canonical gospel could transform our understanding of first-century Christianity. To them, longer Mark was an imitation gospel containing "fake traditions," one of those "late and spurious Gospel tracts" for which "Alexandria was a breeding ground."[22] Many of the reviewers of Smith's books instinctively relegated longer Mark to the abyss of second-century heresy by arbitrarily declaring it gnostic, Carpocratian, or Encratite; it was whatever the scholars' preconceptions about non-canonical gospels and Alexandrian Christianity told them it should be. Even before the letter was published, F.F. Bruce had written, "In so far as it is possible to say anything about this report [the story in LGM 1 and 2] while the document remains unpublished, it may be said that this expanded Gospel of Mark bears all the signs of Gnostic editing."[23]

It is not obvious that we need to invoke the standard second-century heresies in order to account for a depiction of Jesus teaching a follower attired in linen (cf. Mark 14:51–52) the mystery he reserved for his closest associates and taught in private (4:10–12). After all, LGM 1b is not unlike Jesus' private, nocturnal, and gratuitously esoteric instruction of Nicodemus about the kingdom of God in John 3:1–12. It was not the contents of LGM 1 and 2 themselves that led reviewers to a mid-second-century dating but rather a timeworn chain of fallacious reasoning: non-canonical gospel=imitation gospel=mid-second-century gospel=heretical gospel. For scholars who applied this simple heuristic, a negative verdict on the value of Smith's discovery required neither research nor demonstration: "Smith has found a turnip in the root cellar of ancient literature."[24] "The manuscript Smith discovered adds a bit to our knowledge of second-century Christianity...."[25] "And that's where it all belongs!"[26]

Although many of the reviewers attempted to discredit the "secret" gospel with pejorative rhetoric and gratuitous talk of heresy, others knew that this gospel would not just disappear with the tide of bad press. Aware that the raising miracle in LGM 1a looks more like unembellished oral tradition than does the raising of Lazarus, a handful of scholars set out to confront the obvious problem that LGM 1 poses to the view that the canonical gospels contain the only authentic narratives about Jesus. Their solution was to argue that longer Mark was a mid-second-century concoction by an author who derived his materials from all four canonical gospels in the most direct and unimaginative way possible: free association. Thus, "*SGM* borrows the youth of the rich man from Matt 19:16–22; and his youth reminds *SGM* of the young man in Mark 14:51–52, from where *SGM* now borrows the wearing of a linen cloth on a naked body."[27] The speculations about literary borrowings sometimes go on like this until nothing remains in LGM 1 and 2 that was not taken from the canonical gospels. Then Morton Smith's theories are denounced as needlessly complicated and "hypothetical."

Variants of this explanation were put forward by such notable scholars as F.F. Bruce, Robert M. Grant, Raymond E. Brown, and Frans Neirynck. Their reputations supplied the footnote documentation that other scholars would use for the next thirty years to excuse themselves from the task of analyzing this evidence and familiarizing themselves with the secondary literature. With the backing of these experts, some two dozen scholars confidently proclaimed that everything in LGM 1 and 2 was derived in some way or other from the canonical gospels. Their musings about how this text was produced envision such a clumsy, uninspired, and artificial process that it could not possibly be of any importance to our understanding of early Christianity:

> Robin Scroggs: "a crude collage of phrases found elsewhere in the Gospel of Mark." Daryl Schmidt: "artificial literary mosaic"; "a new tale…rather mechanically constructed from individual constituents." Edward C. Hobbs : "a patchwork of phrases…quilted from pieces in our four Gospels"; "what one would expect to be concocted by a person with all the stories in front of him"; "[the author] is not one who freely composes. He has a pair of scissors to cut up manuscripts and glue them down, although the antecedents of pronouns may turn out to be different." F.F. Bruce: "such an obvious pastiche, with its internal contradiction and confusion, …a thoroughly artificial composition, quite out of keeping with Mark's quality as a story-teller." Patrick W. Skehan: "a parody of the raising of Lazarus as told in the canonical John"; "the distorted Lazarus story." André Méhat: "a cento made up of pieces borrowed from the canonical Gospels and welded together." Ernest Best: "It looks as if its author thumbed through Mark until he found the phrase he wanted." Frans Neirynck: "it could almost be said that the story has been composed with the aid of a concordance of the gospels." James D.G. Dunn: "a reworked amalgam of elements from Mark 10…and the story of Lazarus in John 11." Per Beskow: "This strange splicing of bits and pieces from the Gospels of Mark and John…" Robert H. Gundry: "largely a confused pastiche," "expansions of the sort we find everywhere in apocryphal literature." Craig A. Evans: "[probably] an artificial and secondary blend of Marcan and Johannine elements." Frederick W. Baltz: "details and phrases from the Gospels have been cut-and-pasted into a basic story line."[28]

I doubt that these scholars would use the same logic to dismiss the Sermon on the Mount as "an artificial and secondary blend" of elements from Mark, Q, and Matthew's special materials or to argue that Matt 9:27–34 is an obvious, second-century interpolation into Matthew because an even higher percentage of its phrasing is exactly paralleled in the four canonical gospels.[29] Smith commented upon the special logic engendered by the canonical bias back in 1961. Writing to A.D. Nock he noted that some of his colleagues who were studying the longer gospel quotations "take it for granted that anything similar to the canonical Gospels is derivative, and anything not similar, secondary. Thus they cover the field completely with only two false assumptions."[30]

Not everyone who looked at longer Mark saw a worthless patchwork fabrication. Roughly the same number of scholars (more than two dozen) were more impressed by LGM 1's undeveloped appearance (both literarily and theologically), resemblance to miracle stories in the synoptic gospels, and lack of Johannine features. Rather than seeing an "artificial literary mosaic" consisting of individual words, commonplace phrases, and approximate conceptual parallels, these scholars saw a typical healing story that develops in a smooth, uncomplicated, and economical manner, without the "duplications, inconsistencies, and rough connections" that characterize its Johannine counterpart.[31] This other group of scholars agreed with Smith that the raising miracle in longer Mark is based on oral tradition, although few endorsed his postulate of an Aramaic proto-gospel.

Commentators had obvious difficulty accounting for the creation of LGM 1 and its appearance in a form of Mark's gospel. Most of the scholars who subscribed to the pastiche theory did not consider the matter worthy of attention. They let the author's supposed use of scissors and paste speak for his mental condition at the time of the offence. Still, a few of these scholars proposed that the author was seeking to establish the identities of anonymous gospel personalities, identifying Lazarus, for instance, as the rich man in Mark 10:17–22, the streaker in 14:51–52, and "the disciple whom Jesus loved" from John's gospel. Among scholars who thought this story was independent of the canonical gospels, the dominant perspective was that LGM 1 was devised for liturgical use in ordinary baptism. Whether or not they realized it, most of these scholars had rejected Smith's thesis that the longer text was the liturgy for a second baptism, a rite confined to a secret sect of libertines within the Alexandrian church, in favour of Cyril C. Richardson's suggestion about its use in neophyte baptism. Yet they continued to call the text *Secret Mark*, apparently without wondering why a passage used in ordinary baptism would need to be hidden away in a secret gospel, especially when the pericope corresponding to the Eucharist appears in canonical Mark 14:22–25. The scandalous aspects of Smith's historical theories found their way into the occasional exposé of Christianity's suppressed origins, but scholars tended either to ignore these idiosyncrasies or to exaggerate them as a means of discrediting the whole affair. Very few scholars believed that LGM 1 or 2 can tell us anything about the historical Jesus or ventured to use this story to reconstruct the tradition that lay behind John 11. The general reluctance to make use of these gospel passages might seem surprising, even irresponsible. But the debate over whether longer Mark contains authentic oral tradition was quickly undercut by a more sensational hypothesis, namely, that the whole *Letter to Theodore* is just an impressive forgery.

Some of the scholars Smith consulted in the 1960s thought the letter was an ancient forgery, although they had difficulty explaining how an ancient author would benefit by creating it. Smith dealt with their arguments in his book. However, the spectre of forgery came back with a vengeance in 1975, when two scholars offered influential arguments that the letter was a modern hoax. Quentin Quesnell suggested that an erudite scholar who had access to Otto Stählin's 1936 index of Clement's vocabulary and other modern studies of Clement's style could have produced the document, especially if he had the help of someone skilled in imitating handwriting. Quesnell added that any scholarly apparatus Smith used to "authenticate" the document could have assisted a forger in imitating Clement. And he pointed out that Smith's ability to gain access to the tower library at Mar Saba shows that a forger could have planted it there. Quesnell was not clear about a motive, but he suggested that a scholar might devise such a text if he was interested in studying how his peers respond to new discoveries. As an example of that sort of interest, Quesnell noted that Smith himself had requested in the preface of his scholarly book that his peers send him their publications on this subject.[32] Quesnell's main point was that we need to examine the manuscript for signs of forgery before we can accept it as authentic. Not surprisingly, the way he made this point did not go over well with Smith, who was annoyed with the fact that Quesnell's hypothetical forger was a person who had the same expertise, resources, opportunities, and motives as Smith himself. New Testament scholars were greatly distracted by the notion that one of their own had accused Smith of forgery, and many agreed with Quesnell that the manuscript should be subjected to forensic testing before it is deemed authentic. Their suspicions only increased when Charles Murgia offered arguments for modern forgery based on the content of the letter. Murgia suggested that the letter consisted mostly of information that was suspiciously self-authenticating, and noted that the manuscript lacks the major errors that result from a long period of scribal transmission. In his opinion, the letter looks more like an original composition than a copy of a copy of a copy. So as years passed without anyone else claiming to have seen the manuscript, a rumour was born that Smith was withholding it so that no one could perform the tests that Quesnell had outlined. Scholars who were ignorant of the published photos often imagined that there never was a manuscript. The folklore of forgery took on a life of its own.

In general, scholars of Clement and scholars of the gospels responded to the suggestions of forgery in different ways. Although some experts on Clement who belonged to the generation of Smith's teachers were inclined to think the letter contradicted Clement's universalism, most belonging to Smith's generation or later were inclined to believe that the letter was authentic. Since these scholars were more interested in Clement than in the longer gospel, they tended to mention the letter only as an illustration of Clement's esotericism and openness to writings that were later deemed non-canonical. The situation was very different among New Testament scholars, most of whom have too little knowledge of Clement's writings or eighteenth-century Greek handwriting to develop an informed opinion on the letter's authenticity. They generally responded by showing an astonishing credulity about unsubstantiated rumours and a stoic scepticism about indications that the letter might be authentic. That is not to say that most New Testament scholars considered it to be a forgery: they just did not know what to make of the evidence. Rather than study matters about which they had no expertise, these scholars tended to trade stories about Smith's character, which was something they knew firsthand or had heard a great deal about. Some pointed to Smith's sense of humour and irreverence as potential signs of intellectual dishonesty, and speculated about whether Smith had a plausible motive or enough proficiency in classical Greek. (Those most proficient in classical Greek tended to think that the letter surpassed Smith's ability.) The thirst for scandal is typified by an incident recorded in the minutes of a colloquium on the longer text; the agenda for discussion was established on the basis of a dream that one of the participants had about Morton Smith:

> In this dream, Professor Smith met the man responsible for the Piltdown skull. Then Professor Smith broke down and admitted that he himself had written the supposed letter from Clement.
>
> As a result of that dream, I naturally seized upon the whole question of the criteria for detecting a forgery, as Professor Murgia did. That is points 1 and 2 on the list.[33]

For some scholars, the notion that Smith's discovery was just an astonishing hoax was too good not to be true. Having outgrown Sasquatch and the Loch Ness monster, they yearned to believe in at least one fantastic tale. This irrepressible form of credulity is well summed up by the caption of a famous poster depicting a fuzzy photograph of a UFO: "I Want To Believe."

The theory of forgery even proved attractive to scholars who were uninterested in the controversy. Scholars who felt obliged to comment on the relevance of the longer text to another subject, such as Mark 14:51–52 or John 11, often just wrote a footnote expressing reservations about the letter's authenticity and the longer gospel's independence from the canonical gospels, as if the *possibility* that a text might prove irrelevant were sufficient reason not to study it and find that out. The scholars who debunk the apocryphal gospels as second-century fabrications were likewise drawn to the theory of forgery, although for apologetic reasons:

> But, apart from the possibility that the so-called Marcan fragment is little more than a semi-Gnostic fabrication, I do not think that Professor Smith has sufficiently explored the contingency that the entire letter of Clement is a forgery."[34]

> On the whole, so-called *Secret Mark* appears to be a forgery, although whether modern or ancient is difficult to say…a forgery by Smith might be expected to produce a less fragmentary extract and one even more conducive to his views of Jesus as a magician. It thus may be that *Secret Mark* is an ancient forgery, typical of the additions and adulterations of the canonical Gospels that arose especially during the heyday of Gnosticism in the second century.[35]

For these scholars, the question was never What does this text tell us about Christian origins? but Wherein lies its irrelevance? Is longer Mark the product of a modern forger too brilliant to be unmasked, or of a second-century imbecile who composed with a pair of scissors? It is remarkable that so many scholars have vacillated between these two options. Why would a competent modern forger create a gospel extract that supposedly looks like a worthless pastiche? To claim that either possibility might be true is to admit that neither is very compelling. But even though these scholars could not decide what kind of counterfeit gospel they were discrediting, they recognized that one of these wands must be waved in the correct fashion in order to send this text back to the abyss.

By the end of the 1970s, New Testament scholars still mentioned "secret" Mark in an incidental manner, but were generally reluctant to take the gospel *too* seriously and risk looking foolish should it be proved a fake. The widely dismissive reactions of conservative scholars and the spectre of forgery had put an end to serious discussion, and Smith himself had turned his attention to other evidence, having re-evaluated the importance of longer Mark to his theories about Jesus. The longer Gospel of Mark might have slipped silently into the netherworld of the apocrypha (or should I say, pseudo-apocrypha?) were it not for a provocative thesis advanced by Helmut Koester in 1980. Through a study of the minor agreements of Matthew and Luke against Mark in the triple tradition (the stories and sayings shared by Matthew, Mark, and Luke), Koester concluded that the canonical Gospel of Mark was not the version of Mark that Matthew and Luke used as a source for their own gospels; canonical Mark was a mid-second-century abbreviation of the longer gospel. Koester proposed that Matthew and Luke used a proto-gospel, an edition of Mark lacking elements in the canonical gospel that are characteristic of LGM 1. The author of longer Mark must therefore have revised this proto-gospel in the early second century by adding LGM 1 and 2 and some of the features of Mark's text that diverge from the parallel passages in Matthew and Luke. Canonical Mark came about through the removal of LGM 1 and 2.[36]

Koester's thesis generated enormous interest in North America due to its theological implications, which were extremely attractive to liberal scholars. As individuals who define themselves over against traditional forms of Christianity, liberals prefer to believe that Christianity was, at the time of its pristine beginnings, a movement that contained and tolerated theological diversity. According to the liberal myth of Christian origins, proto-orthodox Christians, such as Paul, were originally one voice (or one choir of harmonious voices) among many, but over the course of a few centuries, this form of Christianity rose to dominance through the suppression of legitimate but less pretentious Jesus movements. This reconstruction of Christian origins is how dispassionate historians imply that liberal Christianity is as legitimate as traditional orthodoxy. So with the publication of Koester's initial paper in 1983, longer Mark became highly *theologically* relevant as a potential example of how the canonical gospels not only presented a selective picture of Jesus but also experienced extensive revisions prior to the emergence of standard text types.

Koester himself emphasized the instability of the texts of the canonical gospels in the second century. But another eminent scholar soon developed a different theory of longer Markan priority that gave church censorship a vital role in the production of the canonical gospel. John Dominic Crossan postulated that LGM 1 and 2 were part of the earliest edition of Mark's gospel and conjectured that the private initiation depicted in LGM 1b (in his view, a baptism) quickly became a proof text for sexual libertinism among proto-Carpocratians in Alexandria.[37] This scandal led Mark himself to dismember and scatter the pieces of LGM 1 and 2 throughout his gospel in order to deceive the libertines into thinking that the story *he* composed was really their own impious fabrication made out of pieces of his gospel.[38] Although this was probably not Crossan's original intention, his theory calls into question both the integrity of canonical Mark *and* that of the evangelist who composed it. With similarly unsettling implications, Hans-Martin Schenke modified Koester's thesis by drawing the inference that the Carpocratian longer Gospel of Mark was the ancestor of both the purified longer gospel used in the Alexandrian catechetical school and the later canonical gospel.[39] Schenke's idea that the orthodox longer gospel was merely a purified form of a Carpocratian text was not actually new. A few scholars had already offered that suggestion, convinced that longer Mark was the product of a libertine, gnostic mentality.[40] Of course, those scholars thought that canonical Mark was the original text. Schenke's combination of this theory with Koester's made canonical Mark the by-product of two attempts to remove the "utterly shameless lies" (II.7–9) that "early nonorthodox" Alexandrians had added to the proto-gospel.[41]

Although most scholars in Europe (especially Germany and England) continued to disregard the entire subject, Koester's less radical version of the theory of longer Markan priority inspired a brief renaissance of original research in North America during the 1980s and early 1990s. Whereas the research conducted in the 1970s was more preoccupied with genre, source criticism, and form criticism, that inspired by Koester focused on composition history and redaction criticism. Of course, there were several critical reactions to Koester's theory, which targeted his premise that Matthew and Luke used a copy of Mark that differed from the canonical gospel.[42] The evaluations by David Peabody and Philip Sellew, however, incidentally underscored the Markan qualities of the passages cited in Clement's letter, questioning whether passages composed by this author are readily distinguishable from passages composed by Mark. Yet despite their interest in redaction criticism, proponents of longer Markan priority were no more interested in how LGM 1 and 2 function literarily within the larger context of the Gospel of Mark than were proponents of pastiche composition or forgery. The theologically charged issue of relative priority led liberal scholars to focus more on why these longer Markan traditions were removed than on what they were doing in a form of Mark in the first place.[43] Most just assumed that LGM 1 was part of a baptismal lection and as such did not have an integral connection to the rest of the gospel. Nevertheless, Hans-Martin Schenke and Marvin Meyer explored the effect LGM 1 and 2 have on the larger *narrative*, as had Frank Kermode, a well-respected literary critic who discussed longer Mark in his 1979 book *The Genesis of Secrecy*. These three scholars viewed two or all three of the passages in longer Mark involving a "young man" as developments in a subplot.[44]

By the mid-1980s, "secret" Mark had found a place within a broader, liberal thesis that many of the non-canonical gospels were as ancient and historically important as the canonical gospels. By the early 1990s, this thesis was reaching a wider audience. When Crossan wrote his popular and prodigious book *The Historical Jesus* (published in 1991), he assigned longer Mark and numerous other non-canonical texts to the earliest strata of historical evidence.[45] That same year, the controversial and media-friendly assemblage of scholars called the Jesus Seminar started endorsing Helmut Koester's theory of longer Markan priority in its publications, which purported to give a representative picture of modern Jesus scholarship.[46] In response to this trend, conservative scholars became more insistent that only the canonical gospels contain reliable information about Jesus. Already in 1987, Raymond E. Brown noted with alarm that many scholars were calling into question the "traditional priority and value of the canonical NT books," and cited the various arguments for longer Markan priority as one of these "challenges to the canon."[47] The tone of conservative New Testament scholarship on longer Mark in the 1990s was set in 1991 by John Meier, who published a survey of "The *Agrapha* and the Apocryphal Gospels" in his book *A Marginal Jew*, wherein he caricatured the "revisionists" and their contradictory arguments about longer Mark and accused them of "selling" the apocryphal gospels "under the guise of NT research and the quest for the historical Jesus." Like so many scholars before him, Meier played up the myth of longer Mark's "dubious origins," depicted Clement as unreliable on matters of gospel authorship, and selectively referenced the scholars who argued for longer Mark's dependence upon the canonical gospels.[48] Yet his one-sided survey of "secret" Mark scholarship struck many as a model of scholarly judiciousness, and became a template for similar surveys in subsequent books on Jesus.

Thus began a second wave of attempts to convince the academy and the lay audience of the Jesus Seminar that the longer text is historically worthless. But now Smith's find was entangled in a debate over the value of non-canonical gospels in the reconstruction of the historical Jesus. Throughout the 1990s, the use of non-canonical gospels by liberal Jesus scholars was widely criticized for producing a picture of Jesus that lacked distinctively Christian and Jewish elements. To a large extent this portrait relied on the combined weight of Q and the Gospel of Thomas, since their double attestation of Jesus' wisdom sayings supported a portrait of Jesus as a generic sage rather than as an eschatological prophet (an element lacking in Thomas) or messianic figure (an element lacking in Thomas and Q). Liberal Jesus scholars who studied the longer gospel did not actually conclude that LGM 1 and 2 contain useful evidence concerning the historical Jesus (as opposed to the composition history of Mark), but since they had *examined* this non-canonical gospel, their critics felt justified in playing up its infamy as a means of discrediting their liberal opponents:

> The history of the controversy surrounding the discovery and publication of the purported letter of Clement…need not be rehearsed here. The lack of scholarly verification of the find is as well known as Clement's credulity. Thus, in

my view it is extremely precarious to build complicated theories of Gospel development, as Crossan and Koester have done, on the basis of *Secret Mark*'s alleged relationship to canonical Mark....In all probability *Secret Mark*, if such really existed, is a second century revision of canonical Mark. As such it has nothing to offer serious Jesus research.[49]

But, as a test of the competence of allegedly leading-edge North American scholars, what makes this [secret gospel] simultaneously frightening and revealing is that *even if one knew nothing of its diagnostically-fraudulent provenance*, one still would immediately recognize it not only as inauthentic, but as part of a very nasty, but very funny, knife-sharp joke....What we have here [in LGM 1 and 2] is a nice ironic gay joke at the expense of all of the self-important scholars who not only miss the irony, but believe that this alleged piece of gospel comes to us in the first-known letter of the great Clement of Alexandria.[50]

The problem is that there are serious and enduring doubts about the Clementine text involved, which has not been made available to scholars except in photographic form, and there are unresolved rumors of forgery....With so many doubts surrounding the document, it is surprising to see the evidence of Secret Mark included here [in a publication of the Jesus Seminar] as authoritative, and as proof of the late date of a canonical text.[51]

Behind this tendency to disparage the "secret" gospel and the scholars who study it is a theological preoccupation. Debates about the historical Jesus are frequently debates over the *true* myth of Christian origins: In the Beginning, did God create orthodoxy (a unified church that correctly interpreted God's act of salvation through Jesus as canonized in the New Testament writings and faithfully preserved by us conservatives) or heterodoxy (a variety of Jesus movements with enough diversity in their interpretations of Jesus' significance to be inclusive of people with unorthodox conceptions of "the gospel," like us liberals)? To search for Jesus within the gospels that were *not* included in the New Testament is to question the validity of the image of Jesus presented by "the Church." That, at least, seems to be the wisdom motivating much of the scholarship on longer Mark, which tends to be radically liberal or staunchly apologetic. Both camps see longer Mark as a heterodox gospel, and embrace it or revile it because it was not canonized. Few scholars have seriously entertained the possibility that Clement was right, that a canonical author actually did write a second, orthodox version of his gospel. This fact is rather odd, since LGM 1 and 2 have the form and style of a Markan composition, and the notion that Mark wrote another, lost version of his gospel is no stranger than the reality that Paul wrote letters that were not included in the New Testament (note 1 Cor 5:9; Col 4:16). It would be rather surprising if Luke was the only one of the four evangelists to write a second work. It would also be strange if these authors completely refrained from making revisions and additions to their gospels after the initial publication.

Today, forty-five years after the discovery of the manuscript, there is no general paradigm that most scholars agree on, and most frankly have no idea what to make of this text. Confused about the facts and unaware of the extensive secondary literature on this subject, the majority of commentators simply pledge allegiance to one or more of five mutually exclusive paradigms: forgery; pointless, apocryphal pastiche; pre-canonical version of Mark; secret and elitist gnostic gospel; catechetical supplements for neophyte baptism. The present predicament owes much to the fact that scholars have tended to engage Smith's characterizations of the issues rather than independently examine the evidence. In the thirty years since the publication of Smith's work, no comprehensive study of the letter and its gospel quotations has been published. The options that are presently being considered were all identified and addressed by Smith in the early 1960s, and their continued viability is largely the consequence of certain questionable assumptions in his research that most investigators have accepted without comment. For example, the scholars of Clement who suspected forgery were to some extent reacting against Smith's suppositions that Clement approved of a secret writing and that this writing legitimized an unseemly rite. That these notions are substantiated by the letter is not questioned. Likewise, many of the scholars who accept the letter as authentic also accept Smith's view that the gospel additions were used as catechetical or lectionary readings for a rite. And most have accepted Smith's assumption that the quoted pericopae are Markan only in terms of form and style; with Smith, they view this Markan appearance as a superficial imitation intended to make these materials appear to have been written by Mark. The author of the longer gospel is typically imagined to be either "Markanizing" traditional cultic materials for storage in an established gospel or just foolishly rewriting Johannine stories using Markan language.

## A Literary Thesis

The nature and purpose of the longer gospel appears quite different, however, when the issue of the Markan characteristics of these excerpts is considered at a level exceeding sentence construction. The author of LGM 1 and 2 not only wrote with Markan syntax and vocabulary but also used distinctively Markan literary techniques. Most notably, this author used Mark's favourite techniques for juxtaposing episodes and framing sections of narrative. For instance, he placed the two parts of the story involving the young man and his sister around the incident in which James and John ask for positions of honour. Mark liked to put one story inside (or around) another story as a means of suggesting that the two stories interpret each other, as when he placed the two parts of the cursing of the fig tree around the story of Jesus clearing the temple (Mark 11:12–25). Knowing that the same literary technique is being used in longer Mark effectively solves the problem of why the young man twice returned to Jesus with a linen sheet wrapped around his naked body (LGM 1:11; Mark 14:51–52). He answered "yes" to the question Jesus posed to James and John (Mark 10:38). Longer Mark likewise uses Mark's technique of echoing phrases from earlier incidents as a means of associating widely dispersed but thematically related incidents. The more pronounced verbal echoes within LGM 1 are to incidents that are relevant to the interpretation of LGM 1 and 2. Finally, LGM 1 and 2 create an interpretative bracket around the passion narrative by framing this section of the story with two very similar raising miracles involving Jesus, an anonymous young man, a tomb sealed with a stone, and a group of three women, one of whom is Salome. The central journey section of Mark's gospel is similarly bracketed with two stories about the healing of blind men (8:22–10:52). Other, smaller-scale Markan literary techniques also exist in LGM 1 and 2. The use of these devices implies that the extant passages are best conceptualized as aspects of a literary production, that is, as episodes in a text that was meant to be appreciated *as a story* and therefore read or heard in its entirety.[52]

The validity of this literary paradigm for the study of the longer gospel is the main thing I will endeavour to establish through this study. Specifically, I develop the thesis that the longer Gospel of Mark was designed to lead readers of the shorter version to a more profound appreciation of the essential message of the Markan narrative by elaborating and elucidating important themes and symbolism pertaining to discipleship and christology, including elements which are deliberately ambiguous or obscure in the shorter version, especially the mystery of the kingdom of God (Mark 4:11) and the appearance and naked flight of the young man in Gethsemane (14:51–52). In other words, this text was aptly suited to an environment like Alexandria where many literate Christians viewed their faith as a philosophy and therefore sought its deeper truths (the esoteric teachings of its system) anagogically within sacred writings (see, for instance, *Strom.* V.4.21.4). It was through the exposition of esoteric knowledge hidden in the scriptures that Christians in Alexandria were "initiated in the great mysteries" of Alexandrian Christian philosophy (II.2).

The thoroughly Markan quality of the longer text raises a secondary issue that will be addressed at the conclusion of this study: Did Mark actually write the longer gospel? Scholars have rightly noted that Markan vocabulary and syntax are not too difficult to imitate. But Mark's distinctive literary techniques are aspects of his composition that people rarely notice unless they know what to look for. Many of the elements of Markan literary technique that are used to good effect in LGM 1 and 2 had not been identified by scholars of Mark until long after the letter was discovered. These techniques were probably no more obvious to the earliest readers of canonical Mark, who spoke of its author as someone with little literary sophistication; the evangelist Mark was imagined as a follower of Peter who accurately reproduced Peter's anecdotes about Jesus but arranged them in a less than artful manner. Moreover, it is hard to envision anyone other than Mark wanting to amplify this gospel in a manner that wholly accords with *Mark's* theology. Someone other than Mark would be apt to have a different theological agenda. So the consistency of literary technique and theology between these two versions of the Gospel of Mark strongly suggests common authorship.

The following analysis is divided into two parts. Part 1 addresses the main paradigms for understanding the longer gospel that appear in the secondary literature. These chapters will deconstruct the prevailing conceptions of forgery (chap. 2), "artificial literary mosaic,"[53] pre-canonical version of Mark (chap. 3), *secret* gospel (chap. 4), and baptismal lection (chap. 5). For different reasons, each of these misconceptions has obscured the literary character of the longer gospel. So it is necessary to begin by cleaning up the mess that I described in the preceding pages. Even scholars who are wedded to the notion that the longer gospel, if not the whole letter, is "late and spurious" recognize that *someone* needs to work through all of the primary and secondary literature in order to weed out the false premises and misinformation that support so many contradictory paradigms.

Part 2 of this book consists of a demonstration that the passages quoted in the letter develop and elucidate aspects of Markan theology, including features of the story that readers of the shorter version have often found perplexing. Chapters 6 through 8 each demonstrate the effective use of a distinctively Markan literary technique by the author of LGM 1 and 2. Chapter 6 will demonstrate that the placement of LGM 1 and 2 around Mark 10:35–45 constitutes a Markan-style intercalation, both in form and function. Chapter 7 will argue that the raising of the young man at his tomb in LGM 1a and the resurrection announced by this same young man at Jesus' tomb in Mark 16:1–8 function as a matched pair or frame around the passion narrative, and that this structure is built upon an existing *inclusio* involving the imagery of Jesus leading his disciples in the way to life through death (10:32 and 16:7–8). This device creates a theological framework for the reader's comprehension of what transpires in the passion narrative. Chapter 8 will interpret the more pronounced verbal repetitions or echoes in LGM 1 and 2 as "cross-references" intended to draw the reader's attention to similarities between LGM 1 and 2 and other stories in the gospel. The final chapter will synthesize the implications of this study with special attention to the question of longer Mark's authorship, as well as outline the areas in which this text is relevant to the study of early Christianity.

## Comments on Method

The Markan literary techniques examined in this study were recognized by redaction critics and elaborated theoretically by narrative critics. Because my interest is in elucidating the nature of this gospel by demonstrating the use of these techniques and describing their effects, the method of my analysis is not "purely" literary-critical but rather a hybrid of composition criticism and narrative criticism, or a theoretically informed use of composition criticism— one that pays more attention to the reading process. Readers interested in learning more about the theory behind narrative criticism can consult a variety of good introductory works that apply this methodology to Mark's gospel.[54]

Certain caveats need to be stated concerning the viability of applying literary criticism to a work whose text type and precise contents are not known.[55] Obviously, this analysis cannot concentrate on the whole story because Clement quoted only two of the many additions that distinguished longer Mark from the canonical gospel. What is possible is a study of how the known LGM passages interact with the known materials of their context, that is, with the canonical gospel. A concentration on literary devices rather than on the entire reading experience should permit conclusions that would not be falsified by knowledge of the other passages unique to the longer gospel, though such knowledge would necessitate some refinement of these conclusions.

# ⇥2⇤

# The Question of the Authenticity
# of the *Letter to Theodore*

For decades, discussion of the "secret" gospel has been dominated by two notions: It is a highly dubious document. It is the predecessor of the canonical gospel. Not surprisingly, to the degree that liberal scholars endorse the latter idea, conservative scholars invoke the former. But suspicions about forgery are hardly limited to conservatives, who are more apt to declare longer Mark a worthless second-century pastiche. Scholars of all theological persuasions are drawn to the forgery debate, albeit mostly as a diversion.

So who does reject the authenticity of this letter? If you were to consult the two scholars who have spoken most confidently on this subject—a Professor of Judaica named Jacob Neusner and a Professor of Irish History named Donald Harman Akenson—you would learn either that practically no one was duped into taking Smith's discovery seriously (Neusner) or that "a veritable Who's Who of top biblical scholars have been hoodwinked by a fraudulent secret gospel that implies Jesus was a homosexual" (Akenson).[1] You would learn, in other words, that it is better to concentrate on the published arguments of people who might actually know the difference between an authentic and an inauthentic work of Clement. Should you do that, you would find at least eleven well-informed scholars who have given *reasons* to deny Clement's authorship of the *Letter to Theodore*: J. Munck, W. Völker, A.D. Nock, H. Musurillo, Q. Quesnell, W. Kümmel, C.E. Murgia, P. Beskow, E. Osborn, A.H. Criddle, and A. Jakab. This list might be overstated, since Musurillo admitted that the letter "sounds marvelously like Clement," gave no reasons why Clement could not have written it, and concentrated instead on conceivable motives and persons capable of producing a perfect forgery of Clement (which begs the question);[2] likewise, Quesnell did not claim that the text *is* a forgery or that Clement could not have written it—only that we

Notes to chapter 2 start on page 243

cannot draw a positive conclusion without first examining the physical manuscript;[3] and Nock could not formulate his objection to authenticity more concretely than "intuition"; apparently, he thought the discovery was too good
to be true.[4]

Three of these scholars offered their opinions in the 1960s while Smith
was preparing his commentary (Munck, Völker, Nock), another four, in the
three years following the publication of that book in 1973 (Musurillo,
Quesnell, Kümmel, Murgia). Since then, to the best of my knowledge,
only four reasonably well-informed scholars elaborated arguments against
Clement's authorship in the secondary literature: Per Beskow, Eric Osborn,
and Attila Jakab, who are patristic scholars, and Andrew Criddle, an independent researcher who carefully studied the letter. So the number of
experts who have contested the authenticity of this letter in print is relatively small and has been growing disproportionately slowly compared to
the number of experts who have come to accept the document as authentic or possibly authentic. However, in the long drought of serious study
of this question, the popular conception that longer Mark might be a forgery has become quite strong, to the point of obscuring the reality that most
scholars *who have actually studied the letter and written on the subject* are
inclined to believe that it was written by Clement. What really matters,
though, is not the number of scholars in either camp or even their proficiency in the relevant subjects, but the arguments themselves, most of
which have not been critically examined.

The allegations of forgery have taken two main forms. Some scholars
have proposed that Smith's document is indeed an eighteenth-century copy
of an earlier manuscript, but that the original letter was an ancient forgery
produced within a few centuries of Clement. The alternative is that the
pages Smith photographed are themselves a forgery that was produced
sometime within the last two hundred years. These scenarios have different
implications for the authenticity of the gospel quotations. The most plausible motive for an ancient forgery would be to use Clement's authority to
validate a different version of Mark's gospel.[5] Thus an ancient forgery would
most likely contain authentic excerpts from a lost version of Mark. A modern forgery, on the other hand, would contain nothing but prevarication, so
that possibility has much graver implications for the authenticity of the
gospel excerpts. Nevertheless, since both scenarios bear on the question of
the longer gospel's origins and authorship, both scenarios must be thoroughly explored. We begin, however, with the question of what happened
to the manuscript.

# The Manuscript

One of the most enduring aspects of the folklore that surrounds this document is the notion that Morton Smith prevented other scholars from examining it. The complaint that no one but Smith has ever seen the manuscript is voiced so often and with such moral affectation that many scholars mistake it for a fact. The truth is that at least three other scholars and two members of the Greek Patriarchate handled the manuscript. The information obtained by various inquirers, moreover, corroborates Smith's account that he left the book containing the manuscript among the seventy items that he catalogued in the library at Mar Saba.[6] In 1980, Thomas Talley learned that the Archimandrite Meliton retrieved this book from Mar Saba and brought it to the Patriarchate library in Jerusalem sometime after Smith's two books on the *Letter to Theodore* were published. The librarian, Father Kallistos Dourvas, told Talley that the two pages containing the manuscript had subsequently been removed from the book and were being repaired.[7] In 1996, Willy Rordorf spoke to another librarian, Father Aristarchos, who was able to produce the book but did not know what happened to the manuscript.[8] James H. Charlesworth also made an unsuccessful attempt to locate the manuscript at this library, as have James Edwards (January 1999), Shaye Cohen (June 1999), and John Dart (March 2000).[9]

More detailed information about the manuscript was obtained by Charles W. Hedrick and Nikolaos Olympiou, who have made a number of attempts to locate the manuscript since 1990. They learned from Kallistos that the book was moved to the Patriarchate library in 1977 and that Kallistos himself detached the manuscript in the same year in order to photograph it. After that, the manuscript was kept with the book as separate items, at least as long as Kallistos was librarian (until 1990). He no longer knows where to find it, but he is optimistic that it could still be in the library, and passed along his colour photographs of the manuscript, which Hedrick and Olympiou published in *The Fourth R*. Olympiou speculated that persons in the Patriarchate library may be withholding the manuscript because of the irreverent use made of it in Morton Smith's interpretation.[10]

The latest information about the manuscript is also the most surprising. Guy Stroumsa reported that he, the late Professors David Flusser and Shlomo Pines of the Hebrew University of Jerusalem, and Archimandrite Meliton travelled to Mar Saba in the spring of 1976 in search of the manuscript.[11] There, with the help of a monk, they located the volume by Voss, complete with the manuscript, in the tower library, exactly where Smith left it. It occurred to them that the book would be safer in Jerusalem, so they brought it back with them, and Meliton took it to the library. Stroumsa and the two professors inquired about having the ink tested, but when they discovered that the Israeli police had the only people equipped to do such testing, Meliton objected to leaving the book in the care of the police, so no testing was performed. Twenty-five years later, Stroumsa learned from his American colleagues that he was the only living Western scholar to have seen the manuscript, and was persuaded to publish his account.

It would appear, then, that the manuscript was found at Mar Saba in 1976 rather than 1977, or eighteen years after Smith photographed it, and it disappeared many years after the Archimandrite took it to Jerusalem and a librarian removed it from the book. These facts show how preposterous it is to suggest that *Smith* prevented other scholars from examining the manuscript. The fact that professors other than Smith could have analyzed the ink had their options not been so limited likewise makes it hard to sustain the fantasy that there was a conspiracy between Smith and members of the Patriarchate library to keep scholars from studying it. Yet many purveyors of the folklore still claim that "no one but Smith ever saw the document" and blame Smith for its disappearance.[12] Some prefer not to know any better.[13]

A striking feature revealed by the colour photographs is the extent to which the paper of the manuscript is browning around the edges, which had been cropped out in Smith's commentary volume. This is normally an indication that the book had been shelved for long periods in places where sunlight could irradiate into the edges of the paper, which is not likely to have occurred in the dark tower library at Mar Saba. The darker appearance of the edges of the paper is much more pronounced in the photos by Kallistos than in a newer set of colour photos provided by Hedrick of pages from the same book in 2000. Since we are dealing with two different sets of photographs taken twenty-three years apart under different lighting conditions and using different quality film, it is probably not possible to determine whether this fact has any significance. The new photos also reveal that the third page was severely torn where it was attached to the spine, sometime after Smith took his photos.

Of more importance is the fact that the colour photos allow us to perceive how the chemical composition of the ink has changed from black to lighter shades of rusty brown in the places where Smith's photos convey shades of grey. The ink is nearly black where it occurs in higher concentrations, presumably points where the scribe pressed harder or had just reinked his quill; where the least ink was used, the letters are a very light shade of rusty brown. So the ink has visibly faded, but the fading is evident in both sets of photos, despite the fact that they were taken under different lighting conditions. This new information weighs strongly against the possibility that the text could be a twentieth-century forgery of an eighteenth-century hand. The ways in which the ink and paper of manuscripts deteriorate has been studied extensively at the W.J. Barrow Research Laboratory in Richmond, Virginia. Barrow himself devoted thirty years to the study of the durability of different types of paper and ink, and his research on the deterioration and restoration of documents composed between 1400 and 1850 is pertinent to our assessment of the photographic evidence. Most writing during this period was done using iron gall inks. Barrow noted that these inks produce writings that remain quite legible for many centuries, but when these inks are improperly compounded with an insufficient proportion of gallic and tannic acids, they tend to fade over time from black to rusty brown, especially when stored in adverse conditions—sunlight, mould, and bacteria being the main causes of this deterioration. The relevance of this information becomes clear when we realize just how long this process takes: "The usual time varies from about twenty-five to one hundred years. The factors effecting this change are the proportions of the ink ingredients, the amount deposited on the paper, and the composition of the paper; each of these may be accelerated by poor storage conditions." Once the incorrectly compounded iron gall ink has finished turning brown, its colour remains stable and the writing does not fade further if properly stored.[14] Since both sets of photos depict the same pattern of fading in the ink, and the colour photos show that the ink is rusty brown, the manuscript gives the impression of being no younger than a quarter century at the time Smith photographed it.

Although the ink depicted in the colour photos is the expected colour of oxidized iron or "rust," the paper on which the *Letter to Theodore* was written also appears quite brown in Kallistos's photos. The browning of paper inscribed in iron gall ink is a well known phenomenon; it is the result of a slow process of oxidation of paper caused by the acidity of iron gall inks. This slow "burning" of the paper is a principle factor in the deterioration of manuscripts, and their preservation normally involves neutralizing the acidity. Though Barrow did not state how long it takes for the paper itself to become brown as a consequence of oxidation, it would make sense that this is a very lengthy process since the paper of manuscripts becomes darker and more brittle over time.[15] It may not be possible, however, to determine whether the ink is responsible for the brown colour of the paper on which the manuscript is written, since we have no means of determining the relative difference in colour between the manuscript pages and other pages in the book or verifying that the photos accurately depict the colour of the manuscript. Unfortunately, the photos provided by Kallistos do not include a picture of the last page of the book (318) open beside the first page of the manuscript (the black and white reproduction of page 318 that also appears in *The Fourth R* is from a colour photo secured by Hedrick in 2000).

In view of what is known about the fading and browning of inks and the browning of paper in contact with ink, we can conclude that the photos depict a manuscript that looks like it is a few hundred years old. It remains to be seen whether the generally brown appearance of the manuscript in the photos is in some way a reflection of poor quality film or the age of the photographs. A die-hard sceptic will, of course, entertain the possibility that these indications of ageing could have been faked by Smith. Barrow's research indicates that some formulas of iron gall inks result in writings that would turn brown quite rapidly through exposure to sunlight. Unfortunately, we cannot know what formula was used in the production of this manuscript without physically examining it. But even if the ink was of a composition that could turn brown very rapidly, that would not explain the browning of the paper. Both ink that remains black over the centuries and ink that turns brown affect paper in the same way, though the blacker, or more concentrated, inks are more acidic and therefore more damaging.[16] There was a way of ageing paper artificially that was used in the 1950s by experienced researchers such as Barrow. But this process involved subjecting loose papers to an extremely high temperature (100°C) for periods of up to a few days. It is also possible to age paper and ink using chemicals that oxidize the ink and paper. In the early 1980s, Mark William Hofmann, the forger of the *Oath of a Freeman* and the *Salamander Letter*, used hydrogen peroxide to age documents.[17] It would take a sophisticated method like that to produce a document like the *Letter to Theodore* where the ink is blacker in the higher concentrations (most forgers simply stain their documents with tea or dirt, under the false premise that very old documents look very dirty). It is hard to envision anyone managing to age the manuscript pages artificially in such ways without the pages coming loose from the binding or other damage occurring to the book. So the combination of faded rust-brown ink and browning paper that is characteristic of centuries-old manuscripts is not readily dismissed.

## The Possibility of Modern Forgery

### *The Arguments of Charles Murgia*

When considering the possibility of modern forgery, it is best to begin with a paper written in 1975 by Charles E. Murgia, then Chairman (now Professor Emeritus) of the Department of Classics at Berkeley, for a Colloquium arranged by Edward C. Hobbs on the question of whether LGM 1 represents primitive gospel tradition. Murgia noted parallels between the letter and

"Classical fakes," which raised the possibility that this manuscript was written much later than it appears to be. Most importantly, he noted that classical forgeries often contain information that rationalizes their own existence and late emergence, and that this information does not always harmonize with elements in the undisputed corpus. He also noted that when such forgeries take the form of interpolations within existing texts, they may attempt to authenticate themselves by filling obvious gaps or omissions (lacunas).[18]

Murgia's observations about how forgeries provide self-authenticating information gave scholars a reason to wonder whether the *Letter to Theodore* might actually be a forgery:

> To me it seems that every sentence of the letter, other than the actual quotation of secret Mark, is admirably designed to provide A SEAL OF AUTHENTICITY for the passage of secret Mark. Great care is taken to convince the modern reader of why he has never heard of this gospel before. (1) It is only known at Alexandria, (2) it is carefully guarded, (3) it is read only to the initiates, (4) its very existence should be denied in public, and (5) even perjury should be committed to maintain the secret of its existence.[19]

At first sight, this argument is quite compelling. Smith himself commented in 1976 that Murgia's "theory of a 'seal of authenticity' is the strongest case I have yet seen for the supposition that the letter is a forgery. I think it would persuade me if I could think of a plausible forger (someone capable of doing the job), a plausible reason for the forgery, and a plausible explanation of why, if launched by somebody for some reason, the document has never hitherto been heard of."[20] Six years later, however, Smith treated the question of a seal of authenticity more lightly, and noted that Murgia "fell into a few factual errors."[21] These errors become apparent when one examines Murgia's characterizations of the letter.

Let us consider Murgia's points in order. (1) According to the letter, the gospel is not known only in Alexandria but is also becoming known wherever Theodore lived because Carpocratians discussed it openly. This was not a "secret Gospel," as Smith translated *mystikon euangelion* (II.6, 12), but a mystic gospel whose *essential truths* were hidden beneath the literal level of the narrative. (2) This mistranslation unfortunately led Smith to read the notions of physical guarding and secrecy into the statement that the gospel was "very securely kept" within the church (ἀσφαλῶς εὖ μάλα τηρεῖται; II.1).[22] I doubt we are supposed to imagine guards perpetually posted outside a locked room, preventing the curious from discovering a secret text! The point, rather, is that this text was not made available to persons of unproven character. The reference to Mark bequeathing his text to the church and the fanciful account of how Carpocrates obtained his own copy similarly imply that the original longer text was never copied for larger distribution (i.e., published). (3) The restriction to "those being initiated into the great mysteries" specifically excludes anyone who had not studied the minor mysteries of cosmology from attending readings of this text. But there is no indication in the letter of any attempt to keep catechumens and ordinary Christians unaware of the existence of this gospel. (4) In no sense—not even by implication—is Theodore enjoined "to maintain the secret of its existence."[23] He is told to deny *to the Carpocratians* that their falsifications are Mark's *mystikon euangelion*.[24] The existence of *a mystikon euangelion* is taken for granted in these debates with Carpocratians, for the Carpocratians have it. They are the ones who told Theodore about it in the first place! Moreover, the rationale that the implied author gave for quoting the contents of the longer gospel to Theodore suggests that any *proper* Christian may know its contents:

> But we are "children of light," having been illuminated by the "dayspring" of the spirit of the Lord "from on high," and "Where the Spirit of the Lord is," it says, "there is liberty," for "All things are pure to the pure." To you, therefore, I shall not hesitate to answer the questions you have asked, refuting the falsifications by the very words of the Gospel. (II.16–20)

In his *Paedagogus* Clement used the phrases "children of light" and "having been illuminated" in reference to ordinary Christians, not gnostics (II.9.80.1; 9.79.3; cf. 9.80.4). Illumination is mentioned as a consequence of baptism in *Paed.* I.6.26.1; it is baptized believers who possess "the spirit of the Lord."[25] Thus the persons to whom the mystic text rightly belongs ("we," "the pure") are the *real* Christians who received illumination and liberty from the holy spirit through baptism. Since Theodore is a proper Christian, the implied author has no qualms about divulging the contents of the mystic gospel to him: "To you, therefore, I shall not hesitate…" As far as the incomplete fragment goes (Murgia assumed the fragment is the whole text), there is no direction to Theodore not to share his knowledge of the longer text with other legitimate Christians.

(5) Murgia's last point concerning the implied author's recommendation of a false oath (II.11–12) deserves special attention. According to Murgia, the forger's need to explain why this gospel is otherwise unheard-of has resulted in a highly implausible scenario that conflicts with Clement's position that a true Christian would not use oaths: "The rhetoric of urging someone to commit perjury to preserve the secrecy of something which you are in the process of disclosing is ludicrous." Murgia made an error in supposing that Theodore is being asked to keep this gospel a secret from the people who informed him about it. But Theodore *is* being enjoined to use an oath to bolster the half-truth that Mark did not write the adulterated Carpocratian text,

and Murgia is not alone in supposing that this contradicts what Clement said about oaths in *Strom*. VII.8.[26] It would be helpful, then, to review this passage. In VII.8, Clement reasoned that oaths are sworn by people whose way of life does not instill sufficient confidence in others. An honest life is itself "a sure and decisive oath." A Christian "ought, I think, to maintain a life calculated to inspire confidence towards those without, so that an oath may not even be asked; and towards himself and with those with whom he associates, good feeling, which is voluntary righteousness." Clement went on to say that "The Gnostic swears truly, but is not apt to swear, having rarely recourse to an oath, just as we have said." As this comment demonstrates, Clement acknowledged that there are times when a Christian *would* swear an oath. Presumably, he had in mind situations in which the other party has had insufficient opportunity to appreciate the Christian's truthfulness through witness of prior conduct. Theodore's dealings with Carpocratians would probably be so limited as to qualify as such a circumstance. These opponents, moreover, are not potential converts who might be impressed with a Christian's day-to-day truthfulness but a despised sect whose practices threatened to discredit Christianity. The implied author's strategy for dealing with Carpocratians was to inform them with a solemn oath that their principles are not founded on an authentic apostolic writing. The letter writer attempts to characterize this assertion as essentially the truth, reasoning that the longer gospel that the Carpocratians possess has been adulterated to the point that it is not really the gospel Mark wrote (I.11–15; II.6–12). The telling of a half truth is not at all devious for Clement. In the chapter of the *Stromateis* that follows the discussion of oaths, Clement went on to note that sometimes the gnostic will, "medicinally, as a physician for the safety of the sick,…deceive or tell an untruth" (VII.9.53.2). If lying to Christians for their own good was acceptable to Clement, it is hard to doubt that telling half-truths to heretics for the good of the church would not be. We can agree with Judith L. Kovacs that the letter sounds very much like Clement in this respect.[27]

Murgia's proposed seal of authenticity does not hold up under examination. We may agree that the gospel was known *mainly* in Alexandria, and, among the orthodox, was *read* only to the true gnostics. We can infer that the officials in the church were more circumspect than the Carpocratians about divulging its contents to outsiders and did not distribute it outside Alexandria. But we need not suppose that most Alexandrian Christians of Clement's day knew nothing about it. The stated and implied restrictions on its use do not amount to a sufficient explanation for why modern (or ancient) readers had never heard of the text, though they do help explain why no copies now exist. This silence is not too surprising in view of the fact that six other previously unknown gospels were rediscovered in the twentieth century.[28]

Murgia's observation about how interpolators will fill existing lacunas is still worth considering in view of the fact that the addition of LGM 2 to Mark 10:46 makes the canonical account of Jesus entering and leaving Jericho seem deficient, and the addition of LGM 1 provides an identity for the young man who appears out of nowhere in canonical Mark 14:51–52. But without considerable additional evidence for why the letter should be viewed as a forgery, these facts can only appear ambiguous. The author of LGM 1 and 2 may have been attempting to elucidate elements in the narrative that seemed puzzling. The evidence in fact supports that position. The letter itself does not present LGM 1 and 2 as elements that had been lost from the original gospel; it presents them as subsequent additions made by the original author for the purpose of producing a second, distinct edition of his gospel.

In addition to noting similarities between the letter and classical forgeries, Murgia raised the issue that the manuscript of the letter contains no serious errors indicative of a normal history of scribal transmission. Because scribes are prone to make errors, and errors tend to be compounded as imperfect copies are made from imperfect copies, manuscripts tend to have the occasional serious error in addition to numerous trivial ones. This is especially true of non-standard works, such as the lesser-known works of Clement, which were copied so infrequently that the scribes could not find other copies to use for comparison and correction. But whereas Smith's manuscript has its share of inconsequential errors, it appears to have no blunders. Moreover, in Murgia's opinion, this manuscript's inconsequential errors are not the type an ancient scribe would make but rather the type a modern *author* would make; for instance, "The author, like most modern Greeks, cannot tell his smooth from his rough breathings."[29]

The lack of conspicuous errors was already noted by Smith in his commentary. In Smith's opinion there are numerous indications that the scribe who produced the Mar Saba fragment was a well-trained scholar who made few expected errors and might therefore have been meticulous enough to have studied and corrected the manuscript that he copied.[30] Smith had also noticed the presence of modern errors in breathings; this is his interpretation of both facts: "These [modern] errors [in breathings] do not prove that the manuscript he [the scribe] copied was incorrect in these points; nor does the usual correctness of his spelling prove that it was generally correct. He probably copied by reading the phrases and then repeating them as he wrote them down. Therefore it is not surprising that what he wrote should sometimes reflect either his knowledge or his pronunciation, rather than the reading of the text he was copying."³¹ Scribes normally copied manuscripts by this procedure.³² They would read a phrase and then repeat it to themselves until they finished writing it down, much the way we repeat a phone number to ourselves between looking it up and dialling it. Smith also suggested that the manuscript upon which the copy is based may have lain in the monastery for a millennium without being copied and therefore did not have a lengthy transmission history.³³ Smith's interpretation of the evidence is plausible, and there is no doubt that the person who made this manuscript was a scholar, but the lack of serious errors indicative of transmission weighs in Murgia's favour.

Murgia's perspective on the document, however, lacks a convincing rationale for why such a letter would be forged in the first place. His explanation appears to be that the document was created in the eighteenth century for the purpose of satire or self-amusement, for the letter seemed to him to read as a humorous parody of both Clement and Mark.³⁴ Interestingly, some of the things that Murgia found funny about the letter—such as the reference to Mark using "notes," the ambiguity concerning whether the young man was dead, and the comment in LGM 1:9 that Jesus and the young man returned to the man's house "for he was rich"—are actually consistent with what we know about Clement's views and the peculiarities of Mark's style. According to Eusebius, Clement's *Hypotyposeis* contained a story in which Peter's Roman audience implored Mark to produce for them a memorandum of Peter's preaching (ὑπομνήμα), which became the occasion for his gospel (*Church History* II.15.1–2). The same term is used in the *Letter to Theodore*. So if this is a forgery, the author was knowledgeable enough to draw upon a fragment of Clement's writings preserved by Eusebius. As for the ambiguity concerning whether the young man was dead, which is created by the loud voice from the tomb, the same uncertainty occurs in connection with two other individuals whom Jesus raises by the hand: Jairus's daughter and the epileptic boy (Mark 5:39, 41; 9:26–27). Finally, Mark's tendency to offer peculiar and sometimes embarrassing explanations beginning with the word *for* (γάρ) was pointed out by C.H. Bird in 1953.³⁵ The odd explanation in LGM 1:9 is very similar to the ones in Mark 5:42; 11:13; and 16:4. I share Murgia's amusement with the comment "But 'naked man with naked man,' and the other things about which you wrote, are not found" (III.13–14). Yet Clement often comes across like the straight man in a lurid skit, and *much* funnier lines showcasing his homophobia appear in *Paed.* III.11. So we need to ask whether an interest in making Mark and Clement look a little funnier can account for all the effort involved in preparing a forgery that so successfully imitates Clement's vocabulary, verbal associations, comparisons and metaphors, forms of reference, formulas for beginning sentences, use and frequency of prepositions, syntax, and basic thought,[36] along with Mark's style, redactional tendencies, theological emphases, and literary techniques.[37] We should also ask how this forger benefited from his labour. If this is an eighteenth-century forgery, then "some anonymous scribe has waited patiently for his joke to see the light of day."[38]

## The Arguments of Quentin Quesnell

The widespread suspicion directed against the letter is founded not so much in legitimate concerns about its contents as in gossip about a tantalizing article that appeared in the *Catholic Biblical Quarterly* a few months prior to the Colloquy attended by Murgia.[39] Its author is a man of diverse interests, ranging from philosophy and Catholic theology to the history and archaeology of southwest Florida and even the disappearance of Smith College founder, Sophia Smith, but in the field of New Testament scholarship Quentin Quesnell (pronounced keh-NELL) is best known for his 1967 doctoral thesis *The Mind of Mark* and his memorable exchange with Morton Smith.

The famed article had its genesis in 1973, when Quesnell prepared a review of *The Secret Gospel* for the *National Catholic Reporter*. He had recently read some studies of forgeries, and when he encountered Smith's work on the *Letter to Theodore* "everything seemed so familiar. All the characteristics of a hoax were present; all the classic mistakes that popular summaries like Goodspeed's warn against were being made. I listed them and drew the scientific conclusion that had to be drawn—until further and better evidence appears, this has to be judged a forgery."[40]

Quesnell's book review made no (obvious) suggestion that the letter might be a forgery, but he was intrigued enough by the possibility to write Smith a letter on 15 November 1973 in order to see if Smith would confirm his suspicion. Supposing that Smith might have produced the letter himself with the help of someone who could imitate eighteenth-century Greek handwriting ("the one who knows," to whom *SG* was dedicated), Quesnell conjectured that Smith was conducting a controlled experiment in how scholars respond to new evidence. Quesnell thought that if his suspicion was correct, Smith might ask him to keep this information to himself until the experiment was finished. Smith did not, however, respond with a confession, so Quesnell decided to raise a challenge to the document's authenticity in print. On 27 December 1973, he sent a précis of his article to the journal *New Testament Studies*, suggesting that "Perhaps if a serious scholar became convinced that a controlled study of diverging apologetic interpretations was needed for the improvement of scientific method, he might consider that adequate justification for creating one strictly controllable piece of evidence with which to get the study under way" (that scenario was eventually outlined on pp. 57–58 of his article).

In the finished article, Quesnell argued that the evidence, as Smith presented it, leaves forgery a very real possibility. He did not, however, accuse Smith of forging the letter, because he recognized that such a conclusion would go beyond the evidence: "Did I personally think Smith (in collaboration with 'the one who knows') had forged the document? Of course I did. But that was not the point of the article. Why did I not make it the point of the article? Because it was a conclusion based on negative evidence. All that followed from the evidence made available was that the document could have been produced anywhere between 1936 [when the first index of Clement's vocabulary had been published] and 1958 [when the letter was discovered]." The notion that Quesnell set out to prove that Smith forged the *Letter to Theodore* is a long-standing misconception of Quesnell's article, one that derives in large measure from Smith's intemperate response. Smith's knowledge of Quesnell's private suspicions led him to read more into Quesnell's public arguments than Quesnell intended. So in 1976, Smith offered a brief rejoinder in *CBQ* in which he asserted that "Quesnell insinuates that I forged the [manuscript]."[41] In the same issue Quesnell was allotted 1500 words to set the record straight, but few observers of the dispute were disposed to believe him, for they relished the thought that someone had publicly accused Smith of forgery:

> Dr. Smith feels the point of my article was to prove that he forged the Clement text. If that had been my point, I would have stated it clearly. He would not have had to compose his reply in terms like "insinuates…suggests…insinuation…suspicion…etc."
>
> I did state the real point clearly. It was a general point of scientific method, which is why it interested me….The point was—and remains—that a person who introduces an exciting new manuscript find to the world has the basic responsibility to make the manuscript available for scientific examination.[42]

Quesnell did not "skitter…away from alleging fraud," as the scandalmongers insist.[43] He never intended to make his personal and unsubstantiated suspicions an issue in his article. What did concern him was Smith's decision to present his colleagues with mere photographs of the text. According to Quesnell, Smith's approach of not producing the original for scientific study and restricting his analysis to the content is congruent with the pattern of known forgers; that fact raises the possibility of recent forgery.[44] Hence physical analysis is necessary to rule out a modern origin (e.g., analysis of the ink, the smoothness of the pen strokes, etc.). This concern for how an important manuscript discovery should be presented to the scientific community is what led Quesnell to argue that if Smith had the necessary resources to find and authenticate the document in the late 1950s, then so did a potential forger have them to create and plant the document.[45]

For the most part Quesnell maintained a distinction between this hypothetical forger and the person who authenticated the document, but here and there he buttressed his case by casting suspicion on Smith. Quesnell noted, for instance, that Smith's interest in how scholars respond to new evidence is something that might have motivated a forger. Here Smith is said "to tell a story on himself" when he narrated the reactions of two of his teachers to his discovery.[46] More pointedly, Quesnell wondered aloud whether the dedications of Smith's two books are meant to be understood together, pointing out that the scholarly book was dedicated to someone who Smith knew did not accept Clement's authorship of the letter (A.D. Nock) and that the popular version was written "For The One Who Knows." Quesnell implied that Smith supplied a hint about what this anonymous person knows.[47] More generally, Quesnell characterized Smith's presentation of the evidence as "puzzling" for a serious study,[48] implying that it might not be so serious.

Quesnell had no problem with the contents of the manuscript, which struck him as "quite harmless and in no way implausible for the period in question."[49] His reasons for casting doubt on its authenticity were hypothetical. Instead of convincing someone connected to the Patriarchate to arrange to test the manuscript, or uncovering evidence that Smith had been studying Clement before 1958 (e.g., library records, publications), Quesnell put the onus entirely on Smith, claiming that he "had a responsibility to make the manuscript available for scientific examination." That expectation makes little sense.[50] Regardless of how item 65 found its way into the tower library, Smith could not take it home with him in order to present it to his peers. His ties with the Patriarchate were with people he knew in his mid-twenties. When he desired to return to Mar Saba in 1958, the new Patriarch, His Beatitude Benedict, granted his request to catalogue the manuscripts not in the interests of Western science but in recognition of volunteer work Smith had done for Orthodox refugees ten years earlier.[51] Once that debt to Smith was repaid, Smith had no more influence within the Patriarchate than anyone else who has tried—in vain—to see the manuscript. So what more could Smith do besides publish photographs, report the precise location of the manuscript, and inform the Patriarchate of its importance? Unfortunately, Quesnell's unrealistic demand that Smith produce the manuscript metamorphosed into the myth that Smith refused to let anyone examine it and even into scepticism that it ever existed.

Quesnell's reason for rejecting arguments of authorship based on content also makes little sense. Even if we grant the notion that "a contemporary might always possess as much information about plausible form and content as the would-be detector, possess the same tools, know as much about the uncovering of earlier hoaxes,"[52] the premise that a forger could fool all of his or her contemporaries has past its expiry date. Present-day Clement scholars, with forty-five more years of research at their disposal, should have the necessary resources to detect problems with the content of the letter. Yet they are generally *more* inclined to accept the letter's authenticity, precisely because they now better appreciate the letter's conformity to Clement's thought. Quesnell cited Goodspeed in support of the importance of examining the physical manuscript, but Goodspeed himself conceded that the content and visual appearance of a manuscript usually supply a professional document examiner with enough information for detecting forgery: "What the scholar really desires is to see the very document itself, but failing that a photograph of it will usually answer the purposes of his investigation."[53] Goodspeed had little difficulty exposing fraudulent discoveries strictly on the basis of anachronisms and other irregularities in their *contents*, and his demonstrations of decisive errors often filled several pages. Manuscript or not, there is usually something in the content of a fraudulent ancient text that will stand out as an obvious give-away even to contemporary authorities on the purported author, and such works rarely fool more than a few inattentive experts. Professional document examiners, moreover, can and do find anomalies in the appearance of a manuscript on the basis of photographs. Although people like to romanticize about the perfect forgery, the reality is that "perfect forgeries are so rare that it is doubtful if many document examiners have ever seen one."[54]

Quesnell's contention that Smith's actions conformed to the standard pattern of forgers is likewise problematic. In marked contrast to Smith, the discoverers of the alleged ancient Christian texts discussed by Goodspeed supplied no transcriptions of the texts in the original languages, no photographs of the alleged manuscripts, and no clear information about where to find them. In other words, they merely pretended that they had seen manuscripts. The more knowledgeable charlatans who can forge believable manuscripts, on the other hand, rarely stop at one. It takes an enormous amount of practice to cut a serviceable quill pen, to write naturally and elegantly with feather and ink, and to devise a formula for ink that can be faded artificially, in this case on two types of paper (the last blank page of the book and a page of binder's paper) that are bound into a book. The people who bother to master such things normally forge documents on a regular basis if not for a living; the need for fame or fortune that motivates great forgers is rarely satisfied with a single "discovery." Some, like Mark Hofmann, produced more forgeries than they could remember (and his errors were detected from photographs).[55] When they come under suspicion, such forgers normally resort to greater deceit, such as forging corroborating evidence. When we consider the fact that Smith discovered only one highly significant document, published photographs, carefully preserved those photographs in his safe deposit box, informed the Patriarchate of the manuscript's importance, gave the world accurate information about its whereabouts, and never appealed to "new" corroborating evidence, it is hard to justify the suggestion that we are dealing with a pattern typical of forgers.

## *The Controversy Sparked by Quesnell's Article*

Quesnell did not intend to accuse Smith of forgery or to offer a veiled hypothesis about how Smith could have manufactured the text. He made a case that the manuscript cannot be accepted as authentic in the absence of forensic examination. Nevertheless, during the 1980s some scholars who were venturing to conduct independent research on the document began to play up this dispute, partly to show that they were aware of the possibility of forgery, but also as a means of reviving interest in the subject. The intrigue of Smith's discovery grew with every retelling. In 1979, a Swedish patristic scholar, Per Beskow, capitalized on the mystique of forgery by discussing the longer gospel in a book that addressed the problems involved in detecting modern forgeries.[56] Quesnell's reasons for querying the authenticity of the document figure prominently in this discussion. In 1984, Hans-Martin Schenke began his overview of the scholarly reception of the letter by quoting a page and a half of visceral comments about Smith's theories by three German scholars, then turned to Quesnell and proclaimed "Quesnell makes no secret of his suspicion that Smith might have forged the Clementine letter himself."[57] The year after that, in another review of Quesnell's concerns about authenticity, John Crossan reiterated Smith's slant on the point of one of Quesnell's arguments: "If the text is a forgery, then, one might presume that the scholarship used by Smith to authenticate the document in 1973 [*sic*] was actually prepared to forge it in 1958."[58] That is quite a presumption considering that Smith published nothing on Clement prior to the 1970s and showed little interest in patristics in the period leading up to his discovery. Next Marvin Meyer added to this popular impression of controversy with his comment, "From the well-known statements of Quentin Quesnell to the more recent dispute over insinuations in Per Beskow's *Strange Tales about Jesus*, the scholarly discussions concerning the Mar Saba manuscript have been conducted within the context of expressed doubts and uncertainties about the authenticity of the text."[59] This vague comment, wherein Beskow's "insinuations" establish the meaning of Quesnell's "well-known statements," conjures the thought of veiled accusations, but Beskow insinuated nothing and explained the reasons why he did not suspect Smith.[60]

The constant references to suspicion and controversy were self-fulfilling. Although intended in part to revive interest in the subject, the sensationalism ultimately had the opposite effect, and fewer scholars ventured to make use of a document that might one day be proved a forgery. Despite the dearth of new arguments against the letter's authenticity, the talk of controversy had itself become sufficient evidence that something is amiss, at least for scholars who did not have the appropriate expertise to develop an informed opinion. This growing deference to scholarly folklore, together with Smith's death in 1991, cleared the way for one of Smith's former students to declare him "a charlatan and a fraud, and his discovery a hoax."[61]

Jacob Neusner has made this allegation in a variety of contexts, most notably as part of a review of books by John Meier and John Crossan on the historical Jesus. Under the pretence of defending the enterprise of historical Jesus research against the "disgrace" brought to it by Smith's fraud,[62] Neusner felt free not only to refer to the *Letter to Theodore* as "what must now be declared the forgery of the century," but even to claim that this "brilliant forgery," this "out-and-out fakery," was "exposed" by Quesnell.[63] Neusner did not hesitate to assure us that Quesnell's "Further Questions for Smith" were a discreet way of accusing Smith of forgery, a ploy adopted in order to avoid getting "sued for libel."[64] Yet apart from rephrasing Quesnell's points to make them sound incriminating, Neusner offered no evidence of his own aside from baseless characterizations of Smith's intentions, and numerous, egregious misrepresentations of fact. Where most scholars would do research, Neusner consulted the one famous opinion, then confabulated a new version of the reception of Smith's scholarship that suited his agenda:

> The very quest [for the historical Jesus] met its defining disgrace by Smith, whose "historical" results—Jesus was "really" a homosexual magician—depended upon a selective believing in whatever Smith thought was historical. Even at the time, some of us told Smith to his face that he was an upside-down fundamentalist, believing anything bad anybody said about Jesus, but nothing good. And no one who so rebuked him objected to the campaigns of character assassination that Smith spent his remaining years conducting; there is a moment at which, after all, truth does matter....
>
> ...As a matter of fact, Smith's presentation of the evidence for his homosexual magician, a Clement fragment he supposedly turned up in a library in

Sinai [*sic*] in 1958, ranks as one of the most slovenly presentations of an allegedly important document in recent memory; and, to understate matters, it left open the very plausible possibility of forgery. Smith himself was an expert on such matters, having devoted scholarly essays to great forgeries in antiquity.[65]

This first assault was published as many times as Neusner could find new ways to introduce it. In subsequent attacks upon Smith's memory, Neusner took it for granted that his allegations had had their intended effect. Hence he set aside the pretence of having evidence, and referred to the supposed fraud and imaginary scandal as facts: "As to the scholarly fraud, who speaks of it any more, or imagines that the work pertains to the study of the New Testament at all? I need not remind readers…of the scandal of Smith's 'sensational discovery' of the Clement fragment, the original of which no one but Smith was permitted to examine. Purporting, in Smith's report, to demonstrate that the historical Jesus was 'really' a homosexual magician, the work has not outlived its perpetrator. In the end many were silenced—who wanted to get sued?—but few were gulled."[66]

This is an astonishing assessment of the *Letter to Theodore* and its discoverer—all the more so when we consider that Neusner expressed the exact opposite opinions when he wrote the dust jacket endorsement for *The Secret Gospel*:

> This is a brilliant account of how Morton Smith reached a major discovery in the study of first-century Christianity. We have not only his conclusions and the way in which these are argued, but also his own life and thought as he reached them. The discovery itself ranks with Qumran and Nag Hammadi, Masada and the Cairo Geniza, but required more learning and sheer erudition than all of these together, both in the recognition of what has been found, and in the interpretation and explanation of the meaning of the find. All this Smith has done—and he tells us about it in a narrative of exceptional charm and simplicity.[67]

In addition to writing this radiant endorsement, Neusner had assisted with the proofreading of *CA* before its publication.[68] So when we contemplate the sincerity of his opinion that very few scholars were fooled by this self-evident fraud, we cannot help but wonder whether Neusner categorizes himself among the many who were cowed or the few who were gulled, or whether instead he wants us to believe that he willingly contributed to and endorsed research that he considered fraudulent. I suspect that he knows full well that most knowledgeable scholars then and now could find little reason to doubt the authenticity of the letter and has gambled that the memory of his wholehearted endorsement of this text vanished with Smith and the dust jackets.

Except for the less outlandish remarks in the dust-jacket endorsement, none of the sentences by Neusner that I have just quoted could be deemed accurate. What he offers us is a combination of standard academic folklore and his own far-fetched invention. Much of his first assault was pointed out to him to be either false or unbelievable shortly after he wrote it. When Neusner published "Who Needs 'the Historical Jesus,'" the invited respondent, Craig Evans, pointed out that there was never any scandal caused by the "secret" gospel in the context of historical Jesus research, that "several patristic scholars" consider the letter authentic, and that it is "hard to believe that anyone would devote years of painstaking labor to the production of a 450-page technical book that studies a writing that the author himself faked."[69] In 1996, Shaye Cohen pointed out that "homosexual magician" was "a caricature of Smith's view" and that the longer gospel continues to interest New Testament scholars.[70] Unfortunately, these objections did not deter Neusner from repeating the same notions in the attack on Smith that he contributed to the reprint of Birger Gerhardsson's book *Memory and Manuscript*. Nor will mine, I expect. But since we all agree that "truth does matter," I will point out some other statements that are demonstrably false. Neusner's recollection that the manuscript "supposedly turned up in a library in Sinai" is a good indication that he did not even review the facts about the manuscript before declaring it a forgery. His description of *CA* as "one of the most slovenly presentations of an allegedly important document in recent memory" is an absurd generalization derived from Quesnell's view that *CA* contained "an extraordinarily high proportion of inaccuracies." Quesnell was the only scholar to express a negative opinion of Smith's technical competence, and he substantiated his opinion by noting the errors in Smith's treatment of less than one sentence of the letter.[71] Most reviewers who commented on the book's technical merits were highly impressed; some were nearly as impressed as Neusner had been himself.[72] Neusner's statement that "Smith himself was an expert on" forgery, "having devoted scholarly essays to great forgeries in antiquity" was, of course, offered as incriminating evidence, and was wisely left undocumented. Apart from a study of Deuteronomy and some discussions of Jewish pseudepigraphical writings, there are no such studies in the bibliographies of Smith's published and unpublished writings.

Of particular interest is Neusner's claim to have "told Smith to his face that he was an upside-down fundamentalist, believing anything bad anybody said about Jesus, but nothing good." Here Neusner was talking about Smith's 1978 follow-up book, *Jesus the Magician*, indicating that the rift between himself and Smith came when Neusner decided to criticize this book in defence of Christianity:

I thought and told him to his face that his results were nothing more than anti-Christian propaganda and, in a simple, but uncompromising, footnote, as I said, in the published version of my 1979 SBL address, dismissed Smith's account of Jesus, calling it not history but ideology. In our time a great many Christian scholars have done...no less for Judaism than I meant to do for Christianity: label prejudice and bigotry for what they are, so remove from scholarly discourse what does not belong among decent people. I did not regret then, and do not regret now, enduring Smith's vengeance for doing what I knew, and now know [*sic*], was right and also required of me.

In his day, many feared Smith and his clones, and only a very, very few in the world he dominated defied him. I am proud that, when the occasion demanded, I was one of the few. By publicly condemning his *Secret Gospel*'s outcome, *Jesus the Magician*, I opposed anti-Christianism [*sic*] just as so many Christian scholars, from Moore through Sanders, have opposed anti-Judaism. I take pride that, when it was time to stand up and be counted, I said in print that Smith's portrait of Jesus was not history but contemptible, hateful ideology.[73]

In a more popular book, Neusner added more information about this valiant footnote: Smith "chose to believe everything bad he could about Jesus, perhaps making up what he could not read into the sources. Since I had done my dissertation with him, I bore a special responsibility to say that that was what I thought. So, when I published that lecture, I said so in footnote 18 (the number eighteen standing for *life* in its Hebrew character)."[74]

Whether Neusner privately said anything like this to Smith, I do not know. But since he offered proof for this explanation of the break between himself and Smith, we can compare his story with the published footnote:

At this point [referring to his dictum "what we cannot show we do not know"] I regret I have to part company with my teacher, Morton Smith. Compare the opening chapters of his *Jesus the Magician*..., pp. 1–67, with his discourse on magic, pp. 68–139. The former discussion is tendentious; Smith sets out not to analyse a possibility but to prove a proposition. The shift in the tone of the book and in the character of the discussion when Smith turns to an academic account of magic in antiquity is stunning. This other part of the book is a model of academic clarity and deep learning, while the discussion on "the historical Jesus" is a morass of "proofs" of propositions.[75]

Clearly, there is a discrepancy between Neusner's descriptions of this note and the note itself. The footnote contains no suggestion that Smith made up evidence, praises his discussion of ancient magic, and faintly criticizes his discussion of the historical Jesus as "tendentious" and "a morass of 'proofs' of propositions." One might gather that Neusner thought *Jesus the Magician* was biased and methodologically flawed or that it contained assumptions that were inadequately substantiated. But clearly in this published version of his 1979 SBL address, Neusner made no valiant, public defence of Christianity against the "contemptible, hateful ideology" of *Jesus the Magician* and no intimation that he thought Smith had committed fraud—not even in a footnote. The fact that the 1981 paperback edition of *Jesus the Magician* sports Neusner's endorsement of Smith's "compelling and powerful historical argument" makes it even harder to believe that the rift between Smith and Neusner was the result of Neusner's noble condemnation of this book, rather than the other way around. Neusner has misrepresented not only the facts pertaining to the scholarly reception of the "secret" gospel but also his own prior views about this text and the time and manner in which he came to think of Smith and the *Letter to Theodore* as academic frauds.

So what really happened? What led Neusner to stop thinking of Smith as "the first, the only, and the last authentic teacher I ever had" and start thinking of Smith as "a crank and a crackpot," a "nasty old fool," a "conceptual bungler," a "know-nothing," and a "fraud"?[76] I doubt all the pieces of the puzzle are available in the secondary literature, but Smith's public denunciation of Neusner in 1984 for academic incompetence is the best-attested factor and is sufficient reason in itself.

In order to understand that event, one must know something about the history of these two scholars. Smith was one of the supervisors of Neusner's doctoral dissertation. Neusner learned from Smith's dissertation *Tannaitic Parallels to the Gospels* that the methodologies of New Testament scholarship were relevant to the study of rabbinic literature, and this insight "shaped" "the entire course" of Neusner's career.[77] During the decade after Neusner's graduation, Smith promoted Neusner's work in book reviews, and defended Neusner against his critics. But as far back as 1967 and 1970 Smith's positive reviews of Neusner's books were tempered with references to Neusner's "constant carelessness of execution," inexcusable "inaccuracies," and "slovenliness in details."[78] Smith stopped promoting Neusner's work after favourably reviewing *Development of a Legend* but noting that there were so many errors that "one cannot rely on the statements of fact and would be advised to check everything."[79] Smith put great emphasis on accuracy, and would sometimes look up hundreds of references in the course of preparing a book review. But Neusner did not heed Smith's criticism, so in 1973 Smith very politely informed Neusner that he was no longer going to read his books.[80] For many years Neusner continued to pay homage to his teacher, and even edited a four-volume *Festschrift* in Smith's honour, but their admiration became less mutual as the pace of Neusner's publications became more manic. Neusner is reluctant to admit that his distinction of being the world's most published scholar in the humanities, averaging one book every seventeen days over the entire course of his career, does not suggest only *good* things about his scholarship, and that some scholars would rather not be associated with him because of this.[81]

As long as Smith showed restraint in the way he expressed his disapproval, Neusner paid no attention to Smith's opinion about his careless scholarship. So in 1979, Smith made his first public demonstration. He stood up, turned around, and sauntered out during a plenary address that Neusner gave at an SBL meeting—a calculated gesture of disapproval. This attempt to sever their connection proved inadequate, as one can see from Neusner's feeble attempt to "part company" with his teacher, now enshrined in note 18 of the published version of that address. So Smith staged a second, unmistakable public demonstration at the 1984 AAR-SBL meeting. Prior to that meeting Smith explained his reason to Shaye J.D. Cohen, who recounted this information in a review of Neusner's book on Smith: "Smith explained to me that, because he had been instrumental in launching Neusner's career, he felt responsible for the 'slovenliness' of Neusner's scholarship, which had grown worse over the years. Neusner had proven to be incorrigible in this matter, and therefore Smith wanted to dissociate himself publicly from his student."[82] So at the conclusion of a session honouring Neusner's work, Smith took the podium to denounce Neusner's *The Talmud of the Land of Israel: A Preliminary Translation and Explanation* as "a serious misfortune for Jewish studies, because the people who use it will not only repeat Neusner's mistakes, but make new ones based on the misinformation his work will provide them."[83] Smith then passed out copies of a review by Saul Lieberman of two volumes of this (now) thirty-five volume translation, in which Lieberman undertook to illustrate Neusner's "ignorance of rabbinic Hebrew, of Aramaic grammar, and above all of the subject matter with which he deals."[84] This was more than a public dissociation; it was an attack on Neusner's reputation and influence. The lamentable event was a major humiliation to Neusner and one in a rapid series of blows to his ego. That year he felt he was being "shoved down the memory-hole."[85] His response was to do whatever he could to reclaim his reputation and discredit the people who had threatened it.

When Hershel Shanks recounted Smith's escapade in *Biblical Archaeology Review* in a report on the annul meeting, Neusner likened the journal to *Hustler* magazine and wrote a letter threatening a lawsuit for defamation.[86] He also informed Shanks that he was contemplating suing Smith and Lieberman's estate (Lieberman died before his review was published).[87] William M.

Calder III, a long-time friend of Smith, recalled that Smith showed him a letter from Neusner's lawyer threatening litigation, and that Smith found the threat greatly amusing. Smith responded by writing a letter to *Biblical Archaeology Review* in which he pointed out a slight error in this journal's description of Lieberman's review: "Saul Lieberman's review did not say that Neusner's essays *in this book* 'abound in brilliant insights,' etc. That praise…referred to Neusner's earlier works. In the present volume he found nothing to recommend, but recommended the whole 'for the wastebasket.'"[88] Neusner's writings thereafter contain the occasional insult directed at Smith, but he waited until Smith could not reply before he set out to destroy his reputation. Within two years of Smith's death, Scholars Press released the book *Are There Really Tannaitic Parallels to the Gospels: A Refutation of Morton Smith*, in which Neusner critiqued Smith's then half-century old dissertation, characterizing it as "trivial and, where interesting, quite wrong, ignorant, and misleading." The book abounds with spiteful characterizations such as "surpassingly commonplace triviality,…ignorant and incompetent,…insufficient, shoddy work," "a mess of contradiction and confusion," and—not surprisingly—"fraudulent."[89] The claim that Smith forged his important discovery is of a piece with the book's theme that Smith led a "tragic, fruitless career" and "died a figure of ridicule."[90] That Neusner's assessments of Smith's work have always been indistinguishable from his feelings about Smith should now be obvious, but in case there is any doubt, I will point out that prior to 1984, Neusner described the same dissertation as "the most beautifully argued work of historical reason I know."[91]

I must, therefore, disagree with Romano Penna, who, when borrowing Neusner's phrase "forgery of the century" second-hand from Graham Stanton, remarked "it is natural to agree with an impartial author such as the famous Jewish scholar Jacob Neusner."[92] It is hard to mistake Neusner's opinions on this subject as either knowledgeable or impartial, yet at least six other scholars have noted Neusner's opinion about this document and appealed to his knowledge of Smith—without mentioning his defamatory purpose.[93] Neusner's false witness is taking the place of incriminating evidence.

Neusner's attacks on Smith's memory have proved especially useful to his protégé, Donald Harman Akenson, who utilized Neusner's "secret" gospel scandalmongering as a weapon against liberal Jesus scholars. With a flare for righteous indignation, Akenson rendered this temerarious verdict upon "anyone" who would take this gospel seriously:

> the Secret Mark issue…is a rare moment, a clear adjudication point that
> allows laymen…to judge the competence of the leading scholars in the field:
> not the technical competence in small matters, but on the big matters; and

to determine, not to put too fine a line on it, whether they have at least as much common sense as God gives to a goose.

For look: Secret Mark is a forgery and not one that requires forensic methods and high magnification to detect. Anyone who could not spot it as a forgery from a height of 3,000 feet should not be allowed to make authoritative pronouncements on the authenticity of texts that relate to Yeshua of Nazareth.[94]

Akenson went on to explain to his lay readership that the inability of most biblical scholars to recognize longer Mark for what it is—"a nice ironic gay joke at the expense of all of the self-important scholars"—is proof that "some of the most powerful, most influential persons in the so-called 'liberal' wing of the field…are far from being omniscient or, often, even ordinarily shrewd. Vain, yes; credulous, yes; shrewd, no."[95]

Although admitting that the majority of North American Jesus scholars, liberal and conservative, consider "secret" Mark to be a real gospel, Akenson was mainly interested in using "the gimcrack false-antiquities of the sort exemplified by Secret Mark" to embarrass Crossan, Koester, and the Jesus Seminar.[96] He did not tell us *how* this gospel has influenced liberal portraits of the historical Jesus, but that is not surprising since none of his ideological opponents do in fact view LGM 1 and 2 as reliable evidence *about Jesus*. Koester's writings on the subject have mostly concentrated on the question of the composition history of the Gospel of Mark. Crossan decided that the whole of LGM 1 was invented to justify Christian baptism. And the Jesus Seminar gave every sentence of LGM 1 and 2 a black vote (meaning "largely or entirely fictive") except for those that have structural parallels to the raising of Lazarus (LGM 1:4–7), which were voted grey (meaning "possible but unreliable"). It would appear that for the Jesus seminar, longer Mark merely bolstered the credibility of a passage in John that they would not otherwise have considered credible.[97] Most other Jesus researchers do not mention longer Mark, or do little more than reiterate the standard reasons not to make use of it. Smith appears to be the only Jesus scholar to have factored LGM 1 into his reconstruction of the historical Jesus, and even he devoted only twelve lines to this text in his book *Jesus the Magician*. So it is quite unclear how anyone familiar with New Testament scholarship could think this text played an important part in Jesus research, let alone state that "Secret Mark…cruised into most of the work on the Historical Jesus and upon early Christian texts conducted in the 1980s and 1990s"![98] A more plausible figure would be a fraction of one percent. But the notion that liberal Jesus scholars have embarrassed themselves by relying on a bogus text is useful as propaganda; accordingly, Neusner's contrivance that "the spectacle" of historical Jesus research was "exposed" by its inability to distinguish longer Mark as a forgery is brought to its natural, if illogical, conclusion:[99] the majority of scholars who have not dismissed the *Letter to Theodore* as a worthless fraud are less rigorous and less competent than the few who have: "The field of the Quest for the Historical Jesus would be considerably clarified if (a) someone would definitively drive a stake into the heart of this particular scholarly vampire and thereafter (b) those scholars who have affirmed the work would publicly recant and then examine how they might recalibrate their own scholarly standards so as to avoid being gulled in the future."[100] If this sounds like a misguided inquisition against scholars allegedly, but not really, guilty of confounding historical Jesus research through their acceptance of a brief description of Jesus teaching the young man from Gethsemane the same mystery he gave his closest followers (Mark 14:51; 4:11), that would probably not be too far from the truth.

The premise sustaining the most recent comments by Akenson and Neusner is that the *Letter to Theodore* is an *obvious* forgery. If that were the case, they should have no problem providing definitive *proof*, but both avoided that responsibility by describing the document as so obviously fraudulent that proof would be superfluous. Neusner wrote as if he could will the fact of fraud into existence by declaring it forcefully. Akenson held out the hope that someone else will slay the vampire by doing the requisite research. However, in lieu of the anticipated proof, he listed some "obvious flags" of fraud:

> (a) the only person ever known to have seen the document in question was Professor Morton Smith; (b) there are no known letters of Clement of Alexandria preserved in their original form. Although some of his theological works survive, the nature and content of Clement's letters are known only through their being cited in other men's writings; (c) the text in question was produced not on a first- [*sic*] or second-century piece of writing material, but in the end leaf of a book made of seventeenth-century paper; (d) this obviated the need for ancient handwriting and no one flinched when the text was adjudged to be that of a mid-eighteenth-century hand. (The hand-writing expert was, not surprisingly, Professor Morton Smith); (e) though, in the actual event, no one but Smith ever saw the document, the inks would, of course, have been eighteenth-century inks, chemicals readily obtainable.[101]

Once again, the most incriminating elements of this presentation of suspicious evidence are the least accurate. Akenson should know that the manuscript remained at Mar Saba and was later moved to Jerusalem, since he quoted from one of the articles containing that information.[102] It is deceptive for him to imply that Smith prevented others from seeing the document. The fact that no other letters of Clement exist apart from second-hand quotations is irrelevant, particularly since a large collection of Clement's letters once existed in the very monastery in which this manuscript was catalogued. The second-hand quotations come from one writing, *Sacra Parallela*, which John of Damascus produced when he resided in Mar Saba (716–749).[103] The notion that a mid-eighteenth-century Greek hand would be easier to imitate than ancient Greek handwriting is illogical. If Akenson wants to challenge the dating of this hand, he needs to do something more than suppress the opinions of the nine experts in Greek handwriting whose views are summarized on the first page of *CA*;[104] he needs to present contrary assessments by experts in Greek palaeography. As far as I am aware, no one has offered any reasons to dispute Smith's position on the century of the handwriting. In fact, in 1991, Father Joseph Paramelle, the former director of the Section Grecque at the Institut de Recherche et d'Histoire des Textes anciens in Paris, offered his opinion that the manuscript looks very authentic and typical of the eighteenth century.[105] Essentially, Akenson's only valid point is that the manuscript was written in a seventeenth-century book rather than on papyrus or parchment. Of course, considering that Clement's *Stromateis* is preserved principally in one eleventh-century manuscript, we would not expect to have a manuscript earlier than the middle ages. But the lateness of our first and only witness to this letter is a legitimate concern.

Fortunately for Akenson, his coup de grâce does not concern the manuscript. The decisive point for him is the observation that the gospel excerpts read like a "gay joke." He is fully aware that few North American scholars perceive this joke, but in his opinion, the fact that they are not laughing with him does not belie the obviousness of his interpretation. Quite the contrary, "the burlesque of scholars and scholarship…is the basis of the joke." That is, the real joke is that so many formally trained New Testament and patristic scholars missed such an obvious joke (Akenson is a Professor of History: *Irish* history). This, indeed, was Smith's intention: to expose the pretentiousness of "the most powerful figures in the liberal wing of the Quest establishment" with a text that an untrained observer can immediately spot as a fake.[106] Smith's agenda, in other words, perfectly complemented Akenson's.

The people who now parade the "secret" gospel as an obvious hoax perpetrated by Smith have had some success convincing non-specialists. But the paucity of so-called "more rigorous scholars who see it as a chimera" remains an awkward incongruity for them, particularly since this shortage includes both New Testament scholars and authorities on Clement.[107] In general, the scholars who most confidently ascribe this letter to Clement are ones noted for their facility in patristic Greek, including several who have published translations of Clement's writings and articles on his thought.[108] That the inverse would hold true should only be expected. The real scandal here is that such unscholarly substitutes for expertise and analysis reach publication.

### Is Suspicion of Smith Reasonable?

To this day, most people who suspect Smith of having forged the document have reasoned "he published it, so he could have forged it, so it must be a forgery."[109] It is time to think this supposition through. The premise that Smith forged the document is a hypothesis, and any constructive hypothesis has implications that can be evaluated. We can begin this process by making two plausible deductions from this premise. First, as Goodspeed noted, the most compelling incentive for someone to forge an early Christian text is the fame and prestige that comes from being the discoverer of an important historical document.[110] The *Letter to Theodore* brought Smith international recognition and status, which he capitalized on when he published his popular account of the discovery. Hardly any other motive for forgery could account for the monumental effort Smith put into preparing his analysis of the gospel fragments and the letter. So there is at least one plausible motive, which has often been passed over in favour of less plausible ones (such as that Smith wanted to discredit Christianity by showing that Jesus was gay). Second, it is logical to suppose that if Smith did fabricate the letter, he began by developing the theories he offered to account for its historical significance and constructed the document so that it would substantiate those theories. It is certainly hard to imagine Smith creating the Clementine letter and the Markan gospel quotations *and only then* attempting to work out his elaborate theories about the emergence of Christianity that relate the two together. Smith's sustained interest in showing that the theories he presented in *CA* are better than all competing explanations demonstrates his concern for the plausibility of his analysis of this document. He never tired of clarifying his theories when others misrepresented them,[111] and was particularly hostile in person to two professional acquaintances who had argued that his theories were not only extravagantly complicated but also founded on an historically worthless, late-second-century concoction (namely, Edward C. Hobbs and Pierson Parker). Many of Smith's later articles on Jesus and Paul attempted to provide better support for theories he had argued in connection with the longer gospel.[112] Smith wanted his theories to be taken seriously. It is possible, then, for us to assess the plausibility of the notion that he fabricated the letter by considering whether prior to 1958 Smith held the views that he later used the letter to support, and whether the evidence of the letter seems tailor-made for his theories.

### Smith's Beliefs about Jesus and Mark's Gospel prior to 1958

Smith's writings prior to 1958 express views about Jesus and the reliability of the Gospel of Mark that are very different from those expressed in *CA* and later in *Jesus the Magician*.[113] In his 1956 article "The Jewish Elements in the Gospels," Smith classified Jesus as a "divinely inspired disturber of the established order" belonging to "the long line of prophets and rebels and religious individualists of the stamp of Spinoza and the Baal Shem Tov"; Jesus' motivation was explained in terms of "the individual's response to the guidance of the Holy Spirit, in defiance of the customs and authorities of the society around him."[114] That is, Smith thought that Jesus understood his own activities in relation to the will of the God of Israel. This differs from Smith's later view of Jesus as "one possessed by *a* spirit and thereby made the son of *a* god," one whose miracles required intrinsically efficacious "magical procedures."[115] Indeed, prior to 1958, Smith did not select magic as the best paradigm for the miracle tradition. Like other scholars, he recognized that there were magical elements in the gospel stories and placed no particular emphasis on them. When referring to these activities he regularly chose the sanguine term "miracles," with its mainstream theological implications, and the neutral term "exorcisms";[116] Smith conceptualized the stories of Jesus' miracles and exorcisms—magical elements and all—within the framework of monotheistic Jewish religion. At the time when Smith started to work on the letter, he was in the midst of examining Jesus in relation to the more Hellenistic concept of a "divine man" and decided to put that work on hold. In the course of writing *CA*, however, he came to prefer the word *magician*, although he believed that Jesus belonged to a distinct social type that his contemporaries apprehended in different ways. Divine man and Son of God represent the categories through which Jesus' pagan and Jewish admirers comprehended him. His enemies witnessed the same supernatural wonders but labelled him a magician. If there is an objective difference between a divine man and a magician, it is one of "social status and success."[117] Smith later attempted to prove this thesis in *Jesus the Magician*. Moreover, in 1955 Smith argued the contentious point that it is *improbable* that Jesus himself was interested in sinners and kept their company.[118] In *CA* Smith affirmed this interest as congruent with the picture of a libertine or a magician.[119] As far as I am aware, Smith first expressed his libertine understanding of Jesus in two articles published in 1967.[120]

Smith's views about the Gospel of Mark were likewise different in the years before he catalogued the manuscripts in Mar Saba. In his 1955 article on Vincent Taylor's *The Gospel According to St. Mark*, Smith constantly criticized Taylor for treating the Markan text as historically reliable. This criticism included Taylor's tendency to treat stories that do not conform to stereotyped storytelling patterns as accurate eyewitness memories.[121] After writing *CA*, however, Smith was compelled to justify his own historicizing reading of Mark and LGM 1b by arguing that accounts of actual events in the life of

Jesus were not always preserved in the conventional storytelling forms.[122] In 1955 he criticized Taylor's argument that the saying in Mark 4:11 originally had nothing to do with parables. Smith complained that this theory was designed to eliminate the offensive notion that Jesus told parables as a way of confusing his audience so that they would not repent and be saved (4:12).[123] In *CA*, this very theory is vital to Smith's (strained) argument that "the mystery of the kingdom of God" originally referred to the rite of baptism. Smith even cited Taylor in support, saying nothing about his own page-long refutation of Taylor's position.[124] Finally, in 1955 Smith criticized Taylor for accepting the historicity of two incidents in which Jesus tells two disciples what they will find when they go to make preparations for him in a village and in Jerusalem (i.e., a colt tied up; a man carrying a jar of water). Indeed, Smith ridiculed Taylor for thinking that these two stories were something other than "unmistakable folk-tale material" and for overlooking the historical implausibilities they involve.[125] In *The Secret Gospel*, Smith listed the latter story as evidence of Jesus' secrecy.[126]

There is a great difference between the views Smith submitted to print just a few years before the *Letter to Theodore* came to light and those he expressed by the time *CA* was completed. The prior views are fairly standard and offer good arguments of his own making that can be used against his subsequent magical and libertine reading of the gospels and selectively historicizing reading of Mark within that perspective.

### How Well Does Longer Mark Support Smith's Theories?

Our next consideration is how well the evidence supplied by the letter supports the new theories Smith based on this evidence. When we consider this matter, the hypothesis that Smith forged the document appears very improbable. The element in longer Mark that was essential to Smith's historical reconstruction was LGM 1b. In order to use this incident as evidence for a secret rite of the historical Jesus, Smith had to treat it as a fair depiction of an activity Jesus practised. But this decision conflicted with the prevailing logic of gospel form criticism. For much of the twentieth century, it was standard to assume that stories about Jesus circulated orally for decades before they were recorded on paper. Form critics, who studied and classified the types of stories found in the gospels, believed that each story was originally fashioned in conformity with standard storytelling patterns and was a pure representative of its type. When stories varied from the standard templates, scholars assumed that the deviating elements represented later adaptations of the story to a new function within the evolving church. A miraculous healing story, for example, should narrate the arrival of Jesus or the sick person, the performance of the healing, and some confirmation that the healing was successful. Consequently, when a miracle story such as LGM 1 continues on after the proof of the miracle (1:7–8), form critics assume that the remainder of the story was added at a later time and is therefore not as likely to be based on an authentic oral tradition. As it happens, when healing stories in the canonical gospels continue on beyond the proof of a miracle, they display qualities of redaction.[127]

Within the framework of form criticism, the historicity of the account of Jesus returning to the young man's house in LGM 1b is obviously difficult to maintain because the original story should have concluded when the miracle was accomplished.[128] And since the account of what happens in the young man's house does not itself fit any classic form, it does not exhibit any indication of having had an independent existence as oral tradition (Smith did not adduce John 1:35–40 as a parallel). Smith dealt with these problems by rebutting the assumption that primitive stories always conform to a limited range of types. At the same time, however, he asserted the validity of other assumptions that form critics use to distinguish secondary developments so that he could demonstrate that LGM 1a represented a more primitive, and therefore independent, version of the raising of Lazarus.[129] Smith's rationalism prevented him from suggesting that Jesus actually raised this young man from the dead. But that fact, too, created a difficulty, for Smith was claiming that an historically reliable depiction of Jesus baptizing a disciple existed as an original component within a legend.

The form-critical paradigm was only one obstacle confronting Smith's use of this evidence. In the 1950s, redaction criticism was emerging as a distinct methodological procedure. When analyzed from the perspective of redaction criticism, the fragment looks even less like reliable tradition. Smith believed that the reference to Jesus *teaching* the young man did not fit the context of mystery initiation. He therefore claimed that the verb "was teaching" (ἐδίδασκε) is a scribal corruption and that the text should read "for he *gave* him the mystery of the kingdom of God" (ἔδωκεν).[130] This manoeuvre was actually the crux of Smith's argument, for without it, LGM 1b offers no evidence for Jesus doing anything apart from teaching.[131] But the verb "was teaching" makes sense in its literary context. LGM 1 is set within a section of discipleship teaching (Mark 10:32–45), and the central section as a whole (8:22–10:52) is constructed to highlight Jesus' discipleship teachings. Removal to a house followed by privileged instruction is a distinctively Markan motif (7:17, 9:28, 10:10; cf. 4:10).[132] In that respect LGM 1 resembles Mark 9:14–29, where Jesus symbolically raises a boy who appears to be dead (vv. 26–27) then enters a house with his disciples to give them special *teaching*. LGM 1 also ends with the remark that Jesus got up and went away to a different geopolitical region, which parallels the transitional statements used in 7:24 and 10:1 to conclude instances of Jesus privately teaching his disciples in a house. *Teaching* is clearly the right word for this context. LGM 1:12 would only seem to contain a scribal error to someone intent upon treating it as a factual report about Jesus conducting some kind of mystery initiation.

On the whole, LGM 1b looks much more like a Markan redactional elaboration of an independent resuscitation tradition than it does an unadulterated recollection. The problem which this fact creates for Smith's historical reconstruction is magnified when we consider the theories Smith derived from this text, namely, that Jesus was a magician who offered hypnotically induced experiences of union with his spirit and ascension into the kingdom of God, culminating in freedom from the Law. Beskow stated the problem succinctly: "The odd thing about Morton Smith's theses is that none of them have any worthwhile support in the fragment."[133] Apparently Smith conceded this common criticism, for he barely mentioned the secret gospel in his follow-up book, *Jesus the Magician*.[134] After the mid-1970s, only a few of Smith's articles on Jesus and Pauline Christianity mention this evidence,[135] and only one of them makes substantial use of LGM 1b, namely, "Two Ascended to Heaven—Jesus and the Author of 4Q491." But even there, Smith favoured the evidence of a passage discovered at Qumran. Moreover, a significant element of the original theory became scarce in Smith's writings after 1977, namely, the idea that Jesus performed a baptism that differed from John the Baptist's.[136] This idea did not appear even in *Jesus the Magician*, though, again, it did factor in the article "Two Ascended." Although Smith continued to argue that Jesus performed a rite of mystical ascent (a point for which LGM 1 and 2 clearly supply no evidence), Smith seems to have had no stake in defending the baptismal element of his original theory.

One may also question whether Smith would have created a proof text that many scholars have been able to dismiss as a second-century pastiche. It would have been much easier for Smith to claim that the longer gospel excerpts contain historically reliable information if they did not have so many exact parallels to phrases in Mark and contacts with unique elements in all three synoptic versions of "the rich young ruler." This problem was quite significant for Smith, for the argument that LGM 1 was constructed out of elements in the canonical gospels has frequently been used to dismiss every conclusion about Jesus and early Christianity that he based upon this text. Clearly, if Smith wanted to create a text that gave firm support for his revolutionary views about Jesus, he did a really poor job.

Finally, it should be noted that Smith did not endorse the theory of longer Markan priority, a position which would have strengthened his claim that LGM 1 offers historically reliable information and increased the importance of his find. Although he initially suspected that canonical Mark was a censored form of his discovery and he subscribed to the theory that the proto-orthodox rewrote Christian history by suppressing embarrassing documents, when he weighted the evidence for and against longer Markan priority, he concluded that longer Mark was a later imitation of the canonical gospel produced by someone who had access to one of Mark's sources.[137] For Smith, LGM 1 was a Markanized version of a story taken from a Greek recension of a hypothetical Aramaic proto-gospel used in a different Greek recension by John. That theory hardly strengthened his position that LGM 1b is historically reliable in its details.

### A.H. Criddle's Statistical Study

It might seem by this point that most arguments for a modern forgery fall far short of the ideal of disinterested, careful scholarship, but one important study remains to be treated. Interestingly, this exemplary study comes not from a professor of patristics or New Testament but from a man who studies church history as a pastime, having earned his doctorate in biochemistry. In 1995 Andrew H. Criddle published the findings of his statistical analysis of the letter, in which he argued that "the letter proper (i.e., excluding the heading and the extracts from the secret gospel), contains too high a ratio of Clementine to non-Clementine traits to be authentic and should be regarded as a deliberate imitation of Clement's style."[138]

According to Criddle, an authentic but hitherto unknown work of a particular author should possess a particular ratio of words not previously occurring in that author's corpus to words previously occurring only once; the ratio is generated from the percentage of unique words known to have been used by that author. Applying the datum that 37.5 percent of the words in Clement's undisputed writings occur only once, the statistical model Criddle developed predicts that a genuine work of Clement should have a ratio of eight new words to five previously unique words. The ratio Criddle obtained from the letter is four to nine, which means that "there are too many words previously used only once and not enough previously unknown."[139]

Criddle pointed out that some of the words previously occurring only once in Clement but now found again in the letter are rare words for any writer of that time and postulated that they were selected from diverse passages in Clement precisely because they are practically unique to him. This is how Criddle accounted for both the high number of words previously occurring only once in Clement and the low number of new words: "The only plausible explanation of the above facts is that the author of the letter, in imitating the style of Clement, sought to use words found in Clement but not in other Patristic writers and to avoid words not found in Clement but present in other Patristic writers. In doing so the writer brought together more rare words and phrases [*sic*] scattered throughout the authentic works of Clement than are compatible with genuine Clementine authorship."[140] In other words, someone deliberately attempted to sound like Clement by using words distinctive of Clement. Notice that Criddle did not show "that this letter of Clement is more like Clement than Clement ever is." Bart Ehrman mischaracterized Criddle's study when he claimed that the author of the letter overused Clement's favourite words.[141]

Is this a plausible interpretation of the evidence? It is hard to picture why a forger attempting to sound more like Clement than anyone else would include words (three of the nine otherwise unique words) that are almost as rare in Clement as they are in other patristic writers. More importantly, the theory that the letter's vocabulary was derived through a selection of words distinctive of Clement as determined by a comparison with all the patristic writings implies an unrealistic amount of work. A pre-modern writer would have to have checked all of Clement's corpus and the corpora of the other church fathers for most of the words used. The notion of extensive checking only becomes conceivable if we suppose that this was a modern forger who checked most of the words he used in the letter against Stählin's 1936 index of Clement's vocabulary to ensure that Clement used them *and* regularly examined a modern patristic lexicon to make sure that this vocabulary was more or less distinctive of Clement. That scenario still stretches credulity.

But Criddle has not proven that this author did for the most part use words that are not found in other patristic writers: Criddle merely inferred this conclusion, by way of generalization, from the fact that six of the thirteen words isolated by his model are rare in patristic writings. To demonstrate this point, Criddle would have to show that it is generally true also for those words which appear more than once in the accepted corpus, and that Clement's undisputed writings on the whole do not display the same degree of distinctiveness in relation to other patristic writings. In fact, it is only the words which Clement used several times that could establish the point, for it is precarious to argue that words found only once in Clement's undisputed writings are distinctively Clement-sounding.

To bolster his interpretation of the evidence Criddle factored into his argument the assertion that "The letter brings together words scattered throughout Clement's works and uses them often with new meanings, to put across rather non-Clementine ideas."[142] Since most experts on Clement consider the substance of the letter to be typical of Clement, it appears that Criddle made another unwarranted generalization, presumably based on Eric Osborn's opinion that the author misunderstood Clement's writings. Osborn's opinion was supported by one example—the implausible suggestion that the letter's account of Carpocrates' theft reflects a literalistic misconception of Clement's figurative comment that heretics "cut a side door and break secretly through the wall of the church."[143]

Criddle's interpretation of the ratio generated by his statistical model takes us well beyond the evidence. What this ratio does demonstrate is difficult to decide. Certainly the numbers are practically a reversal of what his model predicts for an authentic work of Clement. The problem is that the ratio is based on an exceptionally small excerpt. According to Criddle's criteria of what constitutes a new word, there were *only* four new words in the letter. The ratio 4:9 is not based on a larger number of words than the four new words he found and the total of nine words previously occurring once. In his own estimate, "the numbers of words in the various categories [are] low, at the margin of real statistical significance."[144]

The high percentage of unique words in Clement's undisputed corpus to some extent reflects Clement's need to impress people with his encyclopaedic learning, particularly with his ability to converse with pagan authors. He may not have felt that need to the same extent when composing private letters. Clement's writings are peppered with citations and allusions culled from biblical and pagan authors, and this fact complicates any analysis of his vocabulary. Criddle understandably eliminated the longer gospel citations from consideration, pointing out that one could not reasonably conclude that the text is *not* sufficiently Clementine because it contains these Markan-sounding sentences.[145] But the highly intertextual nature of Clement's writing forces Criddle to accept as Clementine the various allusions and quotations involved in "Clement's practice of free citation" and therefore to factor into the vocabulary statistics the other, briefer direct quotations in the letter.[146] The length of a citation is a problematic basis for deciding whether its words are Clementine. The problem of deciding what words belong to Clement's vocabulary and, just as important, what words are used only once is complicated by the fact that Stählin did not usually index the words contained in Clement's direct quotations from other authors. The index which forms the basis for statistics about word use has itself been skewed somewhat by Stählin's own decisions about what words are relevant to Clement's vocabulary.

Criddle's approach to the issue of authenticity is commendable. However, this application of vocabulary statistics involves too many uncertainties and unwarranted generalizations for us to accept the results as evidence of forgery.

### The Mystery of Mar Saba

Experts in Christian origins often feel like strangers in a strange land when they ponder statistical studies, but the world of mathematical abstractions is not the strangest place through which we must wander in search of evidence bearing on the letter's authenticity. This is, after all, "secret" Mark we are talking about—a ten-ton magnet for the bizarre and controversial. It may be disorienting, but we must momentarily leave reality behind altogether and enter the fantastic world of an evangelical Christian spy novel.

In 1940, a Canadian evangelical writer named James Hogg Hunter published a fictional novel about a 1936 Nazi conspiracy to dishearten and debilitate the British Empire by discrediting Christianity. The dastardly scheme involved the forging of a manuscript that refuted the resurrection of Christ and the engineering of its discovery by a highly respected British scholar who was known to be visiting monasteries in search of important manuscripts. Hunter named his tale *The Mystery of Mar Saba*. In Hunter's story, degenerate monks at Mar Saba conspire with an evil German "Higher Critic and archaeologist" (11), who coerced a hapless Greek scholar into forging the manuscript. Philip Jenkins, who drew attention to the novel, pointed out that this story sounds familiar.[147] Although the novel consists mainly of espionage, romance, and cliff-hanger adventures, the premise of a scholar finding a forged manuscript at Mar Saba sounds like it was loosely based on the folklore that grew up around Smith's discovery. Yet the book was published the year before Smith's first visit to the monastery. The document in the novel contains a sworn statement by Nicodemus that before sunrise on the first day of the week he and Joseph of Arimathea prudently moved Christ's body to another location because an earthquake had caused the stone to roll away from the tomb's opening. The manuscript is offered to the respected scholar by a monk who pretended that he had found it "in an old chapel buried behind a moveable stone" (281). So, no, we are not dealing with a letter fragment contained in a book that was found by chance in the tower library, or with a different form of a canonical gospel. Still, the similarities are intriguing.

The most noteworthy similarity between the novel and Smith's book *The Secret Gospel* is their respective accounts of how the manuscript was discovered: a scholar comes to Mar Saba in search of manuscripts and at the end of his stay discovers a text that he thinks will have revolutionary implications (281, 293). Yet this similarity is easily exaggerated. In Hunter's story, the respected scholar is horribly disheartened by his discovery, and the whole civilized world is thrown into chaos at the thought that the bodily resurrection of Christ did not occur. The plot hinges on a peculiar evangelical conception of reality, namely, that "this world cannot go on without Christianity. If it should go, everything would go—all that makes life worth living, love, kindliness, brotherhood, our hopes for this life and that which is to come. Without the Christian hope and faith, the world will revert to a paganism and barbarism, aided by all the scientific devilishness of demon-inspired men that will eventuate in a struggle and carnage the like of which has never been seen since man appeared upon the earth" (319). Accordingly, just days after the newspapers describe the "Shed of Nicodemus," stock markets begin to crash, the ranks of Atheists and Communists swell, crime rates surge, the Nationalist party in India demands "the expulsion of all Christian missionaries," and riots break out in major cities in the United States (301, 309, 314, 317). The authentication of this manuscript portends "the destruction of civilization as we know it" (294, 408). Smith's conception of the importance of his discovery was not nearly so dramatic. He thought that the "secret" gospel necessitated a radical rethinking of Christian origins, which is what we might expect from the discoverer of a new gospel. Few of his peers discerned anything quite so revolutionary in the letter, and after forty-five years, the majority of experts still consider it to be authentic. So except for the premise of a scholar discovering a previously unknown ancient Christian manuscript at Mar Saba, there are few parallels between Smith's story and Hunter's that do not depend upon a romantic desire to read Smith's popular book as if it were a mystery steeped in intrigue.

Unfortunately, this desire can be overwhelming for some scholars, particularly those who prefer fantastic explanations to mundane ones. I cannot say I was surprised to see Robert M. Price transform this novel into incriminating evidence against Smith by seriously misrepresenting its plot. To hear him tell it, "the Shred of Nicodemus is a hoax engineered by its 'discoverer,' a hater of the Christian religion."[148] In other words, Price made the discoverer and (now) forger of the Shred match the irreverent Professor Smith by replacing Sir William Bracebridge, the pious evangelical scholar who made the discovery at Mar Saba, with Professor Heimworth, the evil German Higher Critic who planned the forgery out of hatred for the British Empire, and by glossing over the fact that the forgery itself was produced by a third individual, Yphantis, the brother of the hero's love interest. I know that facts rarely get in the way of an incredible theory, but I would have thought that anyone who can imagine Smith producing the perfect forgery would at least have difficulty picturing him reading an anti-intellectual evangelical Christian spy novel.

## The Possibility of Ancient Forgery

To this point we have examined the photographic evidence of the manuscript, the reasonableness of suspecting Smith, the overall rhetorical impact of the letter, vocabulary statistics, and the premise of life imitating "art." But we have barely touched on the question of whether the contents of the letter accord with our knowledge of Clement of Alexandria. That question interested the various authorities on Clement who assisted Smith during the earliest period of his research, and many other experts have since voiced their opinions. The majority agree with Smith that the author is in fact Clement. But the verdict is not unanimous.

### Mark and Alexandria

I will begin with a common argument for dissent. Johannes Munck rejected Clementine authorship in part because he believed that the letter's reference to Mark coming to Alexandria demonstrates dependence on the fourth-century author Eusebius.[149] This matter was noted as a point of suspicion by Edwin Yamauchi and Per Beskow, and more recently by Eric Osborn, Andrew Criddle, and Dieter Lührmann.[150] Osborn and Criddle stated that the tradition connecting Mark with Alexandria is "unknown" before Eusebius. But as F.F. Bruce pointed out, Eusebius quotes this information as a tradition, introducing it with the expression "they say."[151] Bruce noted further that the tradition in the letter contrasts with the one given by Eusebius by not making Mark Alexandria's first bishop;[152] the letter in fact implies that a church already existed when Mark arrived in Alexandria following Peter's death.[153] So the letter's more modest picture of Mark's role in Alexandria is something that could have been elaborated into the more elevated picture offered by Eusebius. What is more, "they say" need not refer to *anonymous* tradition at all but to the individuals whose witness Eusebius adduced in the preceding paragraph, namely, Papias and (surprise) Clement of Alexandria. Scholars have been remarkably reluctant to consider that possibility, despite the fact that in Greek idiom "they say" (φασί) does not normally connote hearsay or even oral tradition but information taken from books.[154] What Eusebius wrote deserves to be quoted at length:

> And it is said [φασί] that the apostle, when the fact [of Mark's writing of the gospel] became known to him through the revelation of the Spirit, was

pleased with the eagerness of the men [who persuaded Mark to do this] and approved the writing for use in the churches.

Clement relates the anecdote in the sixth book of the *Outlines*, and Papias, bishop of Hierapolis, also bears witness to it and to Peter mentioning Mark in his earlier letter. Indeed they say [φασίν] that he composed it at Rome itself, and that he indicates this when referring figuratively to the city as Babylon in the words: "The elect [church] that is in Babylon greets you and so does my son Mark" [1 Peter 5:13].

They also say [φασίν] that this Mark set out for Egypt and was the first to proclaim the gospel which he had written, and the first to set up churches in Alexandria itself. (*Church History* II.15.2–16.1)[155]

We notice here that the first occurrence of the verb in question (φημί) is specifically connected in the next sentence with Clement and Papias; the second occurrence would quite naturally refer specifically to Clement and Papias as well; the third occurrence is similar to the second and provides no indication that impersonal "hearsay" is now in view. Scholars sometimes read the third occurrence of "they say" as an impersonal because the lateness of this first preserved reference to a connection between Mark and Alexandria makes it hard to believe that the tradition could be as ancient as Clement and, especially, Papias. But now that this connection is found in a letter purporting to be by Clement, the rationale for assuming that Eusebius cannot be referring to Clement becomes circular. Once this bias is discarded, it becomes apparent that the letter reinforces Eusebius's claim that Clement associated Mark with Alexandria in his lost work *Hypotyposeis* (the English title is *Outlines*). That Clement, an "orthodox" Alexandrian, strongly concerned with the apostolic heritage of the universal church, would be Eusebius's source for a tradition giving apostolic pedigree to the church in Alexandria makes perfect sense.

## *Clarifying the Issue of Secrecy*

The preceding objection was not an especially important challenge. The major arguments for an ancient forgery are based on presumed discrepancies between Clement's undisputed writings and the *Letter to Theodore*. The strongest assertion of incongruity was voiced by Massey H. Shepherd and Eric Osborn. The letter refers to secret oral traditions, and Clement's perpetuation of such teachings without making them public through his writings seemed incomprehensible to Shepherd and Osborn. Both claimed that Clement would not have had anything to do with a gospel that could not be revealed to the general public.[156]

In order to evaluate the merits of this position, we must first distinguish between what the letter says about secret oral traditions and what it says about the contents of the longer gospel. The author relates an account of Mark's creation of a "more spiritual" gospel by incorporating more narratives of the sort found in the first version, but also, and more importantly, certain passages "of which he knew the interpretation would, as a mystagogue, lead the hearers into the innermost sanctuary of that truth hidden by seven veils" (I.24–26). Mark did not, however, include "the things not to be uttered, nor did he write down the hierophantic teaching of the Lord" (I.22–24). Since the author is using the language of the mystery religions, his terms require some explanation.

Let us begin with what Mark *did not* include. The "things not to be uttered" (τὰ ἀπόρρητα) are esoteric teachings that initiates are forbidden to discuss with the uninitiated.[157] In *Strom.* I.2.21.2 and V.9.58.1 Clement used this term in reference to the secret philosophical teachings of the Christians and Epicureans, respectively. "Hierophantic teaching," on the other hand, has to do with the revelation of mysteries and the exposition of symbols. Clement used the word *hierophant* in reference to the priests of the mystery religions who were in charge of explaining the symbols involved in initiations (e.g., *Prot.* 7.74.3; 2.22.7); but he also applied it to "Moses, the hierophant of the truth," whose words are revelations to those who can perceive their intended allegorical meanings (2.25.1). The highly symbolic image of Jesus as a hierophant revealing divine realities appears in *Prot.* 12.120.1–2. In Clement's day, mystery-religion imagery of initiation was appropriated by philosophical schools to describe the transmission of their secret teachings to qualified members of the school. Thus the implied author of the letter is talking about secret philosophical or theological teachings that originated with Jesus ("the hierophantic teachings *of the Lord*") and were transmitted orally to qualified individuals (presumably beginning with Jesus' disciples, but that is not stated explicitly in the letter). Clement frequently referred to such teachings as gnosis (from the Greek noun *gnōsis,* meaning "knowledge") or gnostic (from the adjective *gnōstikos*) or "the gnostic tradition," so scholars of Clement sometimes refer to these secret teachings as the unwritten gnostic tradition.

That material is what Mark did not include in his more spiritual gospel; it was not to be put in writing. What he did include were "certain traditions" whose *interpretation* could function like a mystagogue (I.25), which is a person who initiates others into mysteries or who comprehends and teaches mystical doctrines. The activity of expounding the hidden meanings of these special passages is an initiation for the hearer inasmuch as it discloses the truths of the unwritten gnostic tradition. Hence this process is likened to the removal of veils obscuring the divine presence in the inner sanctuary of a temple (I.25–26). The same metaphor is used in *Strom.* V.4.19.3 to describe the way the essential religious truths are concealed beneath the literal level of the scriptures; only individuals who have been "consecrated" through their devotion to God and mastery of the passions can enter "the inner sanctuary" of the text by penetrating the figurative level. The special passages that made the longer text a more spiritual gospel were therefore ones that were apt to disclose the hierophantic teachings of the Lord—but only through their proper exposition. The secrets lay beneath the surface, available only to persons who knew what to look for. Mark was careful *not* to covey the unutterable teachings in a more overt form.

In the letter, this more spiritual gospel is also called the *mystikon euangelion* (II.6, 12). In English this is usually and misleadingly translated "the secret Gospel," but *mystikos* had a *different*, richer sense in Clement, especially when used in connection with writings. The fourth chapter of this book will demonstrate that this expression describes the longer gospel as relatively more concerned with the figurative dimension of interpretation. For now it must suffice to say that the so-called "secret" Gospel of Mark is not described as—nor do the quoted passages reveal it to be—a work that was designed to be kept hidden from the public. Nor can we rightly conclude that it was treated as a book of secret material by the Alexandrian community. The implied author describes it as a gospel that had proved effective in revealing the deeper Christian truths, teachings that Clement discussed only with persons worthy of receiving them (*Strom.* V.10.66.1–5; VII.10.55.6–56.2). That group would not have included catechumens, who were essentially undergoing a probationary period in order to demonstrate their sincerity and character. But baptized Christians would presumably be permitted to hear this version of Mark, provided that they had advanced in their studies as far as "the great mysteries" (II.2).[158] At any given time these may well have been a minority of the congregation (*Strom.* V.3.17.4–6), but we are still a long way off from an elitist, secret society.

When we consider how the *Letter to Theodore* portrays the concept of secret tradition, we must therefore differentiate between two issues: the idea that the church possessed secret, strictly oral traditions believed to derive from Jesus and the idea that Mark prepared a more spiritual version of his gospel *that contains none of that secret material*, at least not in an overt form. What we need now to decide is whether preservation of a secret, not-to-be-published oral tradition is compatible with what we know of Clement, and whether he might have accepted a more spiritual version of Mark that was read only to advanced Christians.

## Clement's Esotericism and the
## Letter to Theodore

Although experts on Clement are sometimes uncomfortable about the notion, few have gone so far as to deny that Clement attests to the existence of a secret, unwritten tradition in the Alexandrian church, which was deemed most important for gnostic instruction. This unwritten tradition is referred to in the *Stromateis* as having been passed on to worthy individuals through a chain of oral transmission (V.10.61.1, 62.1; VI.7.61.1, 3; and VI.15.131.2–5). Christ delivered these secret teachings to the apostles, and the apostles delivered them to the fathers of the church (I.1.11.3). As Raoul Mortley recognized, the gnostic tradition was connected with the concealed meaning of the scriptures:

> It is clear that Clement has borrowed his concept of gnosis, in this aspect at least, from the Epistle of Barnabas, which he considered an authentic epistle of the New Testament: a passage from the Fifth Book of the *Stromateis* [chapter 10] designates the Epistle of Barnabas the clearest source of the gnostic tradition....In the perspective of that writing, gnosis is interpreted as the comprehension of hidden truths: the study of these truths is conducted through the christological interpretation of Scripture, that is, of the Old Testament. The true meaning of Scripture is gnosis; in effect, the term *gnōsis* is a synonym for the term "signification" [i.e., the latent meaning].[159]

The existence of a secret gnostic tradition is not really at issue. The issue is whether Clement would have perpetuated the inherited secret oral teaching as secret oral teaching. Some scholars are under the impression that Clement took it upon himself to change the process of secret, oral transmission by *publicizing* the gnostic truths in writing. So, for instance, W. Völker, J. Munck, and E. Osborn had difficulty accepting Clement's authorship of this letter because the letter appeared to them to endorse secrecy about the gnostic tradition.[160]

In responding to Smith's work, Massy Shepherd quoted Jesus' saying about proclaiming from the housetop the things you hear in secret (Matt 10:26–27; Luke 12:2–3). His point was that secrecy was incompatible with Christianity.[161] The question, though, is whether Clement would have agreed. Shepherd quoted one of Clement's favourite sayings, though perhaps not the part of it Clement liked to emphasize. Here is what Clement made of the first half of this saying, the statement that there is nothing hidden that will not be revealed:

> [The Lord] did not reveal to the people in the street what was not for them; only to a few, to whom he knew it to be apposite, those who could accept the

mysteries and be conformed to them. The secrets, like God himself, are entrusted not to writing but to the expressed word. If anyone says that it is written in Scripture: "There is nothing hidden which shall not be revealed, nothing veiled which shall not be unveiled," he must listen to us too when we say that in this pronouncement he foretold that the hidden secret shall be revealed to the one who listens in secret, and all that is veiled, like the truth, shall be shown to the one who is capable of receiving the traditions under a veil, and that which is hidden from the majority shall become clear to a minority....No, the mysteries are transmitted mysteriously, so that they may be on the lips of speaker and listener—or rather not in their voices at all, but in their minds. (*Strom.* I.1.13.1–4)

Clement clearly was at pains to make this saying say something other than what most people, perhaps too facilely, see as its evident meaning. In Clement's view, the veiled truths are most appropriately conveyed in private. They are to be spoken to those few who have proven themselves willing to be conformed to the mysteries, privately ("in secret"), under a veil, and are best left not on their lips but in their minds. "The secrets, like God himself, are entrusted not to writing but to the expressed word." Notice that the word here translated as "the secrets" (τὰ ἀπόρρητα) is the same term used in the letter to denote the things Mark was careful *not* to put in writing (I.22–23). Here is what Clement had to say about the second part of this saying about the revelation of things concealed:

Since our tradition is not held in common or open to all, least of all when you realize the magnificence of the Word, it follows that we have to keep secret "the wisdom which is imparted in the context of a mystery," taught by God's Son....But "announce from the housetops what you hear whispered in your ear," says the Lord. He is telling us to receive the secret traditions of revealed knowledge, interpreted with outstanding loftiness and, as we have heard them whispered in our ears, to pass them on to appropriate people, not to offer them to all without reserve, when he only pronounced thoughts in parables to them. (*Strom.* I.12.55.1, 56.2)

Here Clement treats the imagery of height in the phrase "proclaim on the housetops" as if it were a figure for the *loftiness* of the private ("whispered") exposition, thereby managing to elude the actual point of Jesus' saying (cf. VI.15.124.5–125.2). As John Ferguson remarked, "It must be confessed that Clement's explaining away of his Lord's injunction to proclaim from the housetops is not free from sophistry."[162]

The Markan (hence synoptic) picture of Christ using parables to conceal the truth from the masses is the model for Clement's own *Stromateis*. The passage quoted above continues: "But in fact, my present outline of memoranda [i.e., the *Stromateis*] contains the truth in a kind of sporadic and dispersed fashion [cf. Mark 4:3–9], so as to avoid the attention of those who pick up ideas like jackdaws [cf. Mark 4:4, 15]. When it lights on good farmers [cf. Mark 4:20, 26], each of the germs of truth will grow and show the full-grown grain [only Mark 4:28]" (I.12.56.3). Clement was not prepared to record in his *Stromateis* all of the Christian mysteries, even cryptically, for he strongly feared the implications of exposing the deeper teachings to the general public in a medium that is especially susceptible to misinterpretation. This he made clear in I.1.14.2–4:

> There is a promise, not to give a full interpretation of the secrets [τὰ ἀπόρ–ρητα]—far from it—but simply to offer a reminder, either when we forget, or to prevent us from forgetting in the first place. I am very well aware that many things have passed away from us into oblivion in a long lapse of time through not being written down. That is why I have tried to reduce the effect of my weak memory, by providing myself with a systematic exposition in chapters as a salutary *aide-mémoire*....There are things which I have not recorded—those blessed men were endowed with great power....Others were growing faint to the point of extinction in my mind, since service of this kind is not easy for those who are not qualified experts. These I took good care to rekindle by making notes. Some I am deliberately putting to one side, making my selection scientifically out of fear of writing what I have refrained from speaking—not in a spirit of grudging (that would be wrong), but in the fear that my companions might misunderstand them and go astray and that I might be found offering a dagger to a child (as those who write proverbs put it). "Once a thing is written there is no way of keeping it from the public," even if it remains unpublished by me, and in its scrolls it employs no voice except the one single writing forevermore. It can make no response to a questioner beyond what is written. It cannot help needing support either from the writer or some other person following in his footsteps.

Clement's stated intention, then, was not to publicize the truth indiscriminately for all, but, quite the contrary, to produce a personal *memory aid* to assist in the recollection of oral teachings he had started to forget (cf. I.1.11.1–12.1). His objective that "the discovery of the sacred traditions may not be easy to any one of the uninitiated" is repeated at the close of the *Stromateis*, where he explained that the seemingly unplanned nature of his "composition aims at concealment, on account of those who have the daring to pilfer and steal the ripe fruits."[163] The impression he creates is that when Christian *mysteries* are involved, the *Stromateis* is meant principally to facilitate selective *oral* teaching through the preservation of this material in adumbrations, and secondarily to lead *worthy* uninstructed readers *toward* the truth:

Let these notes of ours, as we have often said for the sake of those that consult them carelessly and unskilfully, be of varied character—and as the name
itself indicates, patched together—passing constantly from one thing to
another, and in the series of discussions hinting at one thing and demonstrating another. "For those who seek for gold," says Heraclitus, "dig much
earth and find little gold." But those who are of the truly golden race, in
mining for what is allied to them, will find much in little. For the word will
find one to understand it. The Miscellanies of notes contribute, then, to the
recollection and expression of truth in the case of him who is able to investigate with reason. (*Strom*. IV.2.4.1–3)[164]

Clement often referred to Christianity as "the true philosophy" (I.5.32.4;
I.18.90.1; II.11.48.1; VI.7.58.2; VI.11.89.3; VII.16.98.2) and firmly held
to the Greek philosophical convention of requiring probation and silence
about the essential doctrines, a practice adapted from the mystery religions.
Clement clearly had no intention of proclaiming to the masses every bit of
authentic tradition he knew, so the fact that the letter endorses Mark's decision
not to put the secret teachings in writing is not an argument *against* the letter's authenticity, but *for* it. This particular objection is a vestige of a phase in
patristics when scholars found it difficult to believe that secrecy and esotericism were compatible with emerging orthodoxy. In 1963 E.L. Fortin complained that "the vast majority" of patristic scholars of his day were inclined
to deny that Clement really knew secret oral teachings, and cited Eric Osborn
as an example. Fortin noted that earlier generations of patristic scholars had
not taken that position.[165] Around the same time, the noted classicist Werner
Jaeger expressed to Smith his concern that this issue would be a sticking point
among patristic scholars of his generation: "The letter seems to contradict
those who have a tendency to interpret away or attenuate the existence in
Clement of a theory of an esoteric Christian doctrine, because they feel that
it is not consistent with his belief in the Christian religion as a universal message to all....We should refrain from letting our modern ideas or preferences
influence our historical judgment. There was a strong tendency at Clement's
time, and in him most of all, to construe Christianity as a philosophy; and...contemporary philosophical schools insisted on finding an esoteric and an exoteric
form of teaching in almost every system."[166] Clement's esotericism was already
a contentious issue within Clement scholarship at the time the *Letter to Theodore*
came to light, so the fact that most authorities before and since then have
taken it for granted that Clement preserved secret doctrines and traditions
and accepted myriad non-canonical writings is relevant here.[167]

It is not surprising that Osborn would assert that "There is nothing in
Clement that could allow this to be a secret Gospel, or to be something that

Clement might write," considering that Osborn managed to segregate, down-play, or else tendentiously reinterpret the various passages from Book One of the *Stromateis* in which Clement rationalizes his refusal to put the gnostic tradition in writing. In an influential paper on this chapter, Osborn van-quished the secret tradition with the remark "There is an esoteric attitude in much that he says and this attitude has its roots in the New Testament; but there is no esoteric doctrine."[168]

That was Osborn's position at the time of Smith's discovery. But in an earlier writing Osborn conceded the various things he played down in that 1959 article. One passage from his 1957 book *The Philosophy of Clement of Alexandria* is worth reproducing, for it conveys the same impression of Clement that the *Letter to Theodore* conveys:

> The most important parts of truth are "hidden." Some are not written down at all but are reserved for the oral instruction of the initiated. Others are writ-ten in an enigmatic and obscure way. The Lord did not reveal to the many the things which belonged to the few. He revealed these things to the few by word of mouth and not in writing. On the other hand what has been writ-ten about ultimate things is expressed in a mysterious form. In Scripture there is enigma, allegory and symbol. Some things are clear, unveiled, and con-vey definite moral teaching, but other things are expressed in riddles and parables and there is need of an interpreter. The *Paidagogos* teaches us clear and definite moral precepts; but we need a *Didaskalos* to handle the riddles and symbols.[169]

It is difficult to see how the *Letter to Theodore* is anything but in agreement with this picture. The letter refers to secret teachings that Mark did not com-mit to writing (I.22–24), but also to symbolic materials that can disclose the gnostic truth to those who are properly instructed (I.25–26, and probably also the "mystic" materials mentioned in I.16–17). Like the *Stromateis*, the mys-tic gospel does not contain the gnostic tradition in its overt form, but points the way to the deeper truths through its *interpretation* in accordance with "the true philosophy." The *Letter to Theodore* presents a very Clement-like picture of the esoteric instruction ("initiation") of advanced Christians in the orally transmitted theological mysteries of the Alexandrian Christian philos-ophy through exposition of the spiritual or veiled sense of scripture.

As far as I am aware, Eric Osborn is the only authority on Clement who still claims that the letter contradicts Clement's conception of gnostic instruc-tion, although the objections he raised in the *Journal of Early Christian Stud-ies* have been repeated by Andrew Criddle and Bart Ehrman in the same journal. All three presume that longer Mark was a *secret* gospel containing some form of secret *written* tradition rather than a *mystic* gospel containing passages whose *interpretation* can disclose the unwritten gnostic tradition. What they claim is true of Clement but not of the letter is actually a reality that the letter presupposes, namely, that for Clement "the 'gnostic' Christian differs from the simple believer, not by access to written texts forbidden to the latter, but by an increased insight into the hidden meanings of texts which are available in principle to simple and advanced believers alike."[170] The source of this confusion is not hard to locate. The notion that the letter describes a secret ritual text that was kept hidden from ordinary Christians pervades Morton Smith's translation and commentary, as well as his study of the "background" of the longer gospel. It is this scenario that led Osborn to declare that "the attribution of the document to Clement is a case of nescience [*sic*] fiction,"[171] although these notions have not seemed problematic to other authorities on Clement. To this point, patristic scholars have done a poor job of differentiating Smith's eccentric views from the actual evidence, although the recent contributions by the French authors Le Boulluec, Kaestli, and Stroumsa show that this is changing.

Most patristic scholars who have mentioned this evidence side with the late John Ferguson, who wrote that the letter, "in manner and in matter, seems clearly to have been written by Clement." Similar comments have been offered by Werner Jaeger, Claude Mondésert, Cyril C. Richardson, William H.C. Frend, Robert M. Grant, R.P.C. Hanson, Salvatore Lilla, André Méhat, Jean-Daniel Kaestli, Alain Le Boulluec (with some hesitancy), Guy G. Stroumsa, Annewies van den Hoek, and Judith L. Kovacs.[172] Lilla's comment is especially interesting:

> ...the "true message," the highest aspect of Christianity, does not consist for him [Clement] simply in some general conceptions about God, or in what can be read and understood by everyone but, first of all, in the ἀλήθεια [truth] which is one and the same thing with the divine Logos, i.e. in a system of doctrines which can be known only by a select few and which, therefore, represent the object of an esoteric *gnosis*.

> The esoteric character of Clement's *gnosis* enables us also to understand why he insists on the existence of a "secret" or "gnostic" tradition different from the ordinary Christian tradition. Christ—Clement says—spoke in parables in order to prevent his teaching from being divulged and communicated secret doctrines to those few among his disciples who were worthy of apprehending them....This view is confirmed by what Clement himself says in a letter rediscovered only recently, in which he draws attention to the existence of a secret version of the Gospel of Mark.[173]

Compare Lilla's description with the longer gospel's picture of Jesus concealing the mystery of the kingdom of God from outsiders using parables

(Mark 4:10–12) but revealing the mystery privately to a worthy individual (LGM 1:10–12). The mystery that Jesus imparts to the young man, however, is not divulged directly to the reader—it is not committed to writing in an overt form. Could Clement *not* have welcomed such a gospel?

There might even be evidence that he did. Consider this passage from *Stromateis* V: "For the prophet says, 'Who shall understand the Lord's parable but the wise and understanding, and he that loves his Lord?' It is but for few to comprehend these things. For it is not in the way of envy that the Lord announced in a Gospel, 'My mystery is to me, and to the sons of my house'" (10.63.6–7). Clement's rejection of envy as the Lord's motive for concealment is reminiscent of the *Letter to Theodore* I.27, where Mark's decision not to include the secret teachings is said not to have been made grudgingly. More importantly, the use of *mystery* in the singular and the way Clement introduced it with reference to comprehension of the Lord's parable is clearly reminiscent of Mark 4:10–12 (Matthew and Luke both use the plural, *mysteries*), but this saying is not from canonical Mark, nor is it found in any other extant gospel. A different version of this saying appears in the *Clementine Homilies* 19.20.1 in connection with an allusion to Mark 4:34, as if both came from the same source (the allusion also contains elements of Matt 13:11): "And Peter said: 'We remember that our Lord and Teacher, commanding us, said, "Keep the mysteries for me and the sons of my house." Wherefore also He explained to His disciples privately the mysteries of the kingdom of heaven.'"[174] Of course, Clement could not have attributed this saying to the Gospel of Mark without digressing to explain why it is not found in everyone else's copy of that gospel, so the odd fact that he omitted the title is explicable, too. It may not be possible to determine whether this saying is a vestige of the mystic gospel, though Clement's endorsement of this non-canonical saying of the Lord makes it hard to believe that he would have had nothing to do with a text such as longer Mark, which contains a passage that conveys the same attitude.[175]

## The Lack of References to the Longer Gospel in Alexandrian Writings

When assessing the possibility of ancient forgery, we need to consider not only the letter's congruence with Clement's style and thought but also the absence of explicit references to the longer gospel in other writings. No other Alexandrian writers mentioned this gospel, and no *clear* reference to it occurs in Clement's undisputed writings. Moreover, Clement's three undisputed accounts of Mark's writing activities make no reference to a second gospel. The famous tradition that John composed a spiritual gospel after the other evangelists had recorded the bodily facts says nothing of Mark composing a relatively more spiritual gospel as well. If the gospel is authentic, why is there only one extant reference to it?

Clement was the first "orthodox" Alexandrian father whose writings have been preserved, so the silence before Clement is not a problem. The silence after Clement is more problematic, although perhaps not unexpected, for the longer gospel might have disappeared from Alexandria during the persecution of Christians under Septimius Severus, as Smith suggested.[176] The letter gives the impression that a single copy of this gospel existed in Alexandria—the original document attributed to Mark—and was under the custodianship of elders who used it within the catechetical school (I.28–II.2, 4–6). Since Clement was an elder and the head of the catechetical school,[177] it follows that he would have been the person most responsible for the preservation of this document. According to the standard view, Clement left Alexandria about the year 202, when "multitudes" of believers "won crowns from God through their great patience under many tortures and every mode of death" (Origen desperately attempting to be one of them). After the exodus of instructors, the catechetical school was closed until Origen revived it (Eusebius, *Church History* VI.1–3). So if the letter is authentic and Eusebius was not exaggerating *too* much, it would be natural to suppose that Clement either left the only copy of the longer text in a safe location within the city or took it with him in order to ensure its preservation. In any event, he did not return to Alexandria, so the use of the longer text in that community might have ended with his departure. Origen either did not know or did not accept the longer text. As Smith pointed out, it is doubtful that Origen was actually Clement's student.[178] Even if he was, he may not have advanced to the level of "the great mysteries" by the time of Clement's departure. (Eusebius depicts Origen as an impulsive teenager at the time of the Severn persecution and the closing of the school.) Furthermore, this was the period when the orthodox were beginning to define themselves and their canon over against the heretics and the non-canonical scriptures. The four-gospel canon was becoming normative around the beginning of the third century, so if a longer text of Mark still existed in the city, there would have been pressure to stop treating it as inspired scripture, particularly in view of its importance to Carpocratian theology.

The fact that Clement's other traditions about Mark do not refer to a second gospel is again not entirely surprising. These traditions are not preserved in Clement's major works but as fragments in the writings of other authors, who presumably quoted what appealed to them. The tradition about John writing a more spiritual gospel comes to us via Eusebius (*Church History* VI.14.5–7), a noted pragmatist in his use of sources. Consequently, we should not presume that everything Clement said about Mark the evangelist has been preserved. The second-hand traditions, moreover, concern the version of Mark that was known to all Christians. Clement, or the persons quoting him, would not have needed to mention Mark's other gospel when discussing the origins of the four generally accepted gospels. Conceivably, the scandalous use of the longer text by the Carpocratians made discussing this gospel in public writings more trouble than it was worth, as the exceptionally defensive and apologetic stance taken in the *Letter to Theodore* itself suggests. Interestingly, Clement's tradition about how John composed a spiritual gospel is preceded by an account of Mark's activities that concludes on a defensive note. After describing how Mark had been persuaded by Peter's hearers to produce and distribute a record of Peter's preaching, Clement commented, "and when the matter came to Peter's knowledge, he neither actively prevented it nor promoted it."[179] This awkward remark is part of a general phenomenon observed by C. Clifton Black: "Among the fascinating characteristics of the early traditions about Mark are their proliferation and oddity: relative to their references to the other Evangelists and Gospels, patristic texts seem to discuss Mark more yet use his Gospel less. Furthermore, in their comments about the Evangelist, the majority seem noticeably awkward, apologetic, and sometimes even pejorative. Even if it proves beyond our ability to recover completely, something's afoot in all of this; compounding the mystery is the reticence of New Testament investigators to pursue it."[180] In this connection we must also consider the fact that, apart from Clement's discussion of Mark 10:17–31 in *Quis dives salvetur?* and a reference to Mark 14:61–62 in his lost *Hypotyposeis*, there are only two indubitable citations from Mark in Clement's extant writings (Mark 8:38 and 9:7). It appears that Clement was reluctant to quote from Mark's gospel.[181] Oddly enough, so was Origen. A mere four percent of their quotations from the canonical gospels come from Mark.[182] The Gospel of Mark was the least quoted and most apologized-for gospel of the traditional four. The *Letter to Theodore* may give us some insight into why that was.

As others have pointed out, the letter's story about Mark can account for John Chrysostom's assertion that Mark wrote his gospel in Egypt and the contradictory claims that Mark wrote his gospel before and after Peter's death.[183]

## Conclusions

Now that we have sifted through the secondary literature and removed the weak, the misinformed, the fanciful, and the intellectually dishonest arguments, we are left with one substantial reason to suspect forgery, namely, the fact that our first and only evidence for this letter is a manuscript that was written in a seventeenth-century book. Compounding this problem is the fact that this manuscript contains no serious errors indicative of a lengthy history of transmission. But we are also left with many positive indications of authenticity.

The arguments in favour of an ancient forgery were predicated on tendentious readings of Eusebius, the *Letter to Theodore*, and Clement's undisputed works. It is dubious to suggest that the letter depends upon Eusebius for the tradition connecting Mark with Alexandria when Eusebius appears to be citing Papias and Clement's own lost *Hypotyposeis*. On the discomfiting issue of secret tradition in the Alexandrian church, the letter and the undisputed works are conspicuously harmonious. At the heart of Clement's philosophy was the unwritten, gnostic tradition, which was the foundation for the "truest" exposition of the exoteric tradition recorded in the gospels and in scripture generally. Clement believed that Jesus denied these esoteric mysteries to the masses by concealing them in parables but imparted them in private to his disciples, who in turn passed them on to worthy Christian teachers. In Clement's day, this secret oral tradition was disclosed only to persons who had advanced through preliminary stages of instruction in "the true philosophy." Clement was careful not to set this tradition in writing for fear that it could be harmful to an uninstructed reader. Consequently, when he wrote his *Stromateis*, he concealed "the secrets" (τὰ ἀπόρρητα) using indirection, discussing them obliquely when appearing to talk about other things. In accordance with this scenario, the *Letter to Theodore* depicts Mark as knowing better than to record the gnostic tradition in an overt form. Like Clement when he wrote the *Stromateis*, Mark conveyed the unutterable teachings indirectly by adding certain passages whose *interpretation* could "lead the hearers into the innermost sanctuary of that truth hidden by seven veils." These mystic passages included a depiction of Jesus imparting a "mystery" privately to a disciple (LGM 1b), the way Clement insisted these mysteries should be transmitted ("privately"; "whispered in our ears"). The actual mystery taught to the young man is concealed from careless or unworthy readers, who will not know how to interpret this episode, and the mystic gospel itself was read only to the most advanced students—the ones least likely to misinterpret it. In keeping with Clement's reluctance to publish the gnostic tradition, the manuscript breaks off precisely where the implied author begins to expound "the true explanation and that which accords with the true philosophy." It is conceivable that Clement or someone after him removed his gnostic exposition of LGM 1 and 2 when a copy of this private letter was published as one of "the letters of the most holy Clement, the author of the *Stromateis*." We know that John of Damascus had access to an extensive collection of Clement's letters when he worked at Mar Saba. *The Letter to Theodore* may be a remnant of that collection.

The arguments in favour of an early modern forgery are no more compelling. This position can account for the lateness of the only manuscript and the lack of serious errors, but makes little sense in view of where and when the manuscript came to light. Why would anyone produce a completely compelling forgery and keep it secret? We can rule out money, fame, the satisfaction of fooling experts, and the advancement of a theological agenda. Charles Murgia's scenario of rainy day amusement and Herbert Musurillo's comment about "anything from pure vanity to an exercise in virtuosity" underscore that as an eighteenth- or nineteenth-century forgery the letter has no evident purpose.[184]

For a plausible motive, we must turn to the twentieth century and the person who became more famous as a consequence of its discovery. But motive is not evidence, and Smith's fabrication of this document remains an exceptionally unlikely scenario. The newer colour photographs reveal characteristics of the manuscript that strongly suggest a dating prior to the twentieth century. The people who foster the romantic notion that Smith was capable of imitating the handwriting and the aged appearance of an eighteenth-century manuscript have not produced any supporting evidence, let alone demonstrated that Smith had developed any expertise in Clement prior to 1958. Quesnell's contention that Smith operated in a manner typical of forgers is confuted by the facts. Contrary to popular belief, Smith neither retained possession of the manuscript nor prevented scholars from inspecting it. Instead, he catalogued it, offered photographs, and published the information that led three Western scholars to locate it. A person capable of producing "the forgery of the century" probably would have created something of greater significance and not been content with only one important "find." Smith did use the document to support a sensational reconstruction of Christian origins, but his radical conclusions cannot be found in his writings before he catalogued the manuscript (Quesnell's distorted citations notwithstanding) and are only weakly supported by the gospel excerpts. LGM 1b is the only part of the gospel quotations that plays a significant role in Smith's theories, but in order to see a mystery-religion initiation in this nocturnal encounter, Smith had to rewrite the evidence, replacing a verb that was appropriate to its larger context ("was teaching") with a verb that was required by his interpretation ("gave"). He also needed to side-step the established methods for analyzing the evolution of gospel traditions, methods he championed only a few years earlier. His historicizing reading of an encounter that looks both secondary and redactional was so easily controverted by his peers that he all but gave up using longer Mark to support his theories about Jesus. He had better success arguing the same points using passages in the New Testament and the Dead Sea Scrolls. It will become clearer in subsequent chapters that Smith misunderstood what the letter conveys about the nature and use of the longer gospel and had a very limited appreciation of the gospel extracts. He was a brilliant and erudite scholar, but he did not comprehend the *Letter to Theodore* well enough to have composed it.

The special insight that the author of the gospel quotations had into Markan composition and theology provides positive evidence for the authenticity of both this letter and the longer text of Mark. Part 2 of this book will demonstrate that when the gospel excerpts are set in their Markan context and interpreted in relation to recent narrative-critical research on Mark, they support the letter's explanation that their author created "a more spiritual gospel," meaning a gospel focused more on the inner, theological meaning (the spirit) than on the outer facts (the body). The excerpts moreover conform to aspects of Markan compositional technique and theology that scholars began to articulate in the decades after the letter was discovered, subtleties that Smith could hardly be accused of having recognized.[185] The use of intercalation, for instance, produces a surprisingly cogent interpretation of Mark 14:51–52. The upshot of this literary analysis is that the letter's gospel quotations make the most sense when viewed as real redactional expansions of Mark's gospel that amplify theological motifs of the canonical text.

It is my position that the evidence in favour of viewing this document as an authentic letter by Clement about an early, expanded version of Mark greatly outweighs the existing evidence against that conclusion. Consequently, I am going to proceed on the assumption that the two longer versions of the Gospel of Mark did exist, and that Clement wrote the letter.

# ⊰3⊱

# Longer Mark's Relation
# to Other Gospels

The longer gospel's version of the raising of a dead man in Bethany is strikingly different from the story in John 11. LGM 1a is much shorter, less elaborate, and frequently at odds with John's details. Quite naturally, scholars have attempted to puzzle out the relationship between these two accounts. Numerous scenarios can be imagined. One possibility is that both stories were derived independently from oral tradition, which tends to be highly variable. Another possibility is that they are related literarily in a direct or indirect way. Perhaps both authors used the same written source, such as a collection of miracles recorded in a notebook. If that is the case, then it is conceivable that they used different editions of the same written source. Or possibly one of these authors copied the story directly from the other's gospel, in which case all the differences must be ascribed to the author who did the copying. However, we do not need to assume that a relationship of direct dependence between these gospels would be literary: most reading in antiquity was done publicly before an audience, so perhaps one author knew the other's gospel from hearing it, but did not have access to a manuscript. In that case, some of the differences could derive from a faulty memory, whereas others could be deliberate. More complicated scenarios are possible, too. Since the writing of gospels did not put an end to word-of-mouth transmission of stories and information about Jesus, it is possible that one of these two authors knew this story not only through acquaintance with the other's gospel or a shared written source but also as an anecdote that Christians around him liked to tell (possibly in many different ways). We must even consider the possibility that one of these two authors encountered this story second- or third-hand from someone who knew someone who heard the other author's gospel read in public, in which case the second author may have heard a

Notes to chapter 3 start on page 255

hybrid account of the miracle: an oral tradition derived from a written tradition. Or, if an intermediary who heard the hybrid tradition was already quite familiar with the oral tradition, he may have passed on to the second author an oral tradition that had only a few reminiscences of the written account (scholars refer to the influence of written tradition upon oral tradition as secondary orality). With so many potential variables and uncertainties, it may not be possible to determine the precise relationship between LGM 1 and John 11, although the evidence strongly suggests that neither author knew the other's text, even indirectly. If there was a relationship of dependence, the dependent gospel was John.[1]

## Longer Mark's Basis in Oral Tradition

Scholars have long realized that the authors of the canonical gospels were not eyewitnesses to the events and words they recorded but second- or third-generation ear-witnesses to the traditions about Jesus that were preserved within various Christian communities. This collective memory existed primarily in the form of memorable stories and sayings. In a predominantly oral culture, tradition is the vehicle of knowledge and wisdom, and tradition must be fashioned in a memorable way or it will not be remembered and transmitted. The more memorable sayings and stories of Jesus are not only thought-provoking but also crafted with a mnemonic structure that assists recollection. People cannot normally remember spoken discourse word for word. Out of the constant stream of information that enters our immediate awareness or short-term memory, only the elements that we reflect upon and repeat in our minds stay with us. Under the best conditions, we find it difficult to remember a sentence verbatim for more than a moment after hearing it. Moreover, the process of contemplating the words we are hearing interferes with our ability to pay attention to what is still being said. So we simply are not capable of remembering discourses verbatim. Although we understand each sentence, we quickly forget most of the actual words and retain only the train of thought and whatever phrases and ideas we are able to reflect upon as we are listening. When the discourse is over, we forget most of the train of thought but remember the gist of what was said and whatever phrases and ideas we continued to think about after the discourse concluded.

That is the case with ordinary spoken discourse. The situation is somewhat different when we listen to anecdotes and sayings, which are generally fashioned in conventional forms. Our familiarity with these conventional forms helps us recognize what we need to remember in order to reproduce the saying or story successfully. Beatitudes, for example, are quite simple to remember because we are familiar with the beatitude form: Blessed are the/you (persons of a certain type), for they/you will (receive some reward). Should we hear a new beatitude, such as "Blessed are the solitary and elect, for [they] will find the Kingdom" (Thomas 49), we only need to remember the variables (solitary and elect; find the Kingdom); in this way, the essential information about the beatitude is encoded in our memories, ready to be reproduced by recombining the variables with the form. Jesus' sayings often fall into discernible forms, and our ability to remember these sayings is greatly assisted by our subconscious awareness of those forms, as were the memories of the people who passed on these sayings in the periods before and after they were first recorded in writing.

The same is true of the stories that appear in the synoptic tradition. Regardless of whether these incidents actually happened, the individuals who first told these stories fashioned them according to the standard storytelling forms of their day so that others who heard these stories could remember them and successfully pass them on. But in contrast to brief sayings, which can be remembered verbatim, stories are seldom remembered word for word, and people are not apt to tell stories exactly the same way twice. Instead, the hearers remember the core of the story and the essential elements—those elements that must be remembered and correctly reproduced for the story to have its intended effect. The other details are inessential and are therefore not committed to memory: these are invented spontaneously in the act of telling the story, and quite often consist of stock phrases and motifs. The supplicant's cry "Son of David, have mercy on me" is one such stock phrase (Matt 9:27; 15:22; 20:30, 31; Mark 10:47, 48; LGM 1:2; Luke 17:13).

The formulaic nature of pre-synoptic oral tradition finds a ready analogy in joke telling. Someone who is good at telling jokes understands the different types or formulas of jokes and what elements are essential to telling a particular joke properly. Someone who is bad at telling jokes will not have a good sense of what elements have to be remembered and of their right order. The bad joke teller is often interrupted with "No, you're saying it wrong..." by someone who already knows the joke, better appreciates how it works, and realizes that on its present course, it will not end up being funny. You have probably heard a joke told wrong, but understood the type of joke well enough that you were able to figure out how the joke should have been told, then managed to tell it properly yourself.[2]

The traditional stories about Jesus that appear in early Christian gospels were to some extent shaped by such a process of transmission. These stories were preserved because the people who heard them appreciated the conventions that apply to each story type and managed to remember (or recon-struct) the essential variables. Of necessity, the synoptic tradition consisted of brief, economical, and conventional materials that ordinary people could remember and pass on without the aid of writing or rote memorization. The wording of a story varied with each telling, but the core or skeleton remained more stable, particularly the elements that had to be preserved for the story to have its desired effect. That is not to say that the stories were always told in the briefest, most economical way possible. Eyewitnesses might have pep-pered their stories with historically accurate but inessential details. Subse-quent tellers might have embellished and elaborated these stories the way good storytellers do today. But it is unlikely that many of the inessential details and embellishments were faithfully transmitted from person to person over the years; whatever was inessential quickly became variable and conven-tional. Consequently, the "original" stories did not progressively evolve into the more elaborate forms that sometimes appear in the synoptic gospels and frequently appear in John. The "secondary" features that appear in the gospels (the unconventional elements that would not be preserved in the course of oral transmission) are more likely products of the stage of writing and derive from the evangelists themselves or their written sources.

With these considerations in mind, let us compare LGM 1 to the stan-dard healing story. In the most basic terms, a healing story has an exposition of the illness, a description of the miracle worker's intervention, and proof that the intervention was successful. These three component parts are worked out using a variety of conventional, auxiliary motifs. Kelber's analysis of Mark's healing narratives yielded the following general formula:

I  Exposition of Healing
    a) arrival of healer and sick person
    b) staging of public forum (onlookers)
    c) explication of sickness
    d) request for help
    e) public scorn or skepticism

II  Performance of Healing
    a) utterance of healing formula
    b) healing gestures
    c) statement of cure

III  Confirmation of Healing
    a) admiration/confirmation formula
    b) dismissal of healed person
    c) injunction of secrecy
    d) propagation of healer's fame[3]

Each of Mark's ten healing narratives fits this threefold pattern. The raising of Jairus's daughter, for example, has the following combination of elements: I-d, a, e; II-a, c; III-a, c. Comparison of longer Mark's account of the raising of a dead man in Bethany with the healing story formula demonstrates that LGM 1a contains little that is uncharacteristic of oral tradition:

| | | |
|---|---|---|
| I-a | 1 | And they come to Bethany. |
| I-c | | And there was there a certain woman whose brother of hers had died. |
| I-d | 2 | And coming, she prostrated before Jesus and says to him, "Son of David have mercy on me." |
| I-e? | 3 | But the disciples rebuked her. |
| I-a | 4 | And having become angry Jesus went away with her into the garden where the tomb was. |
| | 5 | And immediately was heard from the tomb a great cry. |
| I-a | 6 | And approaching, Jesus rolled the stone from the door of the tomb, 7 and going in immediately where the young man was, |
| II-b, c | | he stretched out the hand and raised him, having grasped the hand. |
| III-a | 8 | But the young man, having looked upon him, loved him and began to beg him that he might be with him. |
| | 9 | And going out from the tomb they went into the house of the young man; for he was rich. |

The function of LGM 1:3 within this scheme is debatable. The disciples' rebuke of the woman might involve scepticism on their part about Jesus' ability to help her, even though Jesus has already raised Jairus's daughter (cf. the disciples' hardhearted scepticism about Jesus' ability to feed the second multitude in Mark 8:4). If so, it is consistent with the healing story formula. More likely, though, the rebuke reflects the same attitude that is behind the rebukes in Mark 10:13 and 10:48, namely, that Jesus is too important to be troubled by insignificant people, regardless of whether he can do something for them. In that case, the verse does not fit the formula.

The verses in LGM 1:4–7a are somewhat atypical because Jesus normally encounters the person in need of healing at the beginning of the episode. In this case, Jesus' walk to the garden, removal of the stone, and entrance into the tomb are necessitated by the fact that the young man had been buried, the same way that Jesus' walk to Jairus's house and entry into the little girl's room (which Kelber includes under I-a) were necessary because the deceased was in her bed. So verses 4, 6, and 7a can be grouped under I-a. The loud voice in 1:5, on the other hand, is extraneous to the healing story formula, but is a conventional element in Markan exorcism stories, where it denotes a conflict between the powers of good and evil (1:26; 5:7). A number of scholars have suggested that the loud voice from the tomb is a representation of the demonic realm.[4] LGM 1, then, may combine features of two distinct story types.

Some scholars suspect that Mark 1:40–45 is a like case. In that story, Jesus is confronted by a leper, who asks to be healed. Rather inexplicably, Jesus becomes angry as he heals the man, then rebukes him and casts him out (καὶ ὀργισθεὶς...ἐμβριμησάμενος αὐτῷ εὐθὺς ἐξέβαλεν αὐτόν).[5] Jesus' response seems entirely out of keeping with the situation. It is not clear why the leper's request should elicit anger, yet apart from Mark 3:5, this is the only reference to Jesus becoming outright angry in the canonical gospels.[6] The verb used here to describe Jesus' rebuke of the leper is not the one Mark normally uses when one character censures another. Rather, it is an uncommon and much stronger term that literally means to snort or to growl and implies a menacing reprimand, if not a threat; in colloquial English we might say Jesus "snapped at him." And the verb "to cast out" has the sense of expulsion in all of its other occurrences in Mark, ten of which refer to the expulsion of demons (1:34, 39; 3:15, 22, 23; 6:13; 7:26; 9:18, 28, 38). In the remaining five instances, the casting out is done to humans. Three of these instances involve forceful expulsion (9:47: "thrown into hell"; 11:15: "and [Jesus] began to drive out those who sold and those who bought in the temple"; 12:8: "And they took him and killed him, and cast him out of the vineyard"). In the fourth, the holy spirit casts Jesus out into the wilderness (1:12); the verb *cast out* is evocative of exorcism here, since it is by the holy spirit that Jesus casts out demons (3:28–30). Only in 5:40 is the expulsion more coercive than forcible: when Jesus arrives at Jairus's house, he sends the mourners on their way.

Understandably, translators have had difficulty making sense of the three terms in Mark 1:40–45 that are better suited to an exorcism story. Most opt for the more congenial manuscript variant "moved with pity" in place of the more difficult reading "and becoming angry,"[7] and render the verbs "to rebuke" and "to cast out" almost euphemistically: "And he sternly charged him, and sent him away at once" (RSV). But the conjunction of these strong terms still puzzles most commentators, some of whom have detected an exorcistic conception.[8] So there are good reasons to suspect that this story about the healing of leprosy originally involved a demonic conception of the nature of the disease and that Mark altered this conception by shifting the rebuke and casting out from a demon to a person.[9]

The fact that the healing miracles in LGM 1a and Mark 1:40–45 have exorcistic overtones is especially intriguing in view of the fact that they both contain the phrase "and becoming angry" between the request for help and the miracle. No less intriguing is the fact that John's account of the raising of the dead man in Bethany likewise has an exorcistic phrase using the strong form of the verb "to rebuke" as well as a parallel to longer Mark's loud cry, and these occur at roughly the same places relative to the structure of LGM 1a. John 11:33 states that when Jesus saw Mary weeping together with the Jews who came with her, he "rebuked the spirit and troubled himself" (ἐνε-βριμήσατο τῷ πνεύματι καὶ ἐτάραξεν ἑαυτόν). Again, translators have had great difficulty making sense of these words in the context of John 11. The standard translations presume that "the spirit" has something to do with emotion and could mean "he was greatly disturbed in spirit" (NRSV; cf. RSV, NEB, JB, and KJV). But as Barnabas Lindars determined using the *Thesaurus Linguae Graecae*, "ἐμβριμᾶσθαι with dative of the person means to rebuke" or to threaten (cf. Mark 14:5).[10] So it makes sense grammatically to treat "the spirit" as the object of a rebuke, as in the Acts of Matthew 14, where the same verb is used and the direct object in the dative is a "demonic spirit" (ἐμβριμήσεται τῇ δαιμονικῇ φύσει).

Considering that there are no exorcisms in John, it is unlikely that its author intended the words in question to mean "rebuked the spirit." That he did not read them so seems to be confirmed a few verses later. When the verb appears again in 11:38, Jesus is "rebuking in himself" (ἐμβριμώμενος ἐν ἑαυτῷ), which is apparently a reference to him controlling his sadness (v. 35). The reiteration of this rare verb functions to make the earlier phrase refer to Jesus rebuking an emotion rather than an entity.[11] On this basis Lindars proposed that John's source for the raising of Lazarus was a primitive, synoptic-style incident that involved an exorcistic confrontation, and that the phrase "rebuked the spirit" is the only feature of the original story that survived John's extensive revisions. However, the statement that Jesus "troubled himself" (ἐτάραξεν ἑαυτόν) is also peculiar. As an active construction with Jesus himself as both subject and object, this expression does not naturally suggest that Jesus was *troubled by* something else, such as the sadness of those around him.[12] Rather, Jesus appears to be working himself up into an agitated state while he rebukes the spirit. Edwyn Bevan recognized the underlying dynamics of the story when he compared the use of the form of the verb "to rebuke" in John 11:33, 38 with the reference to Jesus' anger in Mark 1:41: "the verb [rebuke] ἐμβριμοῦσθαι properly connotes rather indignation than sorrow....I would suggest that here too what lies behind the phrase is the idea that in the encounter of Jesus with Death, from whom he is going to rescue the prey, as Herakles rescued Alcestis, Jesus is about to close with the Satanic power. What is suggested is the hard, angry breathing of the man who is bracing himself to meet and overthrow a tremendous enemy."[13] The enemy Bevan detected behind John 11:38 is arguably the same thing represented by the loud voice in LGM 1:5: Death personified.

John's parallel to the loud voice in longer Mark is that of Jesus calling Lazarus out of the tomb: "he cried with a loud voice, 'Lazarus, come out'" (11:43). This, too, may be a remnant of an underlying tradition, for, as Crossan reasoned, the words "loud voice" appear only here in John but are associated with demons and the prospect of imminent demise in canonical and longer Mark (1:26; 5:7; cf. 15:34, 37).[14]

These observations are certainly intriguing. Both accounts of the raising of a dead man in Bethany have different, puzzling details with exorcistic connotations and parallels to Mark 1:40–45. Consideration of these different exorcistic details has led scholars comparing John 11 and canonical Mark 1:41, 43 (Barnabas Lindars, Edwyn Bevan), scholars discussing longer Mark (Morton Smith, Wayne Shumaker, and John S. Coolidge), and scholars comparing John 11 and LGM 1 (John Crossan, Lawrence M. Wills) to detect an underlying conflict with "the demonic power of death."[15] The utility of construing these odd details as vestiges of an earlier form of this story is suggested by the fact that the strong rebuke and the loud voice combine to form a coherent picture of Jesus "rebuking the spirit" on his way to the grave, resulting in a demonic cry from the tomb. Unfortunately, the reconstruction of narrative sources is a notoriously speculative enterprise, so I am reluctant to push the matter. But I do think it is important to compare the explanatory power of this premise with that of the pastiche theory, which proposes that the author of longer Mark revised John 11 by replacing Johannine details with elements drawn almost randomly from the other canonical gospels. Differences that seem inexplicable within the framework of the pastiche theory become intelligible using the premise that an editor with Johannine interests and an editor with Markan interests independently modified a more primitive story that involved an exorcistic confrontation.

If we take that premise as our hypothesis, it follows that the remnants of an exorcistic rebuke are preserved in both John and longer Mark. In John's story, Jesus' frenzied rebuke on the way to the tomb is reinterpreted such that it is directed inward as an act of self-control rather than outward at a demon, and this state of frustration is triggered by the inability of Mary and the bystanders to appreciate the need for Lazarus' death. A similar suppression of Jesus' indignant rebuke on the way to the tomb occurs in longer Mark. Like the author of the canonical gospel, this author does not depict Jesus as an *ecstatic* healer and exorcist who gets worked up before confronting a malignant power, although a trace of this conception appears in the charge that Jesus was "beside himself" and using a demon to cast out demons (Mark

3:21, 22; cf. John 8:48; 10:20–21). Accordingly, this author transformed Jesus' snarling rebuke of the demon into the disciples' rebuke of the sister, not unlike the way exorcism language apparently was transferred from the "demonic" disease to the leper in Mark 1:43. One consequence of this trans-ference is that the rebuke in LGM 1:3 no longer fits within the scheme of a healing story with a demonic conception of the illness; the verse now func-tions redactionally as another indication of the disciples' spiritual short-sight-edness and as a more sanguine explanation for Jesus' anger at this point. Another consequence is that the loud cry from the tomb becomes a response to Jesus' mere proximity: it is triggered by who he is rather than what he does and says (cf. Mark 1:24; 3:11). By virtue of their ability to "see" the holy spirit within Jesus, the unclean spirits recognize "the Holy One of God" who has come to destroy them.

The great cry that precedes the miracle is not problematic in the context of the Markan gospel, where it is unclear whether two other persons were actu-ally dead when Jesus raised them by the hand. In the raising of Jairus's daugh-ter, the miracle is preceded by Jesus' question, "Why do you make a tumult and weep? The child is not dead but sleeping" (Mark 5:39). The reader is left to decide whether Jesus was telling the truth or attempting to forestall the unwanted publicity by pretending that the child was not dead. Similarly, when Jesus exorcises a demon from the young boy with epilepsy, we read, "And after crying out and convulsing him terribly, it came out, and the boy was like a corpse; so that most of them said, 'He is dead'" (9:26). Whether or not their impression is correct is left to the reader to decide. (Interestingly, these three ambiguously dead persons are described using over a dozen diminutives.)[16] So the great cry from the entombed young man is par for the course.

Such a cry would have been wholly inappropriate in the context of John's story, however. John's Jesus is not engaged in a conflict with Satan's minions, for Jesus' "kingship is not of this world" (18:36) and does not need to be established by the overthrow of a "this-worldly" supernatural order. Besides, exorcism is too ordinary a practice for John's messiah, who specializes in extraordinary signs that distinguish him from everyone else.[17] The raising of Lazarus is the greatest of these signs and forms the climax of Jesus' public min-istry. Its impressiveness is what leads the Sanhedrin to decide to kill Jesus so that his popularity will not spark a war with the Romans (11:46–53). Given John's agenda, any detail that raises the possibility that Lazarus was not dead simply would not fit. So an author with Johannine interests would have had good reason to change the loud voice, indeed, to stress that Lazarus was already decomposing (11:39). It is not at all difficult to imagine a Johannine author transferring the "great cry" from the tomb to Jesus, thereby fulfilling the apocalyptic prediction of 5:28–29: "the hour is coming when all who are in the tombs *will hear his voice and come forth*, those who have done good, to the resurrection of life, and those who have done evil, to the resurrection of judgment." This saying conveys the traditional, apocalyptic conception of a general resurrection of the dead; the same conception appears in Matthew's passion narrative, where Jesus' "loud voice" from the cross coincides with an earthquake and the opening of the tombs of the saints, who rise and (after Jesus' resurrection) come out of their tombs (Matt 27:50–53), prefiguring the general resurrection on the last day. In John, however, this apocalyptic theme is given a present dimension. Thus John 5:25 says: "Truly, truly, I say to you, the hour is coming, *and now is*, when the dead will hear the voice of the Son of God, and those who hear will live." The truth of this statement is drama-tized when Jesus calls Lazarus from the tomb "in a loud voice," demonstrat-ing that he himself is "the resurrection and the life" (11:23–26). If John composed 5:25 in order to add a realized dimension to the apocalypticism of 5:28–29, we have reason to suspect that he is also responsible for the fulfill-ment of this prophecy in the call to Lazarus.

I am not claiming that these redaction-critical *speculations* are correct. I am merely demonstrating that if we postulate that both authors began with a tradition about Jesus rebuking a spirit that in turn cried out from a tomb, some very puzzling elements that would be unintelligible according to a the-ory of direct literary dependence can be accounted for as intelligible redactional decisions in keeping with Markan and Johannine interests. We can be quite certain that neither John nor longer Mark derived its patently exorcistic ele-ment from the other, since these details are different (a rebuke of a spirit; a demonic cry from a tomb) and the shared elements of anger and rebuking are expressed in different words and developed in divergent ways. Certainly, the assumption that John used LGM 1 cannot explain how the troublesome phrase "rebuked the spirit and troubled himself" got into his story, nor can the longer text's dependence upon John readily explain why Jesus' cry to Lazarus "in a loud voice" to come out became an inarticulate "loud voice" from a dead man. Lindars made a good case that the raising of Lazarus originally included an exorcistic rebuke, but he did not need to propose that the whole episode in John was composed out of something similar to the exorcism/rais-ing story in Mark 9:14–29.[18] LGM 1a much more closely resembles the syn-optic-style tradition Lindars sought.

The last verse to consider in relation to the typical form of a healing story is LGM 1:9. The shift in setting to the young man's house extends the story beyond the proof of healing, which is uncharacteristic of oral tradi-tion.[19] Although some healing stories in the gospels likewise extend beyond the proof of healing, this kind of departure from type is most likely a literary development. When the evangelists combined disparate oral traditions into single, continuous narratives, they sometimes modified the standard story types in order to allow intrinsically independent episodes to function as sequences within a larger plot. When this happened, characteristic signs of the author's editing usually appear in the story.[20] This is the case with LGM 1:9, too. Redaction critics view the motif of a return to a house for private instruction as a redactional feature in Mark's narrative, not an element stemming from tradition or a written source (cf. LGM 1b with Mark 9:28–29). LGM 1b, moreover, does not fit any recognized story type, and compared to LGM 1a contains a higher proportion of phrases that are *not* conventional in oral storytelling yet are found elsewhere in Mark's story.[21] LGM 1b strongly resembles the private discussion of the mystery of the kingdom of God in Mark 4:10–12, which, together with 4:34 (and perhaps all of 4:13–25 as well), appears to be a Markan insertion within the parable discourse; the shift in setting at 4:10 to "when he was alone" looks like a redactional insertion because it contradicts the indications that the parables before and after this change in setting (4:3–9, 26–33) were addressed to the large crowd from the boat (4:1–2, 33, 36). In other words, LGM 1b does not resemble oral tradition so much as situations within canonical Mark that were created by Mark in order to elaborate upon the preceding incident.

At this point we may conclude that LGM 1 has the expected form of a Markan healing story, displaying the conventional motifs of oral tradition and the peculiarities of Markan redaction. Should we conclude that LGM 1 is an oral tradition reworked by Mark? Before we reach a verdict we need to consider other possible explanations for the similarities between LGM 1a and John 11, particularly whether the former could be an abbreviation of the latter.

## Longer Mark's Relation to John

That an evangelist might abbreviate a story he derived from another gospel is not an unlikely scenario. Matthew and Luke sometimes abbreviated Mark by excising unnecessary details. The result of such abbreviation, however, is usually a shorter version that sounds a great deal like the longer one; the signs of literary dependence are still quite clear. What we have in LGM 1a, however, is a thoroughly Markan version of a thoroughly Johannine story. What is missing is the evidence that either author was acquainted with the other's version of this miracle. Similarity of content does not by itself prove a literary relationship, since two versions of a story derived independently from oral tradition would naturally be similar. Canonical Mark and John relate many of the same episodes in similar ways and frequently in the same order. But even though canonical Mark was probably completed two to three decades before John, scholars disagree over whether even the verbatim parallels between John and Mark prove that John used Mark as a source. Nevertheless, if LGM 1 were found to contain some of the same secondary elements found in John 11 or elements typical of Johannine redaction or style, those elements would support the possibility that the author of LGM 1 was acquainted with John's version, directly or indirectly. So it is very telling that LGM 1 has none of the secondary or distinctively Johannine elements that appear in John 11.[22]

The complete absence of these features from LGM 1 would be truly astonishing if the author of LGM 1 had the text of John open in front of him. That is because John's story consists *mostly* of secondary and Johannine elements. As Smith noted, John 11 is dominated by lengthy conversations and by "psychological and moral and theological interests [that are] all unknown to the simple, primitive miracle story."[23] A liberal estimate of the secondary and typically Johannine features would include the following elements: the second supplicant (Mary), whose plea repeats that of the first (11:28–29, 31–32);[24] the second proof that Lazarus was truly dead (11: 39b; cf. 11:17); most of the direct speech of Jesus, including the christological discussions between Jesus and his disciples (11:4, 7–16) and between Jesus and the women (11:23–27, 40), and Jesus' prayer before performing the miracle (11:41b–42);[25] the proper names of the participants (except for Jesus);[26] the five references to the actions and attitudes of "the Jews" (11:8, 19, 31, 45, 46; these all appear in verses that may be considered redactional on other grounds); the cross-references to Jesus' anointing by Mary (12:3–8) and his healing of the man born blind (9:1–41), which presuppose a larger, textual framework (11:2, 37); the narration connecting these possibly secondary or Johannine elements together (11:5–6, 18, 20, 30, 38a); the reference to the miracle resulting in belief in Jesus and a polarization among the witnesses, which are Johannine themes (11:45–46); and, finally, the Jerusalem leaders' plot to destroy Jesus and Jesus' response (11:47–54), which take the story beyond the proof of the miracle. I want to stress that this is a liberal estimate of possibly secondary and Johannine features, and I am not claiming that all of these features are inconceivable as oral tradition. My point is that with so much possibly redactional material in the Johannine version (41 of 54 verses, or 76%), it would be extraordinarily unlikely that an author using this gospel as his literary source would happen to omit all of it.[27]

The independence of LGM 1 and 2 from John 11 is also suggested by the numerous discrepancies and contradictions between these two accounts. In longer Mark, Jesus does not initially know either the young man or his sister, and the mutual love between Jesus and the young man develops during the story (1:8; 2:1), whereas in the Gospel of John, Jesus already knows and loves Mary, Martha, and Lazarus (11:3, 5, 36). In LGM 2, Jesus snubs two (three?) of the young man's female relatives after he leaves Bethany, whereas in John, Jesus returns to their home for a meal hosted by the sisters and defends Mary's controversial act of anointing his feet with costly oil and drying them with her hair (12:1–8). In longer Mark, the request for help comes directly from the sister, the brother is already buried when Jesus hears about his condition, and the miracle takes place in the same location. In John, however, Jesus is solicited by messenger, the brother remains alive for two days after Jesus learns of his condition, and Jesus travels for four days to reach the tomb. In LGM 1:4, Jesus' anger is triggered by his disciples' lack of empathy for the sister's grief, whereas in John, Jesus' intense agitation (denoted by the verb ἐμβριμᾶσθαι) is triggered by the grief itself (11:33). In longer Mark, Jesus rolls back the stone himself and raises the young man by grasping his hand. In John, Jesus orders others to move the stone and performs the miracle with the command, "Lazarus come out." The "loud voice" in longer Mark comes from the tomb before Jesus reaches it (1:5), not from Jesus as he commands the dead man (John 11:43).

Scholars who think longer Mark is dependent upon John normally characterize these differences as "confusions" on the part of the non-canonical author.[28] But it is hard to see how anyone could get that confused. These discrepancies are more easily explained if we do not suppose a relationship of literary dependence, for uniformity of details and conventional motifs is the hallmark of direct literary dependence, whereas variability in these things is the hallmark of oral storytelling.[29] The synoptic gospels, for example, are most uniform where Matthew and Luke used Mark and Q, and least uniform where Matthew and Luke did not share written sources. The infancy narratives and resurrection appearances in Matthew and Luke, for instance, diverge enormously despite their common subject matter, precisely because Mark and Q did not contain such narratives. Likewise, these two authors' accounts of the death of Judas (Matt 27:1–10; Acts 1:15–20) have many similar elements (Judas betrays Jesus for money, the money is used to purchase a field, Judas shortly thereafter dies an unnatural death, the field is subsequently nicknamed Field of Blood, and the incident fulfils scripture), yet all but the first and last of these common elements are developed in contradictory ways. Some of these differences reflect the variability of oral tradition; others reflect the freedom with which Matthew and Luke revised those traditions. Regardless of how one explains this phenomenon, the fact that independent accounts are often highly contradictory supports the position that LGM 1a represents an authentic Markan tradition, particularly since canonical Mark and John themselves frequently diverge in their accounts of the same incidents.

Consider, for example, the story of Jesus' anointing in Bethany in John 12:1–8 and Mark 14:3–9. It occurs at about the same time relative to the passover in both texts, but before the procession to Jerusalem in John and after the procession in Mark. Both authors agree on the town, but presumably not on the house, for the host is Simon the leper in Mark but Mary, Martha, and Lazarus in John. Jesus knows the woman who anoints him in John's version, just as he already knew the supplicants in John 11 (the woman is in fact one of those supplicants), but that does not appear to be the case in Mark, where the woman is unnamed, as is the sister in LGM 1:1 (the woman who anoints Jesus is probably not the young man's sister). The woman anoints Jesus' feet in John, his head in Mark. John specifies that Judas objected to the anointing; Mark does not specify an individual, and refers more generally to "some" of the people present.

The Markan and Johannine accounts of Jesus' arrest likewise differ in many of their details. In Mark, the arresting party is "a crowd with swords and clubs, from the chief priests and the scribes and the elders," but in John, the group consists of a Roman cohort (i.e., 600 soldiers) in addition to "some officers from the chief priests and the Pharisees." In Mark, Jesus is identified by the prearranged sign of Judas's kiss, yet in John, Judas stands with the arresting party (18:5) while Jesus himself takes the initiative, asking whom they seek and informing them that he is the one they want. Jesus' initiative actually frightens the soldiers in John, who draw back and fall to the ground (18:6)! In Mark, Jesus is reluctant to accept his fate and prays that "this cup" might be removed from him (14:36); in John, Jesus reacts to Peter's attempt to protect him with the retort "shall I not drink the cup which the Father has given me?" (18:11; cf. 12:27). And again, only John supplies the names of the one who used his sword and the slave whose ear was struck.

Numerous differences also appear in the Markan and Johannine accounts of the calling of the disciples, the last supper, the trials, the crucifixion, and the discovery of the open tomb.[30] What is particularly striking about these differences is that they are so often incomprehensible from the perspective of redaction criticism since they do not always coincide with what we know of John's theological interests. But however one accounts for the frequent and often pointless differences between Markan and Johannine renditions of the same incidents, the longer gospel's conformity to this pattern is consistent with the other indications that LGM 1a is an independent tradition, and inconsistent with the view that it depends literally upon John 11.

Some of the specific differences between LGM 1 and 2 and John are worth exploring. Certainly the absence of the names Lazarus, Mary, and Martha from longer Mark would be surprising if John were the source. But it is normal for inessential details such as the names and occupations of minor characters to drop out or vary in the course of oral transmission. So, for instance, the centurion's servant (or slave) in Q appears as an official's son in John (Matt 8:5; Luke 7:2; John 4:46), although the town remains the same (Capernaum). Such details become less variable in the course of written transmission (which is why Matthew and Luke agree). So we might expect anonymous characters to appear in LGM 1 if it is based on oral tradition, but the names Mary, Martha, and Lazarus to appear if the Gospel of John is the source. However, we do not need to rely on abstractions to establish this fact, since there are indications that John did not expect his readers to associate any of these names with the miracle Jesus performed in Bethany. The only named character whom the author expects his readers to know is Mary, who is introduced as the person "who anointed the Lord with ointment and wiped his feet with her hair" (11:2). Lazarus is introduced as "a certain man...of Bethany" and as Mary's brother, and is later reintroduced twice as the person "whom Jesus had raised from the dead" (12:1, 9). Martha, likewise, is introduced as Mary's sister. Thus the author assumes that his readers are already familiar with one of these three characters, but he does not assume that they will recognize that character *from her role in this story*. Instead, she is introduced as the woman from an episode that has not yet been narrated but would already be familiar to a Christian audience (i.e., from oral tradition or an earlier gospel). Since Lazarus and Martha are introduced in relation to the sister who is known from another incident, and the next pericope contains two reminders that Lazarus was the man raised by Jesus, it would appear that John did not expect his Christian audience to associate these three names with this story.

Whether or not John expected his readers to know that the woman who anointed Jesus was named Mary or that a pair of sisters named Mary and Martha lived in the village of Bethany is not clear. In the synoptics, the woman who anoints Jesus is anonymous (Matt 26:6–13; Mark 14:3–9; Luke 7:36–50), and Luke's pair of sisters named Mary and Martha do not live in Bethany; Luke's chronology favours a location for their home in Samaria (10:38–42). Moreover, Luke situates the story of the anointing in a city of Galilee, and he and Matthew agree with their source, Mark, that the host was "Simon," although Luke depicts Simon as a Pharisee rather than a leper.

So it is not at all clear that the original readers of the Gospel of John associated the names Mary, Martha, and Lazarus with a village named Bethany or with the story of the raising of a dead man in Bethany. These details may have been created by the author of John 11. We have reason to suppose, then, that the anonymity of the young man and his sister in LGM 1 and 2 is not a deliberate omission of two names that few readers could forget, but, rather, reflects independent reliance upon oral tradition.

Another difference worth exploring is one that scholars have entirely misunderstood, namely, that the place called Bethany in LGM 1:1 is not the village situated "at the Mount of Olives" in the Gospel of Mark (11:1) and the place where Lazarus is raised in the Gospel of John, but the place east of the Jordan River where Jesus is residing when he is informed of Lazarus' illness.[31] In John 10:40, this locale is described as "the place where John at first baptized," and in the opening sequence of John's gospel, the place is called "Bethany beyond the Jordan" (1:28). In other words, both John's story about Lazarus and longer Mark's story about the young man begin in the same village called Bethany, but only John's version has Jesus travel to a different Bethany in order to raise the brother. A location for LGM 1 east of the Jordan is apparent from the Markan itinerary. At Mark 10:1, Jesus enters northern Judea, then crosses the Jordan eastwards into Peraea. He then travels south through Peraea until he reaches the road that runs between Livias and Jericho, whereupon he turns west. At some point Jesus returns to the other side of the Jordan then comes to Jericho (10:46). The moment when he re-enters Judea is unclear in canonical Mark, but in longer Mark the westward crossing of the Jordan occurs at LGM 1:13. Scholars have misunderstood this because they have confused the narrator's reference to Jesus returning "to the other side of the Jordan" (εἰς τὸ πέραν τοῦ Ἰορδάνου) with the standard synonym for Peraea (πέραν τοῦ Ἰορδάνου or "across the Jordan"), which in the New Testament never has the definite article before it (e.g., Mark 3:8; 10:1; Matt 4:25; John 1:28; 3:26; 10:40; cf. Josephus, *Antiquities* 13.398; *Life* 33); the phrase in LGM 1:13 is instead a relative description whose direction depends on where the action begins. It functions the same way the similar phrase "to the other side of the sea" functions in Mark 5:1 (εἰς τὸ πέραν τῆς θαλάσσης).

The observation that LGM 1 is set in Peraea has significant implications for longer Mark's chronology, a subject about which there has been considerable confusion. With an eye to Jesus' movements in Mark 10, most scholars have reasoned that the redactor of the longer text put the raising story in the wrong place, for if Jesus is travelling southward through Peraea, he should arrive at Jericho before he arrives at Bethany in Judea. They imagined, therefore, that LGM 1:1 presupposes an unnarrated crossing of the Jordan into Judea in order for Jesus to arrive at Bethany, which would entail that at 1:13 Jesus crosses back again into Peraea only to double back across the Jordan (again unnarrated) in order to arrive in Jericho (10:46) then proceed to Jerusalem and Bethany (11:1–11). This "glaring anachronism in the text of Mark" is even offered as proof "that *Secret Mark* is a later addition to canonical Mark."[32] Once we realize that LGM 1 is actually set in Peraea, it becomes apparent that the confusion is confined to the scholars who needlessly posit two unnarrated crossings of the Jordan, and that LGM 1 appears exactly where it should—at the point in the narrative where Jesus would be passing by Bethany beyond the Jordan.[33] In longer Mark, Jesus travels south through Peraea (10:1), turns westward toward Jerusalem (10:32?), arrives at Bethany beyond the Jordan (LGM 1:1–12), crosses the Jordan into Judea where Joshua and the Israelites crossed into the promised land (LGM 1:13), responds to the request by James and John for places of honour on the 7 km stretch between the Makhadat Hajla ford and Jericho (10:35–45), then arrives in Jericho, where he refuses to welcome the young man's sister, his mother, and Salome (Mark 10:46 +LGM 2). This is not a confusion of the Markan chronology but a clarification of where Mark 10:35–45 took place. If either evangelist is confused about location, it is John, who depicts the 34 km journey between these two Bethanies as taking four days (11:14–17) rather than just one, but imagines that Jesus could travel from Bethany beyond the Jordan to Cana in Galilee (at least 120 km) in less than three days (1:43; 2:1). Presumably, John mistakenly thought that Bethany beyond the Jordan was in northern Peraea or just to the north or south of the Sea of Galilee.[34]

The disagreement between LGM 1 and John on the setting of the raising miracle would be hard to explain by a theory of canonical dependence. John clearly situated not only the conversations between Jesus and the sisters but also the miracle itself in the better known Bethany in Judea, which he described as "near Jerusalem, about three kilometres off" (John 11:18). An author dependent upon John would presumably have located the raising miracle in that Bethany as well, particularly if he were writing in the middle of the second century, as proponents of the pastiche theory invariably imagine. If either author had a good reason to shift the setting, it was John, for the four-day journey to Bethany of Judea following Lazarus' demise makes this an undeniably impressive miracle, which in turn sets the stage for the conflict that leads to Jesus' crucifixion. We have good reason to wonder whether the entire story was originally set in Bethany beyond the Jordan.

The location of LGM 1 in Bethany beyond the Jordan suggests a connection between LGM 1b and John 1:35–40. In the former, Jesus remains with an anonymous would-be disciple overnight in Bethany beyond the Jordan. In the latter, two disciples, one of them anonymous, meet Jesus in Bethany beyond the Jordan, follow him to see where he is staying, then remain with him "that day" (i.e., overnight) because the hour was late. The shared detail of Jesus staying overnight with an anonymous disciple would be insignificant were it not for the fact that in both gospels this occurs in the same desert oasis. It appears, then, that both halves of LGM 1 find their closest parallels in John. But the points of contact between LGM 1b and John 1:35–40 are even more nebulous than those between LGM 1a and John 11. Neither account seems to be more "primitive" or "original," and the contacts are too tenuous to suggest a literary connection.

The affinity between LGM 1 and two sections of the Gospel of John that mention or allude to Bethany beyond the Jordan (1:28; 10:40) is interesting, but not entirely surprising, since John and canonical Mark share numerous traditions (especially in the passion narrative), and John's similarities with the synoptics are normally closer to Mark than to Matthew or Luke. The fact that the Johannine parallels are not contiguous is also not surprising, given the observation recorded in the title of Raymond Brown's article "Incidents That Are Units in the Synoptic Gospels but Dispersed in St. John."[35] Brown offered four examples of this phenomenon. I think he found more scattered Johannine parallels than actually exist, but his basic point that elements within contiguous passages in the synoptic gospels are sometimes dispersed in John still holds.

### The Pastiche Explanation

Insofar as LGM 1 is more primitive in form than the raising of Lazarus, lacks distinctively Johannine elements, gratuitously contradicts John 11 and 1:35–40, and combines incidents that are dispersed in John's gospel, it reproduces patterns of relationship that exist between John and the synoptics, patterns which an imitator of Mark's style would not likely think to replicate. So given the fact that LGM 1 also lacks the secondary features found in John 11, such as a second sister and the names that John did not expect his audience to associate with this story, but contains an odd detail that supports Lindars' suggestion that the raising of Lazarus once involved an exorcistic confrontation, the conclusion that LGM 1a represents an independent witness to an oral tradition is eminently reasonable. Indeed, for the Jesus Seminar and two dozen other scholars, this conclusion has seemed too obvious to require demonstration. I belaboured the point because it contradicts the inveterate belief that the non-canonical gospels were written decades after the four canonical gospels and in complete dependence upon them. Defenders of this view know better than to suggest that John's fifty-four-verse christological drama more closely resembles oral tradition than longer Mark's nine-verse account. But the implication that LGM 1a offers a more primitive version of the raising of Lazarus has been countered with arguments that the author of longer Mark abbreviated John 11. In 1974 F.F. Bruce declared this opinion to be self-evident: "The raising of the young man of Bethany is too evidently based—and clumsily based at that—on the Johannine story of the raising of Lazarus for us to regard it as in any sense an independent Markan counterpart to the Johannine story (not to speak of our regarding it as a *source* of the Johannine story)." Later that year Helmut Merkel and Raymond E. Brown developed arguments for longer Mark's complete dependence on the four canonical gospels, and they were followed by Robert M. Grant, Edward C. Hobbs, Daryl Schmidt, and Frans Neirynck.[36] At present, the theory that longer Mark is a second-century cento or pastiche dependent on all four canonical gospels is one of the most frequently voiced opinions on the subject, having roughly as many proponents as the theory that it derives from oral tradition (at least thirty-two).

The arguments in support of direct canonical dependence take a variety of forms. Most often these scholars imagined how, by a process of free association, the author of longer Mark could have been led from one phrase or feature in one canonical gospel to another phrase or feature in another canonical gospel, accumulating details until nothing unparalleled remained that could derive from oral tradition. So, for example, Raymond Brown explained the nocturnal encounter in LGM 1:12 as a "rephrasing in Marcan language" of some "information from the Johannine Nicodemus scene," namely, the concept of teaching (because Nicodemus calls Jesus "teacher"), the concept of the kingdom of God, and the nighttime setting. The author borrowed the phrase "and when it was evening" (1:11) from the introduction to Joseph of Arimathea in Matt 27:57, a connection that occurred to him because both the young man and Joseph are "rich." The notion of "remaining with" Jesus is taken from John 1:39 because there it "is applied to the disciples" and in Mark 4:11 the mystery is given to "the disciples."[37]

Brown's explanation of the origin of LGM 1b as a revision of Jesus' nocturnal encounter with Nicodemus is reminiscent of the way some scholars have explained unique Johannine passages as hybrids of similar stories in the synoptics. Ironically, Benjamin W. Bacon explained Nicodemus as a hybrid of the man with many possessions (Mark 10:17–22), the scribe who was "not far from the kingdom of God" (Mark 12:28–34), and the Pharisee Gamaliel, who defended Jesus' apostles in the Sanhedrin (Acts 5:34–42; cf. John 7:50–52).[38] Thomas L. Brodie's attempt to demonstrate that the entire Gospel of John is a systematic reworking not only of Mark and Matthew but also of Ephesians, the Pentateuch, and part of Luke-Acts shows that any gospel story can be construed as a deliberate revision of other stories.[39] When this form of explanation is applied to *canonical* gospels, scholars rightly object that conceivable scenarios of editorial borrowings are wantonly speculative and methodologically uncontrollable.

When scholars cite rough, random parallels as evidence of literary dependence, they are engaging in parallelomania, "that extravagance among scholars which first overdoes the supposed similarity in passages and then proceeds to describe source and derivation as if implying literary connection flowing in an inevitable or predetermined direction."[40] People who educe vague parallels as evidence that the apocryphal gospels are dependent upon the canonical gospels would do well to remember that the same procedure has been used to argue that the Gospel of Mark is a refashioning of myths derived from the *Odyssey* and the *Iliad* and that the Gospel of John is the product of a Near Eastern form of Buddhism.[41] The listing of trivial, inexact parallels is the sine qua non of improbable theories of literary dependence.

The folly of offering partial parallels and conceivable redactional scenarios as evidence of literary dependence becomes apparent when we compare the various attempts to derive the contents of LGM 2 from Matthew, Luke, and John. Raymond Brown argued that "the sister of the young man whom Jesus loved, and his mother, and Salome" draws upon the description of the women at the foot of the cross in John 19:25–26, since one of these women is described as "his mother," albeit Jesus' mother and not the mother of the young man; this commonplace verbal parallel is not insignificant because the tension between Jesus and his mother in John resembles the tension between Jesus and these women in LGM 2. Moreover, the women at the cross include a sister, albeit Jesus' mother's sister and not the sister of the young man. This parallel, too, is "not so far-fetched," since the sister in LGM 2:1 is "the sister of the young man whom Jesus loved," and John's "disciple whom Jesus loved" is also at the cross. So maybe the author of longer Mark thought Mary of Clopas was Jesus' mother's sister, and confused her with Mary Magdalene, whom tradition confused with Mary the sister of Lazarus. The words "and Salome," however, come from Mark's parallel to this scene (15:40).[42] Edward C. Hobbs, on the other hand, tentatively suggested that the young man's mother comes from the mother of the young man Jesus raised in Luke 7:11–17.[43] Helmut Merkel deemed "and Jesus did not receive them" (LGM 2:2) an "allusion" to Luke's account of the Samaritan villagers' refusal to receive Jesus (9:53),[44] as did Frans Neirynck, who also adduced Martha's welcome reception of Jesus (Luke 10:38) and Zacchaeus's welcome reception of Jesus *in Jericho* (Luke 19:6) as evidence of Lukan influence on LGM 2. Strangely, none of these Lukan passages involves Jesus not receiving someone or uses the compound form of the verb "to receive" found in LGM 2:2. Daryl Schmidt thought that the element of rejection derived from Luke 8:40, where the same verb does occur, although in a description of a crowd welcoming Jesus.[45] (One might point to 9:11 as an example in which Jesus is actually the subject of this verb, but, again, Jesus receives a crowd rather than rejects people.) Neirynck agreed with Brown that "and Salome" comes from Mark's story of the women watching the crucifixion, but ascribed the common phrase "and there were there" to the synoptic parallel in Matt 27:55, which is slightly closer to LGM 2:1 than is Mark 15:40.[46] F.F. Bruce viewed Jesus' rejection of the women in LGM 2 as an extension of the previous story in which James and John ask for positions of honour, noting that in Matthew's version of that story, it is their mother who makes the request for them, and a comparison between Mark 15:40 and Matt 27:56 could have led this author to suppose that Salome was their mother.[47] So here we have a two-sentence story with no significant verbal parallels to any canonical gospel being derived from every conceivable superficial resemblance in four gospels.

The fact that a dozen or more sources can be imagined for just these two sentences is sufficient proof that vague and trivial parallels cannot establish dependence. There is no way to discriminate between a vague parallel that did influence an author and a vague parallel that did not. And the procedure does not make LGM 1 and 2 more comprehensible. What is the logic of supposing that our author wrote about Jesus refusing to meet three particular women in Jericho because he read a comment in John about three female relatives of Jesus at the cross and a comment in Luke about someone receiving or rejecting Jesus? This mystical form of explanation will not become more persuasive should we multiply the indeterminacies in order to explain LGM 1 this way as well. In order to account for all of LGM 1 and 2 without recourse to oral tradition we would need to imagine an author who composed relatively simple, Markan-sounding episodes by strange feats of mental gymnastics.

Thus, in addition to being speculative and uncontrollable, pastiche explanations are unrealistically complicated. Scholars who study the synoptic problem recognize that when a variety of theories can explain the relationship between two or more gospels, the one that involves the most natural editorial procedures is preferable. For example, the Two Gospel (Griesbach) Hypothesis can explain any Markan passage as a deliberate conflation of its parallels in Matthew and Luke.[48] Yet most scholars reject the Two Gospel Hypothesis because it involves a redactional procedure that seems very odd to them: Mark set out to harmonize and epitomize the Gospels of Matthew and Luke by eliminating their unique or contradictory materials and either carefully conflating their shared materials—except for more than two hundred verses of sayings, which he omitted—or following one of them when their accounts diverged; Mark also made theologically motivated revisions and additions that resulted in a coherent narrative. This scenario is possible, but most scholars prefer the Two (or Four) Source Hypothesis because it envisions a more natural way of reworking written sources: Mark wrote his gospel first, using mostly oral traditions, and then Matthew and Luke independently added the contents of a collection of sayings (Q) and other unique traditions (M, L) to the framework of Mark, making alterations to their sources in the process. The same considerations apply with respect to longer Mark. If the theory that canonical Mark carefully conflated Matthew and Luke seems less plausible than the theory that Matthew and Luke independently expanded Mark, then the theory that longer Mark conflated four gospels must be doubly improbable. It is *possible* that an author abbreviated and deliberately contradicted John 11 by replacing John's details with concepts and phrase fragments he found scattered throughout four gospels. But it is simpler and more natural to imagine the authors of John and longer Mark independently reworking oral traditions.

The success of the Two Source Hypothesis as an explanation for the similarities and differences among the synoptic gospels has led many scholars to suppose that a gospel writer using *literary* sources would be more likely to make discrete, purposeful changes motivated by ideological, stylistic, and literary concerns than to make wanton, random changes guided by free association. "If one cannot accept the hypothesis of a careless or capricious evangelist who gratuitously changed, added, and subtracted details, then one is forced to agree…that the evangelist drew the material for his stories from an independent tradition, similar to but not the same as the traditions represented in the Synoptic Gospels."[49] That was Raymond Brown's rationale for concluding that John did not use the synoptics, and it applies equally well to the relationship between John and longer Mark. As we have seen, many of the differences between LGM 1a and John 11, including the most puzzling ones, can be accounted for using the supposition that a redactor with Markan interests and a redactor with Johannine interests independently revised an oral tradition resembling LGM 1a. The remaining differences can be attributed to the variability of oral tradition. In other words, only the assumption of longer Mark's literary dependence on John requires a redactional procedure that would seem inane and capricious in comparison to how the canonical evangelists used written sources.

At this point we can affirm Smith's conclusion that the author of longer Mark did not know the Gospel of John and that his accounts of the raising and initiation of the young man in Bethany ultimately derive from oral traditions, either directly or via a notebook like the ones mentioned in I.19. Apparently, both authors knew traditions about Jesus and an anonymous individual that were localized in Bethany beyond the Jordan. The question in need of more attention is whether John's source for these traditions was oral tradition or longer Mark.

Certainly the scholars who believe that John freely revised Mark should be asking themselves why they suppose John used the canonical gospel. To those scholars I concede that it is not nearly so difficult to imagine John 11 as a deliberate revision of LGM 1a as it is to imagine LGM 1a as a deliberate revision of John 11. But there are two important problems with the idea that John knew longer Mark. The first problem is that this explanation makes the pervasive differences between LGM 1 and its Johannine parallels harder to explain (especially the different but complementary exorcistic elements). The second problem is the fact that longer Mark probably did not circulate outside the Alexandrian church. The premise that Mark bequeathed this gospel to the church in Alexandria (I.28–II.1) presupposes that he did not permit anyone to make copies of the longer text before his death. The complete absence of manuscript evidence for this gospel likewise implies that this text did not circulate outside Alexandria except in its post-Johannine, Carpocratian form. Even within Alexandria, the hearing of this text was restricted to Christians who had proved their worthiness to learn the unwritten gnostic tradition by advancing through elementary moral training and a preliminary study of natural revelation (what Clement called the lesser mysteries).

So it seems unlikely that any canonical evangelist would have known this text directly without having spent a few years in Alexandria. There is, however, a possibility that a canonical evangelist or redactor could have encountered this gospel indirectly through acquaintance with someone from Alexandria who had heard the text. The vagaries of secondary orality could account for some of the differences between John 11 and LGM 1, and Johannine interests could certainly account for others. It remains to be seen whether any advantage is gained by recourse to secondary orality when independent access to oral tradition can explain the contradictions equally well, and there are no verbal similarities that require a literary connection. In my opinion, the simplest explanation is that longer Mark and John are completely literarily independent.

## Longer Mark's Relation to
## Matthew and Luke

The conclusion that longer Mark is independent of John does not tell us anything about its relationship with the other canonical gospels. Proponents of
the pastiche theory have drawn up lists of verbal parallels between LGM 1
and 2 and Matthew and Luke, but most of these parallels are vague, trivial,
or formulaic. The lengthier and more distinctive parallels that might plausi-
bly suggest literary dependence also appear in canonical Mark, sometimes in
a more exact form.[50] The two exceptions are LGM 1:6 and 1:9b. The reference in 1:6 to Jesus approaching the stone and rolling it back is reminiscent
of Matt 28:2, where an angel does the same thing. The verbal parallels, however, overlap with parallels to Mark 16:3:

> And approaching, Jesus rolled away the stone from the door of the tomb.
> (LGM 1:6)

> For an angel of the Lord descended from heaven, and approaching, rolled away
> the stone, and sat upon it. (Matt 28:2)

> And they were saying to one another, "Who will *roll* away the stone for us
> from the door of the tomb?" (Mark 16:3)

The underlined words indicate exact agreement in Greek, and the word in italics denotes the same word in a different tense.[51] Mark 16:3 includes eight of
the words in LGM 1:6 in the same order, though the verb *roll* has a future
tense. Matt 28:2, on the other hand, includes five of the same words found
in LGM 1:6 in the same order, all of which are identical (apart from a final
nu), and two of which ("the stone") occur in Mark's lengthier parallel "the
stone…from the door of the tomb." It is unnecessary to suppose that the
words "the stone" derive from Matt 28:2 since they are part of Mark's lengthier parallel. So the question is, do we really need to propose knowledge of
Matthew's empty tomb narrative in order to explain why the words "and
approaching" and the past tense of *roll* appear in LGM 1:6? Interestingly,
Helmut Merkel took "and approaching" as evidence that LGM 1:6 was patterned after Luke 7:14, where Jesus approaches a coffin in order to raise a
young man. If this commonplace conjunction of two ordinary words is evidence of longer Mark's dependence upon two different gospels, why is it not
evidence that one of those gospels is dependent upon the other?[52] Is it not
simpler to suppose that "and approaching" might be a natural expression to
use when someone approaches a tomb or a coffin, and that the past tense of
*roll* in LGM 1:6 agrees with the past tense in Matt 28:2 because LGM 1:6
describes a completed action rather than a future possibility?

The only Lukan parallel of note is "for he was rich," which appears together with the adverb *very* in Luke 18:23 (ἦν γὰρ πλούσιος σφόδρα). This is Luke's revision of Mark's cumbersome clause "for he was having many possessions" (ἦν γὰρ ἔχων κτήματα πολλά). Luke shortened and improved Mark's phrasing by eliminating the periphrastic imperfect. The question we must answer is why LGM 1:9b agrees with the changes that Luke made to Mark 10:22. Certainly this could be a coincidence: Matthew and Luke independently made the same minor changes to Markan phrasing in hundreds of places, although not many of these "minor agreements" against Mark are this noticeable. The absence of the adverb *very* from LGM 1:9b supports coincidental revision, but another consideration points to the influence of Luke 18:23, namely, the fact that LGM 1a has parallels to unique elements in the Markan, Matthean, and Lukan forms of the story about the man who asks what he must do to attain eternal life: only Matthew calls that man a "young man" (19:20, 22), only Mark contains the phrase "looking upon him loved him" (10:21), and only Luke has the phrase "for he was rich" (18:23). Even the main proponents of the theory of longer Markan priority have acknowledged how odd it is that unique elements from the three canonical versions of "the rich young ruler" would find parallels in LGM 1.[53]

Smith had no definite solution to this problem, but did suggest that Matthew knew and was influenced by longer Mark whereas Clement confused the original wording of LGM 1:9b ("for he was having many possessions") with Luke's more natural and memorable "for he was rich."[54] Most commentators reject both of these explanations. The fact that Matthew contains ninety percent of Mark's contents implies that if Matthew had had access to the longer text of Mark, he probably would have included LGM 1 and 2 and whatever else existed in that gospel. It is possible, of course, that Matthew had read or heard the longer text but did not have access to a copy of it when he composed his own gospel. However, the evidence suggests that longer Mark never circulated outside Alexandria except in its Carpocratian form, which postdated Matthew. That Clement might have inadvertently assimilated the original wording of LGM 1:9b to Luke's phrase "for he was rich" is entirely plausible. Clement's quotation of Mark 10:17–31 in *Quis dives salvetur?* has twelve contaminations from the versions in Matthew and Luke and is missing fifteen words found in the standard text of Nestle-Kilpatrick.[55] Clement's quotation also has additional words that are not derived from the synoptic parallels. Indeed, Clement incorrectly reproduced the sentence in question, "for he was having many possessions." In *Qds* 4.7 that sentence reads, "for he was having much *wealth, and fields*" (ἦν γὰρ ἔχων **χρήματα** πολλὰ **καὶ** ἀγρούς). So it is reasonable to wonder whether Clement's quotations in the

*Letter to Theodore* might contain some inadvertent reminiscences of phrases from the other canonical gospels, and LGM 1:9b would be an obvious candidate for corruption.

Be that as it may, there are two important problems with the position that 1:9b originally read "for he was having many possessions." The first is that it is methodologically dubious to change the evidence in order to bring it in line with one's assumptions. The second is that if we revise LGM 1:9 to conform with the standard text of Mark 10:22, the verse becomes even more nonsensical: "And going out from the tomb they went into the house of the young man; for he was having many possessions." Clearly the Markan and Lukan phrases are not interchangeable in this context, since being rich and having many possessions are not exactly synonymous concepts: a person who is rich does not necessarily have *more* possessions than a person who is not rich. If the standard text is correct at Mark 10:22, then Mark did not actually state that the man who enquired about eternal life was *rich*; Mark said this man had many possessions (not *great* possessions, as the RSV translates πολλά), and emphasized the condition of owning things by using the periphrastic imperfect. We naturally infer that this man was rich because Jesus responded to this encounter with the teaching "How hard it will be for those who have riches to enter the kingdom of God!" (10:23). But the dilemma underscored by the phrase "for he was having many possessions" is whether this man could part with so many things that were valuable to him. At LGM 1:9, however, a comment that the young man possessed many things would be less apropos than the observation that he was rich, although neither remark makes much sense as an explanation for why Jesus and the young man went into his house (rich people were not the only ones who owned houses).

I doubt, therefore, that 1:9b ever read "for he was having many possessions." Of course, it is still possible that Clement assimilated a differently worded explanatory clause to the wording in Luke 18:23; it is even possible that *Qds* 4.7 represents an assimilation of Mark 10:22 to LGM 1:9b and that the latter read something like "for he was having much wealth." Since this sentence occurs in the D text at Mark 10:22, we should take that possibility seriously: LGM 1 has a close affinity to this text, and in this instance D may preserve the original reading of 1:9b.[56] But it is equally conceivable that the author of longer Mark borrowed "for he was having many possessions" from Mark 10:22, in order to suggest that the young man faces a similar dilemma, but shifted the emphasis to the issue Jesus commented upon in 10:23–31 so that the phrase would fit the new context. The word *rich* may come from Mark 10:25 (πλούσιον).

It would appear, then, that if the author of the longer text read "for he was having many possessions" at Mark 10:22 and wanted to allude to this sentence, he had an obvious reason to shift the emphasis of the phrase from the number of possessions to the amount of wealth, and may therefore have made the same revision that Luke made, apart from the adjective *very*. The fact that LGM 1 and 2 describe the brother as a "young man" would not of itself suggest an allusion to Matthew's rich young man, since the longer text's descriptions of the man raised in Bethany clearly allude to the two figures described as young men in Mark 14:51 and 16:5. Indeed, the three young men in longer Mark appear to be one and the same person: The young man who wished "to be with Jesus," meaning be a disciple (LGM 1:8; cf. Mark 3:14; 5:18), reappears in Gethsemane in order to "follow with" Jesus (14:51), which is what disciples of Jesus do (8:34); the young man who was raised by Jesus in his own tomb announces the raising of Jesus of Nazareth in Jesus' tomb (16:5–7). But the fact remains that LGM 1 as Clement quoted it contains parallels to unique elements in all three synoptic versions of Jesus' encounter with the man with many possessions. Though far from decisive, this coincidence is the most plausible evidence that the author of longer Mark was familiar with the other *synoptic* gospels. Since these contacts might be coincidental, it is best to reserve judgment on this matter until the concluding chapter of this study.

## Longer Mark's Relation to Non-Canonical Gospels

Proponents of the pastiche theory have also adduced similarities between LGM 1 and 2 and second-century gospels as part of their argument that longer Mark is late and dependent. They offer Papyrus Egerton 2, the multiple endings of Mark, and Tatian's Diatessaron (a harmony of the gospels) as the closest analogies to longer Mark's supposed recombining of canonical gospel materials. These scholars do not usually speculate about why an author might create a new gospel by rearranging pieces of existing gospels, although a few have ventured the opinion that the author of longer Mark was exploring thematic and verbal connections within those writings as a means of divining new information. Some scholars suppose, for instance, that LGM 1 and 2 emerged as someone's attempt to learn who the beloved disciple was by relating him to Lazarus and the man with many possessions, two other characters Jesus is said to have loved.[57] Others suggest that longer Mark is an attempt to harmonize the synoptic gospels with John.

None of these analogies makes good sense of the evidence. An author interested in divining hidden information is not likely to produce a new story that contradicts the information found in his sources. As soon as we imagine, for example, that the minor characters in LGM 1 and 2 are supposed to be Mary, Martha, and Lazarus, new dilemmas arise: Why did the author set the raising miracle in the Bethany where the siblings did not live? Why did he include only one sister? Why did he suppress the names Lazarus, Mary, and Martha? Why did he imply that the siblings were initially strangers to Jesus when John depicted them as Jesus' intimate friends? And why did he have Jesus snub the sister after leaving Bethany when John depicted Jesus reuniting with these siblings for a meal? Certainly it is problematic to suppose that the author associated the young man and his sister with Lazarus and Mary. Accordingly, it is also problematic to suppose that he identified Lazarus as the beloved disciple.

A new set of problems materializes if we suppose that this author equated the young man with the man who had many possessions in Mark 10:17–22. The initial reference to the young man as the brother of "a certain woman" discourages this identification, for it implies that neither he nor the sister had appeared before. Moreover, such an identification would require a reader to make the unlikely assumption that a person Jesus met while travelling through Peraea to Jerusalem (10:17, 32) managed to return to his home in the southern Jordan basin, die unexpectedly, and be buried before Jesus and his disciples arrived in his village. Also unlikely is the idea that the author identified the sister as Mary Magdalene (via a confusion of Mary Magdalene with Mary the sister of Lazarus). In longer Mark, Mary Magdalene is one of the women who followed and served Jesus while he was in Galilee and who came up with him to Jerusalem (Mark 15:40–41). The anonymous sister, on the other hand, appears as a mourner whom Jesus meets by chance in Peraea; she is not someone Jesus previously knew. Moreover, Mary Magdalene does not appear to recognize the young man in the tomb, which would be odd if he were her brother.

Inconsistencies like these might not faze those scholars who dismiss the apocryphal gospels as terminally confused. But the text itself does little to encourage the associations between gospel personages that scholars have made while working with the premise that this author wrote in dialogue with the canonical gospels. The only assimilation of characters encouraged by LGM 1 and 2 is that of the young man in Gethsemane and the young man at Jesus' tomb; these figures are not necessarily the same person in canonical Mark, but in longer Mark, the three young men are the same individual. That observation, however, tells us nothing about when the text was written.

Longer Mark makes even less sense when it is imagined to be to a harmony of the gospels. A gospel harmony is a new composition that attempts to *harmonize* or reconcile different accounts of the same incidents so that they do not appear to be in conflict. It is not an expansion of an existing gospel that supposedly brings together diverse phrases from *unrelated* gospel passages in order to create *new* pericopae (like LGM 2, which has no canonical parallel) or different and largely *contradictory* accounts of otherwise unique incidents (like the raising of Lazarus) that were not in need of harmonizing in the first place. Longer Mark is so inharmonious with John that a harmonist would have a difficult time combining John 11 and LGM 1 into a single account. Were the author of longer Mark attempting to harmonize the canonical gospels, he would have treated John's details with more reverence and thus avoided unnecessary and pointless contradictions. The same would be true if he were attempting to equate gospel personages. An author who flagrantly contradicts the canonical gospels could not have held the pious reverence for those texts that is supposed to explain his complete reliance upon them.

Comparison with Papyrus Egerton 2 is also problematic. That text contains synoptic and Johannine features, but unlike longer Mark, it does not accord with the style of just one of these gospels. The contacts between Egerton 2 and John include distinctively Johannine themes and language. By contrast, longer Mark is thoroughly Markan: it shares the basic subject matter of a story that is otherwise exclusive to John, but only the phrase "whom Jesus loved him" has a Johannine ring (the phrase "for he was rich" has an exact parallel in Luke, but the words "for he was" are typically Markan in form and function). The two versions of the raising of a dead man in Bethany are more profitably compared to the Markan and Johannine versions of the feeding of the five thousand and walking on the sea (Mark 6:30–52; John 6), for we are dealing with two markedly different versions of the same tradition, one Johannine in style and emphases, the other Markan.

The three second-century additions that appear in some manuscripts of Mark after 16:8, which scholars call the Long Ending, the Short Ending, and the Freer Ending, have infrequently been offered as analogies to the longer gospel. This comparison is fairly appropriate, since here we have actual expansions of Mark. But the analogy is not particularly close. Only the Long Ending sounds a fair bit like Mark; the other two make no attempt to use Markan style. And these endings are not so much attempts to supplement Mark's story as to bring its seemingly deficient conclusion into conformity with the resurrection appearances related in the other canonical gospels. The existence of the Long Ending at least shows that expansions of Mark in more or less Markan-sounding style occurred in the second century.

As Smith recognized, the nearest analogies to the longer text are found in canonical gospel redaction. Longer Mark is an expansion of Mark with additional synoptic-sounding materials, much like Matthew and Luke are expansions of Mark using Q and other synoptic materials. The obvious difference between longer Mark and these two canonical gospels is that Matthew and Luke had no interest in preserving Mark's style, theology, and literary techniques. They did not attempt to preserve the integrity of Mark as a literary composition but used it as a source for their own compositions. They may actually have been trying to replace Mark. Consequently, a closer analogy to longer Mark is the expansion of the Gospel of John through the incorporation of additional incidents and chapters. We know that the incident of the woman caught in adultery was not originally part of this gospel, since it does not appear in the best manuscripts of John and is stylistically more Lukan than Johannine.[58] However, that story was simply inserted into John because it was worth keeping. Better analogies for longer Mark are the addition of chapters 15–17 to the Gospel of John after the original conclusion of the last supper scene (14:31) and the addition of chapter 21 after the original conclusion of John's gospel (20:31). These are hypothetical expansions; we do not possess any manuscripts of John that do not include these chapters. But if we accept the common conclusion that these passages were added to John's gospel after it was essentially finished, then they provide a good analogy to LGM 1 and 2, for here we have passages with the same style and a similar theological outlook being added in order to supplement the original work rather than transform it into a new work.

The closest gospel analogies to LGM 1 and 2 take us back into the first century, which is not where proponents of the pastiche theory intended to lead us. Most are very reluctant to date longer Mark within fifty years of the first century. Their compulsion to place apocryphal gospels as far away as possible from the golden age of the church has led some to dismiss Clement's information that a version of the longer gospel was used by Carpocrates, who flourished during the reign of Hadrian, 117–138. Werner Georg Kümmel, for instance, declared this gospel "a falsification dating from the end of the 2nd century at the earliest," which is a few decades after Clement's arrival in Alexandria, if not a few years after he wrote this letter.[59] The apologetic utility of the pastiche theory is transparent, for the view that this text was derived haphazardly from all four canonical gospels automatically makes it late, weird, and irrelevant. But this theory makes nonsense of the fact that longer Mark was reserved for Christians undergoing the highest level of theological instruction in a celebrated catechetical school.

## Longer Mark's Relation to Canonical Mark

Although the scholars who sought the origins of longer Mark in all four canonical gospels succumbed to parallelomania, they were not imagining the fact that LGM 1 contains numerous phrases that occur in canonical Mark. This fact should not entirely surprise us: the repetition of exact phrases is a characteristic of Mark, one that has been meticulously documented by David Peabody in his book *Mark as Composer*.[60] Nevertheless, as Smith himself observed, the proportion of this recurrent phraseology is higher in LGM 1 (but not LGM 2) than that which typically occurs within passages of comparable length in the canonical gospel. Smith also noted that the repeated phrases are in some instances fairly lengthy and include "main narrative elements" in addition to the formulaic elements typical of Mark's storytelling. Related to this difference is the fact that LGM 1 and 2 contain fewer unparalleled details that individualize the episodes in Mark's gospel.[61] In the canonical text, the stock phrases and motifs that occur in Markan pericopae are balanced by distinctive elements that give each episode its individuality. LGM 1 and 2 are less distinctive in this respect.

### Too Markan to Be Mark?

Since Mark liked to repeat phrases and sometimes did so as a means of suggesting that two stories are thematically related (see chapter 8), the question that needs to be answered is whether LGM 1 and 2 contain too many of Mark's phrases to have been written by Mark himself. In 1979, Ernest Best answered this question affirmatively through a statistical comparison.[62] He assigned values to the verbal parallels in LGM 1 and repeated the process for three passages from the canonical gospel that resembled LGM 1. Repetitions of two or more significant words (i.e., words that are not articles, common particles, etc.) were given a value of 3 if all the words were identical, 2 if there was a single variation, and 1 if there was more than one variation, or if the parallel was either very common in Mark or "vague." Phrases longer than three words were sometimes split up into shorter sense units so that values higher than 3 could be assigned. The values were then totalled and divided by the number of words in the passages, to generate a number that did not represent the percentage of repeated words, per se, but could be used as a point of comparison. A figure representing the percentage of repeated words was produced by totalling the number of words for which a value of 2 or 3 had been assigned, and dividing that number by the total number of words. The figure for LGM 1 was 58.0 percent, whereas that for Mark 1:40–45 was 23.7 percent, that for 7:24–30 was 13.1 percent, and that for 10:17–22 was 27.7 percent.

Best had the right idea when he developed this means of making a general comparison, but in three respects his methodology needs refining. First, Best's method of quantifying repetition involves an uncomfortable degree of subjectivity in the determination of vague parallels and significant words, and in the dividing up of large phrases. The problem with including vague parallels under the rubric of recurrent language is that scholars make different decisions about whether two phrases are similar; this is evident from the fact that Best and Smith frequently disagreed in their decisions about inexact parallels, for instance when the parallelism involved different words that were conceptually similar (e.g., man and woman) or when the parallelism was broken up in one passage by intervening words. Since the issue is recurrent phrasing, the inclusion of vague parallels merely makes the assessment complicated and subjective. Explicit criteria are also needed for determining which verbal repetitions are significant and which morphological variants of a word should count as parallels. Finally, a more objective means of assigning values to lengthy parallels is essential. It is not clear, for instance, how Best assigned a value to the phrase "the mystery of the kingdom of God." Using his criteria, one could argue either for a value of 0, since "the mystery" contains only one significant word and "the kingdom of God" is a common expression, or for a value of 6, since the expression "the mystery of the kingdom of God" *as a whole* is uncommon yet it occurs in Mark 4:11, albeit with the verb *has been given* appearing in the middle. Best's value of 3 seems like a compromise.

The second problem with Best's methodology is that he did not take all of the extant longer-text passages into consideration. For whatever reason, Best excluded the two sentences of LGM 2, which happen to contain very little repeated phrasing. The third problem is probably the most obvious: Best's selection of three Markan pericopae for comparison is too small to be meaningful. A comparison of the thirteen verses of LGM 1 with seventeen verses, or 2.6 percent, of the canonical gospel cannot be statistically significant. From the percentages Best produced, one could argue not only that LGM 1 has too much repetition but also that Mark 7:24–30 has too little. What his small sample does suggest is the possibility that the percentage of repetition varies significantly among pericopae. In order for comparison with canonical Mark to be meaningful, one must tally the values for all of Mark's pericopae, or at least include the pericopae that involve the most recurrent phrasing. If there is even one extended passage in canonical Mark where the same proportion of repetition occurs, then one cannot claim that the high amount of verbal repetition in longer Mark points to a different author.

I attempted to remedy these deficiencies by devising a more objective method of quantifying parallels. I count all repeated conjoinments of two or more words as parallels and assign a value of 1 to each word in the verbal parallel, with the exception of words that vary in form (e.g., gender, tense, number, case, prefix), prepositions, pronouns, definite articles, particles, and conjunctions, which I valued as ½ (or only ¼ for parallel pronouns that differ in form, e.g., αὐτῷ and αὐτῆς), and parallels which consist *only* of a definite article and a noun (e.g., the Pharisees, the Jesus, the house) or of some two-word combination of a preposition, pronoun, definite article, particle, and conjunction; I do not count the latter as parallels because they occur so frequently by chance. This seems to me to be a better way of distinguishing between significant parallels and insignificant ones. In contrast to the way Best and Smith delineated parallels, I do not consider similar words to be verbal parallels. So, for example, I consider the verbal parallelism between the phrases "and there was there a certain woman" (LGM 1:1) and "and there was there a man" (Mark 3:1) to be limited to "and there was there," since "a certain woman" and "a man" are conceptual rather than verbal parallels (both are humans), and the adjective *certain* breaks up the parallelism. I do, however, count verbs that differ in the prefix as partial parallels comparable to verbs that differ in tense, number, or person, and assign a value of ½ to these parallels. If a full stop intervenes two consecutive words in one passage but not in another passage where the same two words appear together, I do not count the first word after the full stop as part of the parallel. Finally, I do not count phrasing that recurs only within the same pericope, since the point of comparison is the longer text's use of phrases that occur in other Markan pericopae.

In order to calculate the percentage of verbal parallelism within a passage, I assign the same values to the words that are not involved in verbal parallels. So rather than divide the combined values of the paralleled words by the total number of words, I assign a value of 1 to nouns, verbs, adjectives, and adverbs and a value of ½ to particles, prepositions, pronouns, and conjunctions, then divide the combined values of the paralleled words by the combined values of all the words.

Index 2 of David Peabody's book *Mark as Composer* lists each verse in the Gospel of Mark together with the numbers and letters of the tables Peabody constructed in order to display particular instances of recurrent language. Because this index provides a rough, visual representation of the places in Mark where the most recurrent phraseology occurs, it was possible for me to select passages in Mark that have a relatively high percentage of repetition. A scan of this index suggests that the passages Best chose for comparison (Mark 1:40–45, 7:24–30, 10:17–22) were not among those with an especially high percentage of verbal repetition. The passages I chose for comparison are not

individual paragraphs but consecutive sections of canonical Mark that are
the same length as the combined word count of LGM 1 and 2 (181 words).

Interestingly, the figure I arrived at for LGM 1 was 60.9 percent, which
is quite close to Best's figure of 58 percent. Despite the redactional appearance of LGM 1b, the amount of verbal repetition is lower there (56.4%)
than in LGM 1a (62.7%). LGM 2, on the other hand, has a much lower percentage (30.3%). The percentage of verbal repetition over the whole of LGM
1 and 2 is 57 percent.

By comparison, the percentage of verbal repetition in Mark 1:16–28a
(181 words) is 49 percent, which is 8 percent lower than the percentage of
repetition in LGM 1 and 2. I doubt that a higher percentage could be found
for another section of the same length in Mark, but I leave that noble quest
for someone more adept at bean counting.

There are shorter sections with higher percentages of verbal repetition in
canonical Mark. The most obvious is 4:1–2 (40 words), which contains 76.5
percent verbal repetition. The translation below is intended to show the verbal repetitions as they occur in Greek.

### Mark 4:1–2

And again     he began to teach                    beside the sea.
_____ freq._____ 6:2; 6:34; 8:31 _____ 1:16; 2:13; 5:21

And [there] gathered together to him     a very large crowd
_____............_____ 7:1__..............._____ 5:21; 5:24; 9:14

so that he got into a boat and sat [in it] on the sea.
                              _____ 1:16; 5:13

And the whole crowd     was beside the sea     upon the earth.
_____ 2:13     _____ 3:7 _____ freq.

And he was teaching them in parables     many things,
_____ 2:13
                    _____ 3:23
                    .........._____ 12:1
                    _____ 4:11

and he said to them     in his teaching,
_____ freq.     _____ 12:38

The solid underlining represents exact verbal parallels; dotted underlining represents partial verbal parallels, which is to say, the same word but with a minor
change, such as a different number, case, tense, or gender. This passage clearly
illustrates that Mark at times composed almost entirely in formulaic phrases.

Best also attempted to show that LGM 1 has too many Markan *stylistic* features to come from Mark's hand. Essentially, Best noted that ten stylistic traits that E.J. Pryke attributed to the author of Mark (as opposed to tradition) appear in LGM 1, then claimed that these Markan traits are too numerous and too evenly distributed, since in canonical Mark these characteristics "tend to cluster in the seams" (the editorial connections Mark composed in order to link originally independent traditions).[63]

Again, this part of Best's paper suffers from methodological problems. To begin with, he did not show that canonical Markan passages do not contain comparable quantities of stylistic traits or that these traits really do cluster in the seams. Those notions may be truisms of 1970s Markan redaction criticism, but they are not entirely true. Earlier in this study, Best himself mentioned his reservations about the notion that Markan stylistic traits would be limited to discrete redactional additions and changes, pointing out that Mark would have retold the traditions he heard about Jesus in his own distinctive manner, especially if he translated them from Aramaic. Certainly that is what Kelber's study of orality indicates. The idea that Mark's own vocabulary and style is found principally in the seams and in discrete insertions is a vestige of a time when biblical scholars believed that oral traditions were verbally fixed "texts" generated and controlled by a community (*folk* literature).[64] We now realize that there is no sense imagining a fixed oral text, since stories always bear the imprint of the storyteller. Traditions about Jesus were not likely transmitted by rote memorization, so the wording and the auxiliary elements generally varied. Unfortunately, Pryke's methodology presupposed the old notion that Mark revised verbally fixed texts. By correlating earlier studies by Markan scholars who made the same erroneous assumption, Pryke distinguished between redactional and traditional sentences, then examined the redactional sentences for their stylistic traits. He therefore ended up with results that confirmed his premise that Mark's stylistic traits appear more often in the seams. The circularity of Pryke's methodology was demonstrated by Peabody in the course of explaining his own method for determining Markan redactional characteristics without making any presuppositions about the nature of Mark's sources and the way he shaped them.[65] What is interesting about Peabody's results is that the Markan stylistic traits he identified occur to a lesser or greater extent in most verses of the gospel. Higher quantities frequently occur in the seams (since Mark had favourite ways of introducing pericopae), but also throughout particular pericopae and even for extended sections of narrative. Peabody's conclusions accord with the impression held by many scholars of Mark that this gospel as a whole has a distinctive style.

Scholars, like Best, who claim that LGM 1 has an overly high proportion of Markan stylistic traits have not attempted to confirm this impression by quantifying the occurrences of these Markan stylistic traits in the canonical gospel. Index 2 in Peabody's book *Mark as Composer* reveals that Mark's verses frequently contain upwards of 5 distinct verbal constructions that are repeated somewhere in the gospel. Mark 4:1–2 contains 24 of these repeated verbal constructions. Of course, not all of the 252 types of recurrent language identified by Peabody necessarily reflect Mark's redaction; some of these forms of verbal repetition could reflect the writing styles of other authors whose sources Mark used (Peabody left open the possibility that Mark used Matthew and Luke and therefore derived most of his materials from written sources). In Peabody's judgment, only 39 of these stylistic traits can be ascribed to Mark with a high degree of certainty. Of these 39 traits, 17 occur in Mark 4:1–2, and only 4 occur in LGM 1 and 2 (5, if one is adjusted slightly). It is important to note that Peabody's list of 39 traits is not intended to be exhaustive—only certain. But however one determines what is distinctively Markan, the familiar judgment that "in Mark itself the Markan peculiarities of style are nowhere so piled up as in the 'secret Gospel'!" is quite mistaken.[66] The award for the highest pile goes to the much shorter segment Mark 4:1–2, which contains more Markan stylistic traits than does the whole of LGM 1 and 2.

Ironically, the fact that these two verses from the opening of chapter 4 "are full of Markanisms" is the reason for the "almost unanimous" agreement among redaction critics that these verses were composed by Mark. The unusually high proportion suggests to redaction critics "that any vestige of an introduction in a possible pre-Markan source has been completely overlaid by Mark's rewriting."[67] So the criterion scholars use to isolate Mark's handiwork in the canonical gospel—high concentration of Markan traits—is the same criterion used to isolate an imitator's handiwork in the non-canonical gospel. Even more ironic, the scholars who believe that LGM 1 and 2 are too Markan tend also to believe that the words and phrases come from all four canonical gospels. Did the author of longer Mark find too many distinctly Markan phrases in Matthew, Luke, and John?

Even though the Markan stylistic characteristics of LGM 1 are not piled up as high as some scholars believe, the fact remains that an unusually high amount of Markan phases appear in LGM 1 *for its length*. Should we interpret this fact as evidence that Mark himself reworked this pericope to nearly the same extent that he reworked the tradition underlying 4:1–2 and similar passages? Or should we interpret this fact as evidence that someone other than Mark imitated Mark's style too carefully? At this point it is too early to draw a conclusion, because we have yet to examine the compositional techniques and theology displayed by LGM 1 and 2. When we do, we will see that the evidence pertaining to those matters points to Mark as the author. It also suggests a possible reason for the preponderance of lengthy repetitions within LGM 1: Mark used these verbal echoes to relate LGM 1 to a number of thematically related passages in the canonical text, such as the transfiguration, the flight of the young man in Gethsemane, the discovery of the open tomb, and the miracles involving resurrection and exorcism motifs. In other words, in his attempt to create a "more spiritual gospel," Mark added some pericopae that function as hermeneutical keys to other passages, unlocking the "spiritual" dimension of meaning within the canonical text. That, at least, is how I interpret the matter.

## The Theory of Longer Markan Priority

Smith was aware that the relationship between the longer and shorter Gospels of Mark could be explained in terms of expansion or abbreviation. He noted that most of the evidence indicates that longer Mark was an expansion of the canonical gospel, but some of the evidence points to abbreviation, particularly the fact that LGM 2 appears (partially) to fill a lacuna in Mark 10:46.[68] Smith resolved this contradiction by postulating that the authors of canonical Mark and John shared a proto-gospel from which the author of canonical Mark drew stories that were also available to the author of the longer text. Mark initially abbreviated this proto-gospel by omitting some of its stories, such as LGM 1 and 2. The author of the longer text, on the other hand, inserted LGM 1 and LGM 2 where they belonged in the Markan sequence, which he was able to determine from the outline of the proto-gospel. At this point, however, LGM 2 was a more substantial tradition that involved a dialogue between Jesus and Salome. A later Alexandrian author subsequently eliminated that dialogue, retaining only the reference to the three women being in Jericho. He covered his tracks by adding the gloss "and Jesus did not receive them," hence rendering the report devoid of significance. So in Smith's view, longer Mark was a later expansion of the canonical gospel, although at least one of its special traditions had subsequently been abbreviated.

### Helmut Koester's Theory

The position that canonical Mark was a direct descendent of the longer gospel was first argued by Helmut Koester in 1980. Koester's theory about "secret" Mark was one facet of his wider interest in demonstrating that "the text of the Synoptic Gospels was very unstable during the first and second cen-

turies."[69] This argument, as it applies to Mark, is predicated on the opinion
that "the oldest accessible text of the Gospel of Mark is preserved in most
instances in which Matthew and Luke agree in their reproduction of their
source—even if the extant Markan manuscript tradition presents a different
text."[70] Koester offered a subset of the minor agreements of Matthew and Luke
against Mark as proof that the earliest copies of Mark differed from the textual archetypes of this gospel that developed in the latter half of the second
century.[71] Koester did not attempt to deal with every minor agreement, nor
did he try to explain them all the same way. The presumed interpolations
now found at Mark 2:27, 4:26–29, and 12:32–34, for example, are not
assigned to any particular redactor. Other textual anomalies, such as the multiple endings of Mark and the absence of Mark 6:45–8:26 from Luke, are
treated as more purposeful and significant redactions. The Markan peculiarities that are relevant to our discussion are those Koester attributed to a stage
in the composition of Mark that produced the "secret" gospel.

Like Smith's theory, Koester's involves both expansion and abbreviation
and the postulate of a lost proto-gospel. But the resemblance ends there. The
first stage in Koester's theory is the production of a lost version of Mark that
was used by Matthew and Luke in different recensions. This "proto-Mark" was
expanded into the "secret" Gospel of Mark early in the second century by an
author who imitated Mark's style but had a different theological agenda. The
canonical text is a mid-second-century abridged version of the "secret" gospel
that was intended to make Mark "suitable for public reading."[72] This canonical redaction involved the removal of the two passages Clement cited in his
*Letter to Theodore*.[73] Koester's reasons for viewing longer Mark as an intermediary stage are as follows:

> The story of the raising of a youth from the dead and his subsequent initia-
> tion…is closely related to a number of other Markan features which were
> not present in the copies of Proto-Mark used by Matthew and Luke: a spe-
> cial understanding of Jesus' teaching in terms of resurrection and initiation,
> the concept of "mystery" as the sum total of Jesus' message to the disciples
> and probably a similar interpretation of the term εὐαγγέλιον [gospel], and
> the elevation of Jesus to a supernatural being endowed with magical powers
> and with a "new teaching."
>
> …A large number of features which distinguish *Canonical Mark* from Proto-
> Mark are so closely related to the special material of *Secret Mark* quoted by
> Clement of Alexandria that the conclusion is unavoidable: Canonical Mark
> is derived from Secret Mark.[74]

The Markan words and themes which characterize "secret" Mark yet are often
unparalleled by Matthew and Luke are grouped under four main headings:

gospel, teaching, mystery, and baptism. To these Koester added a variety of
other elements, such as the verbs "to be amazed" and "to arise" (as in resurrection), the phrase "looking upon him loved him" in Mark 10:21, and the
flight of the linen-clad young man in 14:51–52.

Koester did not systematically explain the connections between these
themes and the longer gospel, but if I correctly understand him, his reasoning is as follows. Most instances of the word *gospel* in Mark are unparalleled
in Matthew (Luke omits the noun altogether), so this word did not appear
in proto-Mark. This term's affinity with longer Mark is suggested by the
phrase "the mystery of the kingdom of God" in LGM 1:12, which refers not
only to baptism (as a mystery initiation) but also to the general content of
Jesus' preaching, that is, the gospel.[75] The identical phrase in Mark 4:11
must derive from the same redaction that produced the longer text because
Matthew and Luke have a significantly different phrase: "To you it has been
given to know the mysteries of the kingdom of God/heaven" (Matt 13:11;
Luke 8:10). Together with the verb "to know," those evangelists preserve
the more primitive plural form of the noun *mysteries*, a word denoting sayings requiring explanations, as in the Gospel of Thomas 63. The singular in
LGM 1:12 and Mark 4:11 reflects a later usage represented in Ephesians,
where the word *mystery* is also associated with baptism and the gospel. The
baptism motif in Mark 10:38–39 is likely tied in with the "secret" gospel, too,
since it is absent in Matthew's parallel (Luke omits the whole pericope) but
coincides with the baptismal imagery of the young man's linen sheet. The
redactor who added the words "baptized with the baptism with which I am
baptized" in Mark 10:38b, 39b transformed a martyrological statement about
readiness to share Jesus' cup (of suffering or death) into a sacramental statement about accepting baptism and Eucharist, contrary to Mark's focus on following Jesus in his suffering. This new emphasis upon the sacraments is in
keeping with the "secret" gospel's interest in presenting "Jesus as a magician
and an initiator into mysteries [*sic*, pl.]," a man of power who raises persons
from the dead.[76] That redaction is therefore also responsible for the unparalleled raising motif in Mark 9:25–27, which, like LGM 1, is closely associated with a passion prediction, and for the unparalleled appearance of the verb
*to arise* (ἀνίστημι) in Mark's first and second passion predictions (cf. 9:27:
"and he arose"). The language of awe (ἐκθαμβεῖσθαι) in, for example, 9:15;
10:24; and 10:32 likewise derives from this redaction, for wondrous amazement is the typical response to magical power. The same applies to the unparalleled references to *teaching* in canonical Mark, for many of these teachings
have to do with the resurrection and with cultic instruction, which is the
sort of instruction that occurs in LGM 1:12.[77] Finally, "secret" Mark contains

parallels to some sentences in Mark that are absent in Matthew and Luke, namely, the description of the young man who fled naked (14:51–52) and the phrase "looking upon him loved him" (10:21).[78]

Koester's claim that these verses or themes were not present in the copies of Mark known to Matthew and Luke has been disputed by David Peabody, Frans Neirynck, and Robert Gundry, and to a lesser extent by Robert Lee Williams, Philip Sellew, and Joel Marcus.[79] Although these authors countered nearly all of Koester's arguments, their critiques did little to diminish the popularity of his theory among North American liberals, perhaps because the discussion has centred around nebulous probabilities. Koester argued that Matthew and Luke *did not read* certain things in their copies of Mark because they did not reproduce them, and his critics have normally responded that these minor agreements of omission are not unexpected in light of our knowledge of Matthean and Lukan editorial tendencies, so those evangelists *probably did read* these things. Both positions are somewhat illogical and by their nature impossible to prove. Different solutions to the synoptic problem have been pitted against each other, with predictably uncompelling results. Peabody faulted Koester for not treating his selection of minor agreements as part of a much larger problem that is not well explained by the Two Source Hypothesis and thus for making a tendentious selection of relevant examples. Neirynck and Gundry faulted Koester for not adequately exploring the possibility that Matthew and Luke would at times agree in how they revised Mark, although Gundry also appealed to the hypothesis that Luke knew and was influenced by Matthew. Because Koester's premise of a proto-gospel was countered with equally hypothetical explanations of why Matthew and Luke revised the standard text of Mark, Koester's theory was not adequately challenged.

Koester's theory is better evaluated by considering whether the various unparalleled Markan elements are actually "so closely related to the special material of *Secret Mark*" that they must derive from the redaction that produced the longer gospel. In most cases, this is clearly not so. The raising of the young man does not produce general amazement, but, rather, love and admiration from the young man, so there is no reason to propose that the unparalleled occurrences of *to be amazed* (ἐκθαμβεῖσθαι) in Mark derive from this redaction (i.e., Mark 9:15; 10:24, 32; 14:33; 16:5) and no basis for Koester's claim that the author of longer Mark envisioned Jesus as a source of supernatural wonderment. LGM 1a is too similar to the healing miracles in Mark for it to serve as evidence of a more magical kind of christology. Similarly, Clement's citations show no affinity for the verb *to rise up* (ἀνίστημι), which is used only of Jesus' getting up to return to the other side of the Jordan (1:13). The expected form of the verb *to raise up* (ἐγείρειν) occurs in the description of Jesus raising the young man. Accordingly, it makes no sense to connect longer Mark with the unexpected form of the verb that appears in the passion predictions of 8:31 and 9:31 and in the exorcism story in 9:27.

The main elements of Koester's argument require more attention, because his arguments connecting them with LGM 1 are more complex. His claim that between four and six of the seven occurrences of the word *gospel* (εὐαγ–γέλιον) were added by the redactor of the longer text is one of the more surprising elements of his theory, for the word *gospel* does not appear in LGM 1 and 2. Koester himself was ambivalent about whether to ascribe this term to this redactor, so it is significant that his discussion of *gospel* disappears from his argument for longer Markan priority in his follow-up essay, "The Text of the Synoptic Gospels in the Second Century," and is placed elsewhere, in his discussion of the genre of the gospels, in his book *Ancient Christian Gospels*.[80] Moreover, Koester now seems less sure that the word *gospel* did not appear in a pre-Matthean form of the Gospel of Mark at 13:10 and 14:9. In a 1988 article "From the Kerygma-Gospel to Written Gospels," he flatly stated that "The occurrences of the term in Mark 13. 10 and 14. 9 are confirmed as part of the original text of Mark by Matt 24. 14 and 26. 13," and his earlier suggestion that Mark 13:10 may be a scribal corruption of Mark under the influence of Matt 24:14 is relegated to a footnote.[81] Since Koester recognized that the word *gospel* in Mark 1:14–15 could be the basis for its appearance in Matt 9:35[82] and readily acknowledged that Matthew would not have taken over Mark's introductory phrase "beginning of the gospel of Jesus Christ, Son of God" because it did not suit Matthew's literary agenda,[83] we should give up on the notion that the word *gospel* was added by the author of the longer text.

Much of the remainder of Koester's argument is predicated on the view that the author of longer Mark added sacramental elements to proto-Mark in keeping with his picture of Jesus as one who initiates into mysteries. Longer Mark's interest in sacraments accounts for the word *baptism* in Mark 10:38–39, which is unparalleled in Matthew (Luke does not include this scene), and for some unparalleled references to teachings of a sacramental nature. My reasons for rejecting a sacramental conception of LGM 1b will be presented in a later chapter. Here I will point out that a sacramental interpretation of the mystery of the kingdom of God in LGM 1:12 is inconsistent with what this phrase means elsewhere in the same narrative. In Mark 4:11, the mystery of the kingdom of God concerns esoteric knowledge about the way God's reign is being established upon the earth. This knowledge is conveyed publicly "in parables," yet these riddles keep "those outside" from comprehending it. When Jesus expounds the parables privately to "those about him with the twelve," he is teaching them about the eschatological mystery concealed within the parables. Since the parable discourse is as much a part of the longer gospel as it is of the shorter gospel, it follows that LGM 1:12 likewise depicts Jesus expounding an eschatological mystery rather than performing a rite. When Koester reviewed CA he rightly rejected Smith's baptismal inter-pretation of *mystērion* in Mark 4:11, LGM 1:12, and the undisputed letters of Paul,[84] so it is unclear why Koester now cites Smith as having proved "that baptism was widely understood as the mystery of the kingdom of God."[85] In any event, what Smith actually argued was that although *mystērion* is nowhere used this way in extant Christian and Jewish literature in the first century, *it might have been*, since it sometimes denotes a process, and baptism can be thought of as a process. So can the establishment of God's reign.

Koester's last reason for associating longer Mark with a cultic element found in the canonical gospel concerns the fact that twelve of Mark's refer-ences to teaching are unparalleled in Matthew and Luke. Since most of these references to teaching are unelaborated or have functional equivalents in Matthew or Luke, scholars who have discussed this aspect of Koester's the-sis have agreed that there is nothing noteworthy about the references to teaching that have no synoptic parallels.[86] Certainly none of them seem sacra-mental when they are read in their *Markan* contexts (Koester finds their meanings in *other* texts that use the same phrases—an approach that violates a fundamental principal of exegesis). Considering that sacramental teaching does not occur in LGM 1, either, there can be no reason to connect any of the unparalleled instances of "to teach" in canonical Mark with LGM 1:12.

This leaves us with the fact that three and a half verses found in canon-ical Mark have a parallel in LGM 1 but do not appear in Matthew and Luke (Mark 9:27; 14:51–52; and 10:21a) and the latter two evangelists agree against Mark 4:11 and LGM 1:12 in their formulations of the expression "the mystery of the kingdom of God." The fact that these features are found only in canonical Mark and LGM 1 is certainly intriguing, but it cannot support the weight of Koester's explanation. What remains to be considered is whether longer Markan priority is feasible despite the inadequacy of Koester's argu-ments. Elsewhere I have outlined the unlikely implications of any theory that the canonical text is an abbreviation of the longer text and addressed specific problems posed by the variants of Koester's theory produced by Hans-Mar-tin Schenke and John Crossan.[87] Here I will outline the problematic impli-cations of Koester's theory in particular (much of which was adopted by Schenke).

## Problematic Implications of the Theory
## of Longer Markan Priority

The most significant problem with the theory that canonical Mark is an abbreviation of the longer gospel is the fact that the latter probably contained considerably more than the fifteen sentences Clement quoted. Clement's descriptions of the longer text as a "mystic" and "more spiritual gospel" imply that its unique contents altered the *nature* of Mark's gospel, making it less like Matthew and Luke and more like the Gospel of John, which Clement called a "spiritual" gospel in contrast to the "bodily" synoptics (he is cited in Eusebius, *Church History* VI.14.7). Moreover, longer Mark's unique contents made it suitable for a very different audience. Alexandrians used the canonical gospel to instruct catechumens and ordinary Christians (I.15–18). The longer gospel was used to instruct persons being perfected in gnosis, specifically Christians receiving the highest level of esoteric theological instruction, called "the great mysteries," through the anagogical study of scripture (see chapter 4). The longer text outstripped the canonical text as a vehicle for expounding the secret, unwritten traditions of the orthodox Alexandrian community because it contained significantly more passages oriented to the symbolic dimension of meaning. Clement did not say that Mark added just the story that bothered Theodore. Clement said that Mark transferred from "his own notes and those of Peter" (*two* sources) "things [pl.] suitable to those studies [pl.] which make for progress toward knowledge" (I.19–21). These additions included *two* distinct types of materials (*logia* and *praxeis*), only one of which is described as particularly amenable to anagogical exegesis (the *logia*; I.25–26). So in addition to containing more "bodily" materials like those which characterized the shorter text (the *praxeis*; cf. LGM 2), longer Mark must have included enough *logia* of a mystic quality to affect the basic nature of the Gospel of Mark and to make it serviceable for advanced, theological instruction. LGM 1 and 2 do not suffice. The letter gives us every indication that longer Mark differed significantly from the canonical gospel, and since there is no indication that any part of the shorter text was absent from the longer text, this means we are dealing with a much longer version of Mark.

The implications of this conclusion for the composition of the canonical gospel are clear. Canonical Mark cannot be thought of as the product of a small redaction that eliminated LGM 1 and 2. We must imagine a large-scale redaction, which is very hard to reconcile with the existing theories of longer Markan priority. Since canonical Mark and Koester's proto-Mark differ very little from each other, the redactor who produced the canonical text would have to have eliminated precisely the most obvious additions made by the redactor of the longer text. In order to maintain Koester's theory, we would need to suppose that someone removed from longer Mark not only LGM 1 and 2 but also the many other mystical and non-mystical traditions that the author of longer Mark had added to the proto-gospel. Yet this redactor somehow overlooked Mark 14:51–52 and the smaller changes that spawned the minor agreements of Matthew and Luke against Mark upon which Koester built his theory. What advocates of Koester's theory need to explain, then, is *why* someone would do that, and *how* this person would know to eliminate just these traditions. Was he trying to bring canonical Mark into conformity with Matthew and Luke by removing almost everything in Mark that cannot be found in one of the other synoptic gospels? Or was he trying to bring Mark back into conformity with the proto-gospel? The former scenario suggests that canonical Mark is a superfluous epitome of Matthew and Luke. The latter scenario is even more improbable, since anyone who knew and preferred the proto-gospel would simply use it. Why go to the trouble of eliminating the complete pericopae added by the author of longer Mark but retain the minor changes that cause Mark to disagree with Matthew and Luke?

Regardless of how we might imagine a redactor eliminating just the pericopae that were added by the author of the amplified text, the reason for such a redaction will remain elusive. Scholars who think longer Mark contained only fifteen additional verses have no problem explaining their removal. But what the theory of longer Markan priority actually requires us to imagine is the "despiritualization" of longer Mark through the removal of the passages that made it *more spiritual*. What could be so problematic about materials that have a more pronounced spiritual dimension? This theory also requires us to imagine the removal of other passages that were more like the "bodily" traditions in canonical Mark. Why remove the ordinary passages that distinguished longer Mark from Matthew and Luke? It is hard to imagine anyone in the mid-second century transforming a more spiritual gospel with affinities to the Gospel of John into a third bodily text containing very little that cannot be found in Matthew and Luke, and this scenario is especially hard to imagine occurring in Alexandria, where exegesis of the spiritual dimension was a favourite undertaking. Yet Alexandria is precisely where this redaction would need to take place. The letter implies that the longer text did not circulate outside Alexandria except in the Carpocratian version; it is natural to suppose, therefore, that if canonical Mark were a recension of this gospel, the "less spiritual" text, too, was produced in Alexandria. The unreality of this scenario becomes palpable when we remember that Clement believed the canonical gospel was produced in Rome. Why would the church that produced and disseminated the canonical gospel only a few decades earlier claim that Mark produced that text *in Rome*? One would expect the officials in a major Christian centre like Alexandria to do whatever they could to emphasize the apostolic foundations of their own church in response to the growing dominance of the church in Rome. But in Clement's day, the Alexandrian community laid claim only to the lesser-known longer gospel.

Given the Alexandrian proclivity to allegorical exegesis, it would be far more natural for one of the "bodily" synoptic gospels to be transformed into a more spiritual gospel so that it could accommodate Christians who expected to find the essential theological truths concealed beneath the literal level of their scriptures (especially if the Gospel of John did not yet exist). That scenario accords not only with the Alexandrian tradition contained in the letter, but also with the extant manuscript evidence for the three Markan gospels. Our only evidence for the "orthodox" and Carpocratian longer gospels is the *Letter to Theodore*. That is not so surprising if the longer text is in fact an isolated recension of the canonical gospel. But if longer Mark and proto-Mark both preceded the canonical gospel, their total disappearance is harder to account for. As the earliest versions of Mark, longer Mark and, especially, proto-Mark would likely be the ancestors of more manuscripts than would a mid-second-century version. How is it that the form of Mark that was available to Matthew and Luke in different parts of the Roman empire (Syria and Asia Minor?) by the 80s of the first century managed to leave no trace in the manuscript tradition, but a single, mid-second-century recension of an earlier recension of this gospel managed to influence all subsequent copies? The improbability of this situation is evident from the fact that an actual revision of the Gospel of Mark from roughly the same period as Koester's proposed canonical redaction—the Long Ending of Mark (16:9–20)—did not succeed in influencing all subsequent manuscripts. Its rise to prominence within the manuscript tradition took a few centuries. When Eusebius was writing around the early fourth century, most of the Greek manuscripts of Mark known to him still ended at 16:8.[88]

The complete triumph of canonical Mark over an older and widely dispersed proto-gospel would require an official policy of replacement. Yet as Frederik Wisse pointed out, there is no support for the kind of institutional control of manuscript production envisioned by this theory:

> Long after the third century the church was in no position to establish and control the biblical text, let alone eliminate rival forms of the text. Though there may have been an attempt at establishing a standard text as early as the fourth century, only beginning with the twelfth century do we have evidence for a large scale effort. This is von Soden's group $K^r$ which shows evidence of careful control. Even at that late date there was no way to prevent the cre-

ation of many divergent copies. Only a small number of manuscripts were consistently corrected to conform to the text of $K^r$ or to that of other groups or text-types. There is no evidence for the Byzantine period or for an earlier date of efforts to eliminate divergent copies of New Testament manuscripts.

Even official efforts to eradicate heretical texts were not always successful, as in the case of Origen's writings and the Nag Hammadi Library.[89] The tenacity of variant readings within the manuscript tradition belies the notion that one mid-second-century revision influenced all existing manuscripts: "every reading ever occurring in the New Testament textual tradition is stubbornly preserved, even if the result is nonsense."[90] So if there were a proto-gospel that was more in line with Matthew and Luke, we would expect to have manuscripts that do not contain the passages and words Koester ascribed to the author of longer Mark (e.g., Mark 9:14b–16, 26b–27; 10:21a, 38b, 39b; 14:51–52), particularly since scribes preferred Markan readings that harmonized with the better-known text of Matthew. The manuscript evidence better accords with the conclusion that canonical Mark was expanded into a text that was not circulated.

These are the most important reasons for questioning Koester's theory of the creation of canonical Mark by the abbreviation of longer Mark. There are no problems with the Alexandrian position that longer Mark was created second, as a separate version of the same gospel, except that liberal scholars find it suspiciously innocuous. The exponents of longer Markan priority deserve credit for conducting original and insightful research on a text that is usually dismissed out of hand. Their position may not be feasible, but it is less incredible than the theory that this text is a second-century pastiche haphazardly derived from the four canonical gospels. The evidence indicates that longer Mark was an Alexandrian expansion of the canonical gospel by an author who had independent access to oral traditions also used in the Gospel of John. We are not yet in a position to decide whether this author was Mark himself and when the longer text was composed. A definite answer must await the literary-critical examination in part 2.

# ⊰4⊱

# The Nature of the Longer Gospel

The *Letter to Theodore* tells us a great deal about how Clement conceived of the origin and proper use of the longer Gospel of Mark. Elaborating upon received tradition, he informed Theodore that Mark had created this "more spiritual" gospel in Alexandria by expanding the gospel that he had created in order to strengthen the faith of catechumens. The additions were selected for their utility in increasing gnosis and included more *praxeis* as well as certain *logia* whose interpretations functioned like a mystagogue, leading the hearers into the innermost sanctuary of the truth. Clement pointed out, however, that the revised gospel included neither "the things not to be uttered" nor the "hierophantic teaching of the Lord" and that it was "very securely kept" within the church in Alexandria, where it was read "only to those who are being initiated into the great mysteries." Clement also called this revision the *mystikon euangelion*.

These statements provide a window onto the use of the longer text in Alexandria in Clement's day. But just as importantly, they permit us to construct a framework within which to comprehend LGM 1 and 2 and the nature of the longer text as a whole. For although Clement's statements about the genre and intended function of this writing are not those of its author, they nevertheless represent the conceptions of someone who knew the complete gospel and expounded it.

## Clement's Conception of the Genre of the Longer Gospel

Clement initially called the longer text "a more spiritual gospel" (I.21–22). In scholarly discussions, this description has all but been eclipsed by the sec-

Notes to chapter 4 start on page 261

ond description he gave using the words *to mystikon euangelion*. That phrase Smith translated as "the secret Gospel," which became the standard title for this text. The question of what might be more spiritual about a secret gospel has for some reason been treated as irrelevant, and investigators continue to use the words "Secret Gospel" (now with a capital *s*) as if *mystikon* were an established synonym for *apocryphon* (which means hidden, concealed, or obscure). *Mystikon can* mean secret, but was also used in a variety of other senses. When it appears in the writings of the early Greek fathers, translators normally use *mystic* or *mystical*—for lack of a better word. There is no obvious English counterpart for the ideas which writers such as Philo and Clement used this word to denote, although "secret" has rarely seemed appropriate. The English derivatives *mystic* and *mystical* are usually adopted as a convention, but are not meant to suggest mysticism or a transformed state of consciousness experienced through meditation, an association which was not prominent in Christian writings until a few centuries later.[1]

It makes a big difference whether we translate *mystikon* as *secret* or *mystic*, for a mystic text is not necessarily a secret writing, hidden from the masses. Accordingly, we need to determine what Clement meant by calling this text a *mystikon euangelion*, and can do so by answering the following questions: Is *mystikon euangelion* really a title? Is the adjective best translated *secret*? How is *mystikon* related to the terms *mystikai*, *logia*, and *praxeis*, which are also used in the letter to describe the longer gospel's contents? And what is the relationship between *mystikon euangelion* and "more spiritual gospel"? Once the Alexandrian conception of this gospel's genre has been determined, we will better be able to comprehend the nature and purpose of the discretion that surrounded its use.

We may start by asking whether "the *mystikon* gospel" is actually a title. There are prima facie reasons for supposing that this phrase was used only as a convenient, perhaps ad hoc, means of distinguishing the longer version of Mark from the shorter one. I know of no other gospels called *mystikon euangelion* that could attest to the use of *mystikon* as part of a proper title. The common titles using *euangelion* usually did not have an adjective modifying the word *gospel*, nor did they use a genitival phrase to introduce the author, as we have here in the phrase "*of* Mark *mystikon* gospel" (II.11–12). Rather, the word *gospel* was normally modified by the preposition "according to" (κατά), as in "the Gospel according to" someone or some group (e.g., Luke, the Egyptians, the Hebrews). The universal convention of having the names of the evangelists follow the phrase "the Gospel according to" may be an indication that the word *gospel* in these descriptions originally referred not to a specific class of writings (which might be called a genre) but to their subject matter, the "good news." That is, these titles denoted the good news about Christ as seen through the eyes of a particular author or community.[2] Thus if "*mystikon* gospel" is understood as a title, the "good news" becomes something of an oxymoron: the Secret Good News or the Mystic Good News. As a title, then, *mystikon euangelion* would not only be unique, as far as I can tell, but would also be unusual for using an adjective and a genitival phrase to modify "the Gospel" and would not have its usual connotation of the good news of salvation. It is more likely, therefore, that *euangelion* here refers to the genre to which this text belongs, and is in keeping with Clement's references to "the gospels" (e.g., *Strom.* I.21.136.2; *Qds* 4.3) and "a certain gospel" (*Strom.* V.10.63.7) or to John as "a spiritual gospel" (cited in Eusebius, *Church History* VI.14.7) and the longer text as "a more spiritual gospel" (I.21–22).

The way Clement used the phrase "*mystikon* gospel" in the letter strongly supports this conclusion. Note, for instance, that when Clement referred to the two versions of Mark's gospel, he did not distinguish one of them as the authoritative or canonical version. His first reference to either gospel occurs in I.11–12. Here the text that Theodore had inquired about is simply referred to as "the divinely inspired Gospel according to Mark." There is no indication that Theodore was familiar with another title for this text or that Clement thought that only the better-known version was Mark's divinely inspired gospel. The same degree of reverence is exhibited the first time the words *mystikon euangelion* are used. Clement believed that Carpocrates' additions had "polluted" the *mystikon euangelion*, by "mixing with the spotless and holy words utterly shameless lies" (II.6–9). Before Clement quoted passages from the amplified version he referred to "the very words of the Gospel" (II.20). Nowhere does Clement convey the impression that only one version of this gospel is *the* Gospel of Mark. To Clement, *both* versions were the Gospel of Mark.

Not only did Clement not treat one version as more authoritative, but he also tended not to distinguish these texts except for the purpose of clarity. The first time Clement differentiated between the longer text and the version of Mark that Theodore knew, Clement used the relative description "a more spiritual gospel" (I.21–22). The two references to this work as the *mystikon* gospel occur later, after Clement related his account of the text's history, and likewise appear at times when a distinction between the two versions is necessary. In II.6 it was necessary to specify that Carpocrates stole a copy of the *mystikon* gospel, and in II.12 Theodore is instructed not to concede to his Carpocratian opponents that their longer version is Mark's *mystikon* gospel.[3] The two other references to this text as "the secret gospel" in

Smith's English translation (II.22; III.14) were added by way of explanation; neither *mystikon* nor *euangelion* occur at those points in the text. His decision to supply *this* description to clarify the referent has nevertheless reinforced the impression that this phrase is the longer text's title.[4] But in these places the subject is left implicit, as if Clement were inclined not to have to make another specification.

It is also important to note that when *mystikon* is applied to this gospel, the word does not appear out of nowhere, as could be expected of a standard designation known to both Clement and Theodore. Rather, it appears after Clement had used a plural form of the same adjective (namely, *mystikai*) as his description of a certain category of Jesus' "doings" which Mark did not include in the first version: "As for Mark, then, during Peter's stay in Rome he wrote an account of the Lord's doings, not, however, declaring all of them, nor yet hinting at the *mystikai* [ones], but selecting what he thought most useful for increasing the faith of those who were being instructed" (I.15–18). The longer gospel, in other words, may be distinguished as the *mystikon* gospel because it was the gospel that included the *mystikai* doings of the Lord—a distinctive set of materials not included in the first version. Conceivably, the adjective *mystikon* was regularly used to specify this gospel in Alexandria, but Clement's own usage suggests that this phrase was more a description of convenience than an established title. Like the phrase "more spiritual gospel," *mystikon euangelion* is an apt summary of the distinctive contents of the special Alexandrian edition, most likely of what made the longer text more spiritual and more apt to lead its hearers to a more profound comprehension of Christian truths (gnosis). However, we must determine the correct denotation of *mystikon* in this letter before we can draw any conclusions about Clement's conception of the nature of this writing.

The first occurrence of *mystikon* in the letter concerns a type of Jesus' "doings" (*praxeis*) that were not included in the shorter gospel (I.16–17). Smith translated this plural form (*mystikai*) as "secret ones," which might suggest activities Jesus performed in secret. However, the notion that Mark omitted Jesus' secret activities from his first gospel makes little sense, for the canonical gospel is cluttered with secret acts: there are private instructions (4:10–20; 7:17–23; 8:14–21, 31–33; 9:9–13, 28–29, 30–32; 10:10–12, 32–34; 13:3–37; 14:17–31), semi-private healings (e.g., 5:37, 40; 7:33; 8:23), private "epiphanies" (4:39–41; 6:48–52; 9:2–8), a private vigil (14:32–42), private preparations (11:2–3; 14:13–15), and attempts by Jesus to suppress knowledge of his messianic identity (1:25, 34; 3:12; 8:30) and even of certain miracles (1:43–44; 5:43; 7:36; 8:26). If "secret" is meant here, it must mean deeds which were not only private but also not recorded in any gospels or spoken of openly (LGM 1b might qualify but not LGM 1a or 2). Yet deeds of that sort would constitute secret oral traditions, the very traditions Mark was careful *not* to include in his *mystikon* gospel (I.22–24). But here we must pause, for Clement did not actually say that the *mystikai* were included in the second version. What he said—and only in passing—is that Mark added to the previously recorded "doings" (*praxeis*) "others also" (I.24), not "doings" of a special sort. Clement's primary interest was in the passages whose interpretations lead their hearers into the innermost sanctuary of the truth (I.25–26), materials he referred to as *logia*. Clement's terse reference to the "other" *praxeis* suggests that they were *not* of a different sort from the ones included in the first version. That conclusion in turn implies that the *mystikai* doings were not the "other" doings that Mark added to the *mystikon euangelion*.

Are we to conclude, then, that the *mystikai* doings were not included in the *mystikon* gospel? Those who would read *mystikon* in this letter as meaning "secret" apparently assume that *mystikai* refers to the secret teachings that were too secret even to be included in a secret gospel (I.22–24). It seems more natural, however, to suppose that the *mystikai* doings were precisely what distinguished the longer text as a *mystikon* gospel. Yet there is a problem. If the "other" doings contained in the longer gospel are not the *mystikai* ones, then, by elimination, the *mystikai* must be included under the description *logia*, which is normally rendered "sayings."

This dilemma is actually part of a larger issue pertaining to the words *praxeis* and *logia*. Was Clement distinguishing between ordinary *acts* and special *sayings*, as most English translations presume? If so, what does that imply about the fifteen verses Clement quoted, which, apart from the words "Son of David, have mercy on me," contain no direct discourse, no *sayings*, at all? If the other *acts* were not what made this text a *mystikon euangelion*, we would have to conclude that the quoted verses were not important either (and certainly not, therefore, distinguished by secrecy), despite the fact that Clement could expound their higher meaning (III.18).

Happily, there is a simple solution to these problems, which has emerged through studies of *logia* in the terminology of Papias and the early fathers. These studies show that the fathers of the second century used *logoi* ("words") rather than *logia* to distinguish sayings from narratives.[5] *Logia* was normally used to refer to the scriptures as a body of writings.[6] This conclusion holds true for Clement's usage. Though in Clement's writings the singular form of *logia* (*logion*) often refers to an individual saying (e.g., *Strom.* I.1.13.3; II.4.17.4) or, more generally, to a discrete segment of scripture (e.g., II.10.47.1, in reference to Lev 18:1–5), the plural, in most of its eleven occurrences, refers to the scriptures as a body of writings.[7] To be sure, a general reference to the scriptures cannot be what Clement meant when he said that Mark added to his gospel "certain *logia*" from his notes. But there is an exception to this sense, which happens to be the most significant point of comparison to the use of *logia* in the letter. In *Qds* 3.1 Clement used *logia* in reference to passages or pericopae:

> It is the duty, therefore, of those whose minds are set on love of truth and love of the brethren…first, by means of the words of scripture, to banish from [the rich] their unfounded despair and to show, with the necessary exposition of the Lord's [*logia*], that the inheritance of the kingdom of heaven is not completely cut off from them, if they obey the commandments.

As Roger Gryson commented, "at first glance, one might have the impression that Clement speaks specifically of the words of Jesus; but when one reads this short tract in its entirety, one sees that the author here comments upon the pericope of the rich young man…in its entirety and that he does not here explicate just the words of Jesus but also those of the other protagonists of the scene, as well as certain narrative traits."[8] The *logia* referred to in *Qds* 3.1 are not a category based on form, such as sayings, but materials relevant to a particular hermeneutical agenda; the most useful of these *logia* for Clement's purpose—Mark 10:17–31—is a passage which we might call an episode. *Logia*, then, was not used by Clement to refer to sayings in contrast to narrative and was not *just* applied to scripture in general; it could be used to refer to particular passages of scripture, regardless of whether narrative or sayings predominate.

In the case of the letter, therefore, *logia* presumably refers to traditions that have a specific utility, namely, the traditions about Jesus that function to lead their hearers toward the deeper Christian truths; these are the materials in Mark's notes which Mark deemed "suitable to whatever makes for progress toward knowledge" (I.20–21). The "other" acts Mark added would be materials that Clement did not think contained a prominent "spiritual" sense (I.24); these he acknowledged, but without further comment. That Clement was not interested in using *praxeis* and *logia* to make a distinction between acts and sayings is confirmed by his use of *praxeis* to characterize the first version of Mark *as a whole* (I.16). His comment that in Rome Mark wrote down "the acts [*praxeis*] of the Lord" obviously does not mean that Mark neglected to include sayings.

If Clement was not in the habit of using *logia* and *praxeis* to distinguish sayings from stories, but did use these terms in reference to gospel pericopae, then the word *logia* in *Letter to Theodore* I.25 is better translated "passages" or "texts," rather than "sayings" (Smith) or "oracles" (F.F. Bruce).[9] This clarification resolves the aforementioned problems, for we now have a more plausible distinction between additional "doings" (*praxeis*) like those in the earlier gospel and "certain passages" (*logia*) especially suited to mystical exegesis. LGM 1 would represent the latter; LGM 2, the former. What is more, we may presume that the *mystikai* doings that Mark did not hint at in his first version were among the *logia*, and that the longer gospel was called a *mystikon euangelion* because it included many such passages.

But what is the special quality implied by the word *mystikon*? The best way to determine this is to study how Clement used this word in his other writings and then compare the results with what we have learned about the occurrences of *mystikon* in the letter. We can begin by noting that *mystikon* is the adjective corresponding to the noun *mystērion*, the basis for the English word "mystery." The meaning of the adjective, therefore, should be sought with regard to how Clement used the noun *mystērion* and other derivatives of this word.

The noun *mystērion* comes from the mystery religions, where it was almost always used in the plural to refer to the secret rituals of those religions, the mysteries.[10] A great deal has been written about the use of this term by Jewish and Christian writers. Most philological studies of *mystērion* agree that when this word was applied by Christians to aspects of Christianity prior to about the fourth century, the cognitive aspect was in view rather than the cultic. More specifically, the early Christian application of *mystērion* tended to be predominantly theological, focusing on eschatology in the first century (the mysterious aspects of salvation history) and on philosophy in the second and third.[11] Moreover, scholars who have examined the Christian usage of *mystērion* tend to view the translation "secret" as inexact and inadequate, for it minimizes the sense of mysteriousness or inscrutability that normally attaches to this word.[12] The tendency among New Testament scholars to translate *mystērion* as "secret" rather than as "mystery" seems to be rooted in the apologetic defence of earliest Christianity against the charge of having been influenced by the mystery religions; Christian scholars once thought that *secret* was a purely secular denotation of *mystērion*.[13] But as A.E. Harvey argued, "this so-called 'secular' usage is not attested until at least the [second] century, and should not be assumed in the New Testament except as a last resort."[14] *Mystērion* basically meant *mystery*.

The lack of a cultic or sacramental connection in Clement's use of *mystērion* was documented in an article by H.G. Marsh in 1936 and does not need to be demonstrated again here, though certain of his conclusions should be iterated.[15] For Clement, the mysteries were divine truths concealed beneath the literal level of the scriptures (e.g., *Strom*. I.5.32.3).[16] A contrived exposition of the two occurrences of *mystērion* in Col 1:25–27 provided Clement with the basis for his claim that the divine mysteries (he turned the word into a plural) were of two types: the gnostic tradition, which is reserved for the few, and the once hidden message of salvation, which is now openly proclaimed to the Gentiles (V.10.60.1–61.1).[17] On occasion Clement followed Philo and Justin in using *mystērion* as a synonym for the terms *symbol* and *parable* (I.12.55.1; V.12.80.7).[18] But in Clement's writings, *mystērion* does not usually refer to the form or manner by which scripture reveals its truths; that is the function of *mystikon* (the adjective) and *mystikōs* (the adverb). Clement normally used *mystērion* to designate the deeper truths themselves.

Because Clement divided the mysteries into two kinds, he was able to "disclose" the exoteric Christian truths through allegorical exposition, the same method by which the gnostic mysteries were imparted.[19] But he still preserved the distinction between what belongs to the many and what only to a few. Clement sometimes described the different levels of mysteries using mystery-religion language of a gradation of mysteries, including a distinction between "the small and the great mysteries" (*Strom.* IV.1.3.1; V.11.71.1; cf. I.1.15.3).[20] An Alexandrian believer might hear the longer text when being initiated into the latter (*Letter to Theodore* II.2). However, when Clement used mystery-religion terms, he followed the precedent of the philosophies, where "the mysteries are not cultic actions but obscure and secret doctrines whose hidden wisdom may be understood only by those capable of knowledge. The gradual ascent of knowledge to full vision is here the true initiation."[21] Massey Shepherd's description of what Clement meant by the greater and lesser mysteries may serve as a useful introduction to the  passages wherein these terms occur: "But the minor mysteries of the Christians have to do with preliminary instruction, what he describes as 'physical matters,' and then one goes on to the major mysteries that go beyond time and space. Thus 'abstracting all that belongs to bodies and things called incorporeal, we cast ourselves into the greatness of Christ, and thence advance into immensity by holiness' so as to reach somehow 'to the conception of the Almighty, knowing not what He is, but what He is not.'"[22]

Clement's mysteries involved the same general approach and had the same goal as those of the various philosophies, namely, "the vision of the divine."[23] The great mysteries are specifically matters of theology and metaphysics, and culminate in visionary experiences of the divine (*Epopteia*); Clement cited Plato in this respect:

> Moses' philosophy has four divisions: first, history; second, that which is properly called legislation (which would be properly classified under ethics); third, religious observances (a part of natural philosophy); fourth, in general,

the nature of the understanding of the divine, [visionary] revelation [ἡ ἐποπτεία], which Plato places among the really great mysteries. Aristotle calls this form "metaphysics."[24] (*Strom*. I.28.176.1–2)

Accordingly, in *Strom*. IV.1.3.1–3 Clement applied the terms *small* and *great* to the lesser mysteries of the origin of the universe (cosmogony) and the study of the observable world (φυσιολογία) and the great mysteries belonging to "the department of theology":

> On completing, then, the whole of what we propose in the commentaries, on which, if the Spirit will, we…shall address ourselves to the true gnostic science of nature, being initiated into the minor mysteries before the greater; so that nothing may be in the way of the truly divine declaration of sacred things, the subjects requiring preliminary detail and statement being cleared away, and sketched beforehand. The science of nature, then, or rather observation, as contained in the gnostic tradition according to the rule of the truth, depends on the discussion concerning cosmogony, ascending thence to the department of theology. Whence, then, we shall begin our account of what is handed down, with the creation as related by the prophets.[25]

The same philosophical conception of the mysteries is presupposed in V.11.70.7–71.1. Clement drew a conscious analogy between Greek mysteries and those of the Jews and Christians (the βάρβαροι, lit. "barbarians"), but the point of the comparison, apart from baptisms forming the earliest stage, is the fact of "instruction and…preliminary preparation" (cf. V.4.20.1). The "great mysteries" are again described in terms of a profound comprehension of "nature and things." They are also quite clearly differentiated from baptism:

> It is not without reason that in the mysteries that obtain among the Greeks, lustrations hold the first place; as also the laver [τὸ λουτρόν: ceremonial washing with water] among the Barbarians. After these are the minor mysteries, which have some foundation of instruction and of preliminary preparation for what is to come after; and the great mysteries, in which nothing remains to be learned of the universe, but only to contemplate and comprehend nature and things.

It is possible to derive a basic conception of the great mysteries from these passages, even if the distinction between the lesser and the greater is a bit unclear. In the view of Salvatore Lilla, the lesser mysteries involve "the indirect knowledge of God," that is, what humans can perceive about God indirectly through study of his works, or the natural world, whereas the great mysteries involve "the direct knowledge of [God]."[26] Somewhat differently, Walter Wagner explained that the lesser mysteries were the fulfillment of the practical aspect of ethics through instruction in "absolute duties" or general principles, learned after study of the "conditional duties" (the subject of the *Protrepticus* and *Paedagogus*). The lesser mysteries represent the theoretical dimension of ethics, and are more adequately described as philosophy, whereas for Clement and Philo the greater mysteries "transcended philosophy" and belong to "the crowning realm of initiation-vision, *Epopteia*."[27] The words *gnosis* and *wisdom* are more adequate than *philosophy* for conveying the substance of these mysteries.

The fact that Clement's words about the great mysteries refer to a highly advanced stage in gnostic instruction rather than to a ritual or set of rituals is vital for our interpretation of the restriction of the longer text to "those who are being initiated into the great mysteries" (II.1–2). Despite the objections of Massey Shepherd, most New Testament scholars who have studied the letter have supposed that this phrase refers to a cultic practice, usually baptism—the very practice to which the phrase is opposed in *Strom.* V.11.70.7–71.1.[28] The incorrectness of this understanding will be the subject of chapter 5. At this point we need to recognize that Clement drew upon the philosophical precedent of a figurative use of mystery language as a means to describe advancement in "the true philosophy" (III.18), that is, in gnosis. Initiation into the great mysteries refers to an advanced stage in a continuous and lifelong process. We should not, therefore, imagine this gospel being used on a special day or in connection with a special ceremony. The current consensus, unfortunately, is that the statement that the text was "read only to those who are being initiated into the great mysteries" refers to the prescribed *time* of the text's use, as if it were read only on a ceremonial occasion and otherwise locked away. The occasion itself is usually taken to be the Paschal evening, when, so these scholars (mistakenly) believe, baptism was performed in second-century Alexandria.[29] But Clement was actually referring to the *persons* exposed to the longer gospel: those Christians sufficiently advanced in the pursuit of gnosis. They heard this text whenever Clement or another teacher used it to expound the esoteric mysteries of Alexandrian Christian philosophy.

That the "mysteries" pertaining to the *mystikon euangelion* are concealed meanings rather than cultic actions is clear enough from Clement's reference to this gospel's special *logia*, where a personified interpretation "initiates" the hearer into a figurative "innermost sanctuary" of truth hidden by veils. Here, the mystery-religion language of initiation refers explicitly to the *interpretation* of special passages. Clement used the metaphors of sanctuary and veil elsewhere in reference to the hiding (veiling) of the gnostic truth beneath the literal level of the scriptures (*Strom.* V.4.19.3–4; cf. VI.15.126.1–4; VI.15.129.4).[30] The metaphor of the innermost sanctuary aptly signifies both the divine realities concealed by the scriptures and the holiness requisite to entering this "space."

Longer Mark's utility in disclosing secret theological mysteries through anagogical exegesis brings us back to the adjective *mystikon* and the question of what this term means in Clement's other writings. In order to appreciate the lack of a cultic or ritualistic meaning to *mystikon* in the *Letter to Theodore*, it is essential to distinguish between Clement's use of the language of the mysteries on their own terms in order to refer to their own practices, and his figurative (or philosophical) application of this language to aspects of Christianity. When he was writing about the pagan mysteries, his uses of *mystikon* normally mean "pertaining to the mysteries" and accordingly have a cultic dimension, though the connotation of "having a symbolic significance" is sometimes also involved (e.g., *Prot.* 2.22.3, 5; 2.34.5; *Strom.* III.4.27.1). His Christian uses of *mystikon* are generally different and more in keeping with the biblical association of *mystery* with knowledge—theological truths that are mysterious. A few partial exceptions occur in the *Paedagogus* when Clement applied the word to "necessary evils," that is, biblically mandated practices that contravene his gnostic ideal of freedom from emotion (ἀπάθεια), namely, sex (the "mystic rites of nature" ordained in Gen 1:28; *Paed.* II.10.96.2), the holy kiss (III.11.81.3), and Esther's mystical adornment of herself with jewellery and makeup, which Clement interpreted as a symbol for the high price of her people's ransom (III.2.12.5). The theme common to these applications of *mystikon* is the paradox (mystery) that certain behaviours associated with passion are divinely mandated. On the whole, however, Clement's Christian applications of *mystikon* are cognitive. Often they involve the general sense of "having the quality of mystery" or the specialized sense of "pertaining to a mystery of the divine will," but the overwhelming majority refer in a technical way to the figurative dimension of texts. Sometimes simple metaphor or symbol is involved, as in *Paed.* I.6.46.3, where Clement quoted Jesus' discourse upon himself as the true bread from heaven, and explained, "In this passage, we must read a mystic meaning for bread." More commonly, though, *mystikon* refers specifically to the enigmatic, allegorical quality that Clement attributed to all scripture, of overtly saying one thing but, in a more profound and relevant sense, meaning something else. He thought that the Hebrew scriptures in their entirety were composed on two levels: the literal (Hebrew) level and the figurative (Christian) level wherein the mysteries lie. Hence, "the mysteries are transmitted mystically" (*Strom.* I.1.13.4). Accordingly, Clement spoke of "the mystic silence of the prophetic enigmas" (*Prot.* 1.10.1) and, of course, of the "mystic veil" of the non-literal sense of scripture: "'Day utters speech to day' (what is clearly written), 'and night to night proclaims knowledge'

(which is hidden in a mystic veil)" (*Strom*. V.10.64.3). For Clement, all scripture communicates both literally and mystically, including his inclusive New
Testament and any ancient philosophical text in which he perceived the voice
of the Logos speaking allegorically.

Many of the preceding comments are well illustrated by a passage in
*Quis dives salvetur?* These words demonstrate how Clement would have read
a *mystikon euangelion* of Mark:

> And as we are clearly aware that the Saviour teaches [his own] nothing in a
> merely human way, but everything by a divine and mystical wisdom, we
> must not understand his words literally, but with due inquiry and intelli-
> gence we must search out and master their hidden meaning. For the sayings
> which appear to have been simplified by the Lord himself to his disciples
> are found even now, on account of the extraordinary degree of wisdom in
> them, to need not less but more attention than his dark and suggestive utter-
> ances. And when the sayings which are thought to have been fully explained
> by him to the inner circle of disciples, to the very men who are called by him
> the children of the kingdom, still require further reflexion, surely those that
> had the appearance of being delivered in simple form and for that reason
> were not questioned by the hearers, but which are of importance for the
> whole end of salvation, and are enveloped in a wonderful and super-celestial
> depth of thought, should not be taken as they strike the careless ear, but with
> an effort of mind to reach the very spirit of the Saviour and his secret mean-
> ing. (5.2–4)

The Markan portrait of Jesus speaking in riddles to the crowds yet expounding his veiled meanings to a select few had an important influence on Clement's
understanding of scripture.

When Clement used *mystikon* in connection with figurative meanings, he
was usually engaged in allegorical interpretation.[31] He used this word when
his interpretation appealed to the standard tropes employed in allegories to
draw a different meaning out of the obvious or literal one, including symbol
(*Strom*. VII.18.109.1), metaphor (*Paed*. I.5.14.4; I.6.46.3; *Strom*. IV.23.150.2,
151.3), etymology (*Strom*. I.24.164.3), numerology (*Strom*. I.21.147.6;
VI.16.145.3; cf. V.6.33.4, 34.5), and typology (*Paed*. I.5.23.2; II.8.75.1).
Accordingly, Clement referred to his allegorical interpretation of the description in Exodus of the furnishings of the tabernacle as a "mystic interpretation"
(*Strom*. V.6.37.1; cf. *Paed*. II.8.62.3; II.10.100.4).

Clement extended the technical meaning of *mystikon* to encompass not only
the figurative mode of reference but also persons and things related to the
mystic dimension of scripture or the gnosis conveyed therein. Jesus' teachings,
for instance, are called mystic (*Strom*. VI.15.127.3) and Jesus himself, "that
mystic messenger" who long ago spoke through the Jewish law but now has

become flesh (*Paed*. I.7.59.1). Clement referred to the disciplined path to perfection as the "mystic habit" and the "mystic stages" (*Strom*. VI.9.78.4; VII.10.57.1). Likewise, the knowledge that results from this practice is said to come from "the mystic choir of the truth itself" (*Strom*. VII.7.45.1). None of these applications of *mystikon* could rightly be described as cultic.[32]

Clement often spoke as if the literal or historical level of scripture "happened" for the sake of conveying, yet hiding, the more real, Christian significance until Jesus, the incarnate Logos, could disclose this purpose (cf. *Strom*. IV.23.151.3). The various historical figures may have said things with meanings plainly unrelated to Clement's exegesis, but they did so in order that the actual, allegorical meaning pertaining to Christianity would not yet be apparent. Clement claimed that "prophecy, in proclaiming the Lord, in order not to seem to some to blaspheme while speaking what was beyond the ideas of the multitude, embodied its declarations in expressions capable of leading to other conceptions" (VI.15.127.4). That is, the literal level is in the service of the allegorical level; the clear meaning depends on the intended deeper meanings for its existence.

Since the literal level "happened," Clement sometimes attributed its existence to the intention of the character(s) in question to do or say something that would contain the deeper Christian meaning while hiding that sense for the time being, as when he explained that "Isaac rejoiced for a mystical reason, to prefigure the joy with which the Lord has filled us, in saving us from destruction through his blood" (*Paed*. I.5.23.2). The intentions behind things said or done by Moses and the prophets were often treated that way, too. But in a more basic way Clement saw in the scriptures the influence of the preincarnate Logos, who controlled the literal level in one way or another. The same applies to the incarnate Logos and the holy spirit. Clement claimed, for instance, that Jesus allowed certain things to happen to him, such as his being anointed by a sinful woman and being crowned with thorns, because of the mystic symbolism of these details (*Paed*. II.8, esp. 63.1, 75.2). Jesus broke the five loaves of bread "very mystically" because the number five has symbolic significance (*Strom*. V.6.33.4). Concerning the spirit, which mediates for the risen Christ, Clement asserted that the holy spirit "mystically" put the voice of the Lord in the mouth of the apostle, when Paul said "I have given you milk to drink" (*Paed*. I.6.49.2). Therefore, when an act recorded in scripture has a deeper (or just figurative) meaning, the act itself, or the intention behind it, can also be called mystic.

This is what Clement probably meant when he referred to the Lord's mystic acts in I.17: they are acts (and sayings) performed for the purpose of conveying a deeper meaning. Since Clement supposed that anything Jesus did or said could have a mystic meaning (*Qds* 5), it seems likely that the mystic deeds gave some indication of their symbolic orientation. Possibly some, like LGM 1 and 2, provided a series of indeterminate references or gaps for the reader to fill; others perhaps were patently symbolic. The sayings may have included a greater use of tropes, such as hyperbole or parable. One can only speculate.

Similarly, the phrase *mystikon euangelion* emphasizes this gospel's symbolic and theological orientation. As Marsh put it, "the adjective μυστικός attached to a noun invests the latter word with the quality of a hidden treasure which can be enjoyed only by those who are not only aware of [the treasure's] existence but have the key to its discovery."[33] Since Clement believed that all scripture contains hidden mysteries, the expression *mystikon euangelion* must be relative: whereas canonical Mark focused more on the "bodily facts," longer Mark focused more on the theological meaning beneath the external presentation. Thus the descriptions "mystic gospel" and "more spiritual gospel" are essentially synonymous.

Clement's distinction between bodily and spiritual writings is an extension of the Greek conception that humans consist of an immortal essence (spirit) encased within a perishable shell (body). Clement thought that the evangelist John endeavoured to get behind the external facts (body) recorded by Matthew, Mark, and Luke in order to disclose their inner, theological significance (spirit). But whereas the Fourth Gospel brought out the spiritual truth concealed within the three synoptics, "Mark's 'more spiritual Gospel'…brought out the allegorical significance of his first edition."[34]

By now it should be clear that the title "the Secret Gospel of Mark" misconstrues the distinction Clement was making between the two editions of Mark. The words *mystikon euangelion* imply that the important *meanings* of the longer text were concealed within its distinctive narratives, but there is no implication in the adjective that *the text itself* was a guarded secret. That would not be necessary, for Mark did not add the gnostic secrets to his gospel but only mystic materials whose proper interpretation could disclose them (I.22–27). As John M. Dillon tried to clarify, "There is a difference between having secret scrolls somewhere and having public works with a higher meaning only expressible through a succession of oral teachings."[35] A more spiritual text can in principle be read by anyone, as was the case with the Gospel of John. We perpetuate the false impression that this text was concealed from the masses because of its secret or illicit contents when we call it the Secret Gospel of Mark.

Why Smith himself used *secret* is not much of a mystery. Smith regularly translated the noun *mystērion* as secret, and he felt that LGM 1 depicted an

THE NATURE OF THE LONGER GOSPEL

actual, secret ritual. When discussing the translation of this word in his commentary, he considered only three options, each apparently in its non-Christian sense: secret, pertaining to the mysteries, and symbolic. The last option was judged most likely by Nock and Mondésert, but Smith did not appreciate their point; he merely mentioned their opinion in brackets. For Smith the only real issue was whether *mystikon* meant secret or pertaining to the mysteries; in other words, he set up a false dichotomy between an unattested meaning and one that applies only to Clement's non-Christian usages. He ignored the predominant meaning of this word in Clement's writings, the sense related to gnostic exegesis; that sense is supported by everything Clement wrote about the *mystikon euangelion*.

## The Reason for the Discretion Surrounding the Use of the Longer Gospel

Even if a secret gospel used in connection with secret rites is not indicated by *mystikon euangelion* or "the great mysteries," are there not other reasons for viewing the longer text as a secret gospel? Does the letter not say that the longer text was "most carefully guarded" (Smith's translation), or at least hidden away in "a church archive containing secret writings"?[36]

No. A church archive and physical guarding are inferences based on the two subordinate clauses in the sentence "and, dying, [Mark] left his composition to the church in Alexandria, where it even yet is very securely kept, being read only to those who are being initiated into the great mysteries" (I.28–II.2). If one imagines that the Alexandrian church "where" the text was kept refers to a building, then one might infer that Clement was speaking of a special, secure room. But that assumption is unwarranted and probably anachronistic. It is more likely that "the church in Alexandria" refers to the group of interrelated Christian communities that existed in Alexandria. We cannot determine from this comment whether the text resided in a locked room or even if it was kept in just one place, although it would be natural for a book to be stored as part of a collection. As Annewies van den Hoek noted, the fact that Clement could quote from a multitude of Jewish and Christian sources suggests that there was a special collection or library of Jewish and Christian books in Alexandria to which he had access.[37] The real question is whether Clement's description of the church's inheritance of the longer gospel implies that it was relocated to a secret and secure book repository rather than to an ordinary library in a house. Smith's translation "most carefully guarded" would naturally suggest the former. But the verb in this phrase (ἀσφαλῶς εὖ μάλα τηρεῖται) basically means "to keep" and can be translated in a variety of ways—most of them unexciting. Liddell and Scott supply nine possible senses: "guard, keep, preserve; watch, give heed to; watch for, lie in wait for; notice, observe; keep, observe (a law or engagement); keep a secret; have regard for, reverence; retain; and reserve." Many of these senses would work here, including guarded, kept, preserved, respected, and heeded. However, this verb is modified by the adverb *asphalōs*, which usually means "securely" but can also mean "certainly" or "beyond a doubt." Smith noted that in Acts 16:23 both words are combined in the sentence "they threw them into prison, charging the jailer to keep them safely."[38] Here the safe keeping does involve physical guarding, but that sense is made clear from the *context* rather than from the words themselves (a prison and instructions to a jailer; the objects are people; and the point is to keep them from leaving). Put differently, the basic *meaning* in Acts 16:23 is "keep safely"; the *means* of safe keeping is physical guarding. Only the context within which these two words are used in the *Letter to Theodore* can determine the means by which the longer text was "very securely kept," if that is the right translation.

Smith's assumption that the text was a physically guarded secret is logical in terms of the structure of the sentence, which elucidates the manner in which the text was "kept" with reference to the fact that it was read only to certain people. But nothing that Clement said prior to this point would lead us to expect that this text was "most carefully guarded"; indeed, that premise clashes with Clement's explanation that Mark "neither grudgingly nor incautiously" composed a more spiritual gospel that merely *hinted at* the secret teachings it was meant to elucidate. Smith's assumption about physical guarding seems to be a function of his historical conclusions, particularly that the longer text was a product of libertine Christianity and preserved "material from the original, libertine tradition."[39] This position required Smith to conclude that Clement did not really like the longer gospel or the secret oral tradition but reluctantly accepted them because of their antiquity.[40] However, the letter reveals that Clement's attitude toward the longer text was entirely positive (e.g., I.11–12; II.8), and the notion that Clement reluctantly endorsed a text associated with libertinism is inconceivable. Clement was excessively prudish for his time—or any time, for that matter. As the *Paedagogus* reveals, he was deeply suspicious of a wide range of ordinary practices: Christians publicly greeting one another with the holy kiss (III.11.81–82); the wearing of jewellery (II.12; III.11.58; only a signet ring is acceptable); women uncovering their feet or heads in public (II.10.114; II.11.117; III.11.79; the veil itself should not be purple, which is showy and invites attention); hairstyles more fashionable than "a plain hair-pin at the neck" (III.11.62); stylish, colourful clothing (III.11.54, 63; men should dress entirely in white); unrestrained laughter (II.5); the disrobing that occurs in public baths (III.5.32); and men who appear effeminate by shaving their beards, having long or girlish locks of hair (III.3.17, 19; III.11.60–62), walking with a feminine gait, speaking in an unmanly voice (III.11.73–74; III.3.23), and wearing soft clothing or their ring on the joint of the finger (III.11.53, 59). Clement's ideal was to live without passions, so he forsook all pleasures that do not derive from noble pursuits; it was fine to derive pleasure from learning, but not from eating (II.1.10–15), sleeping (II.9), and bathing (III.9.46). It should come as no surprise that he had an unfavourable view of sex, which he considered unlawful except for procreation: "Pleasure sought for its own sake, even within the marriage bonds, is a sin and contrary both to law and to reason" (II.10.92). Accordingly, he instructed married Christians to avoid sexual intercourse in the daytime or at any time when conception cannot occur, such as during the months of a woman's pregnancy (II.10.92–93, 95–96). A man as prudish and repressed as Clement would not have accepted the longer text if he thought that it was in any sense libertine.

The broader literary context and our knowledge of Clement disaffirm the notion that the longer gospel was locked away from other Christians in the Alexandrian church, as if a secret society feared that ordinary believers should find out about this gospel. A more plausible supposition is that the text was "safely kept" or "securely kept" in the sense that it was not made available to people of unproven character.[41] Keeping in mind the apologetic function of this verse, which is to exonerate Mark and the Alexandrian church from the scandal of the Carpocratian longer gospel, Clement's point seems to be that this text was reserved for mature individuals who were not likely to misinterpret it or put it to improper uses. Clement's description of how Carpocrates used magic in order to procure a copy does imply that this text was carefully regulated. But a carefully regulated text is not necessarily one whose existence is kept secret, and we cannot put much weight on Clement's "cock-and-bull story" about a demonic conspiracy.[42]

Much of the tale spun about Carpocrates was likely extrapolated from two of Clement's fundamental convictions about the history of revelation, beliefs from which he derived all sorts of "facts." The first belief was that the true tradition was transmitted from Jesus to his disciples to the orthodox church. The second belief was that most expressions of the true philosophy that were formulated apart from the Judeo-Christian traditions were nevertheless dependent on the Christian truth and often stolen (e.g., *Strom*. I.20.100.4–5). Clement thought that "the true philosophy" had been accessible to the ancient Greeks through such sources as the Hebrew scriptures, revelations to Greek philosophers by the Logos or by other supernatural powers, induced states of ecstasy, and so forth (I.17.81, 87; I.21.135.2). He preferred to believe that "All those before the Lord's coming are robbers and bandits," except for the Hebrew prophets, who were "servants." "Philosophy was not sent out by the Lord, but came, says Scripture, either as an object of theft or a robber's gift. Some power, some angel learned a portion of the truth, but did not remain within the truth, and stole these things and taught them to human beings by way of inspiration" (I.17.81.1, 2, 4). These apologetic arguments were his best defence against the obvious charge, already popularized by Celsus, that Christian philosophy was just a recent, crude imitation of Greek philosophy.[43] Clement's accusations about how the ancient Greeks stole Christian philosophy were formed in as concrete a manner as he could pretend happened.[44] Thus, when Greek texts displayed obvious similarities to the Hebrew scriptures, he claimed straight plagiarism (e.g., I.21.101.1; V.14), suggesting that the Greeks "copied the miracle stories of our history" and "plagiarized our most important doctrines and debased them" (II.1.1.1).

This theory was Clement's preferred explanation for Greek literary parallels that had the potential to discredit Christianity. Since the licentious contents of the Carpocratian longer text similarly threatened to discredit Christianity, he explained away the existence of this text using essentially the same theory. The story of Carpocrates' theft is every bit as implausible as Clement's other accusations of literary theft. But in this case, there might be a kernel of truth to it, since Carpocrates hailed from Alexandria. It would not be unrealistic to suppose that before Carpocrates distinguished himself as beyond the pale he had been a member of the Alexandrian church and managed to persuade an elder to make him a copy of the longer text. In fact, it is hard to imagine how Carpocrates could not have been a member at some point, for, as Clement noted, his infamous son Epiphanes, who died quite young, was "still…listed in our church members' register," and the son's writings were in Clement's possession (*Strom.* III.2.2, 8.4).

The reference in the letter to "the foul demons…devising destruction for the race of men" is an appeal to the complementary theory that the foreknowledge and activity of demons was the cause of contemporary embarrassments for Christianity. Justin frequently asserted that demons inspired certain humans to create demonic parodies of the truth in order to make true things look false:

> But those who hand down the myths which the poets have made, adduce no proof to the youths who learn them; and we proceed to demonstrate that they have been uttered by the influence of the wicked demons, to deceive and lead astray the human race. For having heard it proclaimed through the

prophets that the Christ was to come, and that the ungodly among men were to be punished by fire, they put forward many to be called sons of Jupiter, under the impression that they would be able to produce in men the idea that things which were said with regard to Christ were marvelous tales, like the things which were said by the poets. (*First Apology* 54.1–2; see also 56, 62, 64, and 66; ANF trans.)

Clement's adaptation of the demonic conspiracy theory demonstrates that the Carpocratian parody of the longer text had severely tarnished the reputation of the version used in Clement's church. As an apologetic tale, it can prove little else. The story of Carpocrates' theft owes more to theological inference than to knowledge of the facts, at least where it speaks of demonic planning and magical enslavement. Thus the magical elements in this tale cannot be pressed to prove that in Carpocrates' time the text was a physically guarded secret, or even carefully regulated, though undoubtedly the scandal of the Carpocratian parody proved how necessary it was to keep this text away from persons of unproven character.

Smith's inference that the longer gospel was a closely guarded secret was also based upon a particular reading of II.10–12, Clement's direction to Theodore to offer a firm denial to the Carpocratians backed with an oath. The standard paraphrase of this section is as old as Smith's public announcement of his discovery to the Society of Biblical Literature in 1960: "Clement apparently made an unusual concession in revealing the 'secret gospel.' Clement emphatically lectured Theodore on the necessity of keeping knowledge of the gospel a secret—he 'should even deny it on oath,' Clement wrote."[45] We encountered this understanding earlier, when reviewing Charles Murgia's essay. As a paraphrase of Clement's directive to Theodore, it makes little sense. Theodore cannot keep the Carpocratians ignorant about the existence of a gospel that they told him about. The denial backed with an oath concerns, rather, the *authorship*, hence the authority, of the longer gospel used by the Carpocratians. Theodore knew nothing of this text before the Carpocratians told him about it, so an oath from him could only be effective if he appealed to a knowledgeable third party. Presumably, the Carpocratians suggested that he write to Alexandria for verification that Mark wrote this gospel; the Carpocratians expected that someone in the Alexandrian church would confirm Mark's authorship of the passages they described to Theodore. Taking advantage of the situation, Clement told Theodore to tell his Carpocratian opponents that *they* do not possess Mark's mystic gospel. There is no secrecy here, only a half-truth intended to undermine the legitimacy of one particular libertine sect.

Clement's reference to Mark bequeathing this gospel to the church in Alexandria could also be taken as an indication that the longer text was meant to be secret, since it implies that Mark controlled the only copy and refrained from publishing this work himself. The absence of any references to this text by other authors and the absence of preserved copies likewise indicate that it did not circulate outside Alexandria, except in its unauthorized, Carpocratian form. The letter certainly gives every indication that the longer text was used only in Alexandria. But the restriction of this text to one church need not indicate that the existence of this text was a secret. After all, Clement wrote that Mark bequeathed his gospel "to the church in Alexandria" rather than to some secret society within that church. And longer Mark would not have been the only "spiritual" gospel that was not published by its original author. The Gospel of John appears to have been composed in two or more stages,[46] but we have no evidence that any of its earlier incarnations ever circulated (e.g., all manuscripts include the final chapter, which was apparently added after the death of the original author, whose unanticipated demise is recounted obliquely in John 21:20–24). The lack of external evidence for any earlier editions raises the suspicion that the Gospel of John did not circulate outside the Johannine community for many years, perhaps more than a decade (the author of John 21 may have been the person responsible for introducing this gospel to a broader audience). For whatever reason, it appears that the authors of the spiritual gospels did not publish those gospels themselves.

There is one more issue to consider before dispensing with the epithet "the Secret Gospel." Although the suitability of the longer text to gnostic exposition probably led to this text being used primarily in the context of imparting the secret oral traditions, this utility does not account for why it was read *only* to Christians involved in gnostic study. Clement's theory of the polyvalence of religious writings (*Stromateis* V) implies that any gospel would have a variety of symbolic meanings, some of which could be expounded to ordinary Christians, others only to gnostics. Since the longer gospel concealed its gnostic secrets from uninstructed eyes, it is unclear why it did not just supplant the shorter version of Mark in the decades before the Carpocratian scandal—unless the longer text was never thought to be appropriate for catechumens and ordinary Christians. That inference would adequately explain the letter's premise that access to the manuscript was controlled at first by the author and later by elders in the church, as well as the fact that the custodians of this text probably never made copies for use in churches outside Alexandria.

So what reason could there have been for the initial restriction of this gospel to relatively advanced Christians? An important clue emerges from Clement's references to Mark's caution and forethought, which resemble

Clement's rationale for not putting in writing some of the traditions of his great teachers:[47]

> These [memories] I took good care to rekindle by making notes [ὑπομνήμασι]. Some I am deliberately putting to one side, making my selection [ἐκλέγων] scientifically out of fear of writing what I have refrained from speaking—not in a spirit of grudging [οὖ τί που φθονῶν] (that would be wrong), but in the fear that my companions might misunderstand them and go astray and that I might be found offering a dagger to a child. (*Strom.* I.1.14.3)

> ...not, however, declaring all of them, nor yet hinting at the mystic ones, but selecting [ἐκλεγόμενος] what he thought most useful for increasing the faith.... But when Peter died a martyr, Mark came over to Alexandria, bringing both his own notes [ὑπομνήματα] and those of Peter, from which he transferred to his former book...Thus, in sum, he prepared matters, neither grudgingly [οὖ φθονερῶς] nor incautiously, in my opinion, and, dying, he left his composition to the church in Alexandria, where it even yet is very securely kept, being read only to those who are being initiated into the great mysteries. (*Letter to Theodore* I.17–II.2)

The *Letter to Theodore* goes on to note the abomination that resulted when someone unworthy got his hands on this writing and, albeit wilfully, misinterpreted it. Clement had no access to the mind of the author of the longer gospel. He probably drew upon personal experience of the controversy and damage that results from putting certain things in writing and projected his own prudence onto Mark. In any case, at issue in his comments about Mark not incautiously and not grudgingly preparing the longer text is whether these passages should ever have been added to the gospel, considering what ultimately happened. Although longer Mark did not contain the gnostic tradition, it apparently had the potential to be misconstrued, like the materials Clement omitted from his *Stromateis*. This potential made longer Mark dangerous in the hands of the uninstructed, like a dagger wielded by a child.

So it appears that some of longer Mark's contents invited misunderstanding. Certainly that is true of the passage about which Theodore inquired. A typical Alexandrian might easily have construed LGM 1b as a kind of mystery-religion initiation, since those rites often involved nocturnal revelations to ordinary, anonymous persons dressed in linen. Clement himself viewed secret, nocturnal gatherings by fire light, presided over by hierophants, as characteristic of the Greek mysteries (*Prot.* 2.22.1, 6–7); to him, the darkness and nocturnal setting symbolized the inherent evil of the rites. Long before the Carpocratian scandal, Alexandrian elders probably worried that catechumens might misunderstand passages like LGM 1b, and may therefore have always reserved this text for the students progressing in knowledge. The exclusion of longer Mark from public readings may be compared to the exclusion of certain Jewish scriptures from public readings on account of theological difficulties arising from their contents.[48]

Perhaps the best proof of longer Mark's potential to be misconstrued is its reception by New Testament scholars. Even some "professional" readers unconsciously referred to Jesus teaching the young man the "mysteries" (plural) of the kingdom of God, in consonance with mystery religion terminology (though recollection of the parallel to Mark 4:11 in Matthew and Luke may sometimes be the trigger).[49] John Wenham typified this sort of confusion when he wrote "Can we believe that Mark wrote the ill-fitting insertions attributed to him, which suggest that Jesus initiated nocturnal 'mysteries' [sic] in the nude [sic]?"[50] In an endnote, Karel Hanhart attempted to explain how the (non-existent) plural in "secret" Mark does not contradict Mark's style and what he took to be the Pauline meaning of "mystery" in Mark 4:11.[51] Others imagined that LGM 1:11 depicts the young man as wearing *white* linen, which, as Marvin Meyer noted, some of the mystery religions used as the garment of initiation. This transference of the whiteness of the robe worn by the young man in the tomb to the linen sheet worn by the young man in LGM 1b is fairly common, and probably happened among the original readers.[52] Many other scholars declared the text to be self-evidently gnostic, and some supposed that the incident has homosexual overtones. The gay reading of LGM 1b is very popular among non-scholars. Clearly, LGM 1b is a story that "those outside" are prone to confuse with gnosticism, mystery initiations, and sexual libertinism despite the fact that the troublesome elements are all paralleled in either canonical Mark or the Gospel of John and accord with the Markan theme that Jesus taught the mystery of the kingdom of God in private to "those who were about him with the twelve" (4:10–12).

## Conclusions

Smith misconstrued Clement's comments about the nature of the longer gospel. The *Letter to Theodore* does not refer to a secret gospel but to a mystic gospel that had an affinity to the Gospel of John. Teachers in Alexandria found the longer text of Mark to be especially useful for the instruction of advanced Christians but potentially harmful to catechumens. Presumably its utility in disclosing the secret, unwritten doctrines reserved for advanced Christians and the amenability of its overtly symbolic passages to unedifying interpretations led its custodians to avoid reading it to people of unproven character, and the scandalous use of this text by the Carpocratians eventually made discussing this text in public writings more trouble than it was worth. What is most certain and most important for us to recognize is that the translation "secret gospel" misrepresents and obscures Clement's actual conception of the genre and purpose of this gospel. It is time to replace that title and the misleading connotations it invokes.

# ⚛5⚛

# The Original Purpose and Later Use
# of the Longer Gospel

In the preceding chapter I argued that the *Letter to Theodore* refers not to a secret, ritual text but to a gospel that developed the "spiritual" or concealed meanings of the Markan narrative; in Clement's day it was being expounded anagogically to advanced Christians as a means of communicating the esoteric *theological* mysteries of the Alexandrian church. These conclusions require us to reconsider the appropriateness of the form-critical paradigm as the basic tool for comprehending the setting in which this text was read and—just as important—what is being depicted in LGM 1b. Are LGM 1 and 2 communally shaped traditions that functioned as the liturgy or as catechism for a rite that LGM 1b depicts?

## The Baptismal Reading of LGM 1b

That has been the dominant opinion. Nearly all of the scholars who commented on the significance of the young man's linen sheet decided that LGM 1:11–12 depicts some form of Christian baptism.[1] On the face of it, this idea seems plausible: The private, nocturnal setting and the odd costume suggest an initiation; a linen sheet worn over the naked body could facilitate disrobing for immersion. More importantly, since linen was commonly used as a burial wrapping, the sheet could signify the spiritual death and rebirth effected by the rite of baptism. As Smith noted, the word used to describe the young man's sheet in LGM 1:11 and Mark 14:51 (σινδών) also appears in Mark 15:46 in reference to Jesus' burial wrapping. So the sheet has connotations of death and burial in Mark itself. Moreover, as I noted in chapter 3, Bethany in LGM 1:1 is not the village near Jerusalem where Lazarus is raised but the place beyond the Jordan where Jesus first heard of Lazarus' illness. This

Bethany is the place where John the Baptist witnessed to Jesus in the Gospel of John (1:28; 10:40). Thus in longer Mark, Jesus raises and instructs the young man in the place where Jesus' forerunner first performed baptisms in the Fourth Gospel. The relevant details of Jesus' movements through Peraea before and after LGM 1 accord with the archaeological evidence that this place called Bethany was located in present-day Wadi Kharrar, not far from Jericho. The young man's house would therefore have been close to the Jordan River and four freshwater springs.[2]

That a resident of Bethany beyond the Jordan who is dressed in a linen sheet might be a candidate for baptism is confirmed rather strikingly by records of Christian pilgrimage to this site. Several Christian travellers, including the Pilgrim of Bordeaux (333 CE), specify that this location was the traditional site of Jesus' baptism. The account by the Pilgrim of Piacenza from around the year 570 also describes what Christians wore when they immersed themselves in the Jordan River at Wadi Kharrar after an all-night vigil that began in the evening before Epiphany: "Some wear linen, and some other materials which will serve as their shrouds for burial."[3] It is hard to miss the similarity between Jesus' nighttime instruction of a young man dressed only in linen (presumably the shroud he was wearing when Jesus returned him from the dead) and the nightlong vigil culminating in baptism that was witnessed by the Pilgrim of Piacenza at the same location. Interestingly, the practice of wearing linen funeral shrouds during pilgrimage baptism in the Jordan is an element of Greek Orthodox practice.[4] Bethany's association with John the Baptist, "living" water (the Jordan River and freshwater springs), and a peculiar practice of wearing linen burial shrouds as a symbol of baptismal rebirth is a sufficient basis to conclude that the description of the linen sheet in LGM 1b presupposes Christian baptism, if not a special form of baptism specific to Bethany beyond the Jordan.

But *presupposes* seems to be all. The story is strangely unclear about what is transpiring between Jesus and the young man. There is no mention of water or depiction of a baptism. The narrator merely says, "and when it was evening the young man comes to him donning a linen sheet upon his naked body, and he remained with him that night; for Jesus was teaching him the mystery of the kingdom of God. Now rising, he returned from there to the other side of the Jordan" (1:11–13). The combination of the conjunction *for* and the imperfect tense "was teaching" explains why the young man remained that evening, and implies that only teaching occurred.[5] The earlier occurrence of "the mystery of the kingdom of God" in the parable discourse indicates that this mystery concerns a single theological truth about the reign of God that can be grasped only with great effort (4:10–12, 24–25). Such a mystery is too profound for pre-baptismal catechism,[6] the purpose of which was ethical "resocialization," as Clement himself insisted.[7] And precisely where the reader might expect the depiction of a ritual, the narrator states that Jesus got up and went to the other side of the Jordan.

The young man does reappear in Gethsemane, but he is again wearing a linen sheet, which must represent his readiness *for* initiation. Why would he be wearing the garment that symbolizes the old self abandoned in baptism if he was actually baptized in Bethany?[8] Lest we imagine that the young man is now ready to be baptized in some nearby water, we are told that he "was following with" Jesus as Jesus was being arrested—not a good time to seek baptism. He does disrobe, but only in a struggle to avoid his own arrest. His nudity is not a sublime symbol of a believer's participation in Christ's death and resurrection through baptism,[9] or of a power that death could not conquer,[10] but an ignominious detail that exemplifies the fear and desperation of the disciples as a whole.[11] The loss of his linen sheet implies the absence of the kind of loyalty to Jesus that undergoing baptism would convey.[12]

So the young man's linen sheet has baptismal connotations, but the text discourages every attempt to perceive Jesus literally baptizing him. We should not be surprised by this, for the gospel gave two clear indications that Jesus' baptism is not in water. John the Baptist stated this explicitly in the prologue: "After me comes he who is mightier than I, the thong of whose sandals I am not worthy to stoop down and untie. I have baptized you with water; but he will baptize you with the Holy Spirit" (1:7–8). Likewise, in the immediate context of LGM 1, Jesus spoke of "the baptism with which I am baptized" as a metaphorical immersion (10:38–39). His words to James and John about his cup and baptism certainly *allude* to the sacraments marking entrance into the church, but it is the non-sacramental, metaphorical dimensions to these images that are essential to Mark's point. The cup that Jesus offers his disciples symbolizes his blood (death) in 14:23–24 and his passion in 14:36, so the symbolism of Jesus' cup and baptism in 10:38–39 must connote Jesus' suffering and death as well. Like the imagery of taking up one's cross and following Jesus (8:34), the imagery of drinking Jesus' cup and undergoing his baptism signify sharing his violent fate. It therefore makes sense to ask whether the initiatory imagery of LGM 1b further elaborates this theme by extending the comparison between baptism and the process of following Jesus in his way to life through death. But before we consider this possibility, we need to explore the evidence of the letter.

## The Baptismal Reading of the *Letter to Theodore*

It is time to consider what the *Letter to Theodore* reveals about the actual use of LGM 1 and 2 in late-second-century Alexandria. Clement offers us a rare first-hand account of how a gospel was used in a particular community, so it is quite surprising that scholars have mostly overlooked the "external" evidence of the letter proper by focusing mainly on LGM 1b. Conceivably, the initiatory character of this incident, the sacramental-sounding language Clement employed to describe the way the longer text was used, and the lack of viable alternatives to the baptismal theory have all contributed to the "factualization" of Smith's undocumented assertion that the great mysteries "would most easily be referred to the pascha, the annual occasion for baptism."[13] Some scholars seem to think that Clement as much as stated that longer Mark was used in connection with neophyte baptism.[14] The canonical status of this opinion might explain why most scholars have not noticed that it contradicts another widespread conception, namely, that longer Mark was a secret writing known only to an elite sect within the church.

Knowing that this work was not a *secret* gospel does not, however, resolve the problems posed by the letter for the theory that longer Mark was read as catechism and liturgy in connection with baptism. Another contradiction exists that should have been at least as obvious: the *Letter to Theodore* itself dissociates catechumens from the audience for which the longer gospel was written. According to Clement's Alexandrian tradition, what we call canonical Mark was written for "catechumens" (οἱ κατηχούμενοι) in order to strengthen their faith (I.18). The additional passages of the more spiritual gospel, on the other hand, were added for the use of "those being perfected" (I.22) and were "read only to those who are being initiated into the great mysteries" (II.1–2). Catechumens and those being perfected are very different groups. As Smith himself acknowledged, Clement's unqualified references to being perfected concern gnosis.[15] Likewise, as I demonstrated in the previous chapter, Clement's references to the great mysteries have in view an advanced stage of theological instruction. A person was *figuratively* initiated into these *theological* mysteries on a daily basis through study of the hidden, allegorical meanings of the scriptures. The longer text's suitability, if not its actual use, in advanced theological instruction is clearly conveyed in the statement that Mark "transferred to his former book the things suitable to those studies which make for progress toward gnosis" (I.20–21). It follows that those who heard the longer text were already baptized, and those who were undergoing pre-baptismal instruction were still a long way off from hearing it. The fact that the letter itself dissociates catechumens from the audience of the longer text can only cause us to wonder how the hypothesis that this gospel was read in second-century Alexandria in the context of baptism managed to become an assured result.

The restriction of longer Mark to baptized Christians who were well advanced in gnosis is an important problem for the theory devised by Thomas Talley, which finds in LGM 1 an explanation for the early Alexandrian practice of performing baptisms on the sixth day (Friday) of the sixth week of the fast in imitation of Jesus' fast of forty days after his baptism. Medieval sources indicate that in Alexandria prior to Nicea this fast took place immediately after Epiphany (January 6th) rather than during the forty days leading up to Easter, and concluded with the Feast of Palms on the first Sunday after the baptisms. Hence in Alexandria, Palm Sunday and the preceding Friday of baptism occurred a number of weeks before Pascha and the six-day paschal fast.[16] The origins of this practice of baptizing on the sixth day of the sixth week of the fast are unclear, but a long-standing Coptic tradition, mentioned in the tenth century by Macarius, the Bishop of Memphis, recounts that Jesus baptized his disciples on that day.[17] The basis of that tradition is unknown, but Talley believed that it was the raising and initiation story in longer Mark, for that story depicts, in his view, Jesus baptizing a disciple "after six days." Talley worked this conclusion into a hypothesis that by Clement's time the Gospel of Mark was read in Alexandria according to a liturgical cycle, "beginning on January 6: the Baptism of Jesus on that day, the beginning of the imitation of Jesus' fast on the following day with the continued reading of the gospel during the weeks of the fast so as to arrive at chapter 10 by the sixth week, the reading of the secret gospel inserted into chapter 10 in close conjunction with the conferment of baptism in that sixth week, and the celebration of the entry into Jerusalem with chapter 11 of Mark on the following Sunday."[18] As support for this reconstruction, Talley noted that at Constantinople, the gospel reading for the Sunday before Palm Sunday was Mark 10:32–45, which is the passage in which LGM 1 occurs in longer Mark: "Constantinople's five week Markan course breaks off after Mark 10.32–45 and the next eucharist on the following Saturday abruptly shifts to the only canonical parallel to the secret gospel, the raising of Lazarus in John 11, and this 'Saturday of the Palm-bearer: Memorial of the Holy and Just Lazarus' [i.e., Lazarus Saturday] is, in the medieval typika of Hagia Sophia, a fully baptismal liturgy."[19]

Talley did not offer any new arguments for reading LGM 1 as an account of a literal baptism, nor did he demonstrate that baptism was already being performed on a special day in Clement's time. Rather, he accepted Smith's claim that the great mysteries referred to a day of baptism: "That this initiatory encounter is of a baptismal character is not stated in the text, but the use of this pericope in connection with baptism must have established such an understanding. It is true that the subject of the narrative is but a single individual in the Mar Saba fragment, and that the text does not even say that Jesus baptized him. Yet it was this text that was read, Clement says, 'only to those who are being initiated into the great mysteries,' and it is virtually certain that those disciples of Christ were being baptized."[20] The difficulties with Talley's position are apparent in this quotation. The great mysteries have to do with advanced theological instruction, not baptism. There is a superficial similarity between the one disciple being instructed in a linen sheet after six days and the tradition that Jesus baptized his disciples on the sixth day of the week, but it is not clear how one moves from "after six days" to "on the sixth day of the week." One *could* argue that "after six days" is synonymous with "on the sixth day," since "after three days" in the passion predictions must mean on the third day. But it is more likely that the phrase means "a week later" or "on the seventh day," given the fact that the preposition (μετά) means *after* and not *on* (ἐν). In any case, there is no reason why "after six days" should mean the sixth day *of the week* (Friday), for the six-day interval is relative to when Jesus and the young man entered the house, not relative to the first— or any other—day of the week. Thus the coincidence of the number six is not sufficient justification for associating LGM 1 with a tradition that Jesus baptized his disciples on the sixth day of the week.

There is still the question of how a tradition that Jesus baptized his disciples could be represented by a story involving one disciple, who was not even one of the twelve. Some additional information about Clement's understanding of baptism is relevant here. In a fragment of Clement's *Hypotyposeis* preserved by John Moschus, a Palestinian monk of the seventh century, Clement interpreted 1 Cor 1:14 to imply that Jesus baptized one disciple. That disciple, however, was Peter: "Yes, truly the apostles were baptized, as Clement the Stromatist relates in the fifth book of the *Hypotyposes*. For in explaining the saying of the Apostle, 'I give thanks that I baptized no one of you,' he says that Christ is said to have baptized Peter alone, and Peter, Andrew, and Andrew, James and John, and they the rest."[21] Clement, therefore, did not think that Jesus baptized his disciples (plural) on a particular day, as the Coptic tradition has it.

Does the coincidence that Clement believed that Jesus baptized only *one* disciple perhaps reflect consideration of the longer gospel and a baptismal interpretation? The opposite conclusion seems more likely. We do not know why Clement thought it important to believe that Jesus baptized one disciple. He may have been confronting the same problem in relation to which Moschus offered this quotation, namely, that no scripture relates that the apostles were baptized in water, so, according to John 3:5, they are excluded from the kingdom of God. Whatever the motive, Clement found evidence for a single exception in 1 Cor 1:14, not LGM 1b, and that exception was Peter, not the anonymous young man. Had Clement thought that Jesus baptized the young man whom he had raised from the dead, Clement could not very well conclude that Jesus baptized "Peter alone" (Peter is differentiated from this young man in Mark 14:51–54).

The basic conclusion that can be drawn at this point is that there is no good reason to think that LGM 1 was devised for and shaped within a baptismal life setting or that it was given such a function in Alexandria at any point before the end of the second century. The letter itself indicates that this amplified edition was reserved for Christians who were advanced enough to study the most esoteric theological teachings. Catechumens heard the shorter gospel.

## Alternative Cultic Interpretations

Given the distinctions that Clement drew between baptism and the great mysteries (*Strom.* V.11.70.7–71.1), on the one hand, and between catechumens and the audience of the longer gospel, on the other, it is rather remarkable that only three scholars attempted to devise alternative interpretations that could accommodate these facts. Rather predictably, these scholars proposed new rites of initiation that could correspond to the cultic ritual supposedly depicted in LGM 1b. Morton Smith postulated "a second baptism for the true gnostics, distinct from the rank and file."[22] Raymond E. Brown spoke of "an initiation rite into the mystery of the kingdom, i.e., either a (second) baptism, or, more likely, a secret rite phrased in imagery borrowed from baptismal theology: entrance into the kingdom, dying/rising, new man, white garment, paschal setting."[23] And Cyril C. Richardson abandoned his initial baptism theory for a rite involving elements resembling gnosticism and the mystery cults. Since Brown's alternative to Smith's hypothesis of a second baptism is so vague, I will not deal with it separately.

Smith apparently developed his theory of a second baptism in stages. He began by elaborating Richardson's suggestion that Mark 10:13–45 plus LGM 1 constituted a lection for baptism. Since Richardson's theory envisions longer Mark being read to catechumens, Smith had difficulty with Clement's statements that the shorter gospel was read to "catechumens" and the longer gospel to "those being perfected" (i.e., in gnosis). In the commentary section of his book, Smith addressed this discrepancy by suggesting that the latter category referred to "persons in the process of being baptized," who were no longer catechumens.[24] This conjecture eventually became unnecessary when

Smith decided that the rite depicted in LGM 1b was secret and unseemly and that the longer gospel was known only to a gnostic clique within the church. Those inferences led Smith to assume that LGM 1b was read in connection with a second baptism of a different sort. Christians involved in a *second* baptism would by definition no longer be catechumens and could rightly be called "those being perfected" (in gnosis).

What this second baptism involved is not entirely clear. In a few places Smith suggested that it was derived from, and to a large extent preserved, the baptismal practice he ascribed to the historical Jesus, involving a spiritual ascent into the heavens and the resultant libertine conviction of freedom from the law: "the developments which Jesus had added to the Baptist's baptism fell into disuse or were preserved as 'great mysteries' for more advanced candidates."[25] The supposition of a second baptism led in turn to the supposition that there were two distinct communities in Clement's church: a "well-to-do" esoterically inclined congregation which became an "inner circle"[26] and the larger community of lesser educated, more orthodox Christians. Yet the tolerance of secret, libertine rites in the orthodox Alexandrian church itself required an explanation; Smith offered two theories to account for this:

> Such a practice might have resulted from the coming together—perhaps under the pressure of persecution—of congregations originally distinct. A more hellenized congregation, holding to a philosophical interpretation of the religion and familiar with the practices of the mysteries, might have tried to maintain its individuality as an *ecclesiola in ecclesia* and have admitted candidates from the larger church only after a special course of training, and administration of its peculiarly significant sacraments. Another possibility is that we have here a late example of the way many Christian churches first quarantined and then eliminated the libertine tradition. The dangerous secrets of realizable eschatology—of the immediate accessibility of the kingdom and the liberty of those who entered it—were limited to a few, shut away from the rest by special requirements, and at last quietly forgotten.[27]

"It was probably this libertine wing that both produced and preserved the secret Gospel of Mark—a version of canonical Mark expanded by the addition of material from the original, libertine tradition."[28] How someone as prudish and repressed as Clement could have become a leading figure within an inner circle that transmitted a libertine tradition, Smith did not say.

Whether or not Smith realized it, his theory that longer Mark was a secret text that depicted an archaic and unsavoury mystery initiation is incompatible with Richardson's theory that Mark 10:13–45 was a baptismal lection. All of the arguments that Smith adopted from Richardson assume that this lection was read to persons who were in the process of entering the church—

simple folk who might benefit from instruction that emphasized the importance of becoming like children (Mark 10:14) and the need to observe the ten
commandments (10:19), "practice humility," and "make yourselves useful
in the church" (10:42–45).[29] Yet Smith believed that LGM 1 represents a second baptism confined to a libertine, gnostic clique. Why would a section of
Mark devised for new believers contain a passage that adumbrates a secret,
libertine ritual? How could a section of Mark that inculcates simple virtues
serve the liturgical needs of a group of libertine gnostics? Richardson's interpretation of Mark 10:13–45 and Smith's understanding of LGM 1b were
hardly compatible.

Unlike Smith, Cyril C. Richardson abandoned the baptismal theory altogether when he realized that Clement associated both longer Mark and the
great mysteries with gnostic instruction. The alternative ritual that Richardson reconstructed from LGM 1 and 2 and Clement's words on "the mysteries of love" (presumably *Qds* 36–37) is even more incredible than Smith's secret
baptism. In order to find cultic referents for each detail in the gospel excerpts,
Richardson turned to gnosticism and the mystery religions and concluded that
LGM 1a represents a *mors voluntaria* or voluntary, simulated death, whereas
LGM 1b represents "a sacred kiss in the nude, a form of the 'bridal chamber'
(cf. *Gospel of Philip*)," which "seals the kingdom's mystery of love." Richardson interpreted the linen cloth in terms of the mythology of "a return to Par-
adise"; it signifies "a loincloth to hide the genitals." He added that the
reference to the three women perhaps "reflects an Encratite group which *did*
reject women."[30]

The little evidence we have about *mors voluntaria* suggests that these rites
replicated death by evoking the initiate's fear of dying; this was accomplished through a ritual enactment of death, which may have included a
simulated burial or descent into the underworld.[31] In support of reading
LGM 1a as a *mors voluntaria*, Richardson noted that in longer Mark "the
shriek ['loud voice'] comes from the tomb, whereas in John it comes from
Jesus. The phrase generally signifies a prophetic-magical utterance….But
here it echoes the shriek of Legion among the tombs (Mk 5:7) and suggests
the terror of an actual *mors voluntaria*. Who, for instance, being initiated in
the cult of Isis, would not scream as he was led into the dark room to meet
the terrible Osiris, god of the dead, and behold his penis which the indus-
trious and loving Isis had failed to recover?"[32]

This theory might strike a chord with someone who can imagine Christians burying each other alive as an alternative means of participating in
Jesus' death and resurrection, but this melange of gnostic, Encratite, and Isis-
cult parallels does not make much sense in terms of the unfolding of the story.

Literally, the young man is in a tomb because he is dead, not because he is voluntarily undergoing a rite of transformation. The cry from the tomb appears to be provoked by Jesus' proximity, as in Mark 1:23–24 and 5:6–7, where demons inspire their hosts to cry out because the Holy One of God has come to plunder Satan's possessions (3:27). The scream, therefore, does not concern the (dead) man's fear of death, but Death's own fear of Jesus. The part of the story that *does* have an initiatory character (LGM 1b) does not involve nudity or a kiss; the phrase "naked man with naked man" pertains to the Carpocratian version, so the linen sheet does not come off until Mark 14:52. By forsaking the storyline in favour of disparate and abstruse allegorical connections, Richardson lost sight of the fact that LGM 1a is a typical raising miracle.

## The Need for a Literary Perspective on LGM 1 and 2

Evident in Richardson's strained explanation is a compulsion to identify, if not a single ritual, then one conglomerate of practices that can account for all the strange details in LGM 1 and 2. The common notion that gospel materials were crafted through their use in connection with particular church practices inclines scholars to distinguish, in as transparent a way as possible, whatever community practice might be served by a particular pericope. Thus most scholars consider it to be self-evident the LGM 1b depicts a practice of the Alexandrian church.[33] Certainly this pericope would constitute excellent support for this form-critical presupposition, should we ever discover a rite involving nocturnal instruction in the mystery of the kingdom of God given to initiates wrapped in linen sheets. But the fact that the details pertaining to the young man frustrate every attempt to read LGM 1:10–12 as a depiction of a ritual bids us to reconsider the assumption that this passage was fashioned in a cultic context and depicts an actual ritual.

The premise that LGM 1 has a cultic life setting is made more problematic by the existence of LGM 2. "What purpose of what group of which early church led to its invention? And why did Mark include it?"[34] Smith asked those questions of Mark 14:51–52, but they apply equally well to the similarly brief and enigmatic "story" about Jesus snubbing three women when he came to Jericho. LGM 2 is inexplicable when viewed as a unit of tradition that was transmitted orally for a generation or more because it had some illustrative value. Like 14:51–52, it does not answer any questions; it only elicits them. Nor does it make sense to imagine that LGM 2 is a remnant of an actual event that was preserved for decades simply because it happened. So many really important details about Jesus were completely lost, but *this* one, the bare fact that he did not receive three women one day in Jericho, was remembered. Why?

Most scholars who think that LGM 2 has some traditional basis explain its cultic and didactic irrelevance by suggesting that some redactor eliminated a dialogue between Jesus and Salome with the gloss "and Jesus did not receive them."[35] But theories of suppression simply replace the problem of irrelevance with the question of why a tradition deprived of any function was ever put into a gospel. This dilemma is not resolved by assuming that the passage was doctored only after it was incorporated into the text, for the most sensible solution would have been to remove the offending tradition completely so that nothing remains to draw attention to its suppression.

Among scholars who consider LGM 2 to be a complete tradition, the most common form-critical explanation is that it was devised to rationalize Encratite celibacy.[36] This, too, is not a very plausible explanation for how these two sentences could have survived as oral tradition. Aside from the gratuitousness of evoking a philosophical attitude toward marriage simply because the persons whom Jesus did not receive were women (should we invoke this thesis to explain why Jesus was so rude to the Syrophoenician woman?), this notion overlooks the fact that Jesus initially raised the brother at the sister's request and got angry when his own disciples rebuked her. His attitude toward the sister appears to change after he first encounters her.

Hypotheses about a setting in the life of a church can no more explain the existence of LGM 2 than they can the appearance of the anonymous young man in Gethsemane. Perhaps, then, we should stop trying to situate LGM 2 within the world outside the text and ask how it functions within its literary context. Whatever its meaning, LGM 2 has a literary function with respect to LGM 1: it creates an intercalation. As we will see in chapter 6, comparison of the first sentence of LGM 2 with the opening of LGM 1 reveals an extensive parallelism. Both begin with "and" (καί) + a present tense indicative of "to come" (ἔρχομαι) + "into" (εἰς) + a place name + another "and" (καί) + an imperfect of "to be" (εἰμί) combined with "there" (ἐκεῖ), and then mention the same woman, identify her with respect to her brother, and use the Semitism of a redundant possessive in relation to the brother ("whose brother of hers"; "whom Jesus loved him")—in all, nine points of contact in sequence. The reference to the three women in LGM 2 was shaped in such a way that it calls to mind the preceding resuscitation story, in effect bracketing the intervening story of the request of James and John. Mark used this technique as a means of suggesting that the intercalated stories are mutually interpretative. Longer Mark's use of this technique indicates that the structural parallel between LGM 2:1a and the opening of LGM 1 is redactional; the *form* of 2:1a was fashioned by the author of the longer gospel. The remaining words of LGM 2:1—"and his mother and Salome"—likewise were not crafted in some real-life context. What the words "the sister...and his mother and Salome" *do* is create a group of three women that anticipates the groups of three women mentioned in connection with Jesus' crucifixion (15:40) and resurrection (16:1); this grouping of three women functions as part of a "paired frame" (*inclusio*), whereby the passion narrative is bracketed by two raising miracles involving Jesus, a young man, a stone, a tomb, and three women. The remark in LGM 2:2 "and Jesus did not receive them," on the other hand, is reminiscent of Jesus' refusal to receive his mother and brothers when they sought to take charge of him after hearing that he was "beside himself" (3:20–21, 31–35). In light of that literary precedent, a reader might infer that the sister and mother want to take the young man back home because he has abandoned his family and wealth in order to follow Jesus (LGM 1:8; Mark 14:51–52). Thus, in the context of the Markan gospel, LGM 2 reiterates the point that the only family Jesus will acknowledge is the one consisting of those who do the will of God (3:33–35); apart from this context, LGM 2 has no clear theological meaning. The most reasonable conclusion, then, is that LGM 2 is a literary construct. Its form was not shaped through repeated telling in connection with some Christian activity, and its contents depend upon this gospel for their meaning.

If LGM 2 cannot be understood within the framework of form criticism but is susceptible to narrative analysis, then perhaps a more literary approach can help us make more sense of LGM 1b. Indeed, from a reader-response perspective, the entire subplot involving the young man seems designed to confuse us, for it is packed with unexplained details that goad the reader to ask what is going on. As we read the story, we puzzle over questions such as: What cries out from the tomb? Why is this "loud voice" heard *before* Jesus raises the man? Is he not dead? How does the young man's wealth explain why they retire to his house? Why does Jesus stay for a whole week? What command does he give to the young man? What happened to Jesus' disciples? What is the significance of the linen sheet covering the young man's naked body? Why is this meeting private and nocturnal? What exactly is the setting? (Are they still in the house? Did they ever leave it?) What is the mystery of the kingdom of God? Why does Jesus teach it to *this* individual? Why does the author identify only one of the new characters by name? Who *is* Salome? How is she related to the young man's mother and sister? Why are these three women in Jericho when Jesus arrives? What do they want with him? Why does Jesus not receive them? This persistent indeterminacy continues through the reappearance of the anonymous young man in Gethsemane and inside Jesus' open tomb.

Thus, despite receiving a description of what happened, we must contend with numerous gaps that encumber our understanding of what it all means. We are forced to fill in all the missing connections through a dialectical process of considering the details, constructing tentative hypotheses about what is going on in the story, and evaluating how well our hypotheses can account for all the details that the narrator chose to disclose. Each failure to make sense of all the details requires us to try again with a new theory.[37] It is difficult *not* to engage in this process, for we enjoy a good riddle and do not want to be an outsider to a mystery. Our sheer fascination with making sense of LGM 1 and 2 belies the usual assumptions that the author was just carelessly vague or writing for such a specific audience that he did not need to spell out what everyone knew. Rather, gap-laden narration is a prominent Markan literary technique: "The experience of reading Mark's Gospel is regularly the experience of being enticed to fill in the gaps and places of indeterminacy that the narrative presents to us....Like lace, which is characterized as much by its open spaces as by the tangible threads that outline them, Mark's fabric is so full of gaps that we could look almost anywhere for salient examples."[38]

The transfiguration comes close to the level of indeterminacy produced by the extant longer gospel insertions, as does the sequence of events in the prologue and, of course, the account of the young man in Gethsemane. In these stories the narrator shows us the incident unfolding but withholds the authoritative authorial commentary that would explain what we are witnessing. So, for instance, when reading Mark 9:2–13 we struggle to synthesize all the striking—yet unelaborated—details into a coherent theological point that explains not only the significance of Jesus' metamorphosis but also the appearance of Elijah and Moses, the substance of their private conversation, Jesus' reason for commanding silence about the vision until the rising of the Son of man, and his cryptic words about Elijah on the way down the mountain. It is hard not to identify with the befuddled disciples, who are likewise struggling to make sense of this incident (9:5–6, 10–11).

So our first clue that we should be reading LGM 1b as a deliberate enigma comes from the way we ourselves have been reading it. We are fascinated by its indeterminacies and strive to figure out what the private, nocturnal encounter depicts. LGM 1b and 2 have the same effect on readers that Frank Kermode documented with respect to Mark 14:51–52 and the references to the man in the Macintosh in James Joyce's *Ulysses*. To use Kermode's language, these verses produce fractures in the surface of the narrative; their "narrative elements" are difficult to construe "as part of a larger organization," so the human penchant "to prefer fulfillment to disappointment, the closed to the open" impels readers to find an explanation.[39]

Since LGM 1b is a deliberate enigma achieved through a Markan literary technique, it makes sense to search within the Markan narrative itself for clues to the puzzle of what LGM 1b represents. We can begin with the observation that many of its unexplained story elements echo phrases already used in the gospel. The author of canonical Mark frequently repeated phrases across many episodes as a way of encouraging his readers to perceive thematic relationships among otherwise unconnected incidents. The phrases in longer Mark that occur elsewhere in the story necessarily carry connotations that affect their meaning within LGM 1 and 2, just as their use within LGM 1 and 2 necessarily influences the meaning of these phrases elsewhere.

A detailed analysis of longer Mark's verbal echoes must wait until a later chapter. At this point it will suffice to note that many of the verbal echoes in LGM 1 have overtones of discipleship within the larger narrative. The phrase "and he began to beg him that he might be with him" (LGM 1:8), for instance, suggests that the young man wished to become a disciple (cf. Mark 3:14 and 5:18–20). The removal to a house followed by private teaching suggests that Jesus treated him as one (cf. Mark 7:17–23; 9:28–29, 33–50). The words "and after six days" (LGM 1:10) introduced the transfiguration and are associated with private, christological revelation to Jesus' closest disciples (9:2). The phrase "for he was teaching" is the same formula that introduced the second passion prediction (9:31), which was offered in secret to the disciples (9:30). "The mystery of the kingdom of God" is reserved for disciples and is what separates them from "those outside."

The persistent connection between the phrasing of LGM 1 and discipleship establishes a general interpretive framework for the unelaborated details given in 1b. But the key to making sense of these details as a consistent whole is the intercalation of Jesus' discourse with James and John, where Jesus likens his coming passion to a baptism and asks the sons of Zebedee whether they are able to undergo this experience (10:38–39). The framing of this dialogue within the story about the young man and his mother and sister encourages readers to interpret these two pericopae in light of each other. Those who detect a connection between the young man's unusual apparel and the sacramental imagery in Jesus' reply to James and John will likely infer that the young man has dressed for baptism; those who recognize that Jesus' cup and baptism are metaphors for his passion will likely infer that Jesus was teaching the young man that he must be "baptized with the baptism with which I am baptized" in order to share in Jesus' coming exaltation. This is an initiation into a deeper truth, a mystery. But it is not a rite. In the dramatic situation of the story, Jesus' baptism means his arrest, trial, and execution; accepting this baptism means undergoing a similar fate: "If any man would come after me, let him deny himself and take up his cross and follow me" (8:34). Accordingly, when we next see this young man, he is "following with" Jesus as Jesus is being led away to face trial, and he is dressed as if for baptism in what one might gather is his former burial sheet (cf. 15:46). The sheet signifies his readiness to be "immersed" in Jesus' sufferings and his recognition that the way to life is through death. "He has recognized that following this man will lead to death and has come suitably dressed for the occasion."[40]

## The Original Purpose and Later Use of LGM 1 and 2

The two additional passages Clement disclosed to Theodore significantly affect the meaning of at least two elusive themes in the canonical gospel. The mystery of the kingdom of God (4:11) is now directly associated with the central section's teachings on the necessity of following the example of Christ's selfless death (8:34–35; 10:38, 43–45). And the young man's inappropriate attire in Gethsemane now makes sense as a symbolic embodiment of this teaching and a commentary on the failure of the disciples as a whole. Like the young man, they desired to remain loyal to Jesus to the point of death (14:26–31, 51), but were not yet capable of accepting Jesus' "cup" and "baptism." So the author of LGM 1 and 2 is elucidating perplexing elements in Mark's story. The question of how this redaction affects the story will be addressed in detail in the literary-critical part of this investigation. At this point we need to ask an historical question. Why did this redactor do this?

Study of the way Matthew and Luke revised Mark has led scholars to envision redactors as persons intent on *changing* source material in order to make it serve a different situation or a different theology. Many scholars suppose that Matthew and Luke "were attempting not to clarify and extend Mark's vision but to refute and undermine it"—effectively, "to supplant it."[41] These evangelists used Mark and Q as "sources"; so, for instance, they both eliminated Mark 14:51–52 and reworked 4:11 in a way that limits the mystery of the kingdom of God to the individual mysteries conveyed by the parables of the kingdom. The redactor of the longer text, on the contrary, attempted to preserve the integrity of Mark's vision by expanding his story in a manner consistent with Markan theology and composition. Why did this redaction happen?

We can begin to answer this question by considering where and when this redaction took place. Four lines of evidence suggest that the longer gospel was produced in Alexandria: (1) the only reference we have to this gospel comes from an Alexandrian teacher; (2) outside of Alexandria, it was used by the followers of Carpocrates, another Alexandrian (*Strom*. III.2.5.1–2); (3) Clement's tradition about this gospel's origin affirms that it was written in Alexandria; and (4), unless Theodore's inquiry to Clement was entirely fortuitous, it seems that the Carpocratians either directed Theodore to inquire in Alexandria about the legitimacy of the longer gospel or told him their own version of how Mark created it in Alexandria. For the longer gospel to have been instrumental to Carpocrates, it must have been written before 125 CE.[42] A more precise dating must await the final chapter.

Any theory about why this text was written must be somewhat speculative, but the literary-critical analysis presented in part 2 of this study supports Clement's opinion that the author intended to create a more spiritual gospel, meaning a gospel that is more amenable to mystical exegesis. We have little information about Alexandrian Christianity before the third century, but we can be fairly certain that the Alexandrian penchant for uncovering esoteric theological truths within the scriptures was well established when longer Mark was composed. Even before Mark's time, a "mystical," mainly allegorical, method of exegesis was used in Alexandria by the Jewish writers Aristeas, Aristobulus, and Philo (ca. 20 BCE–50 CE).[43] The fact that this approach was also used by Clement in the late second century is significant, for it suggests that Alexandrian Christianity emerged from within the exceptionally large population of Jews in that city. The "Jewish character of earliest Christianity in Egypt" is now widely recognized.[44]

Philo's description of the Jewish monastic order called the Therapeutae in his *On the Contemplative Life* offers a portrait of an Egyptian form of Judaism that took a profound interest in the study of the figurative meanings of scripture:

> The whole interval, from morning to evening, is for them a time of exercise. For they read the holy Scriptures, and explain the philosophy of their fathers in an allegorical manner, regarding the written words as symbols of hidden truth which is communicated in obscure figures. They have also writings of ancient men, who were the founders of their sect, and who left many monuments of the allegorical method. These they use as models, and imitate their principles....They expound the Sacred Scriptures figuratively by means of allegories. For the whole law seems to these men to resemble a living organism, of which the spoken words constitute the body, while the hidden sense stored up within the words constitutes the soul. This hidden meaning has first

been particularly studied by this sect, which sees, revealed as in a mirror of names, the surpassing beauties of the thoughts. (cited in Eusebius, *Church History* II.17.10–11, 20)

It is unlikely that the earliest Christian communities in Alexandria paralleled the Therapeutae in terms of monasticism and extreme asceticism. But the way some of the educated Alexandrian Christians studied scripture may have been quite similar. As is well known, Eusebius was absolutely, albeit mistakenly, convinced that Philo was describing the community composed of Mark's first converts in Alexandria; Eusebius thought that the scriptures read by the Therapeutae were Christian gospels and letters and that the activities of this community were distinctive of the Christian way of life (*Church History* II.16; 17.12).

The longer gospel seems to be an adaptation of the Gospel of Mark to the distinctive thought-world and historical circumstances of Christians in Alexandria. It extends the theme introduced in Mark 4:10–12 that salvation (the ability to repent and be forgiven) is limited to "insiders" who manage to penetrate a mystery that is concealed in the gospel itself in passages that are meant to be read parabolically (i.e., allegorically, as in 4:14–20, or metaphorically, as in 4:26–32). At the same time, longer Mark reinforces the Markan theme that salvation does not come from deeper, spiritual insight itself but from what that insight leads one *to do*.[45] Once "initiated" into this philosophical mystery, a disciple must attempt to follow Jesus in the way to life through death, just as the young man attempted to do. Such a message would have been highly relevant in the context of Alexandrian Judaism in the aftermath of the Palestinian Jewish revolt of 66–70. Tension and conflict between the Jews and Greeks of this city increased after 70 and continued to build until 115, when the Jewish population in Egypt was nearly annihilated.[46]

Once it is perceived that the mystery-initiation imagery in the *Letter to Theodore* is strictly figurative—not only in the letter proper but also in LGM 1b itself—a new theory about the "use" of LGM 1 and 2 in the Alexandrian church of Clement's day presents itself. Christians advancing in gnosis probably would have viewed the private instruction in 1b as an example of Jesus transmitting the unwritten gnostic tradition to a worthy individual, which is to say, the first link in a long chain of transmission whereby "the hierophantic teaching of the Lord" (I.23–24) was passed down from teacher to student. Alexandrian Christians of the second century probably found in LGM 1b a divine precedent for the practice of teaching the most important esoteric doctrines privately to select individuals. That Clement used LGM 1 as justification for this practice is suggested by the way he used various sayings from Mark's parable discourse, where the mystery that Jesus taught the young man is introduced. Clement justified his esotericism with reference to Jesus' practice of concealing the mysteries from the masses by declaring them in parables, and Clement interpreted Mark's parable of the grain growing secretly in terms of the development of gnosis in a person who is properly instructed (*Strom*. I.2.3; I.12.56.2–3; VI.15.124.6–125.2, 126.2–3). Clement cited Matthew's plural form of Mark's expression "the mystery of the kingdom of God" together with the parable of the leaven to prove that "the truly sacred mystic word, respecting the unbegotten and his powers, ought to be concealed" (*Strom*. V.12.80.3). The context of this quotation suggests that Clement thought that "the mysteries of the kingdom of heaven" were in fact the great mysteries of theology, for he was discussing how God cannot be known or expressed in human terms. Finally, Clement used the phrase "to him who has will more be given" to justify imparting gnosis to those worthy of it, and the phrase "from him who has not will be taken away" to justify withholding truth from the unworthy (Mark 4:25 par; *Strom*. VII.10.55.7; *Letter to Theodore* II.16). Most likely, then, Clement thought that Jesus instructed the young man in the unwritten gnostic tradition, the subject matter of "the great mysteries."

The select individuals who attended readings of the longer text would likely have identified with the young man, since he, too, is a privileged recipient of esoteric instruction. Much as the young man is entering an exclusive group by being initiated into "the mystery of the kingdom of God" (the group called "those who were about [Jesus] with the twelve," who are contrasted with "those outside" in Mark 4:10–12), the hearers of this gospel were being initiated into "the great mysteries" of theology that ordinary Christians were not permitted to hear. The instruction of the young man would therefore have seemed to Alexandrian readers to figure their own efforts to cross the boundary between the simple faithful and the true gnostics through the study of "hierophantic" *logia* such as LGM 1 itself.

The possibility that Alexandrians of the second century saw in LGM 1b both a representation of, and rationalization for, their practice of imparting the secret doctrines to a few worthy individuals would not, of course, exhaust the meaning that LGM 1 and 2 had for its exegetes. They would have endeavoured to discern the actual teaching that Jesus gave the young man that evening. Clement probably conveyed his understanding of the secrets concealed within LGM 1 and 2 in his *Letter to Theodore*, for that would explain why the published letter breaks off rather abruptly where his exegesis begins. I would rather not guess what Clement found in LGM 1 and 2 using the highly arbitrary method of allegorical exegesis, although I suspect that the teachings he discerned in longer Mark are scattered and hidden throughout his *Stromateis* for careful readers to discern.

## Conclusions

The nocturnal encounter between Jesus and the young man contains baptismal imagery, but LGM 1b does not depict and legitimize a Christian ritual; it merely presupposes one. The intratextual associations underscored by longer Mark's use of suggestive narrative gaps, verbal echoes, and intercalation indicate that the young man's strange attire signifies his intention to be "baptized" in Jesus' suffering and death. The loss of this sheet signifies a failure in discipleship.

Once we relinquish the notion that LGM 1:11–12 depicts a real-life ritual, we eliminate the intractable problem of identifying one ritual that fits all the details yet is compatible with what we already know about Clement and the Alexandrian church. The letter tells us precisely how this gospel was used in Alexandria, but we have to pay attention to Clement's discussions of baptism, the (small and great) mysteries, perfection, gnosis, and the parabolic nature of scripture in order to understand it. In both the *Letter to Theodore* and LGM 1b, cultic imagery of initiation is used figuratively to convey the process of learning esoteric theological truths concealed within the scriptures, of crossing the boundary between an outsider, who possesses only the carnal sense, and an insider, who possesses the more essential spiritual meaning.[47] Within the Alexandrian church, LGM 1b may have been used to validate the practice of "initiating" a select few into the unwritten gnostic tradition through anagogical expositions of sacred texts. The longer text as a whole was especially amenable to such exposition and may have been composed to serve the interests of educated believers who expected to find esoteric truths concealed within the scriptures.

# ⪧ PART II ⪦

## Analysis of Markan Literary Techniques

# ❧6❧

# Longer Mark's Use of Intercalation

Clement's description of longer Mark as a "mystic" or "more spiritual gospel" suggests that the added passages focused not so much on the outer facts of Jesus' life (the "body" of the text) as on the inner theological significance (the "spirit"). To a careless or uninstructed reader, Mark's most profound mysteries remained concealed behind a literary veil. To those being initiated into the great mysteries, however, the proper *exposition* of its mystic passages (*logia*) disclosed esoteric theological teachings. We may never know how Clement interpreted the longer text because his "true interpretation" was excised from the *Letter to Theodore*. But as we began to see in the last chapter, LGM 1 and 2 guide their own interpretation by employing literary techniques used elsewhere in the gospel. In order to understand this more spiritual edition of Mark, we need to examine those literary techniques. Accordingly, the following three chapters each examine a distinctively Markan literary technique used in LGM 1 and 2 and describe its implications for the interpretation of the Markan gospel. Chapter 6 demonstrates that these two additions form an intercalation.[1] Chapter 7 shows that the raising miracle and the story of the open tomb form a "matched pair" that functions as an interpretative frame around Mark's passion narrative. And chapter 8 examines the effects of various brief repetitions within LGM 1 and 2 of language and themes that occur elsewhere in the gospel. The upshot of this analysis will surprise most scholars of Mark, many of whom insist that "There is no good reason to regard this expanded version of Mark as any less 'apocryphal' than the other gospels to which [Clement] accorded similar recognition":[2] LGM 1 and 2 are as Markan in a literary sense as they are in their vocabulary and phrasing, and they reinforce and elucidate the theology of the canonical gospel.

---

Notes to chapter 6 start on page 268

# The Formal Characteristics
## of Intercalation

Intercalation (also known as the Markan sandwich technique) is the narrative device of placing one episode (story or scene) within another, separate episode such that the completion of the first episode is delayed by the complete narration of the second episode. Commentators on Mark customarily note six "classic" examples of this procedure: Mark 3:20–35; 5:21–43; 6:7–30 (+ vv. 31–32?); 11:12–22 (+ vv. 23–25?); 14:1–11; 14:53–72.[3] The fact that most scholars label these six passages intercalations does not, however, mean that they agree on the nature and extent of this literary phenomenon. A variety of other passages have been deemed intercalations as well, because many scholars do not differentiate intercalation from similar framing techniques.[4] Some, for instance, confuse intercalations with interpolations, which are sayings or narrative comments (though not an entire pericope) that *on form-critical grounds* were not originally part of the passage in which they appear (e.g., Mark 1:23–26 within 1:21–28; 2:5b–10a within 2:1–12; 4:31b within 4:30–32).[5] Fortunately, a few scholars have attempted to define intercalation precisely by investigating what the six generally agreed upon examples have in common. Despite some disagreement over particular narrative features and literary effects, these studies offer general conclusions that can help us determine whether the addition of LGM 1 and 2 represents an instance of this technique, and, if so, how these verses make sense within this perspective.

James R. Edwards' definition of intercalation is a useful starting point: "Each Markan [intercalation] concerns a larger (usually narrative) unit of material consisting of *two* episodes or stories which are narrated in *three* paragraphs or pericopae. The whole follows an A¹-B-A² schema, in which the B-episode forms an independent unit of material, whereas the flanking A-episodes require one another to complete their narrative. The B-episode consists of only one story; it is not a series of stories, nor itself so long that the reader fails to link A² with A¹. Finally, A² normally contains an allusion at its beginning which refers back to A¹, e.g., repetition of a theme, proper nouns, etc."[6]

LGM 1 and 2 fit this scheme very well. In this case, the A¹-story is LGM 1, the B-story is the request of James and John, which culminates in a discipleship teaching (10:35–40, 41–45), and the A²-story is Mark 10:46 plus LGM 2. The latter has to be observed in context for the bracketing effect to become evident. The insertion of LGM 2 between the two clauses of Mark 10:46 produces an obvious repetition of the language introducing LGM 1:

> And they come to Bethany. And there was there a certain woman whose brother of hers had died. (LGM 1:1–2)

> And he comes to Jericho. And there were there the sister of the young man whom Jesus loved him... (Mark 10:46 plus LGM 2:1)

LGM 2 calls to mind LGM 1, much the way Mark 11:20–21 calls to mind the cursing of the fig tree after the intercalated clearing of the temple:

> On the following day, when they came from Bethany, he was hungry. And seeing in the distance a fig tree in leaf, he went to see if he could find anything on it. When he came to it, he found nothing but leaves... (Mark 11:12–13)

> As they passed by in the morning, they saw the fig tree withered away to its roots. And Peter remembered and said to him, "Master, look! The fig tree which you cursed has withered." (11:20–21)

By alluding to the penultimate incident, both the reference to "the sister of the young man whom Jesus loved" and the recollection of Jesus' curse form a bracket around an independent, intervening pericope. Moreover, both A²-stories are only three sentences long, and quickly shade into something else (the healing of Bartimaeus in Mark 10:46b–52; a discussion of faith and prayer in 11:22–25). In this respect LGM 2 also resembles Mark 6:30, a verse which briefly recalls the mission of the disciples then shades into the story of the feeding of the five thousand: "The apostles returned to Jesus, and told him all that they had done and taught. And he said to them, 'Come away by yourselves to a lonely place, and rest a while.' For many were coming and going." The A²-story in Mark 14:10–11 is likewise very brief. LGM 1 is exceptional, though, in that it is long for an A¹-story.[7]

Edwards' observation that the opening of an A²-story will allude to the A¹-story through the repetition of a theme or proper nouns may be supplemented with observations made by Tom Shepherd, whose doctoral thesis attempted to delineate the definition and function of intercalation: "Upon reentry into the outer story some tie is made to the previous section of the outer story. Also, a previously unmentioned character is introduced, or a new name is given to a group previously introduced in the first part of the outer story. This new character or newly named group is the subject/actor of the first or second sentence of the reentered outer story."[8] It is somewhat surprising to learn that a new or newly named character typically appears as the subject of one of the first two sentences of an A²-story, yet LGM 2:1b fits this criterion by introducing the young man's mother and Salome.

Shepherd further observed that the active characters in the outer story tend not to cross over into the inner story, and vice versa, with the exception of Jesus.[9] More specifically, he noticed that "the only characters to cross between the two stories are Jesus and the disciples" and that "the disciples' appearance in *both* stories of an intercalation (Mark 5 and 11) is limited to minor roles."[10] In longer Mark, the disciples play a major role in the B-story, so it is noteworthy that Clement's text of longer Mark 10:46a differs from most manuscripts of the canonical gospel by reading "and *he* comes into Jericho" rather than "and they come..." This difference curtails the sense of character crossover by removing what otherwise would be an indication that the disciples were involved in the $A^2$-story. Thus Jesus' arrival in Jericho and refusal to welcome the three women briefly re-establishes the sense of Jesus being apart from his disciples, which characterizes the $A^1$-story. When Jesus raises the young man in Bethany, the disciples disappear after they rebuke the bereaved sister and Jesus walks off in a huff. In other words, their foolish response provides an excuse for their remarkable absence during the subsequent week with the young man, and this absence provides a contrast with their active role in Mark 10:35–45. Thus LGM 1 and 2 fit the pattern of minimal active character crossover very well.

The lack of active character crossover between the A- and B-episodes of an intercalation reinforces the sense that the two stories are logically unconnected to each other, which in turn heightens the irony of their thematic parallels and contrasts.[11] Generally speaking, "Parallel actions are done by contrasting groups or contrasting actions are done by parallel groups in the two stories."[12] In this case, the young would-be disciple and the twelve form two parallel "groups" whose actions form a contrast. The young man demonstrates a desire to be obedient to Jesus' instruction; he shows his willingness to face death by putting on his former burial wrapping. Later on, when he shows up in Gethsemane, it is clear that he comprehends the requirement of drinking Jesus' cup and undergoing Jesus' baptism, even if he cannot meet it. James and John, on the other hand, claim to be willing to accept Jesus' fate (10:39), but only because they think a "Yes" response will win them positions of honour. As Jesus' response indicates, they do not know what they are asking (v. 38a), and their request for the best seats itself indicates a fundamental unwillingness to abandon self-concern. The indignant attitude of the ten likewise displays self-preoccupation, for they consider the private negotiation for places of honour to be unfair competition, or at least that seems to be implied by Jesus' ensuing teaching to the twelve that those who desire greatness must become servants and give their lives for others. Thus the juxtaposition of LGM 1 and Mark 10:35–45 highlights a contrast between the actions of parallel figures.

This contrast marks an interesting development in the depiction of minor characters in Mark's gospel. Joel F. Williams drew attention to the fact that in the canonical gospel, the minor characters who appear prior to Bartimaeus are primarily supplicants, exemplars of faith in Jesus' ability to heal and save. When Bartimaeus receives his sight, however, he responds by following Jesus "in the way." With Bartimaeus, the minor characters begin to "exemplify a proper devotion to the values of Jesus. In this way the reader is encouraged to move beyond faith in Jesus to a more faithful following of Jesus." "The reader, like the minor characters, must respond to the general call to follow Jesus through self-denial and a willingness to suffer (8.34)."[13] The transition marked by Bartimaeus in canonical Mark occurs one pericope earlier in longer Mark.

There is one notable area of difference between the defining characteristics discussed so far and the effect achieved by inserting LGM 1 and 2 into Mark's narrative. Whereas in the classic examples of intercalation "the flanking A-episodes require one another to complete their narrative," this is not really the case with the LGM additions. There is no clear reason why LGM 1 should not be considered complete in itself, for LGM 2 is unnecessary *as a conclusion* for LGM 1. This is very different from the raising of Jairus's daughter in Mark 5:35–43, for instance, which remained to be carried out after the healing of the woman with the hemorrhage.

The intercalation in Mark 5:21–43, however, could be called an ideal example of Edwards' point. When all the intercalations are considered, this difference between LGM 1 and 2 and the classic intercalations turns out to be one of degree rather than of kind. Some of the other A[1]-stories offer only vague indications that something remains to occur for the A-story to be complete. For instance, Mark did not need to narrate the return of the disciples from their mission. Their return could have been left as a gap which the reader would fill in once the disciples are reintroduced as being with Jesus again (cf. Matt 12:1, where the disciples suddenly reappear after being sent out on mission). Likewise, the only thing that makes the A[1]-story of the cursing of the fig tree incomplete in 11:12–14 is the comment that follows Jesus' curse: "And his disciples heard it." That comment merely indicates that something more *might* come of this.

LGM 2 is also slightly atypical inasmuch as it *resumes* the A[1]-story but does not complete it; the young man's story continues through his reappearances in Gethsemane and inside the open tomb (14:51–52; 16:5–7). But again, this distinctive quality is not without parallel in the classic examples. In 14:1–2, the motif of the plotting of the chief priests leads only to Judas's taking a first step toward betraying Jesus (negotiating with the chief priests). Moreover, the plotting of these religious leaders did not begin here. That theme is a carry-over from 12:12 (cf. 11:18) and began with the Pharisees and Herodians as early as 3:6. What we have in 14:1–2, 10–11 is the resumption of a subplot, not a self-contained story. That subplot does not end until Jesus is convicted. Likewise, the story of Peter's denial, within which the trial is intercalated, is part of a subplot that began in 14:26–31 with Jesus' prediction of this occurrence. That subplot ends with Peter's rehabilitation as a disciple, which is projected to occur after the gospel's ending (16:7).

It is inadequate, then, to say that the A[1]-story is always obviously incomplete without the A[2]-story or that the A[2]-story always brings the A[1]-story to completion. Tom Shepherd supplied a more refined description of what Edwards was getting at in reference to completeness when he wrote that "There is a unique pattern of focalization and defocalization of the two stories which includes incomplete defocalization of the outer story at the point where break away occurs to the inner story. This creates a 'gap' for the outer story across the inner story."[14] The defocalization of the A[1]-story is "never complete." "Something is 'left hanging' across the inner story's telling."[15]

The defocalization at the close of LGM 1 is incomplete inasmuch as the ending brings no resolution to the many questions the narration has produced; we do not even know what went on that last evening. The abrupt reference to Jesus getting up to go to the other side of the Jordan only aggravates our curiosity about the ritualistic details, leaving us to wonder what is to come of the would-be disciple now that he has undergone this "ritual" initiation.

Be that as it may, there is still a real difference. The feature of incomplete defocalization of the A[1]-story is intimately related to a widely recognized effect of intercalation: the impression that the two stories are occurring simultaneously. Mark creates the impression that something that began in A[1] is still going on while B is being narrated. It is important to stress that the concept of simultaneity—or what Shepherd calls "an ellipsis of the outer story [that] crosses the inner story"[16]—does not mean that the events narrated in the A- and B-stories are portrayed as happening at the same time.[17] The *narrated* events are consecutive. In some of these stories Jesus appears in both the A- and B-stories, and he cannot be in different places doing different things at the same time (e.g., 3:20–35; 5:21–43; and 11:12–25). Similarly, the mission of the disciples mentioned in 6:13 is the cause of Herod's and the others' speculations about Jesus in 6:14–16, so the B-episode does not begin simultaneously with the beginning of A[1] where Jesus calls the twelve and commissions them. Only in the trial scene might one feel that the two stories overlap in time, for there is no "carry over" of Jesus across into the story of Peter.[18] Thus it seems that Jesus' fearless confession that he is the messiah is happening at the same time as Peter's cowardly disavowal of Jesus.

The impression that something mentioned in A[1] is still continuing while the B-story is being narrated is produced in differing degrees in Mark's intercalations. A reader will certainly perceive that Jesus' journey to Jairus's house is going on while Jesus becomes entangled with the woman who touched his garment. And in the narrative in which Jesus' relatives[19] set out to take control of Jesus, we realize when they arrive outside his door that they had been travelling to his house while Jesus was debating with the scribes from Jerusalem (the B-story). But the sense of simultaneity is not particularly strong in 3:20–35, and it exists to an even lesser degree in the other examples. The element of simultaneity in 14:1–11 is limited to the impression that the chief priests and the scribes were still conspiring while Jesus was being anointed. Judas's decision to go to them furthers this conspiracy (vv. 10–11), but was not caused by it, since there is no indication that Judas knew what the authorities were doing in 14:1–2. The death of John the Baptist is not presented as if it occurred while the disciples were on their mission, though Herod's reaction likening Jesus to John is simultaneous with this mission and to some extent a consequence of it. And although the withering of the fig tree is made to correlate with the clearing of the temple, there is no suggestion that the tree was withering concurrently with this demonstration, for Peter discovers the withered tree on the following morning, not in the evening when Jesus and his disciples left the city after the incident in the temple (11:19–20).

Bearing in mind that the element of simultaneity is fairly weak in some of the intercalations, it is still noteworthy that this impression is produced only retrospectively in the LGM intercalation, when the reader realizes that the young man's female relatives now wish to meet Jesus. The A[1]-story does not prepare us to expect this, nor does the lack of resolution to our questions about what was going on that evening translate into a sense that the young man's story is still "going on" in addition to being unresolved. Thus the LGM intercalation does not conform well to the criterion that something relating to the A[1]-story is still going on while the B-story is happening. LGM 2 merely *resumes* the storyline begun in LGM 1. There is no distinct indication that something that had begun earlier carried on through the B-narrative.

The lack of any indication that LGM 1 is still going on while the incident with James and John is occurring is in part a result of the type of narrative involved: LGM 1 consists of a complete miracle story with an attached episode of private teaching. With the exception of 6:7–13, the A[1]-stories in Mark are better classified as *introductions* to stories than as complete stories in themselves. The nearest point of comparison would be Mark 11:1–11, viewed as the initial A[1]-story of a triple intercalation:[20]

| Temple   | 11:1–11   | 11:15–19   | 11:27–12:12 |
|----------|-----------|------------|-------------|
| Fig tree |           | 11:12–14   | 11:20–25    |

Mark 11:1–11 relates the messianic procession to Jerusalem (vv. 1–10) and Jesus' inspection of the temple (v. 11). Together, these events are related in an almost allegorical fashion to the action in 11:12–14 of Jesus approaching the leafy fig tree and inspecting it for fruit. That is, 11:12–14, read as a B-story, provides a symbolic commentary on what was happening in 11:1–11: the messiah arrived at Jerusalem and took note of the "barren" or "fruitless" activities going on in the temple, which he then denounced in 11:15–19. When conceived of as an A²-story, the clearing of the temple gives substance to the condition of unrighteousness symbolized by the barren tree (11:17). So the more familiar intercalation of the clearing of the temple within the cursing of the fig tree is part of a larger structure of overlapping intercalations beginning with the procession to Jerusalem. This structure arguably spans from 11:1 to 12:12, for the clearing of the temple can also be viewed as the A¹-story of a third overlapping intercalation focusing on the religious leaders' plot against Jesus. Their wish to destroy Jesus is expressed at the close of his demonstration in the temple (11:18), and their initial attempt to confront him about this demonstration occurs immediately after the intercalated discovery of the withered fig tree (which in this case functions as a B-story). The dispute in 11:27–33 over Jesus' authority to do "these things" is intimately connected with 12:1–12, which extends Jesus' evasive response to include an indirect answer "in parables." Jesus' parable of the wicked tenants resumes the theme of the messiah (the vineyard owner's "beloved son") coming to Jerusalem for the purpose of "reaping fruit" (12:2, 6), setting Jesus' violent actions against the temple and fig tree within a broader scheme of God's relations with his people Israel; the messiah is the last in a long line of prophetic messengers sent by God to reap the fruit of righteousness. This third intercalation elaborates the nature of the antipathy between Jesus and Jerusalem's religious leaders, implying that they are responsible for the unrighteousness manifested in the temple courtyard and symbolized by the barren fig tree. Missing figs (11:13) and withheld grapes (12:2–8) are interchangeable symbols of unrighteousness in Mark, as they are in both Mic 7:1 and Jer 8:13. The plot of the religious authorities that frames the story of the discovery of the withered tree will again be the content of the A-stories in 14:1–11.

When the structure of 11:1–12:12 is viewed as a triple intercalation, we have two new A¹-stories. Like LGM 1, the first is in two parts (11:1–10, 11) and is basically complete in itself. As with LGM 1, the reader wonders what exactly is happening at the conclusion of Mark 11:1–11, but this pericope lacks clear anticipation of its A$^2$-story (the clearing of the temple); the impression that Jesus blasts the fig tree while he is on his way to the temple to address a problem he witnessed the previous day (11:11) emerges only in retrospect of the clearing. This triple intercalation also shows that Mark's bracketing techniques can defy strict classification, since there is a certain fluidity in his use of such devices. The triple sandwich in 11:1–12:12 could alternatively be described as a single intercalation (11:12–25) framed by two stories that narrate the messiah's arrival in Jerusalem in search of "fruit" (11:1–11; 11:27–12:12). Or the whole structure could be described more simply as a chiasm (A, B, C, B′, A′).

To summarize at this point, the structure produced by the addition of LGM 1 and 2 to Mark 10 exhibits many of the defining features of an intercalation. Its A$^2$-story uses repetition to cause the reader to recollect A$^1$. The B-story is basically a single episode (i.e., a "paragraph" or "pericope"), complete in itself and independent of the A-stories. There is minimal active character crossover between the stories, and the actions of parallel characters are contrasted.

The longer gospel intercalation differs from the norm inasmuch as the A$^1$-story set in Bethany does not seem to be continuing through the narration of the request of James and John. At most, the reader will have a sense that not everything has been said concerning the young man and might still be wondering about the nocturnal encounter while reading Mark 10:35–45. The A$^1$-story, moreover, is longer than usual because it is a complete (miracle) story, not merely an introduction. In this respect the LGM intercalation has affinities to paired frame-stories, which are complete pericopae that form interpretative brackets without creating an impression of simultaneity. Mark 11:1–11, viewed as the first A$^1$-story of a triple intercalation, is a useful point of comparison for LGM 1, for it, too, is a lengthy, basically complete pericope that leaves no element continuing during the succeeding B-episode, the cursing of the fig tree.

LGM 1 and 2 plus Mark 10:35–45 is not, therefore, a perfect example of intercalation, but neither are any of the classic examples. The existing definitions of intercalation describe ideal features and effects that are not evident in all six instances; Markan intercalation might be better construed as a syndrome in the sense that each "case" noticeably resembles the others but no case manifests all of the possible "symptoms." Thus the failure of LGM 1 and 2 to match type in one important respect does not disqualify this structure as an instance of this device, the more so since, as we have already seen, the arrangement does fulfill the most important function of an intercalation: the A-story and the B-story clearly reflect back upon each other as mutually interpretative.

# The Hermeneutical Significance
## of Intercalation

We have arrived at the most important feature of intercalation—its mutually interpretative function. During the 1960s and 1970s redaction critics came to realize that "Mark sandwiches one passage into the middle of another with an intentional and discernible *theological purpose*."[21] In the 1980s and 1990s, literary critics pointed out that "the two related stories illuminate and enrich each other, commenting on and clarifying the meaning, one of the other."[22] Robert M. Fowler compared the relation between the B-story and the A-story to a picture and its frame: "The intercalated episodes…frequently contain so many verbal echoes of each other that the reader can scarcely fail to take up the implicit invitation to read the framed episode in the light of the frame episode and vice versa."[23] The indication that the outer and inner stories reciprocally illuminate each other is found in their common or contrasting features, which include theologically significant words and interrelated motifs.[24] The two stories are logically independent, involving mainly different characters and taking place in different locations; nevertheless, the parallels highlighted by their formal juxtaposition imply that some deeper connection exists between them. These contacts are mostly unapparent to the characters, for the interrelations emerge through the narrator's arrangement of the details and commentary upon them, which are apparent only to the reader. The reader tries to make sense of these similar or contrasting elements by treating them metaphorically and seeking to discover a pattern of meaning or occult configuration beneath the "surface" of the stories. Because the reader is enabled to perceive connections that the characters cannot, this literary technique produces dramatic irony: the characters have no inkling of the meaning that their encounters with Jesus have for the audience.

That a deeper, coherent meaning can be produced by the device is clearest in the overlapping intercalations in chapter 11, whose provocative similarities suggest to the reader that the successive incidents are thematically connected at a symbolic level. In this case, Mark used similar stories to develop different aspects of the same theme. The procession to Jerusalem with its anticlimactic inspection of the temple, the morning walk to Jerusalem and inspection of the fig tree, and the vineyard owner's sending of his beloved son to get some of the produce of the vineyard are all different ways of expressing the idea that the messiah ("beloved son") has come to Jerusalem expecting to find righteousness among God's people. The cursing and withering of the fig tree, the overturning of tables and seats in the temple, and the destruction of the tenants of the vineyard are different ways of expressing the com-

ing destruction of the temple and its caretakers (Jerusalem's religious aristocracy) for perpetually withholding the "fruit" of righteousness. This meaning
is apparent to the reader more so than to any character in the story (except,
presumably, Jesus), because only the reader has this vantage on the events.
The next best example of the mutually interpretative function of Markan
intercalation within canonical Mark is the instance in 5:21–43, though there
is considerably less agreement among scholars over how to interpret this
sandwich. The common conviction that these two miracle stories interpret one
another is based on the strong parallels of similarities and contrasts. The
recipients of these miracles are both female and called "daughter" (5:23, 34),
though the little girl with a rich family contrasts with the lone woman who
spent all that she had on doctors; both females have become permanent
sources of defilement; and the number twelve is prominent in both stories
(5:25, 42), as are the themes of faith (5:34, 36) and "being saved" (5:23, 28).
Yet the deeper significance of these enticing connections is far from obvious,
and the same applies for the remaining intercalations.

The LGM intercalation, however, is as straightforward and striking an
example of mutually interpretative stories as that found in Mark 11. LGM 1
and Mark 10:35–45 are thematically linked through the imagery of death
and ritual initiation. The young man is brought back from the dead, and
after a period of six days he presents himself to Jesus dressed as if for a rite
of initiation. James and John are taught that in order to receive positions of
honour they must be prepared to drink Jesus' cup and be baptized with his
baptism. These words allude to the rites of baptism and Eucharist but are being
used figuratively to connote sharing in Jesus' death. If the two stories interpret each other, then the linen sheet worn by the young man is easily viewed
as a baptismal garment.

When LGM 1 and Mark 10:35–45 are viewed as mutually interpretative,
the mystery of the kingdom of God in LGM 1:12 is illuminated as the discipleship teaching that one saves one's life by losing it. When we recognize
this, we understand why a young man appears in Gethsemane wearing only
a linen sheet, and attempts to "follow with" Jesus at the moment when Jesus
begins to "drink" his cup (cf. 14:35–36). The young man seeks to enter
Jesus' glory (10:37) by being "baptized" in suffering and death, and is therefore attempting, albeit briefly, to do what James and John said they could do—
now that they and the other disciples have run away. The intelligibility of the
young man's attire in light of the baptismal metaphor in 10:38–39 is good
evidence that the author of LGM 1 and 2 was aware of the mutually interpretative function of this Markan bracketing device.

## Excursus on the Relevance of Intercalation to the Question of the Authenticity of the *Letter to Theodore*

The strong likelihood that the author of LGM 1 and 2 was aware of the mutually elucidating function of Markan intercalation has important implications for the authenticity of the *Letter to Theodore*, for this function of intercalation was not widely recognized by biblical scholars before the 1980s.[25] Until very recently, discussions of this device concentrated more on its relevance to the meaning and redaction history of particular passages than on the nature of the phenomenon itself and were limited to parenthetical remarks or footnotes. At present, only a handful of studies have carefully examined intercalation as a subject in its own right, by analyzing the literary effects of select examples. The first dissertation on this technique was written in 1985; since then one other dissertation and a few articles have been produced.[26]

Those who have traced the evolution of the scholarly discussion have pointed out that Mark's tendency to put one story inside another was first recognized to have a narrative function by von Dobschütz in 1928, who noted its utility in creating the illusion of time passing (esp. 6:7–30) or of distance being traversed (esp. 5:21–43).[27] In the case of 14:53–72, however, von Dobschütz perceived that intercalation functions to create the appearance, not of time passing, but of simultaneity.[28] He also reasoned that Mark sometimes put one story inside another story so that the beginning of the outer story would anticipate developments that would occur after the intervening episode or as a way of anticipating later intercalations.[29] And he recognized that intercalation could be used as a means of suggesting an internal connection between two stories (e.g., 3:20–35).[30]

Following von Dobschütz's study, the dominant impression among scholars was that the device was used to create or heighten the sense of time passing between the start of the first story and its resolution.[31] The idea that this device was used by Mark to manipulate the sense of narrative time remained the dominant perspective through the 1960s, though infrequently other aspects of von Dobschütz's discussion appeared in the comments of some authors during this period. E. Klostermann noted in 1950 that the device brings related stories together, and T.A. Burkill observed in 1963 that the technique draws attention to parallels or contrasts in the two episodes.[32] Burkill came close to conscious realization that one story provides hints for the interpretation of the other when he wrote that "Israel stands under the curse of the Messiah…because it failed to bring forth the fruit which one would naturally have expected of a privileged people." As with a number of other scholars, his impression that the cursed fig tree represents an indictment of Israel depended more on his understanding of Luke's parable of "the unproductive fig tree" (13:6–9) than on his awareness of how intercalation causes two stories to illuminate each other.[33]

The earliest reference I found to the mutually interpretative function of this device appeared in a 1953 article by C.H. Bird, an early proponent of Mark's authorial creativity.[34] In this unconventional article Bird mentioned the "Marcan parenthesis" of the temple clearing and cursed fig tree, and noted that the former "should be regarded as elucidating and elucidated by" the latter, adding that this is a "function of a Marcan parenthesis."[35] He extended this insight to the intercalation in Mark 5 as well (he mentioned the one in chapter 3, but did not offer an interpretation).[36] Apart from his interpretations of the intercalations in chapters 11 and 5, Bird's comments about the nature of the device did not extend much beyond what I just quoted.

Bird's understanding of intercalation was uncharacteristic of scholarship in the 1950s, and by 1960 only a few authors had begun to view the device the same way. A progression can be traced from year to year in the commentaries. Sherman E. Johnson (1960) did not see any significance to the device beyond its ability to suggest the passing of time, an effect which he detected only in Mark 5, 6, and 11. Johnson almost perceived more when he wrote, "The cleansing of the Temple and the night, spent presumably in Bethany, provide the necessary lapse of time for the fig tree to be withered. Mark's connexion of this with the cleansing of the Temple is deliberate."[37] Johnson said nothing more about the connection. The closest Philip Carrington came to appreciating this device in his 1960 commentary was his comment, with respect to Mark 14:1–11, that "We recognize immediately a typical specimen of the 'split lection' or interlocking technique of Mark, by which one narrative is enfolded within another so as to add to the suspense and drama of the situation; Mark's characteristic treatment of his material makes the evil designs of the priesthood and the treachery of the trusted disciple a dark background for the romantic story of the anointing."[38] Carrington did not mention the technique in any of his discussions of the other classic examples. Paul S. Minear (1962) noticed that the insertion of the temple cleansing within the fig tree story indicated that Mark saw a "connection" between the two.[39] But he did not see any such significance in the other examples, apart from 14:1–11, concerning which he noted a sharp contrast between the woman and the conspiring religious leaders, and 14:53–72, wherein he perceived a twin trial of Jesus and Peter full of fascinating contrasts (though he said nothing about one story being within the other).[40] Denis Nineham (1963) reasoned that in 5:21–43, 6:7–30, and 14:1–11 "time [is] being…given for the initial action to develop," but he did see a symbolic purpose to 11:12–25, which he explicitly attributed to the device, without explaining how it achieves this effect (he noted the parable of the fig tree in Luke 13:6–9).[41] In the same year, though, Etienne Trocmé stated "There is an obvious relationship between the mysterious episode of the barren fig-tree and that of the cleansing of the Temple (11.15–19) which is sandwiched into it. Whatever meaning is to be attributed to Jesus' attitude to the tree…, it is clear that the curse cast on it and its miraculous effectiveness are designed in Mark to explain the significance of the brutal cleansing of the Temple."[42] In a footnote he added, "It is frequent in Mark for a story to be related in two parts, between which comes a passage relating to some quite different episode. In such a case, even if the conection [sic] between the two is not clear, Mark endeavours to explain one with the help of the other." He then listed all six of the classic examples. He referred to the device as an "elementary…literary technique."[43]

It was during the second half of the 1960s and the 1970s that a sizeable number of scholars came to appreciate intercalation as a device that permits stories to be mutually interpretative. Yet this perspective only began to dominate in the 1980s. As late as 1979, Frank Kermode had to deal with a variety of misconceptions about intercalation, referring often to Howard Clark Kee's 1977 study *Community of the New Age*.[44] Kee's lack of precision in defining the device was typical of scholarship on this subject in the mid-1970s. He lumped the intercalated stories together with the interpolated stories (i.e., 2:1–5a, 5b–10a, 10b–12; 3:1–3, 4–5a, 5b–6) and was unable to detect any consistency in Mark's use of the device.[45] Similar confusion is not uncommon today.[46]

James R. Edwards suggested that this slow evolution in the way scholars understood intercalation paralleled the evolution of the idea that Mark was not just a compiler of traditions but also a creative author.[47] The notion that Mark brought his materials into conformity with a theological agenda did not take hold until the 1970s. Interest in intercalation as a reflection of Mark's theological interests emerged through the efforts of certain redaction critics to refine their criteria for determining where Mark had modified his traditions. In 1965, Ernest Best discussed the device as evidence of Mark's hand. He recognized that the temple/fig tree episode is mutually interpretative, and he came close to applying the same logic to the intercalation of the death of John the Baptist within the mission of the disciples.[48] Robert H. Stein suggested in 1969 that "A Markan redaction history can only be ascertained from a 'sandwich' if in some way the inserted pericope interprets or is interpreted by the pericope into which it is inserted."[49] Stein was interested in this mutually interpretative function as a criterion of Markan redaction, not for what it indicates of Markan technique. His own conclusion was that only 3:20–35 and 11:12–25 had mutually interpretative elements. In 1972, Frans Neirynck classified intercalation as an instance of the pervasive "duality" that characterizes Mark's composition. Neirynck at that time likewise offered no elaboration, only a list.[50]

As far as I can tell, John R. Donahue's 1973 book *Are You the Christ?* offered the first systematic exploration of the idea that "There is a dialectical relationship between the inserted material and its framework whereby the stories serve to interpret each other."[51] This idea is now commonplace among Markan scholars, though it was still in need of demonstration when Edwards wrote his 1989 article, partly because only a few of the six classic examples can clearly be shown to work this way (a point that is not generally conceded).

Longer Mark's additions around Mark 10:35–45 reflect a comprehension of Markan compositional technique that was barely evident in the secondary literature a decade after the *Letter to Theodore* was discovered and was not widely appreciated until two decades later, when gospel scholars began to take an interest in literary theory. This strongly suggests that the letter was not created by a modern scholar. The most important books on the Gospel of Mark at the time the letter surfaced—Vincent Taylor's commentary (1952) and Willi Marxsen's pioneering effort in Markan redaction criticism (1956)—aptly illustrate how ill-prepared scholars were in the 1950s to identify and decipher Mark's literary techniques.[52] This is especially true of the manuscript's discoverer, Morton Smith, whose unMarkan and strangely historicizing interpretation of LGM 1 and 2 led a half dozen reviewers to characterize him as a nineteenth-century rationalist.[53] Like most scholars, Smith did not appreciate the figurative nature of the imagery of initiation in either the letter or the gospel quotations. Indeed, prior to Frank Kermode's 1979 study *The Genesis of Secrecy*, it did not occur to scholars to read LGM 1 and 2 as *episodes in a story*, which is the essential first step toward an appreciation of the literary techniques used in these quotations. So if we agree that LGM 1 and 2 form a typically Markan intercalation, then we can rule out a modern origin for the *Letter to Theodore*.

# ⊰ 7 ⊱

# Longer Mark's Use of
# Framing Stories

Intercalation is not the only Markan framing device employed by the author of LGM 1 and 2. By adding these fifteen verses he managed to situate the final (Jerusalem) section of the gospel between two strikingly similar raising miracles. These stories share many distinctive features. Both take place at rock-hewn tombs. Both draw attention to a stone cover and its removal from the door of the tomb. And both narrate movements into and out from the tomb. In the first story Jesus rolls away the stone himself and, upon entering, raises an unnamed young man. In the second story three women followers of Jesus are wondering who will roll the stone from the door of his tomb, and, upon entering the open tomb, find an unnamed young man who tells them that Jesus has risen from the dead. The verbal contacts are quite close:

> …Jesus <u>rolled</u> <u>the stone</u> from <u>the door of the tomb,</u> <u>and going into</u> immediately where the <u>young man</u> was…<u>going out</u> from <u>the tomb</u>… (LGM 1:6–7, 9)

> "Who will <u>roll</u> for us <u>the stone</u> from <u>the door of the tomb</u>?"…<u>And going into</u> the tomb they saw a <u>young man</u>…<u>going out</u> they fled from <u>the tomb</u>. (Mark 16:3, 5, 8)

The underlined words indicate where both passages use the same Greek words. Two different words meaning "from" (ἀπό and ἐκ) appear in both narratives, but their orders are reversed, so they are not in parallel.

More notable still is the presence in LGM 1 and 2 of words that occur in the canonical gospel only in Mark 14:51–52 and 15:40–16:8. The words "young man" (LGM 1:7, 8, 9, 10; 2:1) and "having put on" (LGM 1:11) occur only in 14:51 and 16:5. "Linen sheet" (LGM 1:11) is used only in 14:51 and 15:46. "Naked body" (LGM 1:11) appears only in 14:51. And "Salome"

---

Notes to chapter 7 start on page 271

(LGM 2:1) occurs only in Mark 15:40 and 16:1. Interestingly, the references to a young man never give his name but always describe what he had "put on." In LGM 1:11 he had put on linen of unspecified form—presumably a sheet wrapped into a sleeveless tunic. In 14:51 he has again put on a linen sheet, which he loses in a panic to escape (the women, too, run away in 16:8). In 15:46 Jesus' corpse is wrapped in a linen sheet, whereas the young man in the tomb has put on a white robe. Like the open tomb story, LGM 2:1 includes a grouping of three women, the last of whom is Salome, a character not found in the other canonical gospels. Finally, there is a reference in 10:32 and 16:5–8 to Jesus "going before" his "frightened" and "amazed" followers (the same three verbs are used). In the former verse, Jesus is going before his disciples on the way from Galilee to Jerusalem; in the latter verses, he is reported to be going before them from Jerusalem back to Galilee.

Clearly, many themes from the end of Mark's story now occur together at an earlier point in the longer gospel. All of these derive from the longer gospel's additions except the image of Jesus going before his frightened and amazed followers. Examination of this specific repetition will reveal that a literary "bracket" or *inclusio* already existed at this point in the canonical gospel. This bracket around the passion narrative is enhanced by the verbal parallels provided by the longer gospel. In longer Mark we find a story about Jesus raising a young man in a tomb as he leads his followers to Jerusalem and a story about this same young man appearing in Jesus' tomb, announcing Jesus' own resurrection and the message that Jesus is leading his followers back to Galilee. Thus, in longer Mark a relatively inconspicuous *inclusio* is supplanted by a more conspicuous pair of framing stories, which enhance the presence and effect of the canonical bracket.[1]

## What Constitutes an *Inclusio*?

The word *inclusio* refers to bracketing repetitions of words or phrases. Joanna Dewey offered a useful definition of the device: "The repetition of the same word or phrase at or near the beginning and ending of some unit, a sentence, a pericope, or a larger section. The form of the word need not be repeated exactly. For instance, one might find a noun and a verb from the same root. Inclusio is by definition an indication of structure, the beginning and end of a rhetorical unit of any size. It is a recognized technique of oral literatures. So the rhetorical critic by designating certain repetitions as inclusios is making a judgment about the limits of some unit of narrative."[2] Commonly noted examples of *inclusio* in Mark are the repetition of "gospel" in 1:1 and 1:14–15, which brackets the prologue, and the parallel phrases "and he taught them many things in parables" in 4:2 and "and with many such parables he spoke the word to them" in 4:33, which mark the start and finish of the parable discourse. Strictly speaking, *inclusio* refers to repeated words or phrases, not to larger units such as pericopae. But the repetition of similar pericopae can have a comparable effect, provided the repetitions bracket a distinct section of a story. Repetitions of that sort are sometimes called framing stories or matched pairs.

Dewey's point that *inclusio*s demarcate the beginning and end of a "section" of related materials is sometimes overlooked. The device indicates to the reader that there is a particular unity to the included material, that it can be understood as a discrete section. This information guides the reader's comprehension, by requiring him or her to recognize the unity. Consequently, not every repetition of words or similar stories creates an *inclusio* or frame—only those that bracket related material. For instance, the very similar stories of Jesus healing a deaf man (7:32–37) and a blind man (8:22–26) do not seem to enclose materials that have some unified quality or feature that sets them apart from the adjacent materials as a section. Neither do the two feeding miracles (6:32–44; 8:1–10). But both of these sets of repetitions may be considered components within a larger section that emphasizes the disciples' inability to comprehend who Jesus is, which is bracketed by narratives offering opinions on that very question (6:14–16; 8:27–30).[3] If the intervening material cannot be comprehended as a unit, the repetitions should not be viewed as either framing or delimiting.

The two accounts of Jesus healing a blind man (8:22–26; 10:46–52) exemplify Mark's use of framing stories. The enclosed material is thematically and structurally related: along with other more or less relevant passages, it consists of three cycles of discipleship material. The section as a whole depicts Jesus' journey from the villages near Caesarea Philippi to Jerusalem. Before this section comes Jesus' itinerant mission based in Galilee, and after it, Jesus' activities in and around Jerusalem. The story of Peter's "confession" (8:27–30), which follows the healing of the first blind man, is the central turning point of the story, the *peripeteia*; it marks a significant transition in the disciples' understanding of who Jesus is.

## Do Mark 10:32 and 16:7-8 Create an *Inclusio*?

It is an often-made but seldom-explored suggestion that the dynamics of Jesus' "going before" (προάγων) his disciples back to Galilee following his resurrection (16:7) can be elucidated by the way Mark used this verb in 10:32.

Both passages conjure an image of Jesus going before his disciples then depict his followers' cowardly fear (ἐφοβοῦντο):

> Now they were in the way, going up to Jerusalem, and Jesus was going before them; and they were amazed, while those who followed were afraid. (10:32)

> "But go, tell his disciples and Peter that he is going before you to Galilee; there you will see him, as he told you." And they went out and fled from the tomb; for trembling and astonishment had come upon them; and they said nothing to any one, for they were afraid. (16:7–8)

The disciples and the frightened followers are in both cases separate groups. Mark 10:32 distinguishes the disciples, who were amazed, from "those who followed," who were afraid.[4] Likewise, at the empty tomb, the disciples are the intended recipients of the message that Jesus is going before them, but it is a group of three women who react fearfully. These three women were introduced as persons who "were following him" in Galilee and who "came up with him to Jerusalem" (15:40–41)—a reminiscence of "going up to Jerusalem" in 10:32, 33. Hence in both 10:32 and 16:8, the fear belongs to a category of followers distinct from the twelve, a feature which strengthens the connection between the two passages. This separate group of disciples apparently represents anyone who would heed the call narrated at 8:34: "And he called to him the multitude with his disciples, and said to them, 'If any man would come after me, let him deny himself and take up his cross and follow me.'" The expression "those who followed" is similar to "those who were about him with the twelve" in 4:10. This broader group of disciples is one with which the reader can identify. The failure of the women to deliver the young man's message forces the reader to consider what she or he will do: follow courageously or turn away. ✗

The likelihood that Mark constructed an interpretative bracket around the passion narrative increases when we consider that the passion prediction attached to 10:32 itself summarizes the whole intervening sequence through a compendium of the most theologically relevant things that will happen to Jesus. Mark 10:33–34 functions as a dramatic program note for the remainder of the story: "Behold, we are going up to Jerusalem; and the Son of man will be delivered to the chief priests and the scribes, and they will condemn him to death, and deliver him to the Gentiles; and they will mock him, and spit upon him, and scourge him, and kill him; and after three days he will rise." This list stretches from the present action of going up to Jerusalem to the reality mentioned in 16:6 of Jesus' rising from the dead, which is to say, everything between 10:32 and 16:7. This last passion prediction is the one that situates the Son of man's sufferings in the context of a trial in Jerusalem.

Before this point Jesus has not explained where they are going and how his death will come about. Mark 10:33–34 thus sets the agenda for the Jerusalem section of the story.

The Jerusalem section begins with Jesus' ride on a colt up to Jerusalem. The fact that that story starts at 11:1 may seem to count against the possibility that 10:32 has a bracketing function. However, as Mary Ann Tolbert noted, ancient rhetoricians believed that smoother narration resulted when divisions within a narrative "overlap...at the edges": "The tendency to supply linking words or phrases, often but not always indicative of major themes, close to the end of one division and near the beginning of the next is a very common rhetorical practice. It serves to alert the reader to the shift in material while at the same time smoothing the transition."[5] The hope of deliverance conveyed in the words "Blessed is he who comes in the name of the Lord! Blessed is the kingdom of our father David that is coming!" (11:9–10) is anticipated in Bartimaeus's plea "Son of David, have mercy on me!" in the pericope that precedes this procession (10:47, 48), and even earlier in the request of James and John for positions of honour when Jesus enters his glory (10:37). Thus Tolbert is correct to perceive in the reference to Jerusalem in 10:32–34 and the use of the title Son of David in 10:46–52 "a clear foreshadowing of the major theme of the second division" and thus an example of how "the close of [one] division overlaps at the edges with the opening of the [next] division."[6] That the leader-and-followers imagery in 10:32 and 16:7–8 produces an *interpretative* bracket around the Jerusalem section will become more apparent once both occurrences of this image have been examined.

## Mark 10:32

The significance of this journey to Jerusalem is developed within another "bracketed" segment overlapping the section just defined, namely, the "central section" (8:22–10:52) separating the Galilean and Jerusalem phases of the narrative. This section incorporates three discipleship teaching cycles (8:31–9:1; 9:30–37; 10:32–45), in relation to which 10:32 forms the introduction to the last. This verse depicts a gesture by Jesus and the responses it invokes: "Now they were on the way, going up to Jerusalem, and Jesus was going before them; and they were amazed, while those who followed were afraid." The remainder of this cycle elaborates a pattern developed in the previous two cycles: Jesus foretells his coming passion (8:31; 9:31; 10:33–34), the disciples demonstrate their inability to accept this message (8:32–33; 9:32–34; 10:35–41), and Jesus responds with a teaching on discipleship (8:34–9:1; 9:35–37; 10:42–45).[7] This threefold development elaborates the figurative significance of both this journey from Galilee to Jerusalem and the foretold return (14:28; 16:7).

The logic to this development emerges in retrospect from the three discipleship teachings. Therein when Jesus "summons" his disciples (8:34; 9:35; 10:42) it is in order to combat a mindset which is preventing them from accepting any thought of his death. In the process of explaining true discipleship, Jesus discloses that the aptitude they lack is that characteristic of his passion: self-abnegation. Through these stereotyped situations Mark contrasts two modes of abiding in community: self-preoccupation and self-denial.

The first discipleship teaching follows Peter's rejection of the fate laid out in the first passion prediction:

> And he called to him the multitude with his disciples, and said to them, "If any man would come after me, let him deny himself and take up his cross and follow me. For whoever would save his life will lose it; and whoever loses his life for my sake and the gospel's will save it. For what does it profit a man, to gain the whole world and forfeit his life? For what can a man give in return for his life? For whoever is ashamed of me and of my words in this adulterous and sinful generation, of him will the Son of man also be ashamed, when he comes in the glory of his Father with the holy angels." (8:34–38)

The phrase "whoever is ashamed of *me and of my words*" (v. 38) reveals the nature of Peter's objection: he is ashamed to follow a Christ who is rejected and killed. The parallel expression "whoever loses his life for *my sake and the gospel's*" (v. 35) establishes self-abnegation as the opposite of this attitude. Peter rejects the passion prediction because he lacks this attitude. His preoccupation with self leads him to associate messiahship with victory and greatness (gaining the whole world).

Jesus counters this attitude with a teaching depicting the road to the cross as the way to salvation. The Hellenistic mythology of the vindicated martyr is evident: only those willing to abandon themselves for the sake of the cause ("for my sake and the gospel's") will secure salvation or "life."[8] That discipleship entails literal risks to one's life is apparent in 13:9–13, where the briefer expressions "for my sake" and "for my name's sake" accompany predictions of Christians being delivered up to death by former associates and family members. However, the call to self-abandonment in 8:34–38 is not strictly literal, for the phrase "for my sake and the gospel's" also occurs in a passage emphasizing the need to abandon one's life in terms of former attachments to people and places (10:28–30). Anyone who abandons house, lands, and family will receive eternal life in the future. So at issue in 8:34–38 is a disciple's willingness to sacrifice everything for the gospel. The paradox is that only those who abandon their lives will save them. Thus, by taking up his cross, Jesus illustrates the principle that the way of death is the road to life.[9]

The same message is conveyed somewhat differently in the second discipleship teaching. The connection between self-preoccupation and the disciples' inability to conceive of Jesus dying is far more explicit here. In a caricature of conceit, the disciples respond to Jesus' passion-and-resurrection prediction with a private discussion of which of them is the greatest. Again, Jesus responds with a teaching depicting humility as the way to exaltation:

> And he sat down and called the twelve; and he said to them, "If any one would be first, he must be last of all and servant of all." And he took a child, and put him in the midst of them; and taking him in his arms, he said to them, "Whoever receives one such child in my name receives me; and whoever receives me, receives not me but him who sent me." (9:35–37)

The imperative of making oneself last in order to become first foregrounds the less literal sense of dying to the self. That the child exemplifies the humility of Jesus' messiahship and the lowly status required of a disciple is suggested by the parallels between the sayings in 9:37; 9:41; and 10:14–15. All of these verses speak of (or are situated in the context of) receiving persons. In 9:37 these persons are children, and receiving them is tantamount to receiving Jesus and God. In 9:41 it is the followers of Jesus who are received and who are thereupon referred to as "little ones" (9:42; cf. the word "children" for disciples in 10:24). In 10:13 the disciples hinder children from meeting Jesus, and in 10:14–15 Jesus states that the kingdom belongs to children. This last passage appears to define the quality of a child that Jesus offers as exemplary of discipleship in 9:37. The children are persons whom the twelve deem too inconsequential to bother someone as important as Jesus. Since "to such belongs the kingdom of God," it follows that to be a disciple is to be without status. The kingdom itself must be accepted as lowly (like a child) in order for one to enter it (10:15).[10] These notions help explain the logic of 9:37 as the conclusion of the second discipleship teaching. Receiving a child (or perhaps a lowly disciple) is the same as receiving Jesus or God (the one who sent him) inasmuch as Jesus is renouncing the status that his disciples expect of him. He is accepting the nominal status of a child, of one who is last of all and servant of all—a nobody; to this lowly status the disciples must aspire if ever they are to be numbered among the first.

The third cycle of discipleship teaching continues the threefold pattern of Jesus predicting his passion, the disciples responding inappropriately, and Jesus summoning them for a lesson on self-denial. But this time the disciples' inappropriate response is not so much a parody of self-preoccupation as a burlesque: James and John ask Jesus to grant them the seats of greatest honour.

Again Jesus responds that his disciples must deny themselves to the point of death (or, metaphorically, die to their *selves*) if they would have future greatness:

> And Jesus called them to him and said to them, "You know that those who are supposed to rule over the Gentiles lord it over them, and their great men exercise authority over them. But it shall not be so among you; but whoever would be great among you must be your servant, and whoever would be first among you must be slave of all. For the Son of man also came not to be served but to serve, and to give his life as a ransom for many." (10:42–45)

Jesus' willingness to serve others to the extent of dying for them is now offered as the appropriate model to be emulated. As in the previous passage, the issue is the means of becoming first or great "among you" (i.e., in a community of disciples) rather than that of attaining salvation itself. Nevertheless, all three discipleship teachings concern a consummate vindication of the way of humility. The statements contrasting greatness and servitude or first and last (9:35; 10:43–44) are reminiscent of the one bringing to a close the section immediately preceding 10:32 ("But many that are first will be last, and the last first") and appear to elucidate the principle upon which this reversal of one's present status is based. Hence, the greatness proffered in these sayings concerns one's status in the eschaton and not (or not merely) the "paradoxical greatness" of those who humble themselves in the community.[11]

In 10:42–45, as in the first discipleship teaching, Mark is interpreting the mechanism of eschatological reversal in accordance with the mythology of the apotheosis of the martyr, which is comparable to (and possibly the historical basis for) the apocalyptic conception of the resurrection of the righteous (e.g., Dan 12:2–3; Rev 20:4–6). The question posed to James and John makes this even clearer: "Are you able to drink the cup that I drink, or to be baptized with the baptism with which I am baptized?" (10:38). The image of the cup in the Hebrew scriptures is used to conjure suffering, joy, and wrath, but here, in conjunction with a second metaphor foretokening Jesus' death, we recognize the influence of Hellenistic thought, wherein a cup can signify "death as a violent end."[12] The transformation achieved through martyrdom is implicit in the baptismal metaphor, for Christian baptism, understood as death and rebirth,[13] signifies a transition to a new quality of life, "that eschatological life with Christ that is perfected at the parousia."[14] Implicit in these two negatively framed metaphors, then, is the promise of salvation or resurrection for those who follow Jesus' example.

In 8:22–10:52 Jesus' words on discipleship stress the need for self-abnegation in the present as the way of attaining exaltation in the future. This theme that life comes through death, or exaltation through humiliation, is the abstract content symbolized in the image of Jesus "going before" his disciples "in the way" (ἐν τῇ ὁδῷ). This leader-and-followers image occurs in relation to each passion prediction, as does the metaphor of the way: The theme of following Jesus is introduced in 8:34 in the call to *follow after* him. The notion that his disciples were following after him is implicit within 9:33, where Jesus asks his disciples what they had been discussing "on the way": if he could not hear what they were talking about as a group, he had probably enacted this teaching by going ahead of them. And the image of Jesus going before his disciples becomes explicit in 10:32, where this gesture and the amazement and fear it provokes become the stimulus for an explanation of where he has been leading them (v. 33). The imagery of the way enters these teaching moments at 8:27; 9:33, 34; and 10:32. It is also mentioned before the encounter with the rich man (10:17) and is what Bartimaeus "followed him in" at the end of the central section (10:52). The leader-and-followers imagery of 10:32 thus dramatizes the message in 8:34: Jesus goes before his disciples as a model to be emulated, for the road to Jerusalem is the way to life through selfless suffering and death.

## Mark 16:7–8

When the leader-and-followers imagery in Mark 10:32 is viewed as a symbolic enactment of 8:34, it becomes natural to presume that the recurrence of this imagery in 16:7–8 also bears a symbolic quality. As a reversal of Jesus' journey through Galilee to Jerusalem, the image of the resurrected Jesus leading his disciples back to Galilee presumably connotes a reversal of the developments embodied within the Jerusalem section. In order to understand the nature of this reversal, however, we must consider it in relation to the movement of the narrative as a whole. Mark's portrayal of Jesus' public career begins with an authoritative and largely successful mission based in Galilee but ends with this authority being subverted through Jesus' rejection by Jerusalem's religious aristocracy and his willing assumption of humility. As soon as Peter confesses that Jesus is the Christ, Jesus starts to subvert his disciples' expectations about his messianic authority, and the journey southward to the place of relinquishment begins. Thus Mark 16:7 looks backward to the status Jesus renounced through his passion, but also forward to the vindication proclaimed in the discipleship teachings. The way to life through death is now depicted auspiciously through a symbolic image of its reward.

The significance of the empty tomb lies not only in the resurrection but also in the information that Jesus' presence can be encountered elsewhere, *on the way to* Galilee, for Jesus is leading his disciples once more. There is an implicit "because" in 16:7b. Jesus is not "here" (v. 6) because he is going before

the disciples to Galilee: *"there* you will see him." These few, choice words of
an anonymous young man convey the impression that the assailed shepherd
is now reassembling his scattered sheep, leading them to Galilee the way a
shepherd walks at the head of his flock (14:27–28).[15] But this time the leadership is spiritual, for the disciples will not see Jesus until they get there. The
unique possibilities for stark and selective description afforded by the medium
of verbal narrative permit Mark to conjure thoughts of restoration and leadership without specifying how these notions are to be imagined realistically.
All the reader needs to perceive is that Jesus' return to Galilee extends the symbolic journey or process patterned upon 8:34.[16]

Three features of 16:7 remain to be examined: the singling out of Peter,
the detail that the messenger was "a young man," and the words "there you
will see him, as he told you."

The young man's directive to the women to tell "his disciples and Peter..."
is often viewed as a passing reference to an early resurrection tradition naming Peter as the first to whom Jesus appeared (1 Cor 15:5; Luke 24:34).
Such an allusion is plausible if we may presume that this tradition is something most readers would be expected to know. But it does not explain why
the mention of Peter should come *after* the reference to the disciples, particularly in view of his pre-eminent position both in the story itself and in the
tradition of an initial appearance to him. The unexpected manner of Peter's
specification seems actually to set awry whatever positive conception of Peter
might be inferred from a tradition naming him first. Does not this wording
insinuate that Peter is presently *not* a disciple?[17] Considered in light of the fore-
going narrative, the special reference to Peter finds ready justification in
Peter's attempts to exempt himself from the part assigned to the disciples in
the very prophecy of which the young man now speaks:

> And Jesus said to them, "You will all fall away; for it is written, 'I will strike
> the shepherd, and the sheep will be scattered.' But after I am raised up, I
> will go before you to Galilee." Peter said to him, "Even though they all fall
> away, I will not." And Jesus said to him, "Truly, I say to you, this very night,
> before the cock crows twice, you will deny me three times." But he said vehe-
> mently, "If I must die with you, I will not deny you." And they all said the
> same. (14:27–31)

The recurrence of the adjective "all" (πάντες) in 14:27 ("You will all fall
away"), 14:29 ("Even though they all fall away, I will not"), 14:31 ("And they
all said the same"), and 14:50 ("And they all forsook him, and fled") ties
together this prophecy and its actualization in Gethsemane and underscores
the representativeness of Peter's role.[18] As Christopher Francis Evans suggested, "the separate mention of Peter in 16.7 reflects the isolation of Peter

amongst the 'all' who will be made to stumble in 14.27–29."[19] Peter's sworn dissociation from those who would fall away like frightened sheep translates briefly into action when he continues to "follow" Jesus after all the disciples have fled (14:54). His autonomous stance, however, becomes a source of burgeoning irony; despite his bravado, Peter follows tentatively and safely "at a distance," only to disown Jesus completely at the first signs of real danger (14:66–72). His confident assertion that *he* will not forsake Jesus thus underscores the tragedy of his failure, though Mark's ironic concentration upon Peter really makes vivid the failure of the disciples as a whole (14:31).

The special mention of Peter therefore reminds the reader of the failure of the disciples. But as part of a message announcing the fulfillment of Jesus' predication "But after I am raised up, I will go before you to Galilee," this reminder draws attention to the polarity and mystery of the transformation whereby the fallen shepherd once more leads his scattered sheep. It is as if to say that Jesus' exemplary sacrifice has now made all things—even the impossible journey of discipleship—possible (cf. 10:23–31).

The miraculousness of this reversal is made all the more apparent by the presence of an anonymous "young man" as the bearer of this message. Recall that an unnamed "young man," similarly described in terms of his surprising actions and clothing, popped up just as inexplicably in Gethsemane. In the longer Gospel of Mark, the figure in Gethsemane is elaborated into an individual: a person with a past, a house, and a family. In that text, the young man at the empty tomb is presumably the same *person* who asked to be with Jesus in Bethany and who followed Jesus briefly in Gethsemane. Considering that Jesus entered the young man's tomb and raised him from the dead, it is only fitting that the young man should enter Jesus' tomb and announce Jesus' resurrection. A reader might even wonder whether the young man rolled back Jesus' stone just as Jesus rolled back his. In the canonical text, however, the unnamed young men are not necessarily the same individual and are not so much *persons* as interrelated symbolic figures. Of the figure in Gethsemane we learn only that he, like Peter, was *following* Jesus, dressed only in a linen sheet on a chilly spring night (14:54, 67), and shamefully fled naked in the face of actual danger. Like Peter, this young man epitomizes the disciples' fear of arrest and their failure to follow in the way to life through death. At the tomb, though, we encounter a young man dressed in a white robe symbolizing the glory common to heavenly beings and vindicated martyrs (see Rev 6:11; 7:9, 13–14).[20] The detail that he was seated "at the right hand side" of the tomb might naturally evoke thoughts of honour and vindication, considering how often the image of sitting on the right side (of Jesus or God) connotes exalted status in this narrative (Mark 10:37, 40; 12:36; 14:62). A symbol of failure to follow in the way has been transformed into a symbol anticipating the reward of this journey: exaltation. Put differently, the two appearances of a young man represent the coming to pass of both elements of the prophecy of 14:27–28 (scattering and restoration), embodying the story of the disciples in both aspects. Mark prepares his readers to believe that these disciples (and anyone else) might finally, truly, follow Jesus as he resumes his leadership in the way.

By viewing the young man at the tomb as a symbol of eschatological vindication, we bypass the pointless debate over whether this figure is human or angelic in the canonical gospel. A young man in a white robe could be construed either way. As Andrew T. Lincoln suggested, the ambiguity is probably deliberate, since it allows this man to function not only as a messenger (which is the primary function of an angel among people) but also as a symbol of resurrection and vindication. The blurring of vindication imagery and supernatural imagery is appropriate here, "since Mark's Jesus tells us that 'when they rise from the dead, they…are like angels in heaven' (12:25)."[21]

It seems reasonable to conclude that Mark chose the verb "to go before" in 16:7 in order to suggest a continuation of the symbolism of Jesus' leadership in the way to life through death. The exalted Jesus continues to "go before" his disciples (and anyone else who would "come after" him) as exemplar of this way, having become the apotheosis of what others may obtain by following his lead.[22] That Mark's emphasis lies in the image of Jesus leading his disciples back to Galilee is apparent from the fact that this "going before" is the only element common to both 14:28 and 16:7 and a condition to which the resurrection itself is twice subordinated: "A curious feature in 14.28, that the resurrection is referred to in a subordinate clause and is used as a time indication ('after I am raised up…'), recurs in the juxtaposition of 16.6 and 16.7, in that the fact of the resurrection…is relegated to second place by the announcement of what is to follow as the climax."[23] Indeed, it is the fact that Jesus is going before his disciples to Galilee that the women are commanded to report to them, not the resurrection itself.[24] The conspicuous change in the tense of the verb "to go before" from future in 14:28 to present in 16:7 further heightens the relevance of this verb, making it not only somewhat more prominent than the new notion of seeing Jesus but also more immediate. Jesus *is* now doing what he said he *would* do after his resurrection. The present participle indicates that Jesus is *between* the tomb and Galilee at the moment of the young man's speaking. As Morna Hooker perceived, "[Mark] is certainly saying something far more significant than that Jesus will arrive in Galilee before the disciples. This is no mere rendezvous, but a call to the disciples to follow Jesus once again. On the way to Jerusalem,

Jesus had gone ahead (10.32 ἦν προάγων), and the disciples had seen him and followed. Now they are called to follow him, even though they cannot see him. What looks like an inconsistency in Mark may be a deliberate attempt on his part to underline that this is what discipleship means, now that Jesus has been raised from the dead."[25]

But if Mark is referring to Jesus' continued spiritual leadership "in the way," to what does "there you will see him" refer? Because the other gospel writers tell us that Jesus appeared bodily to his disciples prior to his ascension, readers of Mark usually imagine a pre-ascension, bodily appearance as well. But not all Christians made that assumption.[26] As a late convert, Paul could not claim to have seen the risen Jesus in bodily form, yet Paul made no distinction between the appearance of Jesus to him and the appearances of Jesus to Cephas, the twelve, more than five hundred believers, James, and the other apostles (1 Cor 15:3–8; 9:1). Whatever Paul experienced seemed to him to be a revelation of Jesus' lordship and a commission to preach to the Gentiles. He could even speak of God revealing his son "in me" (ἐν ἐμοί; Gal 1:16). Paul's apostleship was highly contested, so if he thought that Jesus appeared to other apostles in a more tangible form, he had a motive to downplay that difference. Nevertheless, he is our principle witness to the traditions about the resurrection appearances prior to Matthew, Luke, and John, and his descriptions demonstrate that the word *see* in Mark 16:7 might refer to a vision of the exalted lord—an epiphany of an exalted being.

The story of the transfiguration arguably represents Mark's attempt to convey the nature of this epiphany in narrative form. Therein, Jesus temporarily takes on the form that he will attain following his death: he becomes an exalted, heavenly being in the company of Elijah and Moses. Some of Mark's contemporaries believed that Elijah and Moses existed with Enoch in heaven, all three of them having been taken up alive by God.[27] In light of this belief, many scholars have proposed that the emptiness of Jesus' tomb is significant for Mark because "it conforms to the central motif and proof which lies at the heart of translation stories: the disappearance or absence of the corpse."[28] In other words, the empty tomb and the transfiguration together imply that when the women come to anoint Jesus' body, Jesus is already in heaven, in the company of Israel's immortalized heroes.[29] The transformation of Jesus into the heavenly state of his resurrected condition is perhaps what the transfiguration is meant to represent. By witnessing the transfiguration, Peter, James and John are experiencing something like a proleptic appearance of the risen Jesus from heaven.[30]

The promise that the disciples will see Jesus in Galilee appears to anticipate a vision of the exalted Lord rather than a bodily (pre-ascension) appearance. But there is more to this seeing than the awareness of Jesus' heavenly exaltation, for in accord with Mark's use of the verb "to see" (ὁράω) elsewhere in the story, 16:7 carries the christological connotation of understanding who Jesus really is.[31] Compare the sense of spiritual (albeit demonic) perception of Jesus' true nature in Mark 5:6–7, where Legion ran to Jesus and worshipped him after "he saw Jesus from afar," and the revelatory insight of the centurion in 15:39, which resulted from *seeing* how Jesus died. The opposite sense of misconceiving Jesus' true nature accompanies the verb "to see" in 6:49, 50; 15:32, 36.[32] The association between *seeing* and spiritually *understanding* Jesus is explicit in Mark 4:12: "looking intently they see and do not perceive, listening closely they hear and do not comprehend...." The miracles that frame the central section of the gospel make this association programmatic for the story of the disciples.[33]

The first of these miracles, 8:22–26, uses the imagery of sight-giving to disclose a two-stage development in the disciples' christological understanding. Another form of the verb "to see" (βλέπω) occurs in both this story of Jesus healing a blind man and the immediately preceding story about the disciples' incomprehension of the feeding miracles (8:15, 18, 23, 24, 25). In the latter, Jesus asks them, "Having eyes do you not see, and having ears do you not hear? And do you not remember? ...Do you not yet understand?" These comments effectively compare the disciples to blind and deaf men, that is, to the deaf man (7:32–37) and the blind man (8:22–26) who are healed within the section of the gospel that is bracketed by the opinions about who Jesus is (6:14–16; 8:27–30). Peter's confession therefore marks a transition in the disciples' comprehension of Jesus from the total imperceptiveness about his messiahship that they display in the first half of the story (*blindness*) to the imperfect conception of the nature of this messiahship that dominates thereafter (seeing *imperfectly*). "Like the man in 8,22–26 [Peter] only 'sees' dimly and in a confused way at first. Full 'sight', i.e., insight into the full meaning of Jesus' identity, can only come at the cross (cf. 15,39) and the resurrection (cf. 16:7)."[34] "Peter 'sees' that Jesus is the Messiah, the Christ. But he fails to 'see' that, as the Christ, Jesus must suffer. To heal Peter (and perhaps the implied reader) of that blindness will require a second stage, the second half of Mark's Gospel."[35] Thus the second development is from misconception to true understanding of this messiahship (seeing *plainly*), a state projected in 16:7.[36] The imagery of a blind man attaining imperfect sight symbolizes the abrupt yet partial insight that the disciples are about to have into who Jesus is.

The second story involving a blind man, which forms the closing "bracket" around the central section, presents Jesus' healing of blindness as the catalyst in a man's passage from initial faith and preliminary insight ("Son of David,

Jesus…") to subsequent discipleship. The image of the once-blind Bartimaeus following Jesus "on the way" could hardly present a more fitting complement to the leadership image in 10:32. What this means for 16:7 is clear. The disciples will not only see their risen Lord in Galilee but will also come to appreciate the necessity of his passion and follow him in this way. "To 'see' Jesus is to perceive that being a disciple is following the way that he took, the way on which he is still 'going before' (16:7)."[37]

The gospel concludes with the astonishing statement that the women did not convey to the disciples the message with which they were entrusted. Instead, the women "fled from the tomb; for trembling and astonishment had come upon them; and they said nothing to nobody, for they were afraid" (16:8). This exceptionally negative conclusion complicates the predicted restitution of the disciples, particularly when 16:7 is thought to anticipate a bodily resurrection appearance. Some scholars who subscribe to that view have therefore denied that the silence of the women was as final as Mark emphatically conveyed, reasoning that the disciples surely could not have met up with Jesus without being told to return to Galilee.[38] Other scholars, who reject the traditional view, have instead suggested that the disciples must never have reassembled and seen the risen Jesus in Galilee and were therefore never commissioned as apostles.[39]

These readings of 16:7–8 neglect certain peculiarities of the wording. "Galilee" is too large a locale to serve as a specification for a rendezvous. Moreover, "16.7 is only very indirectly a command to go to Galilee, and 14.28, on which it is based, is hardly a command at all."[40] The message that the young man tells the women to deliver is not the news of Jesus' resurrection, which he mentions in an almost incidental fashion by way of explaining the absence of Jesus' corpse. The message is that Jesus "*is going before you,*" leading the disciples back to Galilee. This is an explanation of what *is* happening, not a command about what *should start* happening or, as some scholars imagine, a description of a potential positive outcome that remains ambiguous. The young man is announcing that the fulfillment of the prediction Jesus made in 14:27–28 *is* now taking place, a reality which does not depend on what the women do. Because prophecy *is* being fulfilled, the reader can presume that Jesus is guiding his disciples back to Galilee and will eventually appear to them there.

What is most troubling to the implied reader is not the fact that the disciples never received this message. Rather, it is the fact that the story ends with the observation that the women were too frightened to take part in the restoration of the disciples under Jesus' leadership, or even to say anything about this at all. Why does the story end on a note of failure and incompre-

hension? Perhaps this startling situation is meant to provoke the reader into ✗
a decision about the way of discipleship. Will she or he flee like the women
or follow like the disciples? The question put earlier to James and John is now
put to the reader: "Are you able to drink the cup that I drink, or to be baptized with the baptism with which I am baptized?"

## LGM 1 and 2 and Mark 16:1-8
## as a Frame for the Passion

The addition of LGM 1 and 2 obviously makes the frame formed by 10:32
and 16:7–8 as apparent as the matched pair around the central section. But
it also develops the significance of this *inclusio* and affects a reader's percep-
tions of 14:51–52 and 16:1–8. In order to appreciate this, we need to consider these additions sequentially, as developments in a subplot.

Following the depiction of Jesus leading his disciples in the way to life
through death (10:32–34), Jesus arrives in Bethany and raises a young man,
who then wishes to become a disciple and receives private instruction. The
placing of LGM 1 and 2 around Jesus' words about his cup and baptism
implies that Jesus taught the young man that honour comes through humiliation, life through death. Elsewhere, when Jesus retires to a house and gives
private instruction, the teaching gives insider information concerning the
preceding incident (7:17–23; 9:28–29, 33–37; 10:10–12). Accordingly, we
may infer that the mystery of the kingdom of God is apropos of the young
man's own rising from the dead.

The relationship between the raising and private teaching on the mystery
of the kingdom of God will be explored in the next chapter. Stated simply, the
young man's return to life becomes the basis for his instruction in the nature
of salvation, the eschatological truth that in order to attain "life" one must first
"die" to the self. His linen sheet signifies the transformation that comes
through death (baptism being a symbolic death by drowning). When Jesus
is betrayed, the young man will again put on this garment and attempt to
accompany Jesus back to Jerusalem in order to undergo Jesus' "baptism" of
suffering and death.

To our surprise, at the first sign of trouble the young man fails in his
resolve, becoming an epitome of the flight of the disciples as a whole.[41] Why
this ideal disciple, who responded so quickly and positively, should fail just
as quickly and miserably is difficult to fathom, though his story is in keeping
with Jesus' analogy of the seed sown upon rocky ground (πετρῶδες), "who,
when they hear the word, immediately receive it with joy; and they have no
root in themselves, but endure for a while; then, when tribulation or perse-

cution arises on account of the word, immediately they fall away" (4:16–17). It is not too surprising that the other disciple to fall this way was nicknamed "Peter" (Πέτρος), meaning rock.[42]

Following the crucifixion, the young man whom Jesus raised from the dead appears once more, this time to proclaim Jesus' resurrection and continuing leadership in the way. Donning the white robe of a vindicated martyr, the one who, with Peter, exemplified the disciples' failure to follow now inexplicably announces the restoration of this group, including Peter, and prefigures their success. A reader of longer Mark will not see this young man as an angel bearing tidings from heaven, but as a man from Peraea whose startling reappearances in Gethsemane and the open tomb validate his message. For quite despite himself, this young man abandoned Jesus, in fulfillment of Jesus' words "You will all fall away; for it is written, 'I will strike the shepherd, and the sheep will be scattered.'" And now he sits nobly and serenely inside an empty tomb, reiterating Jesus' words "But after I am raised up, I will go before you to Galilee" (14:27–28).

The passion narrative is not only framed by the two miracles located at tombs but also subdivided by the appearance of the young man in Gethsemane. Benoît Standaert observed that 14:51–52 marks a transition in the passion narrative. Before the young man's shameful flight, "Jesus is in the circle of his friends." Afterward, he is "in the camp of the opposition."[43] So the start of the passion proper, through which Jesus suffers alone, is signified by this brief appearance of the young man. This three-part structure involving two frame-stories and an inner, transitional episode is comparable to Mark's use of three thematically similar incidents at the beginning, middle, and end of the story in order to develop the theme of Jesus' divine sonship. During Jesus' baptism, a voice from heaven declares to Jesus, "You are my beloved Son; with you I am well pleased" (1:11). During Jesus' transfiguration, that voice is heard again, this time declaring to the disciples "This is my beloved Son; listen to him" (9:7). And during Jesus' crucifixion, after Jesus "expires" and the temple curtain is torn in two, the centurion declares, "Truly this man was a Son of God!" (15:39).[44] It would appear that in the last of these three incidents, the holy spirit, which had "split" the heavens while entering Jesus at his baptism (1:10), now "splits" the temple curtain in two (a tapestry mosaic of the heavens) while departing Jesus (15:37–38). Hence we have a "cosmic *inclusio*" around the entire story, and this story is divided into two parts by a thematically similar inner episode.[45] In the first part, the disciples are blind to Jesus' identity as Son of God. In the second part, they "see" Jesus' sonship imperfectly (the actual transition to imperfect sight occurs just prior to the transfiguration with Peter's recognition of Jesus' messiahship).

The parallelism that allows the baptism, transfiguration, and crucifixion to function like "pillars" that structure the whole gospel is sometimes depicted in a chart like this:[46]

| Baptism | Transfiguration | Crucifixion |
|---|---|---|
| Heavens "split" | | Temple veil "split" |
| Dove descends | Cloud descends | Split in veil descends from top to bottom |
| Voice from heaven | Voice from cloud | Jesus' voice from cross |
| "You are my beloved Son" | "This is my Son, the beloved" | "Truly this man was a son of God" |
| John the Baptist appears dressed like Elijah | Elijah appears to Jesus; Jesus hints that John was Elijah | The onlookers think Jesus is calling Elijah |

A similar chart can be used to depict the similar structure created by the insertion of LGM 1 and 2:

| Mark 10:32–34 and LGM 1 and 2 | Mark 14:50–52 | Mark 15:40–16:8 |
|---|---|---|
| Jesus rolls away the stone from the door of the tomb | | "Who will roll away the stone from the door of the tomb?" |
| A young man is raised by Jesus | | A young man announces Jesus' resurrection |
| Young man returns wearing linen over his naked body | Young man appears wearing linen over his naked body | Young man appears wearing a white robe |
| Two women "and Salome" | | Two women "and Salome" |
| Jesus leads the way to Jerusalem | | Jesus leads the way to Galilee |
| The disciples "were amazed" | | The women "were amazed" |
| Those who follow Jesus are afraid | Young man and Peter follow Jesus fearfully | Women (who were following Jesus in Galilee) are afraid |
| | All of the disciples and the young man flee | The women flee |

Whoever created LGM 1 and 2 had a remarkable feel for canonical Mark's narrative and theological designs.

# ⤞8⤝

# Longer Mark's Use of
# Verbal Echoes

The preceding two chapters examined the longer gospel's use of two familiar Markan framing techniques: intercalation and matched pairs. This
chapter will explore the additional interpretative moves encouraged by the
numerous echoes of Markan phrases that exist within LGM 1. Mark's proclivity to repeat words and phrases across episodes is familiar to interpreters of
the canonical gospel, who often explain the phenomenon in terms of emphasis and cross-referencing:

> The repetition of a limited number of words through the many episodes
> provides echoes which invite the reader to make connections between one
> part of the narrative and another. For example, the "ripping" of the temple
> curtain just before the centurion recognizes Jesus as the Son of God recalls
> by verbal association the "ripping" of the heavens just before God pro-
> nounces Jesus to be his son....Tracing such verbal motifs through the story
> is illuminating. And as the words recur in similar or different contexts, they
> are enriched by repetition and accumulate many nuances of meaning for
> the reader.
>
> The many key words which recur throughout the story are like major and
> minor motifs running through a musical composition.[1]

We have seen how longer Mark's verbal foreshadowings of the young man's
flight from Gethsemane, the burial of Jesus, and the open tomb reinforce a
literary structure. It is reasonable to expect that the verbal echoes of earlier
scenes within LGM 1 might be a means of encouraging the reader to consider
otherwise unrelated incidents in light of each other.

This examination of echoes will begin with some prominent parallels to
stories within the central section, specifically the rich man's question and the

transfiguration, and will conclude with a discussion of the phrases "great cry" and "the mystery of the kingdom of God."[2]

## Reminiscences of the Man
## with Many Possessions

At the end of LGM 1a we encounter two reminiscences of the story of the man with many possessions in Mark 10:17–22. LGM 1:8 repeats the words "but the…, having looked upon him, loved him and" from Mark 10:21, reversing the subject (Jesus) and object (an anonymous man). LGM 1:9 terminates with the phrase "for he was rich," which resembles "for he had many possessions," the final clause of the episode with the rich man. The former echo is peculiar merely for its awkwardness: why repeat this phrase so soon after its initial occurrence and reverse the relationship between the subject and object? The latter echo is more peculiar, since it is an explanation that does not explain: "And going out from the tomb they went into the house of the young man; for he was rich." Taken at face value, this "explanation" implies that Jesus and the young man went into his house for a taste of the good life. The comment even seems ironic, for in the preceding dialogue, Jesus dismissed the possibility of the rich entering the kingdom of God. The reader must suppose that this time the evangelist meant something other than what he seems to convey. But humorously puzzling explanations that begin with the word *gar* ("for" or "because") preceded by the verb "to be" (e.g., ἦν γάρ) are a feature of Mark's style, and a purpose to this clause becomes apparent when we consider other examples.

In 1953 C.H. Bird proposed that Mark used embarrassingly peculiar *gar* clauses to draw attention to statements that have hermeneutical relevance.[3] Compare, for instance, the comment about Jairus's daughter in 5:42: "and immediately the girl got up and walked, for she was twelve years old." Her *age* does not explain why she got up and walked—it is the reason she was *able* to do so (the numerous diminutives in the story might lead one to think she were an infant). The reader must pause to figure out what Mark meant, because what he wrote does not make sense. The strangeness of the explanation draws attention to the number twelve, which is a detail that relates this story to the intercalated incident of the woman who had had a hemorrhage for twelve years. The coincidence that the woman had been suffering as long as the girl had been alive (and stopped suffering when the girl died) is a hint that there is another level of meaning to the story, and the number itself becomes a point of entry into this symbolic dimension.[4] Similarly, in 16:4, the women's concern about who will roll back the stone from the door of Jesus' tomb is followed by the remark, "And looking up, they saw that the stone was rolled back, for it was exceedingly great." The size of the stone does not explain why the stone was rolled back. It explains why the women were wondering how they would get at the body to anoint it. However, the description "for it was exceedingly great" (ἦν γὰρ μέγας σφόδρα) has broader implications. As we will see a little later in this chapter, the word "great" has connotations within Mark of conflict with the powers of death, and here heightens the miraculousness of Jesus' victory over it (like the "great" calm that resulted after Jesus rebuked the "great" wind of the storm that threatened to sink his boat; 4:37, 39). In another *gar* clause Mark accounts for why Jesus found no fruit on a leafy fig tree with the words "for it was not the season for figs" (11:13). This is the most remarkable example, for it manages to make Jesus look foolish for thinking he would find figs out of season, and spiteful for destroying a tree that did not go along with his mistake. This foolishness and misplaced anger conflict with the picture of Jesus presented thus far in the story, but the discrepancy can be resolved if the incident is read symbolically. Many scholars treat this peculiar *gar* clause as a hint that Jesus' encounter with the fig tree is a prophetic commentary on the fate of the temple.[5] Robert Fowler, for instance, categorized Mark 11:13 as a *gar* clause that imparts a symbolic quality to a story, in this case functioning as a clue to the figurative dimension revealed through the sandwich technique.[6] Odd explanatory *gar* clauses occur within the three intercalations that are most readily viewed as mutually interpretative (Mark 5:21–43; 11:12–25; and LGM 1:1–2:2), just before a shift in setting. Since the *gar* clauses in 5:42 and 11:13 appear to function as hints to the reader to seek a concealed meaning, we must consider the possibility that the peculiar *gar* clause in LGM 1:9 functions similarly.

If the words "for he was rich" are a hint, their heuristic relevance should be sought in the pericope of the man with many possessions. There, a man who wants to know "What must I do to inherit eternal life?" is told "Go, sell what you have, and give to the poor, and you will have treasure in heaven; and come, follow me." After this man goes away sorrowful, Jesus says to his disciples, "How hard it will be for those who have riches to enter the kingdom of God!" (10:23). The verbal reminiscences of this story within LGM 1a imply that the young man in Bethany shares the same *dilemma* faced by that other man. "For he was rich" is a hint that the instruction Jesus gave to the young man likewise concerns eternal life and the demand to leave riches and family behind in order to "follow" Jesus (Mark 10:21, 23–31). Robert Gundry reasoned that the command Jesus gave to the young man in LGM 1:10 was to sell everything he owned; in Gundry's opinion, the linen sheet symbolizes the man's utter destitution, for he now possesses only that which belongs to a corpse.[7] These inferences seem reasonable, though we can only be sure that the man has abandoned family and home, and of that only after we see him in Gethsemane "following" Jesus.

## "And After Six Days"

After entering the house, six days pass before Jesus commands the young man and the latter comes to him in the evening for private instruction in a mystery. A period of six days also preceded the private revelation of Jesus' future, exalted condition to Peter, James, and John on the mountain (9:2).[8] Since both instances of the phrase "and after six days" function as introductions to episodes of private revelation, the repetition in LGM 1:10 is probably intended to invoke a comparison between Jesus' transfiguration and the raising and initiation of the young man.[9]

The comparison itself appears to focus on changes in Jesus' and the young man's clothing, to which attention is drawn in the sentences following this phrase. Jesus' clothes are transformed into a brilliant white to make him appear as if he is attaining his exaltation to the right hand of the Father, and the young man wraps a linen sheet around his naked body as part of the baptismal symbolism of his initiation into the mystery of the kingdom of God. Though this mystery is given an eschatological content (Mark 4), the young man's clothing and the private, nocturnal context are also evocative of mystery initiations and therefore suggestive of epiphany and insight; initiations of this sort function as rites of passage, marking a change in ontological status to that of the saved. Through a change in clothing, therefore, both Jesus and the young man are depicted *as if* involved in ontological transformations. These states become actual for both at the end of the gospel, when the young man shows up in Jesus' tomb wearing a white robe (στολή), the colour of Jesus' clothing (ἱμάτιον) on the mountain (the word *white* occurs only in 9:3 and 16:5). The young man now wears the white robe of the vindicated martyr (Rev 6:11; 7:13–14) as he announces Jesus' resurrection.

The point of evoking this comparison between the initiation of the young man and the transfiguration becomes clearer when we notice that both stories involve the themes of suffering and rising from the dead. LGM 1 presents the raising of a dead man followed by a private teaching that is associated with martyrdom (cup and baptism) through the use of intercalation. Since Jesus' private instruction usually relates to something that immediately preceded it (e.g., 4:10–20; 7:17–23; 8:14–21; 9:28–29, 33–37; 10:10–12;

13:3–37), the reader may presume that the mystery of the kingdom of God concerns the transition from death to life. Similarly, Mark 9:2–13 offers a vision of Jesus' resurrected state followed by a private teaching stressing the scriptural necessity "that he should suffer many things and be treated with contempt." The narrator does not explain why Jesus speaks to Peter, James and John about the common fates of Elijah (John the Baptist) and the Son of man while they descend the mountain, but there are indications that Jesus is explicating the vision that these three just witnessed. This discussion is preceded by Jesus' reference to the vision in the form of a charge "to tell no one what they had seen, until the Son of man should have risen from the dead" (9:9), and the disciples' inquiry about Elijah's return is represented as a response to their confusion about "the rising from the dead." Jesus' answer in 9:12–13 indicates that just as it was predicted that Elijah must come first, and did, covertly, in the mission and suffering of John the Baptist, so, too, the Son of man must appear incognito and suffer many things. The reader is left to find the thread that connects the various details, but needs only to look back to the teaching in relation to which this episode happens "after six days." The sayings in 8:34–38 affirm the apocalyptic precept that resurrection is the reward of the martyr. The role of suffering and death as a prelude to the state of exaltation witnessed by the disciples is likewise what the voice from the cloud iterates when it tells the disciples to "Listen to him!" for it was Jesus' words about his passion that Peter had resisted hearing, and Jesus resumes this teaching in 9:12–13. Thus the transfiguration "is meant to reassure the disciples that both for Jesus and for them glory *will* follow suffering but it will not bypass the way of the cross."[10]

Both Mark 9:2–13 and LGM 1 are concerned with resurrection or eternal life and depict Jesus offering a private, yet enigmatic, disclosure of the suffering involved in its attainment. The theme of transformation through suffering and death is likewise prefigured in the story of Jesus' baptism—provided one perceives Jesus' movements within the prologue as a microcosm for the gospel as a whole.[11] Just as the larger narrative presents Jesus journeying from Galilee to Judea to be crucified then returning to Galilee, the prologue presents Jesus journeying from Galilee to Judea to be baptized then returning to Galilee. If the prologue is read as a symbolic plot synopsis, then Jesus' crucifixion is represented figuratively by his baptism, an act of death and rebirth. The parallelism between these two events is deliberately underscored by the fact that both result in a declaration that Jesus is God's Son, but the reader will not perceive this connection until Jesus crosses the Jordan River into Judea (LGM 1:13) and speaks ominously of his "baptism" (Mark 10:38–39).

We saw in the last chapter that the baptism, transfiguration, and crucifixion share a number of verbal and thematic parallels. When these events are
read as variations of the same theme it becomes apparent that "both the Baptismal narrative and that of the Transfiguration are concerned with teaching
that Christ's glory is inextricably bound up with the mystery of his sufferings
and death."[12] I am tempted to suggest that the baptism and transfiguration
form a bracket around the Galilean section (overlapping the start of the central section) much as the known LGM additions and the empty tomb story
bracket the Jerusalem section (and overlap the end of the central section). In
the first pair of brackets, Jesus is involved in a real baptism (1:9–11) and a
symbolic resurrection (9:2–8); in the second, both Jesus and the young man
are involved in a symbolic baptism (Mark 10:38–39; LGM 1b) and a real resurrection (Mark 16:1–8; LGM 1a).

## The "Great Cry" from the Tomb

LGM 1 includes the peculiar detail that a great cry is heard from the tomb
before Jesus reaches it. The timing of this voice naturally causes problems for
commentators. Some suppose that the miracle was performed at a distance[13]
or that the young man was not entirely dead to start with.[14] These interpretations safeguard the literal level of the text from violation by an impossible
detail, but are not encouraged by the narrative. Rather, the reader has been
led to assume that the physical contact gained through Jesus' gesture of
stretching out his hand and touching or raising a person (LGM 1:7) is essential in restoring wholeness and life (e.g., Mark 1:31, 41; 5:23, 41–42; 6:5;
7:32; 8:23, 25; 9:27). Other scholars, presuming the voice to be an impossible detail, construe its presence as a tradition-historical problem, noting
that the words "in a loud voice" are also used in John 11:43 to dramatize the
summoning of Lazarus from the tomb. For them, the pertinent question is
whether a stranger form of the same detail is indicative of a more primitive
or a more developed tradition.[15] John Crossan considered the larger contexts of both gospels in his assessment of the tradition-historical question: "In
Mark…a 'great cry' is uttered both by demons as Jesus exorcises them (1:26;
5:7) and by Jesus himself as he dies (15:34, 37). In [LGM 1], then, it has overtones of the struggle with the demonic power of death. But John never uses
it elsewhere, and in 11:43 it seems at best a residue."[16] The resemblance
between this loud voice and the responses of demons to Jesus' mere presence
recalls previous conflicts with "the demonic power of death," whose minions
were causing their hosts to act in self-destructive ways (1:26; 5:2–5, 13;
9:18, 20, 22, 26).[17] But there is no demon and no exorcism in LGM 1a,

only an unexplained cry in response to Jesus' proximity. So in what sense is this voice the power of death? In order to answer this question it is necessary to consider the connotations of the words voice (φωνή) and great (μέγας) in the Markan gospel.

As Frederick W. Danker noted, the word *voice* "is reserved by Mark for extraordinary communication." It first occurs in 1:3 in reference to the prophetic message of John the Baptist, "the voice of one crying in the wilderness" (Isa 40:3). Subsequently it is used to describe the unexpected intervening voice of God (Bath Qol), which declares Jesus to be "my Son" (1:11; 9:7), and in reference to the alarmed cry of demoniacs, who likewise recognize that Jesus is "the Holy One of God" and "the Son of the Most High God" (1:26; 5:7).[18] The adjective *great*, on the other hand, is frequently used in connection with symbolizations or embodiments of death. The demoniacs who cry out "in a great voice" are the most obvious embodiments of the power of death (1:26; 5:7). But this power is also embodied in more symbolic forms: The storm at sea caused by the "great wind" (4:37) is a metaphor for "the powers of chaos in general," as is frequently the case in the Psalms and in ancient Near Eastern poetry.[19] The "great herd" of possessed pigs (5:11) that drowns in the sea after receiving Legion's demons makes concrete the great number and "destructive nature" of the demons Jesus destroyed.[20] And the "very great stone" that sealed Jesus' tomb (16:4) clearly signifies the power of death that is defeated through Jesus' resurrection.[21] The word *great* is also connected with the theme of exorcism: the demon in Capernaum is rebuked, Legion is sent out, and the great wind on the sea is rebuked. Further, the specific theme of crying out in a great voice is connected with the thought of imminent destruction: Jesus succumbs to death with two great cries, and the Capernaum and Gerasene demoniacs express their fear of destruction (or torment) "in a great voice" (cf. 1:24; 5:7). Thus, within the larger context of the Gospel of Mark, the "great voice" in LGM 1:5 must in some sense represent "death, about to be worsted."[22] The very presence of the messiah now provokes terror not just in the demons who seek human destruction, but in Death itself.

As a personification of the demonic realm, the alarmed cry that emanates from a dead man violates the boundary between literal and poetic, turning this raising miracle into a paradigm for the general conflict between the messiah and the powers of death that is occurring in this gospel. Because Jesus challenges Death itself, the revivification of the young man's corpse acquires eschatological overtones of resurrection, thereby anticipating Jesus' decisive victory, which this young man will announce from Jesus' tomb.

The exorcism-like resurrection in LGM 1a is paralleled by a resurrection-like exorcism in Mark 9:25–27: "And when Jesus saw that a crowd came running together, he rebuked the unclean spirit, saying to it, 'You dumb and deaf spirit, I command you, come out of him, and never enter him again.' And after crying out and convulsing him terribly, it came out, and the boy was like a corpse; so that most of them said, 'He is dead.' But Jesus took him by the hand and lifted him up, and he arose." As James M. Robinson commented, "Following upon the act of exorcism, the scene is depicted so as to make it evident that violence and death itself have been cast out. Jesus' cure of the epileptic boy is described in terms of resurrection."[23] The notion that Jesus' exorcisms are conflicts with the powers of death is unmistakable in this story, a great deal of which recounts the attempts this demon would make on the boy's life (9:18, 20, 22, 26). The symbolism of defeating death is even more explicit in LGM 1a. The resurrection-like exorcism, occurring just before the second passion prediction, and the exorcism-like resurrection, occurring just after the third, together depict salvation as a victory over forces antithetical to life.

## "The Mystery of the Kingdom of God"

In Mark 4:10, an inner circle of Jesus' followers ("those who were about him with the twelve") privately ask Jesus why he speaks to the crowds in parables. Jesus replies that the mystery of the kingdom of God is reserved for his associates; "those outside" experience everything in riddles, so that they cannot understand what they hear and see, and therefore do not repent and receive forgiveness. Jesus then proceeds to explain the parable of the Sower, without specifying how that parable, or any other, conveys the mystery. The situation in LGM 1b is similar. The mystery of the kingdom of God is taught in private to a would-be disciple without the substance of this mystery being disclosed in a direct way to the reader. Excluded from the contents, the reader is apt to find the information about the relative day and hour of this instruction (after six days, in the evening) and the costume in which it was received (linen) more riddling than revealing.[24] Thus LGM 1:12 extends the dilemma created by Mark 4:11: any reader who wishes to be more than an outsider must figure out the mystery of the kingdom of God.

Fortunately, longer Mark offers enough clues to allow the reader to resolve the enigma with some effort. The wrapping of LGM 1 and 2 around the request of James and John connects this mystery to the discipleship theme of following Jesus in the way to life through death, as does the structural parallel between LGM 1 and the transfiguration, an incident which connects Jesus' future glory with "the mystery of his sufferings and death."[25] The two verbal parallels to the man with many possessions imply that this

mystery concerns what the young man must do to inherit eternal life. The
pattern whereby episodes of private instruction concern some aspect of the
preceding incident likewise suggests that the mystery of the kingdom of God
is somehow connected with resurrection. In keeping with the initial reference to this mystery after the parable of the Sower, LGM 1b presumably
treats the raising miracle in LGM 1a as "an acted parable, or allegory, like
the withering of the fruitless fig tree,"[26] that conceals the eschatological
mystery of the kingdom of God from "those outside" but functions to
reveal this truth to insiders like the young man, with the help of private
instruction (cf. 4:1–20).

It is not difficult to imagine LGM 1a as a parable of the kingdom, for the
Markan concept of parable is not limited to the brief verbal narratives that function as extended metaphors for something else. The word *parable* itself is
applied to "any statement that includes an element of indirection, perhaps even
of obscurity, and hence demands explanation."[27] The common denominator
in Mark's usage is that the sayings be capable of a second level of meaning:
the overt sense conceals a more significant point. Moreover, the allusion to
Isa 6:9–10 in Mark 4:12 implies that it is not just what people hear but also
what they *see* that happens parabolically ("in parables"); the further allusions
to this passage from Isaiah in Mark 6:52 and 8:17–21 reinforce the impression that extraordinary actions, such as the miraculous feedings, can have a
deeper, parabolic significance.[28] So a miracle can certainly function as a parable of the kingdom of God. The clue that LGM 1a has such a meaning is provided by the "great voice" from the grave, an intrusion of poetic significance
into the literal level of the text.

As an enacted "parable" of the kingdom, the raising of the young man,
like the symbolic killing and raising of the epileptic boy (9:25–27), illustrates the paradox that one must undergo death in order to defeat it. The private explanation of this "parable" in LGM 1b expounds this insight by using
baptismal imagery of death and rebirth. However, despite the ritualistic, even
mystery-religion imagery, this man is *taught* a mystery, in keeping with the
instruction given to insiders in Mark 4:10–20. Baptism imagery is used here
to interpret the salvific dimension of the young man's rising according to
the analogy of dying (drowning in water) and rising again, though the baptism by which this transformation is attained is not the Christian rite itself but
a metaphorical "immersion" in literal suffering and death. To be baptized
with Jesus' baptism is to live a life of active self-abnegation patterned upon
Jesus' passion (8:34).

It would appear, then, that in the longer Gospel of Mark the mystery
of the kingdom of God is the paradox that one saves one's life by losing

it. This eschatological principle is the rationale that underlies both Mark's christology (15:31–32) and discipleship theology (8:35), the two main themes that appear in the central section of the narrative, where LGM 1 and 2 were placed.

## LGM 1:12 as an Elaboration of Themes Introduced in Mark 4:11–12

A number of Markan scholars have offered similar interpretations of the mystery of the kingdom of God that focus on the necessity of the messiah's death and the way of the cross. Eduard Schweizer interpreted the mystery as "the word of the cross" in articles published in the mid-1960s.[29] Madeleine Boucher decided that the mystery includes "the requirement for the disciple to 'deny himself and take up his cross' (8:34)" but also "a view of the messiahship which involves suffering": "the basic paradox is that he who works miracles with 'authority'…is the one who must suffer and die."[30] Similarly, Priscilla Patten stated that "Mark has interpreted both teachings and events to convey a message about the 'mystery of the kingdom' which was found to be the suffering, rejection, death, and vindication of the Son of Man." In a later article she voiced the suspicion that the secret behind the parables would reveal something about the messianic secret.[31] James G. Williams preferred to stress the christological dimension of the mystery as "the sacrificial suffering of the Son of man," but added, "In one sense, 'the way of the Lord' could be viewed as the theme of Mark, an alternative image appropriate to the 'mystery of the Kingdom.'"[32] John R. Donahue also saw the mystery of the kingdom of God as having both a christological and discipleship dimension. In his view, "the content of the 'mystery of the kingdom' in Mark is that the reign or power of God is now manifest in the brokenness of Jesus on the cross"; this mystery is in effect "the way of the cross."[33]

The congruence between what the mystery of the kingdom of God appears to mean in LGM 1:12 and this increasingly common conception of what this phrase denotes in Mark 4:11 is certainly noteworthy. Unfortunately, interpretations of 4:11–12 have always been difficult to substantiate exegetically. This problem is partly the result of inconsistencies in the parable discourse, the by-product of multiple stages of composition.[34] The resultant text is problematic, and no interpretation of Mark 4:11–12 will conform perfectly with all the details in the discourse as it now stands. Nevertheless, the longer text's equation of the mystery of the kingdom of God with the major discipleship and christological themes of the central section is in many ways consistent with developments in the canonical gospel of concepts intro-

duced in 4:11–12. I intend to demonstrate this consistency without attempting to resolve the numerous issues that pertain to the interpretation of the mystery of the kingdom of God in the canonical gospel.

There are features in the composition of Mark 4–8 that associate the
mystery of the kingdom of God with the important christological and discipleship themes introduced in the central section. To begin with, a connection
is provided implicitly in the use of "the word" (ὁ λόγος) to describe both the
message contained in the parables and the first prediction of the passion. In
4:33–34 the preceding discourse is described in terms of Jesus speaking "the
word" to the crowds through parables of the kingdom, but offering private
explanations to his disciples. In other words, "the word" is synonymous with
the message that "occurs" (γίνεται) to outsiders in riddles but has been given
to "those who were about him with the twelve";[35] it is the mystery of the kingdom of God. By speaking the word in parables, Jesus is taking on the role of
the sower in the explanation of the Sower parable, where "the word" occurs
eight times in reference to his message (4:14–20). Thus, Jesus is "disseminat-
ing" the word or mystery in riddling speech.

But whereas in Mark 4 the narrator tells us that Jesus "spoke the word
to them" using parables, immediately after the first passion prediction the narrator declares that Jesus "spoke the word openly" (8:32). The reference to *open*
speaking of "the word" implies a transition from the paradigm of riddling
speech established in the parable discourse and therefore a different way of
speaking about the same subject.[36] That Mark is suggesting a transition from
parabolic to plain disclosure of the mystery of the kingdom is also supported
by the arrangement of incidents leading up to this section. Beginning with
the parable discourse and culminating in the discussion about bread in the
boat, Mark develops the theme of the disciples' incomprehension.[37] They do
not understand the parable of the Sower, which is the key to understanding
the others (4:13);[38] they wonder who Jesus is in view of his mastery of wind
and sea (4:41); they are astounded that he can walk on the water, precisely
because they also do not understand the first feeding miracle (6:51–52);
they do not comprehend the parable about the true source of defilement,
which should have been a riddle only to the crowds (7:18); and they do not
understand the "parable" of the leaven of the Pharisees and Herod because
they also have not comprehended the second feeding miracle (8:14–21).

It would be difficult to argue that these misunderstandings all involve one
theme. However, one larger implication to the disciples' incomprehension is
developed in the final pericope, 8:14–21. Here Jesus reprimands his disciples
for their *blindness* concerning a reality revealed in the nature miracles: "Do you
not yet perceive or understand? Are your hearts hardened? Having eyes do

you not see, and having ears do you not hear?...Do you not yet understand?" These words echo the Isaian language of blindness in 4:12 and Jesus' rebuke in 4:13, as well as the disciples' hardhearted confusion because of "the loaves" when confronted by Jesus walking on the sea (6:52), which might itself pick up the theme of hardheartedness in Isa 6:9–10. The intratextual linking of 4:12–13; 6:52; and 8:14–21 indicates that the nature miracles, particularly the feedings, are parabolic manifestations of the mystery introduced in the parable discourse.

Jesus' rebuking of his disciples for their blindness concerning the nature miracles is immediately followed by a transitional story (the first "bracket" around the central section) in which a two-stage healing of blindness appears to characterize the disciples' imminent recognition of Jesus' messiahship as a transition from spiritual blindness (having eyes but not seeing) to "fuzzy" perception (note the use of βλέπω in 8:18 and 8:23, 24). Hence "Peter's 'trees-as-men-walking' declaration" should represent a *partial* perception of that same reality about which the disciples were blind when confronted by the nature miracles: the mystery of the kingdom of God.[39] His confession that Jesus is the Christ marks a first step in the disciples' insight into the larger, eschatological mystery of the rule of God which Jesus mediates.

At 8:29 Peter comes to realize *that* redemption is occurring with Jesus. But he does not comprehend what this redemption entails for Jesus and his followers. Jesus therefore begins to re-educate his disciples with instruction in the necessity of the Son of man's death and the paradoxes of salvation. The three "plain" and (mostly) private discipleship teaching cycles appear therefore to constitute the most unambiguous statements about the mystery of the kingdom of God in Mark. These teachings disclose the implications for messiahship and discipleship of the mystery that life comes through suffering and death.[40]

In terms of composition, therefore, it makes sense that LGM 1 should appear in the central section of the Markan gospel and associate this mystery with the way to life through death. This association of the mystery of the kingdom of God with discipleship accords, moreover, with a general shift in the way the kingdom of God is described in the central section. Before the central section, Jesus' proclamation of the kingdom of God concerns the arrival of God's rule and the nature of its coming. In the central section, however, the theme of the coming of the kingdom (or its final glory) occurs only in 9:1; the other kingdom sayings concentrate on the matter of what a disciple must do (or be or receive) in order to enter the kingdom. A disciple must overcome all penchants to sin (9:47), adopt the nominal status of a child (10:14), embrace the kingdom in the trifling form of a child (10:15), and relinquish wealth (10:23–25).

## The Mystery of the Kingdom of God and the Markan Gospel's Imperative of "Spiritual" Understanding

These observations concerning how LGM 1 accords with the mystery/misunderstanding theme in Mark's gospel may be supplemented through a reader-response analysis of how the theme of the disciples' incomprehension affects the implied reader. Throughout Mark 4 and again in the discussion about the loaves in Mark 8, the imperative of understanding is communicated to the reader. This expectation is first conveyed by the Sower parable, which is bracketed by the commands "Listen! Look!" and "Whoever has ears to hear, hear!" (4:3, 9; cf. 7:14). These summonses to attention accentuate the necessity of perceiving a second level of meaning within the parable. The importance of perceiving this meaning is again reinforced by Jesus' reproach of his disciples, the supposed insiders, for not having understood this parable (4:13). Jesus' allegorical explanation likewise places emphasis on understanding; in addition to outlining various barriers to discipleship, it provides a commentary on how it is that some people come to perceive the mystery whereas others do not. The different soils are also different kinds of *hearers*:

> The interpretation of the first parable is devoted to an explanation of...two levels [of comprehension]: the superficial level, called "seeing" and "hearing" (v. 12), is exemplified by those who "hear" the word but then fall away (vv. 15, 16, 18). The deeper level, called "knowing" and "understanding" (v. 12), is itself the objective of the interpretation (v. 13), and is exemplified by the fourth example: "These hear the word and receive it and bear fruit..." (v. 20). Most illuminating are Mark's explanations for the two levels: progress from the first to the second level is blocked by the cosmic enemy of Christ, Satan (v. 15)....The deeper level is given by God (v. 11), and corresponds to the "repentance" and "forgiveness" (v. 12) for which the gospel calls....Thus the struggle for "understanding" is the inner aspect of the struggle between Satan and God constituting the history of Jesus.[41]

The need to work at discerning the mystery concealed in "the word" is the focus of 4:21–25: "And he said to them, 'Is a lamp brought in to be put under a bushel, or under a bed, and not on a stand? For there is nothing hid, except to be made manifest; nor is anything secret, except to come to light. Whoever has ears to hear, hear!' And he said to them, 'Take heed what you hear; the measure you give will be the measure you get, and still more will be given you. For to the one who has will more be given; and from the one who has not, even what that person has will be taken away.'" The explanatory *gar* clauses that follow the parables of the lamp and the measure indicate that these parables are interpreted by the aphorisms that follow them. Thus 4:21–22 and 4:24–25 each form a unit. In context, the reference to the illogicality of taking out a lamp in order to place it under a bushel concerns the mystery concealed in the parables or, more generally, the concealed revelation of the mystery of the kingdom in Jesus' riddling words and actions.[42] Verse 21 indicates that the lamp, or hidden truth about the nature of God's rule, is not supposed to remain hidden, and v. 22 explains, paradoxically, that the hiding occurred *in order that* (ἵνα) the mystery might come to light. Interposed between the two units is another call to listen and discern: "Whoever has ears to hear, hear!" (v. 23). This general call to *anyone* is another indication to the reader that knowledge of the mystery requires a willingness to pay close attention to the parables and the ability to discern their hidden truths. This theme is repeated in the next sentence, "Take heed what you hear," which directs the interpretation of the parable of the measure: "The measure of listening of the reader is the basis for the measure of the reader's understanding of what has been said; according to that measure the secret will be revealed to him and the riddle solved, and he will be able to see even more than he could expect on account of the attention given by him (4:24b). The reader who is attentive is given understanding, but the reader who is not is robbed even of the understanding he has (4:25)."[43]

We see, then, that Mark 4:21–25 develops the theme in 4:14–20 that discipleship is a struggle to "bear fruit" in an environment of forces hostile to "the word" by adding that success depends upon *straining to understand the deeper truths conveyed parabolically in this gospel*. This effort is rewarded with revelation. As 4:11–12 indicated, insight into the mystery is essential for salvation, for this knowledge is what leads a person to repent and be forgiven. The principle that deeper understanding is acquired through concerted effort can account for why this mystery is not spelled out for the reader within Jesus' private explanations of the parables. The reader must discover for him- or herself what vital truth is contained in all the kingdom parables.

Mark returns to the theme of the importance of "spiritual" understanding in 8:14–21. This discussion about bread and understanding is one of the more peculiar incidents in the gospel. On the surface, the unfolding of this passage makes perfect sense. Jesus says something enigmatic about leaven which reminds his disciples of the fact that they have only one loaf of bread with them in the boat. They start to become concerned, and Jesus severely reprimands them for their obduracy, pointing out that he recently fed nine thousand men with a dozen loaves of bread and that the leftovers were greater than the amount of food with which he started.

As straightforward and sensible as this interchange may be, an attentive reader will realize that more is being said. Jesus' protracted comments about the imperceptiveness of his disciples contain allusions to two previous incidents, both of which involve the theme of inability to perceive deeper truths evident in his words and deeds. The question "Are your hearts hardened?" is reminiscent of Mark's perplexing explanation for the disciples' apprehension in seeing Jesus walking on the water: "And they were utterly astounded, for they did not understand about the loaves, but their hearts were hardened" (6:51b–52). And Jesus' further interrogatory "Having eyes do you not see, and having ears do you not hear?" is reminiscent of his earlier allusion to Isa 6:9–10 as an explanation for why outsiders experience everything relating to the mystery of the kingdom of God in riddles (4:11–12). That the feeding miracles prove Jesus capable of providing sustenance for his disciples cannot, therefore, entirely be the point. His disciples should have seen something in these two miracles that would have given them a profound and essential insight into who Jesus is, the sort of insight that would forestall their fears and incomprehension.

What this insight is supposed to be, however, is far from apparent to the reader. As Jouette M. Bassler noticed, Mark's "explanation" that the disciples were astounded at seeing Jesus walking on the sea because "they did not understand about the loaves" is itself remarkably obscure. Instead of offering clarification, this authorial remark manages precisely to promote confusion about *both* the sea-walking episode and the first feeding miracle:

> In the first place, this is not the explanation expected by the reader, who would find more illuminating a reference to the earlier episode where Jesus had demonstrated similar mastery over wind and waves (4:35–41). Furthermore, as Quentin Quesnell has noted, this explanation really clarifies nothing. "It leaves completely unspecified what they had not understood about the [loaves], and 6:30–44 contained no hint that there was anything about the [loaves] which required a special understanding...." At first reading, then, the narrative comment about the loaves has little apparent connection with the sea-walking episode. Its presence is jarring, the flow of the narrative is blocked, and the reader is provoked into considering possible modes of connection yet is unable to resolve the problem with the information given.[44]

After the first feeding story the reader receives this indication that something important was there to be perceived. After the second feeding the point is made again. By alluding to the confounding "explanation" in 6:52, Mark 8:17–18 revives the reader's earlier confusion about the significance of the loaves though hints that this truth is a part of the saving knowledge announced in chapter 4 but, alas, never clearly revealed. The reader, still wondering about the meaning of "the leaven of the Pharisees and the leaven of Herod," is manipulated into recognizing that she or he also does not understand what the two feeding miracles reveal about Jesus or how this knowledge is related to the mystery of the kingdom of God. But far be it from Jesus to offer some words of revelation; instead, he leads his disciples, and the reader, through a patronizing review of the ratios of loaves (he ignores the fish) to people to leftovers involved in the two feeding miracles, a protracted synopsis that culminates in the question "Do you not yet understand?" On this note the pericope ends, leaving the reader as dumfounded as the disciples about what it is that was seen but not perceived when Jesus multiplied the loaves.

The most obvious message implied by the review of quantities is that Jesus' performance has declined sharply, for the second time he used more loaves to feed fewer people and had fewer morsels left over. The christological implications of that fact are difficult to contemplate, and consequently the reader will probably not pursue this line of thought. Frustrated, he or she will probably begin to wonder whether an allegorical clue was supplied in the numbers. Yet here again there seems to be indirection, for it is hardly apparent from the story what the numbers twelve or seven or five could symbolize.[45] "There is," as Frank Kermode recognized, "a strong suggestion that the answer has to do with number," but anyone who offers a solution based on numerology ends up as befuddled as the disciples.[46] In consequence of such narrative manoeuvrings, "the reader is led, at a crucial point in the narrative, to *the same internal disposition that the disciples possess in the narrative: misunderstanding and confusion*."[47] The interchange between Jesus and his disciples concerning bread brings Mark's readers face to face with their own incomprehension, with the fact that they, too, are outsiders to the deeper truths conveyed within this story. This is more than a little peculiar. "As it stands, the story seems self-defeating, unless its point were that proper insight is quite beyond all of us and yet required all the same." This is John Meagher's assessment of Mark 8:14–21, and as counterintuitive as it might seem to scholars working within a tradition-critical framework, it warrants consideration by a literary critic.[48]

Why would an author introduce the notion of a mystery requisite to repentance and salvation, omit a clear explanation of this mystery, then later suggest to his readers that they, like Jesus' dimwitted and hardhearted disciples, are outsiders to the truth? Why hide this truth in the first place? Bassler suggested that Mark wished at the close of the Galilean section to induce his readers to pay close attention to the upcoming central section, where the essential teachings of the gospel are conveyed. While the disciples begin to see the mystery imperfectly, the readers focus hard on the "plain" teachings about "the word," seeking some insight into the feeding miracles.

That rhetorical purpose may be the most obvious solution to the riddle of the loaves. Nevertheless, we may still wonder what was implicit in "the loaves" that the disciples and the reader could have seen. Mark's focus on the loaves to the exclusion of the fish suggests that he considered the loaves to have some special significance. Although I am as obtuse as the disciples about this issue, I suspect that Mark's emphasis upon the loaves points to the resemblance between these feeding miracles and Moses' provision of manna in the wilderness. If so, then the disciples and the crowds have missed the messianic implication that Jesus is leading them in a new Exodus. Accordingly, Peter's recognition that Jesus is the Christ would mark his realization of the redemptive significance of the loaves. But that recognition was only a partial insight. Full insight into the loaves is possible only in retrospect of the last supper, when Jesus once more takes, blesses, breaks, and offers bread (14:22; cf. 6:41; 8:6). There the reader learns that the "parable" of the loaves refers in some way to "Jesus' broken body on the cross."[49]

## Deeper Understanding as a Literary Agenda Shared by the Longer and Shorter Gospels

It is apparent that the shorter Gospel of Mark demands the kind of deeper or "spiritual" understanding of its own narrative that the longer gospel helps provide. The shorter gospel presents this understanding as a prerequisite to repentance and salvation. Yet it also makes its concealed truths difficult to penetrate. The mystery of the kingdom of God and the cameo of the linen-attired young man at Jesus' arrest are enigmas in the shorter gospel. The puzzlement they produce in the reader appears to be quite deliberate. The clearest message that a reader of the canonical version of Mark can discern from Mark 4:11–12; 8:14–21; and 14:51–52 is that she or he does not understand everything. A reader who feels that there is more that can and should be understood will be highly motivated to read "a more spiritual gospel" that offers an initiation into the essential teachings of the Markan gospel. Was that perhaps Mark's intention? It is time to survey the results of this study and determine whether the same person wrote both gospels.

# ⤞9⤝

# Conclusions

## The Nature and Original Purpose
## of the Longer Gospel

The fifteen verses from longer Mark quoted in Clement's letter elaborate the main discipleship teaching of Mark's central section, namely, that whoever would come after Jesus must be willing to deny self in imitation of Jesus' passion. Mark's Jesus describes the way to salvation through self-abnegation, or life through death, metaphorically, using the imagery of taking up one's cross (8:34–35), being a child (10:14), becoming a slave or servant for others (9:35; 10:43–45), and sharing his "cup" and "baptism" of suffering and death (10:38–39). The longer text develops this theme by sandwiching Mark 10:35–45 between LGM 1 and 2, allowing a careful reader to perceive that the young man who appears in Gethsemane symbolizes Jesus' demand that his disciples undergo his "baptism" or passion. Moreover, the positioning of these two additions at the transition between the central section and the passion narrative creates a more obvious frame around the passion narrative than that appearing in canonical Mark, for in the longer text, the image of Jesus leading his followers on the way to life through death (Mark 10:32; 16:7–8) now occurs in connection with two raising miracles involving Jesus, a tomb, a stone that rolls, an unnamed young man, and three women (the third mentioned being Salome). In longer Mark, the young man whom Jesus raised from the dead is also the young man who announces Jesus' resurrection and the restoration of his disciples, whose failure he previously symbolized (14:51–52).

These literary-critical conclusions concur with Clement's conception that longer Mark was a "more spiritual" version of Mark, meaning one that con-

---

Notes to chapter 9 start on page 278

centrates more on the figurative dimension of the Markan text (the spirit or soul) than on the literal level or external "facts" (the body). The pericope Clement quoted elaborates two longstanding mysteries in the Gospel of Mark: the mystery of the kingdom of God and the enigma of the young man dressed in linen. Both the longer and shorter gospels stress the notion that salvation is reserved for those who penetrate the former mystery, which is concealed within Jesus' parabolic discourses and actions (4:10–12; LGM 1:12). This mystery "has been given" to Jesus' disciples, yet they do not comprehend it, and neither does the average reader of the canonical text, who is given no direct explanation and is left to ponder various clues in the narrative, ultimately sympathizing with Jesus' uncomprehending disciples. Because LGM 1 and 2 utilize the Markan technique of ambiguous narration ("gaps"), these fifteen verses initially deepen this mystery, exploiting the enigmas of Mark 4:11 and 14:51–52. But because LGM 1 and 2 also utilize Markan literary techniques that aid interpretation, such as intercalation, framing stories, and verbal echoes, these verses ultimately offer an attentive reader a satisfying solution to these perplexing aspects of the shorter version and assist this person in identifying with, or "joining," the circle of disciples who receive additional instruction—the young man and "those who were about him with the twelve" (4:10). Such a gospel would be of interest to "those who were being perfected" in knowledge within the Alexandrian community (I.20–22). Clement's accurate characterization of the longer gospel's nature probably attests to a profound study of its contents; it is only natural to suppose that he himself was "initiated" into the "great mysteries" through a guided exposition of this and other useful texts.

Since this text appealed to Christians who sought to derive the essential, esoteric teachings of Christianity anagogically from the scriptures, it is plausible that its author took to heart the Alexandrian proclivity to view Christianity as a philosophy containing esoteric teachings.[1] Yet despite this more esoteric orientation, the truths conveyed through LGM 1 and 2 are still available to readers of the canonical gospel. In fact, the same themes are featured in "plain" language in the central section of the Markan gospel. What LGM 1 and 2 do is deepen a reader's appreciation of this gospel's christology and discipleship theology. Moreover, the heightened esotericism of the longer gospel does not signify a belief in salvation through insight and secret knowledge or even a basically cerebral and individualistic approach, since the insights achieved through contemplation of the longer text reinforce the active and community-oriented approach to discipleship espoused in Mark 8:22–10:52.

The longer text's focus on deeper understanding has implications concerning its intended audience. Scholars generally assume that all gospels were written for hearers. Certainly the author of the canonical gospel strove to make his message accessible to a wide and diversified audience, for he wrote the way people speak and used an uncomplicated syntax and vocabulary. But the canonical author's interest in unschooled hearers does not mean that he had only one kind of person in view, and literary-critical scholarship has shown that Mark's story is accommodating to the reader-response presupposition of a visual reading experience. That is, Mark also had educated *readers* in mind. He wrote a text that has something for everyone. The longer Gospel of Mark is written in the same aural and accessible style, but it was directed more toward persons who, like Origen, Clement, Philo, and the members of the Jewish Therapeutae, had the ability to study a text closely and privately, pondering hidden meanings.

In view of Clement's opinion that the longer gospel did not contain any secret materials in an undisguised form, there is no good reason to call this text the Secret Gospel of Mark or to picture it as something whose existence was revealed only to the initiated. Morton Smith simply mistranslated the description *mystikon euangelion* (II.6, 12), giving *mystikon* a sense that does not accord with the way second-century church fathers used the word. When Clement used *mystikos* in connection with sacred texts, he was referring to the "mystic" or figurative meaning concealed within the literal sense. The phrase *mystikon euangelion* is therefore better translated as "the mystic gospel" and understood not as a title but as a synonym for "a more spiritual gospel." The longer text was more esoteric than the shorter text, but it was something that could in theory be read to anyone, since it did not disclose any secrets in an overt fashion. In that sense, the longer Gospel of Mark was like the *Stromateis*, which Clement composed with deliberate obfuscation in full knowledge that "uninitiated" readers would inevitably have access to it. Indeed, the parallelism in Clement's descriptions of how he and Mark composed their respective "theological" works is a good indication that he thought that the longer text was designed to adumbrate the secret oral teachings in a publicly accessible, written form (*Strom.* I.1.14.3; *Letter to Theodore* I.18–27). In both cases Clement described an author making a careful selection of theologically useful materials from a set of personal notes that consist of the author's own recollections of his teacher(s), and in both cases Clement indicated that the decision to exclude certain traditions was made out of prudence rather than a grudging desire to withhold traditions from the uninstructed. Interestingly, Clement's justification for producing his own deliberately obscure work was firmly grounded in his understanding of the Markan theme that Jesus proclaimed the mystery of the kingdom of God in parables: "[The Lord] is telling us to receive the secret traditions of revealed knowledge…and…to pass them on to appropriate people, not to offer them to all without reserve, when he only pronounced thoughts in parables to them [Mark 4:33–34]. But in fact, my present outline of memoranda [i.e., the *Stromateis*] contains the truth in a kind of sporadic and dispersed fashion [cf. Mark 4:3–9], so as to avoid the attention of those who pick up ideas like jackdaws [Mark 4:4, 15]. When it lights on good farmers [Mark 4:20], each of the germs of truth will grow and show the full-grown grain [only Mark 4:28]" (*Strom.* I.12.56.2–3). So when Clement composed his *Stromateis* as a publicly accessible treatise of theological instruction that would neverthe-less withhold its secrets from the uninitiated, or at least casual, reader, he apparently thought that he was composing in a manner similar to the way Mark produced his other gospel.

Longer Mark's special utility in disclosing the secret, unwritten teachings may be the main reason for its confinement to persons who had proved themselves worthy of receiving such instruction, although the potential for misunderstanding passages like LGM 1b was probably a factor as well. Most likely, complications resulting from the use of an even longer and very embar-rassing version of the mystic gospel by the Carpocratians eventually led to greater discretion in the use of this text within the proto-orthodox church and, by Clement's day, a general reluctance to talk about it, not unlike the Jerusalem Patriarchate's present attitude toward the manuscript in response to Smith's controversial interpretation of LGM 1b.

Previous scholarship has misunderstood not only the nature of the longer text but also the manner of its use in Alexandria. The standard pre-supposition that LGM 1 and 2 were read liturgically and mainly in isola-tion from their literary context is simply mistaken. The nocturnal instruction of the young man does involve baptism imagery and is set in Bethany beyond the Jordan, a place where John the Baptist worked. But the linen sheet is metaphorical: to undergo Jesus' baptism is to follow in the way of the cross, as the young man briefly attempts to do in Gethsemane. The longer text frustrates every attempt to read this imagery more literally. Like-wise, although mystery-religion imagery pervades the *Letter to Theodore*, this imagery is metaphorical. It connotes the progressive disclosure of secret theological truths through directed scriptural exegesis (I.25–26). This fig-urative use of mystery-religion language was standard in the writings of Alexandrian Jewish and Christian authors of this period (e.g., Philo and Ori-gen) and should not be taken to imply a cultic setting for readings of the longer text. Clement's belief that Jesus baptized only Peter further under-mines the notion that he interpreted LGM 1b as a baptism, as do his state-ments that Mark wrote his Roman gospel for catechumens and his

Alexandrian gospel for Christians advancing *in gnosis*. Longer Mark's connection with "the great mysteries" concerns the highest stage of theological education. Consequently, this text was not read annually in conjunction with a special festival, such as Easter; rather, it was expounded anagogically on a day-to-day basis as a means of transmitting the secret oral traditions of the "true philosophy."

Given the affinity between longer Mark's account of private teaching and Clement's opinion that the secret teachings be transmitted to select individuals in private, it is reasonable to suspect that Clement saw in LGM 1b a precedent for initiating only worthy individuals into the small and great mysteries of nature and theology. That is how he interpreted elements relating to the mystery of the kingdom of God in the canonical gospel. Unfortunately, the existing copy of the letter breaks off at the point at which Clement began his exegesis of LGM 1 and 2. If Clement's interpretation contained elements of the secret doctrines that longer Mark was used to explicate, this section was probably deliberately omitted by whoever published the collection of Clement's letters of which this one was a part (I.1). Thus, the manuscript Smith found may not be an incomplete copy of a complete exemplar but a complete copy of a private communication that was edited prior to its publication.

Although we have little evidence on which to base conclusions about the longer gospel as a whole, certain generalizations seem warranted. To start with, Clement's descriptions of how and why this text was written imply that it was significantly longer than the canonical gospel. The amplified gospel presumably contained enough material of a "mystic" character to affect the overall nature of the Markan gospel such that it seemed less like the "bodily" synoptic gospels and more like the Gospel of John. Since LGM 1 provides literarily independent accounts of two narratives otherwise unique to the Gospel of John (1:35–40; 10:40–11:54), it is reasonable to suppose that longer Mark's similarity to the Fourth Gospel involved more than its "spiritual" orientation; longer Mark may have had other, independent contacts with Johannine traditions. Clement's comments about the mystic nature of longer Mark suggest, moreover, that it contained additional overtly symbolic (hence "odd") narratives comparable to Mark 14:51–52 and, perhaps, more riddling utterances like Mark's three discourses "in parables" (3:23–30; 4:1–34; 12:1–12). Longer Mark as a whole likely stressed the importance of seeing with discernment, in keeping with the theme in the parable chapter that true insiders are persons who not only see but perceive, not only hear, but comprehend.

## Who Wrote the Longer Gospel?

Morton Smith thought longer Mark was "an imitation [of Mark] of the simplest and most childish sort," and most scholars have agreed.[2] Conservative scholars prefer to view "secret" Mark as "a conscious attempt to ape Markan literary style…that has nothing to do with either Markan provenance or purposes" and to dismiss it as a revision of John 11.[3] The present study calls this pervasive bias into question. The numerous, often pointless, contradictions between LGM 1a and John 11, and between LGM 1b and John 1:35–40, are the sort of thing we find when we compare John and the synoptics. Some of these differences, such as the setting of the miracle in Peraea rather than Judea, the absence of the names Lazarus and Mary, and the absence of a second Bethany and a second sister, are very hard to account for if the author knew the canonical version. A variety of features of LGM 1 are most readily explained if this story is independent of John: the basic conformity of LGM 1a to Markan healing stories; the presence of Markan redactional characteristics where LGM 1 diverges from the healing-story formula; the absence of Johannine language, characteristics, and editorial emphases; and the absence of elements in John 11 that are uncharacteristic of oral tradition. We are probably dealing with a gospel that was written during the same period as the canonical gospels by someone who did not know the Gospel of John but did have access to the collective memories of Christian communities, including stories about Jesus that were set in Bethany beyond the Jordan.

The use of Markan literary techniques supports this conclusion, and points us to Mark himself. Just as canonical Mark uses two stories about Jesus healing blindness to set off the central, discipleship section (8:22–26; 10:46–52), longer Mark uses two stories about Jesus and a young man to frame the passion narrative. Whereas the matched pair of healing stories around the central section implies that Jesus is attempting to "heal" his disciples of their "blindness" concerning his identity (8:18, 27–33), the matched pair of resurrection stories around the Jerusalem section implies that Jesus is leading these disciples in the way to life through death. That much was implied by the *inclusio* formed by 10:32 and 16:7–8. With the addition of LGM 1 and 2, this frame around the passion becomes much more effective, and the significance of the anonymous young man in Gethsemane comes more clearly into focus: he is a disciple symbolically wrapped like a corpse in order to follow the one whose path leads through death to life.

The author of LGM 1 and 2 elucidated the significance of that figure by using Mark's technique of intercalation, aware that Mark used this device to illuminate puzzling incidents, such as the story of the cursing of the fig tree, which surrounds the clearing of the temple. In both of these instances of intercalation, an enigmatic incident becomes symbolic of the central, more intelligible incident. And in both cases, a puzzling explanatory *gar* clause offers a clue to the significance of the enigmatic incident. Interestingly, both of these intercalations were produced by wrapping the outer story around the inner.[4] The intercalation produced by the addition of LGM 1 and 2 conforms well with the criteria scholars have devised within the last fifteen years to distinguish this technique, both in form and function, from other types of interpolations. This congruence is apparent in some rather subtle ways, such as the lack of active character crossover[5] and the tendency of the $A^2$-story to include both "an allusion at its beginning which refers back to $A^1$, e.g., repetition of a theme, proper nouns, etc.,"[6] and a reference to "a new character or newly named group [as] the subject/actor of the first or second sentence of the reentered outer story."[7] LGM 1 and 2 do not conform perfectly to the established criteria, but neither do any of the six classic examples.

The story about the raising and instruction of the young man also uses Mark's technique of echoing phrases from earlier incidents as a way of implying thematic relatedness, as well as that favourite technique among reader-response critics: ambiguous, gap-laden narration. Like Mark 14:51–52, LGM 1b narrates an incident but leaves out the information a reader needs to make sense of what is transpiring—provoking the imagination yet frustrating every attempt to comprehend the details as parts of a larger whole. Finally, LGM 1 contains a few subtle Markan idiosyncrasies. As with two other stories in which Jesus raises a person by the hand, it is curiously unclear whether the person being raised up is actually dead (LGM 1:5; Mark 5:39; 9:26), and that person is described using diminutives (five in LGM 1 and 2; seven in Mark 5:21–24, 35–43; and two in Mark 9:14–27).

In addition to using Markan vocabulary, style, and literary techniques, the extant verses of longer Mark exhibit Markan redactional interests and theology. As is normal in Mark, the disciples come across as thoughtless and uncomprehending (cf. 5:31; 6:49–50; 7:17–18; 8:32; 9:32, 34, 38; 10:13, 35–41), Jesus gets thoroughly annoyed with them (cf. 4:13, 40; 8:4, 17–21, 33; 10:14), and Jesus performs the miracle despite the palpable tension that develops between him and the faithless people around him (cf. 2:5–11; 3:1–6; 4:38–40; 5:38–41; 9:18b–20, 23–25). The miracle concludes with Jesus entering a house and giving private instruction (cf. 9:28), and the movement to a new geo-political region is signalled by Jesus "getting up" and departing (LGM 1:13; Mark 7:24; 10:1). In terms of christology, Jesus is pictured as one who delivers people from the powers of death and destruction. Like Mark's exorcism stories, there is a confrontation with the power of death, during which a demonic voice cries out in fear of its destruction (cf. 1:24; 5:7). The "great cry" personifying death is reminiscent of the "great storm of wind" (4:37), the "great herd of swine" (5:11), and the "very great" stone (16:4), which represent the many faces of death that the messiah overcomes. The exorcistic element in the raising story is also reminiscent of the unexpected exorcistic language that appears in Mark's account of the healing of a leper ("having become angry...and having rebuked him immediately he cast him out"; 1:40–45). In terms discipleship theology, the longer text emphasizes the necessity of discerning the mystery of the kingdom of God and the need for a disciple to abandon self, following the example of Jesus' passion. As in Mark 4:10–12, this mystery is reserved for those who are with Jesus (LGM 1:8), is taught in private, and is not conveyed directly to the reader. The mystery of the kingdom of God and the way to life through death are one and the same thing in the longer gospel, in accordance with the opinions of some recent exegetes. These are arguably the most important discipleship themes in Mark's story, and it is significant that the longer text develops them in the central section, where Mark elaborates these themes.

These agreements with Markan literary technique and theology have to be weighed against the elements in LGM 1 and 2 that are uncharacteristic of how Mark does things. Smith noted the high proportion of repeated phrasing and the lack of features that individualize this story. Although LGM 2 does not repeat many Markan phrases or themes, everything in LGM 1 except the garden is reminiscent of other things or happenings elsewhere in Mark. To a certain extent this makes sense: As a "mystic act" that brings out meanings concealed within the literal level of the narrative, LGM 1 should echo the various aspects of the story that it functions to explicate, such as the loud cries and the oddly attired young man in 14:51–52. As the first of a matched pair framing the passion narrative, it should resemble Mark 16:1–8. This explanation is not entirely satisfying, however, for although Mark used exact verbal repetition as a means of highlighting similarities among episodes (cf. 7:32–37 with 8:22–26; and 11:1–6 with 14:12–16[8]), he did not overuse this technique. So LGM 1 stands out as having too much repetition and too little that is unique.

The exact amount of verbal repetition in LGM 1 and 2 has been overstated in the secondary literature, so it is important to be precise. LGM 1 and 2 contain far fewer of the repeated characteristics of Mark's writing style than can be found in Mark 4:1–2, which is less than one-quarter the length of LGM 1 and 2. Since 4:1–2 is almost universally attributed to the hand of Mark by redaction critics, we would be wise not to pretend to know instinctively how much is too much. LGM 1 and 2 contains 8 percent more exact verbal repetition than can be found for an equally long passage in Mark (181 words), but 19.5 percent less verbal repetition than can be found in Mark 4:1–2 (40 words). One can certainly argue that since redaction critics consider high concentrations of Markan phrasing and stylistic features to be a sure indication of Mark's editorial work, the high proportion of verbal repetition in LGM 1 should point to Mark rather than away from him. The real problem is that there is so little that is unique within LGM 1.

A few other features of LGM 1 seem uncharacteristic of Mark when viewed in their larger context. The phrase "having looked upon him, loved him" stands out not only because it occurs a short time earlier but also because the one loving and the one loved are different. Likewise, the disciples' callous rebuke of the woman occurs quite soon after their callous rebuke of the people who were bringing children to Jesus (10:13), and the sentences used to describe these rebukes are nearly identical. The story involving Bartimaeus has a rebuke as well (10:48). Terence Y. Mullins noted two other awkward elements. First, the woman's petition "Son of David, have mercy on me" is exactly the same as Bartimaeus's petition in 10:48 (cf. v. 47). Elsewhere in Mark's story, supplicants never petition Jesus using the exact same phrase. Second, the proximity of these identical petitions makes Bartimaeus's words seem redundant.[9] These awkward aspects of LGM 1 in context are not typical of Mark, who, as I have indicated, tends to vary his story elements more than this. On the other hand, Clement's statement that Mark expanded his gospel with materials taken from his notes could explain the redundancy that appears when LGM 1 is read in context. The insertion of written pericopae into an already finished narrative could result in some awkward repetitions.

Interestingly, Mullins himself was inclined to believe that Mark could have been the author of both Markan gospels. Before the *Letter to Theodore* was published, Mullins had argued that Papias's description of how Mark composed his gospel differentiated between Mark's translation of Peter's written reminiscences and Mark's own recollections of Peter's preaching ("a few things as he remembered them").[10] So Mullins was partial to the tradi-✝ tion in Clement's letter, which speaks of Mark expanding his gospel using "his own notes and those of Peter." Mullins' theory allows for the conjecture that when Mark was not translating Peter's notes, Mark's style was more distinctly his own.[11] Jean Carmignac agreed with Mullins on this matter and suggested that "The letter of Clement of Alexandria finally gives us the key to the statement of Papias."[12]

A different theory that could explain the higher than normal proportion of Markan phrasing in LGM 1 emerges from David Peabody's response to Helmut Koester's theory. An exponent of the Griesbach Hypothesis, Peabody argued that Mark composed his canonical gospel as a conflation of Matthew and Luke. But Peabody also suggested that LGM 1 and 2 are so Markan that they could have been produced by the author of the canonical gospel (he left open the question of whether it was the same author or an imitator).[13] Given these assumptions, one could argue that LGM 1 and 2 represent Markan pericopae that were not formulated on the basis of written gospel sources and are therefore "purer" examples of Markan style. My own premises do not permit me to adopt this solution or the one suggested by Mullins. I will simply acknowledge that there is more repetition of Markan phrases in LGM 1 than is normal for a passage of the same length and leave the reader to decide what to make of this fact.

I am hard pressed to find uncharacteristic features in the use of Markan literary techniques. One might note that although removal to a house for private instruction is typically Markan, the instruction is not usually delayed ("and after six days...") and is normally preceded by a question from the disciples. On the other hand, the transfiguration is a private revelation relating to an event that occurred six days earlier (the first passion-and-resurrection prediction, in 8:31; NB "Listen to him!" in 9:7), and the central section's private teachings on the way of the cross are initiated by Jesus (8:34–9:1; 9:35–37; 10:42–45); indeed, the one in 9:35–37 occurs after Jesus and his disciples enter a house (v. 33). So the phrase "and after six days" and the absence of a question from the young man in LGM 1b may be subtle indications that the mystery of the kingdom of God concerns the way of the cross.

With respect to Markan style, Pierson Parker claimed that there were fewer instances of the historical present in LGM 1 and 2 than we might expect in Mark.[14] Subsequent scholarship on Mark's use of the historical present has shown that this feature of Mark's style is unevenly distributed and therefore not statistically predictable. Contrary to the dominant opinion, Mark usually did not employ this tense in a colloquial way or for dramatic effect. He usually employed it as a means of marking transitions to new material. Carroll D. Osburn distinguished three functions of the historical present in Mark. Two of these functions occur in LGM 1. The isolated use of the historical present in 1:11 ("and when it was evening the young man comes to him donning a linen sheet upon his naked body") corresponds to the "cataphoric use of isolated historical presents within units dominated by past tense verbs to denote a semantic shift within the account to material of somewhat different nature." That is, the present tense in 1:11 prepares the reader or hearer for a shift in the subject matter of the story, in this case the start of the esoteric teaching incident. Likewise, the individual occurrences of the historical present in 1:1 and 1:2 accord with Mark's use of "the historical present to set the stage for an event, with the account itself given entirely in past tense verbs...." LGM 1 and 2 are not representative of the third, less frequent, Markan usage of the historical present in an episode to mark "the main features of the discourse, culminating in each instance in past tense verbs." Because the historical present has particular narrative functions in this gospel, the frequency of its occurrence within a pericope is irrelevant.[15] The correct question is, Does the usage in longer Mark correspond with Mark's way of doing things? The answer is Yes.

If we just weigh the similarities and the differences, it is clear that longer Mark is far more similar to Mark's way of doing things than different. But we cannot settle the question of authorship in such a simplistic way, because the fact that LGM 1 and 2 are so thoroughly Markan does not in itself prove that Mark is the author. We must bear in mind that in the Greek system of education, students learned to write by imitating important authors. Imitation was a common literary practice, and examples of deliberate imitation can be found in early Christian literature. The second-century author of Mark 16:9–20, for instance, used a style quite similar to the Gospel of Mark, perhaps intending for his addition to appear to be the work of Mark himself. So let us consider the possibility that these Markan characteristics are imitations by another author.

If we try to imagine this author as someone who lived decades after Mark, we run up against the obstacle presented by the absence of Johannine features. One would expect public performances of John's gospel to affect the way the story of the raising of the dead man in Bethany was told and remembered. Who can forget Jesus' cry, "Lazarus, come out" and the image of a man wrapped in burial clothes walking out of a tomb? Who would set the story in Peraea after hearing John's gospel? We actually possess manuscript evidence attesting to the use of John in Egypt early in the second century (P[52]). So a date later than, say, 120 CE is not reasonable.

More importantly, the notion that someone other than Mark would try to think exactly like Mark is contradicted by the existing evidence. Christian theology varied from place to place and did not remain static in any community. It is hard to imagine a much later writer wanting to confine himself to Markan theology when there were so many interesting theologies to draw on. The same would be true of Mark's own associates, whoever they might have been. Christian theology always reflected the individuality and unique experiences of the theologian, regardless of who that person had as a teacher. Few scholars would imagine that Paul's co-workers, such as John Mark, Luke, and Barnabas, held theologies identical with Paul's. So we should not imagine that a disciple or co-worker of Mark was merely a receptacle of his teacher's thought. Theologians are like snowflakes: no two are exactly alike.

The disputed epistles of Paul and the Johannine Epistles provide good analogies. In general, the letters written by Paul's followers and admirers became progressively less Pauline, in both thought and style. If 2 Thessalonians is not by Paul, it is nevertheless the one most like the undisputed letters. But it conveys a very different conception of the circumstances of Christ's return than that expressed in 1 Thessalonians. In my opinion, the failed prophecy in 2 Thess 2:3–4 that the man of lawlessness will enthrone himself in "the temple of God" rules out a late date for this letter, since "the temple of God" would most naturally refer to the temple in Jerusalem, which was destroyed in 70 CE. Colossians presents a like case. It, too, is close enough to Paul's thought that it might have been written by Paul. It does not, however, simply repeat the theology found in the undisputed letters, but develops Paul's theology in ways Paul *might* have developed it. Ephesians, which is an imitation of Colossians, goes even further in the same directions. The Pastorals, on the other hand, hardly contain any distinctly Pauline themes and do not even try to imitate Paul's writing style. But they were written by someone who apparently admired Paul and presumed to speak in Paul's name (I doubt the admiration would have been mutual). A similar situation exists in the Johannine corpus. The letters sound very much like the gospel, but they are preoccupied with a new set of problems and opponents, with the result that the theological emphases shift and favourite terms take on new meanings. For instance, the opponents branded children "of the devil" are not non-Christian Jews, as in John 8:44, but secessionists from the Johannine community (1 John 3:8–10), and the christological emphasis has shifted from Jesus' divinity to his humanity or coming "in the flesh" (1 John 4:2). The theology of the letters is very similar to that of the gospel, but not identical. Scholars are not unanimous that the author of the letters was someone different from the author of the gospel. But either way, these differences provide a good example of the fact that we should not expect even the same author to have identical theological concerns when composing years later.

The situation is the same when we consider examples of expansions of existing texts. Both Matthew and Luke expanded Mark, but made no attempt to preserve Markan vocabulary, style, literary techniques, and theology. Quite the opposite. The author of Mark 16:9–20 likewise made no attempt to preserve Mark's theology, despite his attempt to imitate Mark's style. John 21 sounds like the rest of the gospel and is essentially Johannine in its theology, but its author has different emphases that are more similar to what one encounters in the synoptic gospels and 1 John. For instance, the expectation of Christ's parousia expressed in John 21:21–23 accords with the outlook of 1 John 2:18, 28 but is hard to reconcile with the main gospel's emphasis upon realized eschatology; in John 14:16–23 the second coming has been spiritualized into the notion that Christ will come back to those who love him in order to abide within them. Scribal interpolations found in the manuscript tradition likewise tend not to reinforce the theology of the gospel in which they occur. Scribes who added *new sentences* to the Gospels did so in order to assert their own views. Even brief interpolations often give problematic verses a more congenial meaning.[16] It would be very hard for any redactor to suppress his own ways of thinking even when attempting to imitate someone else.

With these considerations in mind, it becomes apparent that another author would probably have had no interest in propagating Markan theology and no reason to do so. A different author who wished to expand Mark's gospel would probably have imitated Mark's style but pursued his own theological agenda, much like the author of Mark 16:9–20. But the biggest problem for any theory of imitation is the fact that longer Mark contains more Markan characteristics than any imitator living before the 1980s is apt to have noticed. Although Mark has been studied intensively since the theory of Markan priority began to dominate in the last third of the nineteenth century, specialists in Mark have only quite recently begun to discern and articulate many of the Markan literary techniques used in the longer text, such as Mark's tendency to bracket sections of narrative using similar stories (discussed by Lohmeyer in 1936), his penchant for peculiar explanatory clauses beginning with "for" (C.H. Bird in 1953), his tendency to intercalate thematically related stories *for theological reasons* (mid-1960s and early 1970s), and his love of ambiguous gaps (Robert Fowler in 1991). And these scholars have been able to build upon each other's research. Indeed, it is only in the last few decades that scholars of Mark realized that Mark was capable of employing intelligent literary techniques. Some still refuse to entertain such thoughts—either because they think Mark's colloquial and unliterary style reflects Mark's education more so than his intended audience's or because they want to believe that Mark innocently and faithfully reported the anecdotes he heard from Peter.

It is important to be realistic about what an imitator of Mark might have discerned about Mark's writing style. An imitator might have noticed and reproduced the "surface features" of Mark's story, such as his favourite words, phrases, and sentence constructions, and even some of Mark's redactional tendencies. But Mark's compositional techniques would not have been obvious. The fact that experts in the canonical gospels examined LGM 1 and 2 for decades without noticing even the most obvious literary techniques discussed in part 2 of this book is probably a good indication of how much a hypothetical imitator of Mark is likely to have discerned about Markan compositional technique on his own.

One might be tempted to conjecture that an ancient author would have been more sensitive to these things than we are now, but no such awareness is apparent in the earliest Christian commentaries on the gospels or in the exegesis of the fathers. "Despite the Fathers' capacity to read beyond a literary surface and appreciate the complex symbolisms implicit in many biblical narratives, they lacked the capacity to 'read' the surface of a literary narrative in the way that modern readers have been trained to do." Whereas modern narrative critics read the gospels as individual stories conveying unique theologies, the fathers read the gospels "as a single *evangelium*," selectively expounding pericopae "as support for the primary ecclesiastical goals of the period."[17] Conflicting details were glossed over or mentally harmonized, not scrutinized for what they might reveal about the distinctive interests of the evangelists themselves. Consequently, orthodox interpreters were unpractised in discerning the unique theologies and compositional techniques of the evangelists. The various endings of Mark demonstrate how little the interpolators actually did notice of Mark's style and literary technique, and the widespread acceptance of the Long Ending demonstrates that they hardly needed to know such things in order to produce successful imitations.

Even if it were sensible to imagine an ancient imitator who read the gospels like a late-twentieth-century narrative critic, Mark's literary idiosyncrasies made his gospel that much more difficult to imitate. Mark's manner of composition was not typical of authors educated in rhetoric. He used a number of standard rhetorical techniques such as chiasm, *inclusio*, central turning point, and overlapping sections.[18] But his most distinctive and unconventional devices, such as intercalation and odd explanatory *gar* clauses, were not taught in the rhetorical schools.[19] Hence, his first readers would not have been predisposed to recognize and appreciate these techniques, at least consciously.

Indeed, it is highly improbable that an ancient imitator would even have *expected* to find subtle compositional techniques in Mark's gospel. The general consensus was that Mark the evangelist was literarily unsophisticated. The earliest preserved tradition about him is that of Papias (early second century), who referred to Mark as an interpreter or translator (*hermeneutes*) of Peter. According to Papias, Mark set out to record Peter's anecdotes as accurately as possible. Papias was very apologetic about the fact that Mark's arrangement of his traditions is not proper, explaining that since Peter "composed his teachings according to the *chreiae* and not as a rhetorical arrangement (*suntaxin*) of the Lord's sayings, Mark made no mistake in writing some things just as he recollected (*apemnemonesen*) them. For he was careful of this one thing, to leave nothing he heard out and to say nothing falsely."[20] Although this is a notoriously difficult passage to interpret, it would appear that Papias thought that Mark was more interested in accuracy than in arrangement. In light of the technical nature of many of the terms Papias used, some scholars now believe that his comment that Mark wrote "accurately but not in order" (*taxei*) "refers not to chronological order but to what would be a rhetorically and logically effective order."[21] In other words, Papias may not have been preoccupied with the chronological differences among the four gospels but with the fact that Mark's arrangement of his materials seemed rhetorically ineffective by the standards of his day. The fact that Papias needed to defend Mark in this way implies that Mark's gospel had been the subject of criticism for its lack of literary artistry.[22] This general impression had not improved by the time Augustine suggested that Mark might have abbreviated Matthew's gospel: "Mark follows him (Matthew) closely and looks as if he were his servant (*pedisequus*) and epitomist (*breviator*)."[23] Mark was thought of as the evangelist who composed with the least conscious deliberation. When Christians read his gospel they saw the vivid recollections of the apostle Peter as recorded by his faithful lackey.

Given this evidence, we have little reason to suppose that an ancient author might have perceived and reproduced the many distinctive Markan literary devices that become evident when LGM 1 and 2 are set in their Markan context. Nor is a later imitation more plausible, for the opinions that Mark was an abbreviator of Matthew or a simple compiler of traditions predominated until the mid-twentieth century. As late as 1956, Willi Marxsen needed to prove that Mark was sufficiently master of his materials to be called an author. By the close of the 1970s most redaction critics still supposed that Mark made discrete revisions to traditions that were essentially fixed in their wording; Mark the evangelist was still thought of as an editor whose functions were confined to compiling and arranging pericopae, modifying words, and adding occasional phrases and summary statements.[24] Attention was shifting to Mark's methods of relating traditions together (composition criticism), but many scholars still did not *see* Mark's literary techniques as clearly as they do now. Intercalation, for example, was often lumped together with other forms of interpolation, and there was no consensus about whether Mark's central section included one or both of the accounts of the healing of blindness that most scholars now realize frame it.

The literary-critical observations presented in part 2 of this book were made possible by a revolution in gospel scholarship in the 1980s that turned Mark into a true author, and very few of those observations could have been made before the 1970s. So when we contemplate the question of whether LGM 1 and 2 could be the work of an imitator, we need to recognize that we are hypothesizing a redactor who was able to notice and imitate aspects of Markan composition that specialists in Mark have only recently begun to perceive. Clement offered a simpler and more plausible explanation for why this author composed so much like Mark. He was Mark.

The strongest evidence that Mark wrote LGM 1 and 2 is the fact that these verses offer a very satisfying solution to the age-old riddle of why a young man dressed only in a linen sheet follows with Jesus as Jesus is being led away under arrest. There are many painfully improbable interpretations of Mark 14:51–52 and a few fairly good ones, but the only one that seems entirely satisfying to me is the one suggested by the intercalation formed by LGM 1 and 2 around Mark 10:35–45. I would not have thought of relating Mark 10:38–39 to Mark 14:51–52 had I not asked myself whether the central pericope does in fact illuminate the outer one, so I give full credit to the author of longer Mark for "initiating" me into the mystery. I know from experience what Clement meant when he said that Mark added materials "of which he knew the interpretation would, as a mystagogue, lead the hearers into the innermost sanctuary of that truth hidden by seven veils." Not everyone is going to agree with me that the young man who follows Jesus in Gethsemane is wearing his former burial attire (a linen sheet wrapped around a naked body) like a baptismal garment in order to symbolize his intention to undergo Jesus' "baptism" in Jerusalem. But I think that scholars who do agree that this is the best solution to the riddle will have to concede that Mark is the most likely author of LGM 1 and 2.

The question of who Mark was, is another matter altogether. I accept that his name was Mark because his gospel is not called the Gospel of Peter, or of Andrew, or of James or John. There are at least a dozen better candidates for a fictitious attribution than Mark, a name which does not appear in any list of the twelve disciples (the same applies to Luke). Unfortunately, Mark was a very common name, and we do not know whether this Mark was one of the persons referred to by that name in the New Testament. So when I say "Mark" wrote the longer gospel, I mean that this author was the same person who wrote the canonical gospel. Those interested in the question of who Mark was (and was not) should read C. Clifton Black's exemplary study  *Mark: Images of an Apostolic Interpreter.*

## How and When Was the Longer
## Gospel Composed?

Having decided the question of authorship, we are ready to ask how and when the longer gospel was composed. This subject has been dominated by Helmut Koester's theory that the longer text represents a stage in the composition of Mark that preceded the canonical gospel. That scenario presents numerous problems when it is pictured concretely, a major one being the difficulty of explaining why anyone would remove the "mystic" or "more spiritual" stories in Mark in order to create an epitome of Matthew and Luke. Clement's notion that a "bodily" gospel was made more spiritual for the benefit of advanced students makes far more sense, given the likelihood that Mark's Alexandrian audience contained many literate Christians of Jewish background who preferred to discover the most important truths using anagogical exegesis. Clement's description of the intended audience of the longer gospel is entirely plausible and constitutes the most important external evidence we have for a matter about which scholars frequently speculate. It is rather unfortunate that most scholars have dismissed a rare description of the production and intended audience of a gospel by a church father who had carefully studied it and knew local traditions about its production.

One reason for the neglect of Clement's tradition is the tendency among scholars to believe that the evangelists were settled church authorities who wrote only for their own communities. There is good reason to suppose that Matthew and John were written for particular communities, but the Markan community is a much more elusive entity.[25] This scholarly construct has no obvious advantage over the traditional picture of Mark as a missionary who travelled among Christian communities and died in Alexandria. Thus we ought to take seriously Clement's opinion that Mark's two gospels were written for distinct *kinds of* Christians (beginners and gnostics) rather than for specific communities, bearing in mind that the kind of Christian for which longer Mark was written would have been especially abundant in Alexandria.[26]

C. Wilfred Griggs noted another reason for the lordly neglect of Clement's tradition about Mark's activities in Alexandria, namely, "a continued scholarly bias against the traditional role of Mark in Egyptian Christian history."[27] The old view that the connection between Mark and Alexandria must be fictitious because it first appears in the writings of the fourth-century historian Eusebius needs to be replaced with the recognition that this connection appears in a late second-century letter by an Alexandrian writer and that Eusebius was, in fact, citing Clement and Papias as his sources for this information. In other words, external support for this connection can be traced as far back as Papias in the first decade of the second century.[28]

A third reason for the neglect of the tradition recorded in the letter may be the fact that the dates suggested by the letter for when Mark wrote his two gospels do not harmonize with the general consensus that the canonical gospel was written around the year 70 CE. It is certainly hard to believe that a work so preoccupied with the Jewish war with the Romans (66–74) and the destruction of the temple (Mark 11:12–25; 12:9; 13:2, 14–16; 14:58; 15:29, 38) was written before Peter's death (ca. 64). And it is doubtful that Mark was as closely associated with Peter as the Roman tradition claims. Perhaps Clement attempted to harmonize a less reliable Roman tradition about how Mark wrote the canonical gospel with a more reliable Alexandrian tradition about the longer gospel. In any event, Clement associated Mark's arrival in Alexandria with Peter's death, which is too early if Mark wrote the first version of his gospel in Rome around the year 70.

The most transparent reason for this neglect, however, is the orthodox tenet that the four canonical gospels stand alone as the first and only credible witnesses to Jesus. One cannot make the case that non-traditional images of Jesus are "copyright violations" of the canonical gospels without maintaining that all other gospels were written after the first century by individuals who had no access to living traditions about Jesus. The notion that Mark wrote a distinctly Alexandrian edition of his gospel may not be inherently improbable or offensive, yet might seem to concede too much to "the liberals," who use non-canonical gospels to supplement or challenge the picture of Jesus in the canonical texts. There is an apologetic advantage to claiming that longer Mark is late and unorthodox. That remains true even if the evidence suggests that this gospel was written by a beloved saint and presents an orthodox picture of Jesus.

Clement's comment that Mark supplemented his gospel with materials taken from his personal "notes" may strike modern readers as odd, but it is entirely reasonable. As Black pointed out, the procedure imagined in the *Letter to Theodore* accords with the advice given to historians by Lucian of Samosata (ca. 120–180): "By all means [the historian] should be an eyewitness; but, if this is impossible, he should listen to those who relate the more impartial account.... When he has gathered all or most [of the facts], first let him weave them together into some notes [*hypomnēma ti*] and fashion a body [of material] still charmless and disjointed. Then, having laid order [*taxin*] upon it, let him bring in beauty and ornament it with style and figuration and rhythm."[29] Most likely the story about the raising of a dead man in Bethany was already in Mark's notes when he came to Alexandria.

The fact that LGM 1 supplies a cogent explanation for the enigma of the Gethsemane streaker strongly suggests that Mark composed LGM 1 at the same time as Mark 14:51–52, even though he did not include LGM 1 in the canonical gospel. The fact that the raising miracle occurs within the chronology of longer Mark where Jesus would be passing by Bethany beyond the Jordan and where the miracle is able to amplify an existing *inclusio* also accords with this conclusion, as does the fact that LGM 1 and 2, together with 14:51–52 and 16:1–8, have the same effect on the passion narrative that the stories of Jesus' baptism, transfiguration, and crucifixion have on the whole gospel. In both cases, the outer stories function as a matched pair or frame and the inner story denotes a turning point in the plot. More generally, the basic agreement between LGM 1 and 2 and the theology and emphases of the canonical gospel is easier to comprehend if these verses were composed while Mark wrote the canonical gospel; after Mark moved to Alexandria, his theological emphases probably developed and shifted, as Paul's theology apparently developed through the 50s in the course of interacting with communities in different regions and meeting new theological challenges. However, it is clear that Mark had decided not to include LGM 1 and 2 in his original gospel for catechumens before it attained its final form. I have shown elsewhere that LGM 1 does not fit well within the most important structure of Mark's central section because it disrupts a tight, carefully constructed threefold cycle of passion prediction, inappropriate response by the disciples, and discipleship teaching.[30] LGM 1 is clearly a secondary addition with respect to this structure. Likewise, the reference to the young man in chapter 14 as "a certain young man" rather than "the young man" suggests that LGM 1 did not exist in Mark's story when the young man in Gethsemane was added to the passion narrative.[31] The same logic applies to the reference to "a young man" in 16:5. When Mark 14:51–52 and 16:1–8 were composed, the two anonymous young men were not represented as the same young man, which would be odd if LGM 1, the story that equates these individuals, already existed in the narrative.

So what we have in LGM 1 and 2 is a Markan story that is as old as the canonical gospel but was intentionally left out of that gospel. Presumably, Mark recognized that this incident was better suited to a different audience, and when he came to Alexandria he did, in fact, take this and other preformed episodes out of his notes and insert them into his gospel. In the process, he improved some structures in his narrative and spoiled others. It is important to bear in mind that the amplified gospel was intended for persons who had already read the shorter gospel. The threefold cycle still exists in its undisrupted state in the shorter gospel, where it serves the purpose of highlighting the imperative that a follower of Jesus renounce all status and self-concern. Ideally, the rhetorical effect of that construction will already have influenced readers of the longer text, who will perceive LGM 1 and 2 as an elaboration of that theme. Mark had a new agenda for readers of the expanded gospel and so may not have been too concerned to preserve intact the three-fold cycle in the central section. It would, in fact, be difficult for Mark to supplement a finished gospel without spoiling some of his earlier constructions. This appears to have happened in the canonical gospel where Mark inserted an esoteric interlude within the parable chapter. I agree with scholars who think that Mark 4 originally presented Jesus using parables as a means of communicating effectively with the crowd. The introduction to this episode presents Jesus getting in a boat in order to teach a large crowd many things in parables (4:1–2). The word *teach* suggests real communication rather than deliberate obfuscation, as does the first sentence of the concluding comment, "With many such parables he spoke the word to them, *as they were able to hear it*" (4:33).[32] But this scenario is spoiled by Mark 4:10–25, which introduces the theme that Jesus speaks in parables so that "those outside" (who are represented by the crowd) cannot understand him and consequently will not repent and be saved. The very idea that Jesus could be alone with an inner group that includes his disciples makes no sense in the context of Jesus teaching the crowd from a boat, particularly since Jesus is again addressing the crowd by the end of this interlude (4:23, 33) and never does leave the boat: "And leaving the crowd, they took him with them in the boat, just as he was. And other boats were with him" (4:36). So the materials in chapter 4 that stress the use of parables as a means of preventing clear communication come across as an awkward revision. Since, however, both the verses that depict Jesus communicating effectively using parables and the verses that spoil this notion contain numerous Markan characteristics,[33] it would appear that Mark changed his mind about why Jesus used parables, and spoiled his own composition. Interestingly, both LGM 1 and Mark 4:11 contain the esoteric notion of the mystery of the kingdom of God, and Mark 14:51–52 is easily removed from the account of Jesus' arrest without disrupting the flow of the narrative. All of these passages appear to be secondary with respect to their immediate contexts. Perhaps Mark's decision to present Jesus as a mysterious figure and a teacher of concealed truths occurred at a late point in the writing of the canonical gospel. Whatever the case, LGM 1 and 2 were deliberately left aside, and Mark 14:51–52 was included as a deliberate enigma, perhaps as an incentive to read the more spiritual version that can disclose such riddles to attentive readers.

When exactly longer Mark was composed is difficult to decide. If Mark was planning his second version before he finished the first, then we should not picture an interval of many years. However, in chapter 3 we encountered some evidence that the author of LGM 1 might have known the Gospels of Matthew and Luke. If Matthew and Luke wrote their gospels in the 80s, as most scholars think, Mark might have known those gospels, provided he did not die nearly as early as tradition says he did. But the contacts with Matthew and Luke in LGM 1 are not especially compelling. So I think longer Mark should be dated within a few years of the canonical gospel. Within the framework of the Two Source Hypothesis, this conclusion would imply a date in the early 70s and make longer Mark the *true* Second Gospel.

Proponents of the Two Gospel (Griesbach) Hypothesis would necessarily choose a later date for both Markan gospels. For obvious reasons, these scholars have no problem with the possibility that Mark knew Matthew and Luke, just as they have no problem explaining the high proportion of Markan phrasing in LGM 1 (LGM 1 would represent Mark's retelling of oral tradition rather than his conflation of Matthew and Luke). These scholars do not normally fix a date for the writing of canonical Mark; they are more apt to offer a general range of years, such as "no more than a few decades after the martyrdoms of Peter and Paul in 65–68 CE."[34] Within this framework, longer Mark could still be written before the Gospel of John and might appear to represent an intermediate stage between the synoptic gospels and John.

## Longer Mark's Relevance to Scholarship

If, as I have argued, Mark did prepare a much longer version of his gospel in Alexandria, then one of the most important sources of information about Christian origins is lost to us. We do, however, have fifteen verses, and they are quite relevant to a variety of issues. As Charles W. Hedrick pointed out, the parallels between longer Mark and John press the matter of whether the Johannine tradition and the synoptic tradition were originally as separate and distinct as scholars sometimes imagine.[35] LGM 1 supports Barnabas Lindars' stance that John's miracle stories originally circulated in forms more typical of the synoptic tradition. So LGM 1 is relevant to form-critical studies of the Johannine tradition, especially studies of the evolution of John 11. An example of longer Mark's utility in this regard can be found in the attempts by Boismard and Fortna to use LGM 1:1 to reconstruct an earlier form of the opening of the Johannine story.[36]

A related matter is the literary relationship between John and the synoptics. The question of whether any writer involved in the production of the

Gospel of John knew longer Mark deserves further exploration. As a whole, the evidence suggests that those texts were independent, but as with the problem of John's relation to the synoptics, there are some possible indications to the contrary. It is interesting to note, for example, that the raising of Lazarus has structural functions similar to LGM 1. Like the latter, John 10:40–11:54 functions as a transition between Jesus' public ministry and the passion narrative and can be viewed as forming the first of a matched pair of resurrection miracles framing the passion narrative. Even more interesting is the evidence that the raising of Lazarus was not originally part of John's gospel but was added in a second edition.[37] The beloved disciple, who is a partial counterpart to longer Mark's anonymous young man, was likewise elaborated at a later time (his appearances within John 19:35 and John 21 are almost certainly redactional). So it is at least conceivable that a redactor made changes to John after reading longer Mark.

LGM 1 and 2 also have relevance to some historical issues. For instance, since LGM 1:1 and John 1:28 both refer to a Bethany on the east side of the Jordan River, the longer text is highly relevant to the question of where this Bethany lay. John's topographical clues are notoriously indeterminate, but those in longer Mark are much clearer and support the traditional site at Wadi Kharrar. It is rather interesting, therefore, that LGM 1b uses baptismal imagery, for this is "the place where John first baptized" (John 10:40). I argued that LGM 1 was not meant to be taken as a literal depiction of baptism and that Clement did not read it that way. But since longer Mark and John agree that Jesus stayed overnight with an anonymous disciple in Bethany beyond the Jordan (John 1:35–40), it appears that longer Mark's highly redactional picture of Jesus teaching the mystery of the kingdom of God has some nebulous traditional basis, and that this tradition reaffirms the strong Johannine association between Jesus and a place where John the Baptist worked (1:28; 3:26; 10:40). So LGM 1 may have some relevance to historical Jesus scholarship.

Scholars who choose to use LGM 1b as evidence for the historical Jesus would be well advised of two things. First, the presence of characteristically Markan themes and phrases in LGM 1:9–13 prevents us from assuming that this incident is a transcript of something that happened one week. If there is an historical kernel here, it should be sought in relation to the parallel tradition in John 1. Second, LGM 1b was designed to be ambiguous and tends to function like a Rorschach inkblot, revealing whatever the interpreter is inclined to see in it. One person sees a baptism and a mystical rite of assent to the heavens, another sees "a sacred kiss in the nude, a form of the 'bridal chamber' (cf. *Gospel of Philip*)," still another sees a prototype of an Alcoholics

Anonymous meeting.[38] If we are looking for the historical Jesus here, it would be best not to imagine that we have a report of something someone saw while looking in a rich man's window one evening. It would make more sense to pose questions such as, Did Jesus in fact have esoteric teachings that he gave privately to his disciples? Might he have visited Bethany beyond the Jordan in the last weeks of his life (LGM 1; John 10:40)? Might the baptismal movements in this region have influenced his theology (Luke 12:50; Mark 10:38–39)?

Another historical question raised by LGM 1 is whether this text is related to what appears to be a localized Christian practice of undergoing baptism while dressed in one's future funeral shroud. This practice occurs today at the traditional site of Jesus' baptism by John and is known to have occurred in the vicinity of Bethany in the sixth century. A study tracing the history of this practice could make an important contribution to our knowledge of the longer text.

LGM 1 also raises a general question pertaining to the gospels: Why do certain healing and nature miracles have exorcistic elements? It is readily understandable that Jesus might use exorcism in response to diseases that manifest themselves in the form of involuntary seizures or vocalizations (Mark 1:26; 5:5; 9:17–18, 22). But why are there traces of an exorcistic confrontation in cases where there is no obvious reason for Jesus to think that the person he is healing, or the phenomenon he is confronting, is being controlled by demons (e.g., Mark 1:41, 43; 4:39; John 11:33, 38; LGM 1:5)? Are we seeing indications of a popular christology that had been worked over by literate, more theologically minded evangelists?

The *Letter to Theodore* has obvious relevance to the study of earliest Alexandrian Christianity. Walter Bauer's theory that Christianity in Alexandria was mostly heterodox until the third century is still a common position, but a number of experts have found good evidence that the majority of Alexandrian Christians in the second century could be characterized as "proto-orthodox."[39] Since it now appears that Mark really was active in Alexandria in the 70s of the first century, it follows that earliest Alexandrian Christianity was by no means free of orthodox Christians. Ironically, the esotericism and elitism of second-century Alexandrian Christianity probably owes a great deal to Mark's portrait of Jesus privately teaching his disciples a mystery requisite to salvation while using parabolic words and actions as a means of concealing this mystery from outsiders. Mark endorsed an existing Jewish-Christian preoccupation with hidden meanings that proved hard to control.

In 1988 Helmut Koester raised the issue of longer Mark's relevance to textual criticism, and experts in that area have lately followed his lead.[40]

Regardless of one's views about Koester's theory of the origin of canonical Mark, one may agree that the existence of a Carpocratian form of Mark in the second century adds to the growing evidence that Christians felt much freer to revise the gospels in the period before the production of our earliest extant manuscripts.[41] What is more, the tradition about Mark producing a second version of his gospel for a different kind of audience poses the interesting question of whether some of the variants that exist within the manuscript tradition of the gospels might actually reflect revisions or adaptations made by the original authors after the initial copies were distributed.[42] Is it ever the case that the most difficult reading represents the wording of the original copies yet not the wording that the evangelist finally settled on? How often does the quest for the supposedly most authoritative original text lead textual critics to restore literary foibles that the evangelists themselves belatedly identified and fixed?

The widespread perception among New Testament scholars that the apocryphal gospels have little to offer us is clearly self-perpetuating: Those who hold it are loath to dignify these gospels by studying them as meticulously as they do the canonical gospels. They naturally discover little more than they expect to find. The longer text of Mark reminds us that the measure you give is the measure you get (4:24). Its account of the raising and instruction of the young man quite intentionally offers nothing to anyone who will not struggle to discover its secrets, following the principle, "From him who has not shall be taken away" (II.16; Mark 4:25). But to the one who has eyes to see and ears to hear, this pericope is every bit as illuminating as those in the canonical gospels. Imagine what we could learn if we possessed a complete copy of Mark's other gospel.

# ⊰ Notes ⊱

## Preface

1 James E. Davison, "Structural Similarities and Dissimilarities in the Thought of Clement of Alexandria and the Valentinians," *SecCent* 3 (1983): 212.

2 Morton Smith, *Clement of Alexandria and a Secret Gospel of Mark* (Cambridge: Harvard University Press, 1973), 448–52.

3 Smith, *Clement of Alexandria*, 446–47.

4 Robert J. Miller, ed., *The Complete Gospels: Annotated Scholars Version* (Sonoma: Polebridge Press, 1992), 405.

## Chapter 1

1 Isaak Vossius, *Ignatius v. Antiochien, Epistolae genuinae S. Ignatii Martyris*. For Smith's account of the discovery, see Morton Smith, *The Secret Gospel: The Discovery and Interpretation of the Secret Gospel According to Mark* (New York: Harper and Row, 1973) (hereafter cited as *SG*).

2 Subsequent references to the letter will omit the title. See the preface for an explanation of the conventions I use when referring to Clement's works.

3 The Greek term here translated "young man" (*neaniskos*) normally refers to a male in his twenties. Since this character's youth is treated as his defining feature, we can presume that he is noticeably younger than Jesus and his disciples, hence probably in his early-to-mid-twenties. See Marvin W. Meyer, "The Youth in the *Secret Gospel of Mark*," *Semeia* 49 (1990): 139–40.

4 The linen clothing is of an unspecified form. The phrase "having put a linen (something) upon his naked body" would be a very unnatural way to describe someone dressed in a regular garment; however, the same word for linen (*sindōn*) is used in Mark 15:46 to describe the simple sheet in which Joseph of Arimathea wrapped Jesus' corpse, so translators tend to refer to the young man's wrapping as a linen sheet or linen cloth (e.g., the RSV, NRSV, NEB, and JB at Mark 14:51–52).

5 Smith, *SG*, 13.

6 Smith, *Clement of Alexandria and a Secret Gospel of Mark* (Cambridge: Harvard University Press, 1973), 1 (hereafter cited as *CA*); *SG*, 22–23.

7 Pierson Parker, "On Professor Morton Smith's Find at Mar-Saba," *AThR* 56 (1974): 53–57.

8 Parker's opinion was quoted in Sanka Knox, "Expert Disputes 'Secret Gospel,'" *New York Times*, 31 December 1960, p. 7. Parker reasoned that any detail in LGM 1 and 2 that cannot be found in exactly the same form in canonical Mark must be deemed non-Markan, a premise that would make every detail that appears only once in canonical Mark the product of another author. See Parker, "Smith's Find," 53–54; idem, "An Early Christian Cover-up?" *New York Times Book Review* (22 July 1973): 5. Smith explained Parker's methodological confusions in *SG*, 39, 42, 46.

9 Smith, *CA*, 139; *SG*, 42–43.

10 Smith, *CA*, 143. See the whole discussion on pp. 142–44.

11 Morton Smith, "Merkel on the Longer Text of Mark," *ZTK* 72 (1975): 143.

12 Smith, *CA*, 152–58; *SG*, 45–46, 52–56.

13 Smith, *SG*, 46–52, 56–61; idem, "Mark 6:32–15:47 and John 6:1–19:42," in *Society of Biblical Literature 1978 Seminar Papers*, ed. Paul J. Achtemeier (Missoula: Scholars Press, 1978), 2:281–87.

14 Smith, *CA*, 194; idem, response to Reginald Fuller, in *Longer Mark: Forgery, Interpolation, or Old Tradition?* ed. Wilhelm H. Wuellner, Protocol of the Eighteenth Colloquy: 7 December 1975 (Berkeley: Center for Hermeneutical Studies in Hellenistic and Modern Culture, 1976), 12–13 (hereafter, this book will be cited as *LM*). The approximate date of 95 CE that Smith gave in *LM* conflicts with his earlier claim in *SG*, 142 that Matthew knew and used the longer text by the year 90.

15 Smith, "Merkel," 143; *CA*, 114, 135.

16 Smith, *CA*, 121–22, 188–92, 194; *SG*, 41–42, 42–43 n. 2.

17 Smith, *CA*, 183; *SG*, 79. He essentially retracted this suggestion in his book *Jesus the Magician* (San Francisco: Harper and Row, 1978), 207.

18 Smith, *CA*, 176–78. Part of Richardson's letter is reproduced in *SG*, 64–65.

19 Smith, *SG*, 65–66, 113–14, 119–20, 130–31; *CA*, 240 n. 17, 251, 253–54, 263, 283, 284.

20 Shawn Eyer, "The Strange Case of the Secret Gospel According to Mark: How Morton Smith's Discovery of a Lost Letter of Clement of Alexandria Scandalized Biblical Scholarship," *Alexandria* 3 (1995): 109–10; available online at: <http://www-user.uni-bremen.de/~wie/Secret/secmark-engl.html>.

21 See, e.g., Joseph A. Fitzmyer, "How to Exploit a Secret Gospel," *America* 128 (23 June 1973): 572. Smith, "Clement of Alexandria and Secret Mark: The Score at the End of the First Decade," *HTR* 75 (1982): 455.

22 Parker, "Cover-up," 5.

23 F.F. Bruce, *Jesus and Christian Origins outside the New Testament* (London: Hodder and Stoughton, 1974), 165.

24 Joseph A. Gibbons, review of *SG*, *Sign* 53 (September 1973): 48.

25 Paul J. Achtemeier, review of *CA* and *SG*, *JBL* 93 (1974): 628.

26 Fitzmyer, "Exploit," 571.

27 Robert H. Gundry, "Excursus on the Secret Gospel of Mark," in his *Mark: A Commentary on His Apology for the Cross* (Grand Rapids: Eerdmans, 1993), 622.

28  Robin Scroggs, review of *SG*, *CTSR* 64:1 (November 1973): 59; Daryl Schmidt,
    response to Reginald Fuller, in *LM*, 41, 43; Edward C. Hobbs, *LM*, 22, 66;
    F.F. Bruce, *The "Secret" Gospel of Mark* (London: Athlone Press, 1974), 12;
    Patrick W. Skehan, review of *CA*, *CHR* 60 (1974–1975): 452, 453; André
    Méhat, review of *CA*, *Revue de l'histoire des religions* 190 (1976): 197 (my trans-
    lation); Ernest Best, "Uncanonical Mark," in his *Disciples and Discipleship: Stud-
    ies in the Gospel According to Mark* (Edinburgh: T. and T. Clark, 1986), 205;
    Frans Neirynck, "La fuite du jeune homme en Mc 14,51–52," in *Evangelica: Gospel
    Studies–Études d'évangile, Collected Essays*, ed. Frans Van Segbroeck (Leuven:
    Leuven University Press; Uitgeverij Peeters, 1982), 223 (my translation); James
    D.G. Dunn, *The Evidence for Jesus* (Philadelphia: Westminster, 1985), 51; Per
    Beskow, *Strange Tales about Jesus: A Survey of Unfamiliar Gospels* (Philadelphia:
    Fortress, 1983), 99; Gundry, "Excursus," 621, 612; James H. Charlesworth
    and Craig A. Evans, "Jesus in the Agrapha and Apocryphal Gospels," in *Study-
    ing the Historical Jesus: Evaluations of the State of Current Research*, ed. Bruce
    Chilton and Craig A. Evans, NTTS 19 (Leiden: E.J. Brill, 1994), 530; Freder-
    ick W. Baltz, *Lazarus and the Fourth Gospel Community* (Lewiston: Edwin Mellen,
    1996), 104.
29  See Smith, *CA*, 376–77, 140–41.
30  Quoted by Smith in *SG*, 67.
31  Citing Delbert Burkett, "Two Accounts of Lazarus' Resurrection in John 11,"
    *NovT* 36 (1994): 209. Burkett was not discussing John in relation to longer
    Mark.
32  Quentin Quesnell, "The Mar Saba Clementine: A Question of Evidence," *CBQ*
    37 (1975): 55–58 and n. 16.
33  Reginald H. Fuller, in *LM*, 56.
34  Herbert Musurillo, "Morton Smith's Secret Gospel," *Thought* 48 (1973): 329.
35  James R. Edwards, "Appendix: The Secret Gospel of Mark," in his *The Gospel
    According to Mark* (Grand Rapids: Eerdmans, 2002), 511.
36  Helmut Koester, "History and Development of Mark's Gospel (From Mark to
    Secret Mark and 'Canonical' Mark)," in *Colloquy on New Testament Studies: A
    Time for Reappraisal and Fresh Approaches*, ed. Bruce Corley (Macon, GA: Mer-
    cer University Press, 1983), 35–57.
37  John Dominic Crossan, *Four Other Gospels: Shadows on the Contours of Canon*
    (Minneapolis: Winston, 1985), 91–121; idem, "Thoughts on Two Extracanon-
    ical Gospels," *Semeia* 49 (1990): 155–68.
38  Crossan argued both that the empty tomb narrative was an invention of Mark
    the evangelist and that this pericope was composed from the debris of LGM 1
    and 2; if he still maintains both positions, it follows that Mark censored his
    own gospel. See Crossan, "Empty Tomb and Absent Lord (Mark 16:1–8)," in
    *The Passion in Mark: Studies on Mark 14–16*, ed. Werner H. Kelber (Philadelphia:
    Fortress, 1976), 135–52; idem, *The Historical Jesus: The Life of a Mediterranean
    Jewish Peasant* (San Francisco: Harper, 1991), 329, 414–15; idem, "Historical
    Jesus as Risen Lord," in John Dominic Crossan, Luke Timothy Johnson, and
    Werner Kelber, *The Jesus Controversy: Perspectives in Conflict* (Harrisburg: Trin-
    ity Press International, 1999), 1–47.
39  Hans-Martin Schenke, "The Mystery of the Gospel of Mark," *SecCent* 4:2
    (1984): 65–82.

40  E.g., Bruce, *Jesus and Christian Origins*, 165–66; Méhat, review of *CA*, 197. Cf.
    Pieter W. van der Horst, "Het 'Geheime Markusevangelie': Over een nieuwe
    vondst," in his *De onbekende god: Essays over de joodse en hellenistische achtergrond
    van het vroege christendom*, Utrechtse Theologische Reeks 2 (Utrecht: Univer-
    siteitsdrukkerij, 1988), 57–58.

41  Schenke, "Mystery," 76.

42  E.g., David Peabody, "The Late Secondary Redaction of Mark's Gospel and the
    Griesbach Hypothesis: A Response to Helmut Koester," in *Colloquy on New Tes-
    tament Studies: A Time for Reappraisal and Fresh Approaches*, ed. Bruce Corley
    (Macon, GA: Mercer University Press, 1983), 87–132; Frans Neirynck, "The
    Minor Agreements and Proto-Mark: A Response to H. Koester," in *Evangelica
    II 1982–1991 Collected Essays by Frans Neirynck*, ed. Frans Van Segbroeck (Leu-
    ven: Leuven University Press; Uitgeverij Peeters, 1991), 59–73; Gundry, "Excur-
    sus"; Philip Sellew, "*Secret Mark* and the History of Canonical Mark," in *The
    Future of Early Christianity: Essays in Honor of Helmut Koester*, ed. Birger A. Pear-
    son (Minneapolis: Fortress, 1991), 242–57.

43  E.g., Crossan, *Four Other Gospels*, 108–110; Winsome Munro, "Women Disci-
    ples: Light from Secret Mark," *JFSR* 8 (1992): 47–64.

44  Schenke, "Mystery," 76–80; Meyer, "The Youth in the *Secret Gospel of Mark*,"
    138–49; Frank Kermode, *The Genesis of Secrecy: On the Interpretation of Narra-
    tive* (Cambridge: Harvard University Press, 1979), 57–64.

45  Crossan, *Historical Jesus*, 429–30.

46  Helmut Koester and Stephen J. Patterson, "The Secret Gospel of Mark" (draft
    translation, introduction and notes), in *The Complete Gospels: Annotated Scholars
    Version*, ed. Robert J. Miller (Sonoma: Polebridge Press, 1992), 402–405. Ori-
    ginally published as "Secret Mark," *The Fourth R* 4:3 (1991): 14–16.

47  Raymond E. Brown, "The *Gospel of Peter* and Canonical Gospel Priority," *NTS*
    33 (1987): 322–23.

48  John P. Meier, *A Marginal Jew: Rethinking the Historical Jesus*, vol. 1, *The Roots
    of the Problem and the Person* (New York: Doubleday, 1991), 120–23. Scholars
    who object to the use of this document in the reconstruction of early Chris-
    tianity have been stressing the same three points since the early 1970s. See, e.g.,
    Musurillo, "Smith's Secret Gospel," 327–31; Helmut Merkel, "Appendix: The
    'Secret Gospel' of Mark," in *New Testament Apocrypha*, ed. Wilhelm
    Schneemelcher, 2d rev. ed. (Cambridge: James Clarke; Louisville:
    Westminster/John Knox Press, 1991), 106–109; W. Kümmel, "Ein Jahrzehnt
    Jesusforschung (1965–1975)," *TRu*, n.s., 40 (1975): 302; van der Horst, "Het
    'Geheime Markusevangelie,'" 54–56; Dunn, *Evidence*, 51; Petr Pokorný, "Das
    Markusevangelium: Literarische und theologische Einleitung mit Forschungs-
    bericht," *ANRW* II 25:3 (1985): 2001; Charlesworth and Evans, "Agrapha and
    Apocryphal Gospels," 526–32; Graham Stanton, *Gospel Truth? New Light on
    Jesus and the Gospels* (Valley Forge: Trinity Press International, 1995), 93–95.

49  Craig A. Evans, *Jesus and His Contemporaries: Comparative Studies* (Leiden: E.J.
    Brill, 1995), 32–33.

50  Donald Harman Akenson, *Saint Saul: A Skeleton Key to the Historical Jesus* (Oxford
    and New York: Oxford University Press, 2000), 87–88.

51  Philip Jenkins, *Hidden Gospels: How the Search for Jesus Lost Its Way* (New York:
    Oxford University Press, 2001), 102.

52 Because the term *reader* is more apropos of narrative criticism and the phrase "reader or hearer" is cumbersome, I tend to use the word *reader* by itself. However, the word *hearer* should also be understood whenever I refer to the reader. *Letter to Theodore* I.25–26 and II.1–2 appear to indicate that the practice in Alexandria in Clement's day was for someone to read this gospel aloud to others. The reader would presumably explain the hidden meanings, thereby making its mysteries accessible to those whose education did not enable them to read. It is probably the case, though, that the longer gospel was oriented to literate persons more so than the canonical version, and that persons like Clement would read it privately if they wished. The popular view that all reading in antiquity was vocalized and public is an exaggeration; see Frank D. Gilliard, "More Silent Reading in Antiquity: *NON OMNE VERBUM SONABAT*," *JBL* 112 (1993): 689–96.

53 The quoted phrase was used by Daryl Schmidt in his response to Reginald Fuller, in *LM*, 41.

54 E.g., George Aichele, *Jesus Framed*, Biblical Limits (London and New York: Routledge, 1996); Robert M. Fowler, *Let the Reader Understand: Reader-Response Criticism and the Gospel of Mark* (Minneapolis: Fortress, 1991); Christopher D. Marshall, *Faith as a Theme in Mark's Narrative*, SNTSMS 64 (Cambridge: Cambridge University Press, 1989); David Rhoads and Donald Michie, *Mark as Story* (Philadelphia: Fortress, 1982); Robert M. Fowler, "Reader-Response Criticism: Figuring Mark's Reader," in *Mark and Method: New Approaches in Biblical Studies*, ed. Janice Capel Anderson and Stephen D. Moore (Minneapolis: Fortress, 1992), 50–83; Elizabeth Struthers Malbon, "How Does the Story Mean?" in ibid., 23–49.

55 The gospel quotations have an affinity to the Western text Codex Bezae Cantabrigiensis (called D). For instance, the D text has "and they come into Bethany" (= LGM 1:1) instead of "and they come into Bethsaida" (Mark 8:22), "and having become angry" (= LGM 1:4) rather than "and feeling compassion" (Mark 1:41), and "he began to beg him..." (= LGM 1:8) instead of "he begged him that he might be with him" (Mark 5:18). On this subject, see Smith, *CA*, 122–23; Daryl Schmidt, *LM*, 41, 42; and Edward C. Hobbs, *LM*, 21. D as we know it would not have existed in the second century or earlier, so it cannot be assumed that longer Mark in general was a representative of this text type.

# Chapter 2

1 Bob Harvey, "Mark's Secret Gay Gospel a Hoax, Scholar Argues," *The Ottawa Citizen*, 6 August 2000, referring to Donald Harman Akenson's arguments in *Saint Saul: A Skeleton Key to the Historical Jesus* (Oxford and New York: Oxford University Press, 2000).

2 Herbert Musurillo, "Morton Smith's Secret Gospel," *Thought* 48 (1973): 329. As reasons to consider forgery, he noted the lateness of the only manuscript witness and the absence of a reference to the manuscript that the scribe copied (330).

3 Cf. Quentin Quesnell, "A Reply to Morton Smith," *CBQ* 38 (1976): 201: "As for the content, I find it quite harmless and in no way implausible for the period

in question....I do not find the style typical of Clement, in spite of the careful adherence to his vocabulary. But that must be argued elsewhere." (He did not return to the subject and make that argument.)

4 Nock's opinion is recorded in *SG*, 25, 29; *CA*, 67.

5 Helmut Koester, "The Text of the Synoptic Gospels in the Second Century," in *Gospel Traditions in the Second Century: Origins, Recensions, Text, and Transmission*, ed. William L. Petersen (Notre Dame, IN: University of Notre Dame Press, 1989), 34 n. 49.

6 Morton Smith, "On the Authenticity of the Mar Saba Letter of Clement," *CBQ* 38 (1976): 196.

7 Thomas Talley, "Liturgical Time in the Ancient Church: The State of Research," *Studia Liturgica* 14 (1982): 45.

8 See Jean-Daniel Kaestli, "Introduction de l'Évangile secret de Marc," in *Écrits apocryphes chrétiens*, ed. François Bovon and Pierre Geoltrain, 2d ed. (Paris: Gallimard, 1997), 1:59–60 n. 4. He noted that Father Aristarchos is frequently asked about this document.

9 James H. Charlesworth, *Authentic Apocrypha: False and Genuine Christian Apocrypha* (North Richland Hills, TX: Bibal Press, 1998), 30, 32; James R. Edwards, "Appendix: The Secret Gospel of Mark," in his *The Gospel According to Mark* (Grand Rapids: Eerdmans, 2002), 510 n. 2; Shaye Cohen, e-mail to author, 11 July 2002; John Dart, *Decoding Mark* (Harrisburg: Trinity Press International, 2003), 138–39.

10 Charles W. Hedrick and Nikolaos Olympiou, "Secret Mark: New Photographs, New Witnesses," *The Fourth R* 13:5 (2000): 8–9. For additional discussion, see Dart, *Decoding Mark*, 137–39.

11 Guy G. Stroumsa, "Comments on Charles Hedrick's Article: A Testimony," *JECS* 11 (2003):147–53. Stroumsa's story was first announced publicly by Bart D. Ehrman, "Too Good to Be False? A Text Critic Looks at the Secret Gospel of Mark" (paper presented at the annual meeting of the SBL, Toronto, ON, Canada, November 2002). More details are supplied in Ehrman, "The Forgery of an Ancient Discovery? Morton Smith and the Secret Gospel of Mark," in his *Lost Christianities: The Battles for Scripture and the Faiths We Never Knew* (New York: Oxford University Press, 2003), 83–84.

12 Akenson, *Saint Saul*, 87; cf. 85. See also Jacob Neusner, *Are There Really Tannaitic Parallels to the Gospels? A Refutation of Morton Smith*, SFSHJ 80 (Atlanta: Scholars Press, 1993), 27, 29; idem, Forward to Birger Gerhardsson, *Memory and Manuscript: Oral Tradition and Written Transmission in Rabbinic Judaism and Early Christianity* with *Tradition and Transmission in Early Christianity* (1961 and 1964; reprint, Grand Rapids: Eerdmans, 1998), xxvii.

13 Akenson's repeated intimations that Smith withheld the manuscript cannot be blamed on ignorance, for in *Saint Saul*, 273 n. 22, Akenson cited Smith's article "Clement of Alexandria and Secret Mark: The Score at the End of the First Decade," *HTR* 75 (1982): 449–61, which recounts Thomas Talley's information on pp. 458–59.

14 W.J. Barrow, *Manuscripts and Documents: Their Deterioration and Restoration* (Charlottesville: University of Virginia Press, 1955), 13–14, 50–51. My research into this subject was prompted by an observation made by Mahlon H. Smith <mahlonh.smith@worldnet.att.net>, REPLY: [XTalk] Secret Mark," in SYN-

OPTIC-L, <synoptic-l@bham.ac.uk>, 9 October 2000. Archived at: <http://groups.yahoo.com/group/synoptic-l/message/4935>.

15 Barrow, *Manuscripts and Documents*, 15–17.

16 Barrow, *Manuscripts and Documents*, 17.

17 Joseph Rosenblum, *Practice to Deceive: The Amazing Stories of Literary Forgery's Most Notorious Practitioners* (New Castle, DE: Oak Knoll Press, 2000), 338.

18 Charles E. Murgia, "Secret Mark: Real or Fake?" in *LM*, 35–40.

19 Murgia, in *LM*, 38. I added the numbers in parentheses.

20 From a letter to Wilhelm Wuellner, 5 August 1976, as cited in Saul Levin, "The Early History of Christianity, in Light of the 'Secret Gospel' of Mark," *ANRW* II 25:6 (1988): 4274.

21 Smith, "Score," 451.

22 These topics are discussed in chapter 4.

23 Murgia, in *LM*, 38; cf. 60. This error is perpetuated in Bart D. Ehrman, "Response to Charles Hedrick's Stalemate," *JECS* 11 (2003): 161; idem, "Forgery," 85.

24 The relevant words in II.11–12 can be translated either as "nor should one agree that [the Carpocratian version] is Mark's mystic gospel" or "...that the mystic gospel is by Mark." The latter is Smith's translation, which is disputed by Claude Mondésert and Cyril C. Richardson (*CA*, 52, 53). Smith's reading might at most imply a tacit denial that the longer text is used in Alexandria. But lying in order to convince a few Carpocratians that the longer gospel is not accepted in Alexandria is still nowhere near the sort of cover-up that could explain why a modern reader has never heard of the text.

25 Smith, *CA*, 168.

26 Murgia, in *LM*, 38–39, 60. W. Kümmel, "Ein Jahrzehnt Jesusforschung (1965–1975)," *TRu*, n.s., 40 (1975): 302 (citing verbal comments made by H. von Campenhausen); Helmut Merkel, "Appendix: The 'Secret Gospel' of Mark," in *New Testament Apocrypha*, ed. Wilhelm Schneemelcher, 2d rev. ed. (Cambridge: James Clarke and Co.; Louisville: Westminster/John Knox Press, 1991), 1:108 n. 5 (repeating Kümmel's comments); Levin, "Early History," 4273; Ehrman, "Response to Charles Hedrick's Stalemate," 161; idem, "Forgery," 85.

27 Judith L. Kovacs, "Divine Pedagogy and the Gnostic Teacher According to Clement of Alexandria," *JECS* 9 (2001): 18–22. On Clement's limited endorsement of deception for a higher good, see also David Satran, "Pedagogy and Deceit in the Alexandrian Theological Tradition," in *Origeniana Quinta*, ed. Robert J. Daly (Leuven: Leuven University Press, 1992), 119–24 (cited by Kovacs). Bart Ehrman's objection that the letter contradicts Clement because "Clement is quite explicit elsewhere in his writings that Christians should never lie or distort the truth" is a more obvious half truth than that endorsed by the letter ("Response to Charles Hedrick's Stalemate," 161; cf. "Forgery," 85).

28 Charles W. Hedrick and Paul A. Mirecki, *Gospel of the Savior: A New Ancient Gospel* (Santa Rosa, CA: Polebridge Press, 1999), 1. These are the Dialogue of the Saviour, Egerton Papyrus 2, Papyrus Oxyrhynchus 840, Papyrus Oxyrhynchus 1224, the Gospel of Mary, and the Gospel of the Saviour.

29 Murgia, in *LM*, 40, 60.

30 Smith, *CA*, 3–4, 289.

31  Smith, *CA*, 2.

32  See D.C. Parker, *The Living Text of the Gospels* (Cambridge: Cambridge University Press, 1997), 37–38.

33  Smith, "Score," 451. See his conjectures about the text's transmission in *CA*, 285–90 and *SG*, 144–48.

34  Murgia, in *LM*, 39–40, 60, 61, 62.

35  Murgia, in *LM*, 39, 60. C.H. Bird, "Some Gar Clauses in St. Mark's Gospel," *JTS* 4 (1953): 171–87. On Clement's reference to Mark producing notes, see Wayne A. Meeks, "*Hypomnēmata* from an Untamed Sceptic: A Response to George Kennedy," in *The Relationships Among the Gospels: An Interdisciplinary Dialogue*, ed. William O. Walker, Jr., Trinity University Monograph Series in Religion 5 (San Antonio: Trinity University Press, 1978), 167–69; C. Clifton Black, *Mark: Images of an Apostolic Interpreter* (Columbia: University of South Carolina Press, 1994), 141–42.

36  I am citing, almost verbatim, the categories Smith used to analyze the attribution of the letter to Clement (*CA*, 67–75).

37  The congruence with Markan composition will become apparent in the chapters exploring longer Mark's use of Markan literary devices.

38  Frederick W. Danker, review of *SG*, *Dialog* 13 (1974): 316.

39  Quesnell, "The Mar Saba Clementine: A Question of Evidence," *CBQ* 37 (1975): 48–67.

40  Quesnell's personal recollections are quoted from two letters he wrote to me. His review was published as "'Secret Gospel': Improbable Puzzle," *National Catholic Reporter* (30 November 1973): 12.

41  Smith, "Authenticity," 197; cf. idem, "Score," 450.

42  Quesnell, "Reply to Morton Smith," 200.

43  Akenson, *Saint Saul*, 273 n. 22.

44  Quesnell, "Reply to Morton Smith," 200–201.

45  Quesnell, "Question of Evidence," 56 n. 16; "Reply to Morton Smith," 201.

46  Quesnell, "Question of Evidence," 57.

47  Nock's intuition was that the letter was an *ancient* forgery ("not later than the fourth century"), as Quesnell himself noted ("Question of Evidence," 54 n. 11), but Quesnell informed me that the above characterization of his implication is basically accurate, to the best of his recollection.

48  Quesnell, "Question of Evidence," 66, 58, 67.

49  Quesnell, "Reply to Morton Smith," 201; cf. "Question of Evidence," 58–59.

50  See Hedrick and Olympiou, "New Witnesses," 6.

51  Smith, *SG*, 9.

52  Quesnell, "Reply to Morton Smith," 201.

53  Edgar J. Goodspeed, *Strange New Gospels* (Chicago: University of Chicago Press, 1931), 3.

54  Paul L. Kirk, *Crime Investigation*, 2d ed. (New York: Wiley, 1974), 501, as cited by Joel Nickel in *Pen, Ink, and Evidence: A Study of Writing and Writing Materials for the Penman, Collector, and Document Detective* (Lexington: University Press of Kentucky, 1990), 190.

55  Rosenblum, *Practice to Deceive*, 341.

56  Per Beskow, *Strange Tales about Jesus: A Survey of Unfamiliar Gospels* (Philadelphia: Fortress, 1983), 96–103; originally published as *Fynd och fusk i Bibelns värld*

(Stockholm: Proprius förlag, 1979). Beskow's discussion of "secret" Mark was significantly revised in the 1985 reprint of the English edition.

57  Hans-Martin Schenke, "The Mystery of the Gospel of Mark," *SecCent* 4:2 (1984): 71.

58  John Dominic Crossan, *Four Other Gospels: Shadows on the Contours of Canon* (Minneapolis: Winston, 1985), 103.

59  Marvin W. Meyer, "The Youth in Secret Mark and the Beloved Disciple in John," in *Gospel Origins & Christian Beginnings: In Honor of James M. Robinson*, ed. J.E. Goehring et al. (Sonoma: Polebridge Press, 1990), 95; cf. idem, "The Youth in the *Secret Gospel of Mark*," *Semeia* 49 (1990): 130.

60  Beskow, *Strange Tales*, 103, reiterated even more forcefully in the 1985 revised edition on p. 104. Cf. Murgia, *LM*, 60, 65.

61  Jacob Neusner and Noam M.M. Neusner, *The Price of Excellence: Universities in Conflict during the Cold War Era* (New York: Continuum, 1995), 78.

62  Neusner, *Refutation*, 27–31; essentially the same text appears in "Who Needs 'the Historical Jesus'? Two Elegant Works Rehabilitate a Field Disgraced by Fraud," in his *Ancient Judaism: Debates and Disputes: Third Series*, SFSHJ 83 (Atlanta: Scholars Press, 1993), 173–76; "Who Needs 'The Historical Jesus'? An Essay Review," *BBR* 4 (1994): 115–18; and *Rabbinic Literature & the New Testament: What We Cannot Show, We Do Not Know* (Valley Forge, PA: Trinity Press International, 1994), 172–74. It is not clear how or when Jesus research fell into disgrace over this document, for no other Jesus scholars factored its brief gospel excerpt into their reconstructions *of Jesus*. There is a conspicuous irony in Neusner's choice of Crossan as a scholar whose work rehabilitates Jesus scholarship from this imaginary disgrace, since Crossan adopted Smith's designation "magician" for Jesus and decided that the longer text was the most original form of Mark. See John Dominic Crossan, *The Historical Jesus: The Life of a Mediterranean Jewish Peasant* (San Francisco: Harper, 1991), 169.

63  Neusner, *Refutation*, 28, 29, 30.

64  Neusner, *Refutation*, 30. This inference is repeated by Akenson in *Saint Saul*, 273 n. 22. I asked Quesnell whether he had feared being sued; he wrote back, "I don't believe it ever entered my mind."

65  Neusner, *Refutation*, 28.

66  Neusner, Forward to *Memory and Manuscript*, xxvii. Cf. Neusner and Neusner, *Price of Excellence*, 78.

67  Shawn Eyer brought the endorsement to my attention.

68  Smith, *CA*, x. Smith thanked him for the "many corrections" that he made.

69  Craig A. Evans, "The Need for the 'Historical Jesus': A Response to Jacob Neusner's Review of Crossan and Meier," *BBR* 4 (1994): 129.

70  Shaye J.D. Cohen, review of *Are There Really Tannaitic Parallels to the Gospels?* by Jacob Neusner, *JAOS* 116:1 (1996): 87 n. 9.

71  Quesnell examined the documentation accompanying Smith's commentary for six of the words in line I.2 of the letter (see *CA*, 7–8); he showed that five of Smith's twelve citations in this place are in error (Quesnell, "Question of Evidence," 65–66).

72  In the reviews, Smith's "scholarly thoroughness" was described as "monumental" (George MacRae, "Yet Another Jesus," *Commonweal* 99 [25 January 1974]: 417), "overwhelming" (James M. Reese, review of *CA* and *SG*, *CBQ* 36 [1974]:

435), "intimidatingly brilliant" (Norman R. Petersen, review of *CA* and *SG*, *Southern Humanities Review* 8 [1974]: 525), and "un monument d'érudition, disons mieux de science" (André Méhat, review of *CA*, *Revue de l'histoire des religions* 190 [1976]: 196); see esp. Etienne Trocmé, "Trois critiques au miroir de l'Évangile selon Marc," *RHPR* 55 (1975): 292; and Howard Clark Kee, review of *SG*, *JAAR* 43 (1975): 327: "With its textual, statistical, stylistic, and palaeographical analyses and its assembling of biblical, patristic, and heretical parallels, the larger work is a model of responsible publication of an ancient document."

73 Neusner, *Refutation*, 10, 158; cf. 23.

74 Neusner, *Rabbinic Literature*, 4–5.

75 Jacob Neusner, "New Problems, New Solutions. Current Events in Rabbinic Studies," in his *The Academic Study of Judaism: Essays and Reflections, Third Series: Three Contexts of Jewish Learning* (New York: Ktav Publishing House, 1980), 103 n. 18.

76 The quotations come from Neusner, *Refutation*, 7, 39 (elaborated on p. 25), 6, 26 (cf. 19, 27, 31, 39, 135–39), 25, and 167, respectively.

77 Neusner, *Refutation*, 15–17 (the quoted words are from p. 17).

78 Morton Smith, review of *A History of the Jews in Babylonia I*, by Jacob Neusner, *JAAR* 35 (1967): 182; idem, review of *A History of the Jews in Babylonia III, IV, V*, by Jacob Neusner, *JBL* 89 (1970): 492.

79 Morton Smith, review of *Development of a Legend*, by Jacob Neusner, *Conservative Judaism* 26:4 (1970): 76.

80 Neusner, *Refutation*, 19.

81 On 28 May 2002, Neusner's online curriculum vitae boasted over 850 books authored or edited between the years 1962 and 2001 (http://inside.bard.edu/religion/faculty.shtml). If that number is correct, this works out to 21.8 books per year over the course of thirty-nine years, or one book every 16.7 days. However, Neusner's rate of producing books steadily increased over the years, from 2.3 per year over the first decade to the rate of 50 per year, which he averaged in the mid-1990s; that works out to one book every 7.3 days.

82 Cohen, review of *Refutation*, 86. Cohen disputed various elements of Neusner's account of the event, which can be found in *Refutation*, 23–24; Neusner and Neusner, *Price of Excellence*, 226–27.

83 Hershel Shanks, "Annual Meetings Offer Intellectual Bazaar and Moments of High Drama," *BAR* 11:2 (1985): 16, which reproduces Smith's brief speech verbatim.

84 Saul Lieberman, "A Tragedy or a Comedy?" *JAOS* 104 (1984): 315. For an independent but very similar (if less colourful) review of this translation, see Tirzah Meacham, "Neusner's *Talmud of the Land of Israel*," *JQR* 77 (1986): 74–81.

85 Hershel Shanks, "The Neusner Phenomenon—Personality and Substance," *BAR* 11:6 (1985): 60.

86 Shanks, "Neusner Phenomenon," 60; idem, "Neusner Joins Ranks of Superman," *BAR* 11:3 (1985): 8.

87 Hershel Shanks, "Neusner Decides Not to Sue," *BAR* 11:4 (1985): 8.

88 Morton Smith, letter to editor, *BAR* 11:3 (1985): 18.

89 Neusner, *Refutation*, ix, 38, 39, 139. Smith's dissertation was completed in Hebrew in 1944, defended in 1945, and revised and translated into English in 1951.

90 Neusner, *Refutation*, 157, 25; cf. Neusner and Neusner, *Price of Excellence*, 227.

91 Jacob Neusner, *New Review of Books and Religion* 4:3 (1979): 24, cited by Cohen in his review of *Refutation*, 86.

92 Romano Penna, "Homosexuality and the New Testament," in *Christian Anthropology and Homosexuality*, ed. Mario Agnes, L'Osservatore Romano Reprints 38 (Vatican City: L'Osservatore Romano, 1997), 35.

93 James H. Charlesworth and Craig A. Evans, "Jesus in the Agrapha and Apocryphal Gospels," in *Studying the Historical Jesus: Evaluations of the State of Current Research*, ed. Bruce Chilton and Craig A. Evans, NTTS 19 (Leiden: E.J. Brill, 1994), 526 (noting Neusner "knew the late Professor Smith as well as anyone"); Graham Stanton, *Gospel Truth? New Light on Jesus and the Gospels* (Valley Forge: Trinity Press International, 1995), 93; Bruce M. Metzger, *Reminiscences of an Octogenarian* (Peabody, MA: Hendrickson, 1997), 130–31; Akenson, *Saint Saul*, 274 n. 22 (with the assurance that Neusner offers "a fairly definitive description of his mentor"); Ehrman, "Too Good to Be False?" Evans, Stanton, and Metzger did not endorse Neusner's opinion. They merely passed it along as conceivably important.

94 Akenson, *Saint Saul*, 86–87.

95 Akenson, *Saint Saul*, 88, 89.

96 Akenson, *Saint Saul*, 89.

97 Koester, "History and Development of Mark's Gospel (From Mark to *Secret Mark* and 'Canonical' Mark)," in *Colloquy on New Testament Studies: A Time for Reappraisal and Fresh Approaches*, ed. Bruce Corley (Macon, GA: Mercer University Press, 1983), 35–57; Crossan, *Historical Jesus*, 330, 331; Robert W. Funk and the Jesus Seminar, *The Acts of Jesus: The Search for the Authentic Deeds of Jesus* (San Francisco: HarperSanFrancisco, 1998), 1, 114–19, 408–10. Koester initially defended Smith's position that these verses have significance "for our understanding of the historical Jesus" (response to Reginald Fuller, in *LM*, 32), though he was not sure what that significance might be; as far as I am aware, he has not returned to that matter.

98 Akenson, *Saint Saul*, 274 n. 22.

99 Quoting from Neusner, "Disgraced by Fraud," 175.

100 Akenson, *Saint Saul*, 274 n. 22.

101 Akenson, *Saint Saul*, 87.

102 See n. 13, above.

103 See Smith, *CA*, 285–86; *SG*, 144; Musurillo, "Smith's Secret Gospel," 329.

104 See also Smith, *SG*, 22–23.

105 Paramelle's opinion was related to me by Annewies van den Hoek in an e-mail dated 2 December 2002.

106 Akenson, *Saint Saul*, 88, 89.

107 Akenson, *Saint Saul*, 273–74 n. 22. Smith's extraordinary capacity to intimidate his critics (documented with a quotation from Neusner's rhetoric about Smith) and the inability of liberal scholars to think critically figure prominently in Akenson's explanation.

108 See n. 172 in this chapter.

109 Noted by James R. Davila, <jrd4@st-andrews.ac.uk>. "REPLY: Secret Mark." In IOUDAIOS-L. <ioudaios-l@lehigh.edu>. 1 July 1995. Archived at: <ftp://ftp.lehigh.edu/pub/listserv/ioudaios-l/archives/9507a.Z>.

110 Goodspeed, *Strange New Gospels*, 4–5.
111 E.g., Smith, response to Reginald Fuller, in *LM*, 12–13.
112 E.g., Morton Smith, "Ascent to the Heavens and the Beginning of Christianity,"
in *Studies in the Cult of Yahweh*, ed. Shaye J.D. Cohen (Leiden: E.J. Brill, 1996),
2:47–67; idem, "The Origin and History of the Transfiguration Story," *USQR*
36 (1980): 39–44; idem, "Pauline Worship as Seen by Pagans," *HTR* 73 (1980):
241–50; idem, "Paul's Arguments as Evidence of the Christianity from which
He Diverged," *HTR* 79 (1986): 254–60; idem, "Two Ascended to Heaven—
Jesus and the Author of 4Q491," in *Studies in the Cult of Yahweh*, ed. Shaye
J.D. Cohen, 2:68–78.
113 Quesnell's article includes a collection of paraphrases and quotations from three
of Smith's earlier works that produces the impression that prior to 1958 Smith
believed, in essence, that Jesus was a magician who practised libertine rites of a
sexual nature which he and his followers kept secret ("Question of Evidence,"
58–60). This impression is utterly misleading, for seven of these nine proof
texts fundamentally misrepresent what Smith wrote. See Scott G. Brown, "The
More Spiritual Gospel: Markan Literary Techniques in the Longer Gospel of
Mark" (Ph.D. diss., University of Toronto, 1999), 106–14; better yet, spend half
an hour looking up the passages Quesnell quoted.
114 Morton Smith, "The Jewish Elements in the Gospels," *JBR* 24 (1956): 96.
115 Smith, *SG*, 105–106 (emphasis added).
116 At one point in a 1956 essay, Smith discussed Palestinian sects that practised
magic, but even here Smith said nothing about Christians having such practices—this despite including Christian sects in his survey; see Morton Smith,
"Palestinian Judaism in the First Century," in *Studies in the Cult of Yahweh*, ed.
Shaye J.D. Cohen, 1:107–108.
117 Smith, *CA*, 227–29.
118 Morton Smith, "Comments on Taylor's Commentary on Mark," *HTR* 48 (1955):
27–28.
119 Smith, *CA*, 211, 262; see also *Jesus the Magician* (San Francisco: Harper and
Row, 1978), 43, 138.
120 Morton Smith, "Jesus' Attitude towards the Law," in *Papers of the Fourth World
Congress of Jewish Studies*, ed. World Congress of Jewish Studies (Jerusalem:
World Union of Jewish Studies, 1967), 1:241–44 (presented in 1965); idem,
"The Reason for the Persecution of Paul and the Obscurity of Acts," in *Studies
in the Cult of Yahweh*, ed. Shaye J.D. Cohen, 2:87–94.
121 E.g., Smith, "Comments," 24 and n. 6.
122 Smith, *LM*, 13.
123 Smith, "Comments," 30.
124 Smith, *CA*, 178.
125 These are outlined at length in Smith, "Comments," 47.
126 Smith, *SG*, 80. Smith also criticized Taylor for thinking Mark used repetition for
"cross-reference" among pericopae ("Comments," 31–32). This idea is accepted
in *CA* (e.g., 136, 177). I argue in chapter 8 that the author of LGM 1 and 2 made
extensive use of this technique.
127 Werner H. Kelber, *The Oral and the Written Gospel: The Hermeneutics of Speaking and Writing in the Synoptic Tradition, Mark, Paul, and Q* (Philadelphia:
Fortress, 1983), 49.

128 Reginald H. Fuller, "Longer Mark: Forgery, Interpolation, or Old Tradition?" in *LM*, 7.

129 Smith, *CA*, 152–58; *SG*, 53. His critique of form criticism is offered in *CA*, 149. He continued this critique in later writings: *LM*, 13; "Merkel on the Longer Text of Mark," *ZTK* 72 (1975): 146; "Score," 455–56.

130 Smith, *CA*, 178–84 (183); *SG*, 79.

131 Smith later abandoned his claim of textual corruption when he found evidence that διδάσκω and its cognates can mean giving a mystery or magical rite; see Smith, "Authenticity," 199 and n. 12; *Jesus the Magician*, 207; and "Two Ascended," 69 n. 5. The fact remains that "teaching the mystery" is not a normal way to refer to the act of baptism.

132 See M.A. Beavis, *Mark's Audience: The Literary and Social Setting of Mark 4.11–12*, JSNT Sup 33 (Sheffield: JSOT Press, 1989), 91–95; Willem S. Vorster, "Meaning and Reference: The Parables of Jesus in Mark 4," in Bernard C. Lategan and Willem S. Vorster, *Text and Reality: Aspects of Reference in Biblical Texts* (Philadelphia: Fortress; Atlanta: Scholars Press, 1985), 35; David Peabody, *Mark as Composer*, New Gospel Studies 1 (Macon, GA: Mercer University Press, 1987), 163, 164.

133 Beskow, *Strange Tales*, 103. Cf. the similar comments by Ronald J. Sider, "Unfounded 'Secret,'" *CT* 18:3 (9 November 1973): 26 (160); John G. Gibbs, review of *SG*, *ThTo* 30 (1974): 424; Joseph A. Fitzmyer, "How to Exploit a Secret Gospel," *America* 128 (23 June 1973): 570–71; idem, "Mark's 'Secret Gospel'?" *America* 129 (4 August 1973): 65; Musurillo, "Smith's Secret Gospel," 328; Quesnell, "Improbable Puzzle," 12; idem, "Question of Evidence," 58; Kümmel, "Jahrzehnt," 303; and Levin, "Early History," 4281.

134 Smith discussed the longer text initiation story on only two pages of *Jesus the Magician* (ten lines on p. 134, two on p. 138) and briefly mentioned it in five endnotes on pp. 203 (2x), 207 (2x, documenting p. 134) and 210 (the notes are not numbered in this book); Smith alluded to the possibility that the letter supplies evidence for the possession of secret oral traditions in Mark's church on p. 104 (see the endnote on p. 194); approximately twenty other endnotes mention discussions of particular topics found in his books on longer Mark, but do not mention LGM 1 and 2. The basic neglect of longer Mark in *Jesus the Magician* was pointed out by Beskow in *Strange Tales*, 130 n. 135.

135 E.g., Smith, "Pauline Worship," 102 (a subordinate clause); "Ascent to the Heavens," nn. 39 and 53 (two sentences).

136 Brief reference to Jesus' special baptism can be found in Morton Smith, "Salvation in the Gospels, Paul, and the Magical Papyri," in *Studies in the Cult of Yahweh*, ed. Shaye J.D. Cohen, 2:134, 136–37.

137 Smith, *SG*, 61–62; *CA*, 145, 188–92, 194 (postscript). Many scholars erroneously report that Smith thought "secret" Mark was the original form of Mark (e.g., Ehrman, "Forgery," 79, 80), but Smith specifically rejected that conclusion in *LM*, 12–13 and "Merkel," 135.

138 A.H. Criddle, "On the Mar Saba Letter Attributed to Clement of Alexandria," *JECS* 3 (1995): 216. He did not say in the article whether he thought the letter was an ancient or modern forgery, but his inferences about how it must have been composed entail procedures that would be practically impossible for a writer who did not possess lexicons and author indexes (e.g., p. 218). In a fol-

low-up discussion on the Internet ("Secret Mark—Further Comments"), he confirmed this conclusion (http://www-user.uni-bremen.de/~wie/Secret/Crid-dle-Feb99.html).

139  Criddle, "On the Mar Saba Letter," 218.

140  Criddle, "On the Mar Saba Letter," 218. Criddle gave no evidence that the letter contains rare Clementine phrases.

141  Ehrman, "Forgery," 85–86.

142  Criddle, "On the Mar Saba Letter," 218.

143  Eric F. Osborn, "Clement of Alexandria: A Review of Research, 1958–1982," *SecCent* 3 (1983): 224.

144  Criddle, private e-mail to author, 18 February 1999.

145  Criddle, private e-mail to author, 18 February 1999.

146  Criddle, "On the Mar Saba Letter," 217, 219.

147  Philip Jenkins, *Hidden Gospels: How the Search for Jesus Lost Its Way* (New York: Oxford University Press, 2001), 102. Pages in parentheses refer to James H. Hunter, *The Mystery of Mar Saba* (New York: Evangelical, 1940).

148  Robert M. Price, "Second Thoughts on the Secret Gospel," *BBR* 14 (2004): 131. Price also called *The Mystery of Mar Saba* "one of those 'lost Gospel novels,'" implying that the Shred of Nicodemus is a gospel, like Smith's discovery. A short written testimony that *disputes* the resurrection can hardly be characterized as a gospel.

149  Johannes Munck, in *CA*, 27, 33.

150  Edwin M. Yamauchi, "A Secret Gospel of Jesus as 'Magus'? A Review of the Recent Works of Morton Smith," *CSR* 4:3 (1975): 240; Beskow, *Strange Tales*, 101; Osborn, "1958–1982," 224; Criddle, "On the Mar Saba Letter," 216; Dieter Lührmann, "Das 'geheime Markusevangelium' bei Pseudo-Clemens," in his *Fragmente apokryph gewordener Evangelien in griechischer und lateinischer Sprache*, Münchener theologische Studien 59 (Marburg: N.G. Elwert, 2000), 182.

151  F.F. Bruce, *The "Secret" Gospel of Mark* (London: Athlone Press, 1974), 13; cf. the comments by L.W. Barnard in "St. Mark and Alexandria," *HTR* 57 (1964): 149.

152  Bruce, *"Secret" Gospel*, 15.

153  Birger A. Pearson, "Earliest Christianity in Egypt: Some Observations," in *The Roots of Egyptian Christianity*, ed. Birger A. Pearson and James E. Goehring, SAC (Philadelphia: Fortress, 1986), 138.

154  G.M. Lee, "Eusebius on St. Mark and the Beginnings of Christianity in Egypt," in *Studia Patristica XII*, ed. Elizabeth A. Livingston, TU 115 (Berlin: Akademie-Verlag, 1975), 425–27.

155  The translation is from B. Orchard, "Mark and the Fusion of Traditions," in *The Four Gospels 1992: Festschrift Frans Neirynck*, ed. Frans Van Segbroeck et al. (Leuven: Leuven University Press, 1992), 2:793.

156  See Massey H. Shepherd, response to Reginald Fuller, in *LM*, 62–63; Osborn, "1958–1982," 224–25; and Criddle, "On the Mar Saba Letter," 216 (who is following Osborn). Shepherd's objections were usually directed against Smith's interpretations of the letter; Shepherd did not make inferences concerning the letter's authenticity, about which he kept an open mind.

157  Chrys C. Caragounis, *The Ephesian Mysterion: Meaning and Content*, ConBNT 8 (Uppsala: CWK Gleerup, 1977), 11.

158 The "great mysteries" are discussed in *Strom.* IV.1.3.1 and V.11.71.1 (cf. I.1.15.3). In these places their contents are described as theological, not cultic. Chapter 4 will demonstrate that when Clement used the word *mystery* in connection with orthodox Christianity, he did so in reference to esoteric knowledge.

159 Raoul Mortley, *Connaissance religieuse et herméneutique chez Clément d'Alexandrie* (Leiden: E.J. Brill, 1973), 56 (trans. mine). See also Salvatore R.C. Lilla, *Clement of Alexandria: A Study in Christian Platonism and Gnosticism* (Oxford: Oxford University Press, 1971), 56–57, 137–42, 154–60; John E. Steely, *Gnosis: The Doctrine of Christian Perfection in the Writings of Clement of Alexandria* (Louisville: The Microcard Foundation for the American Theological Library Association, 1954), 127–28.

160 See *CA*, 31–32, 37 (for Völker and Munck); Eric F. Osborn, "Teaching and Writing in the First Chapter of the *Stromateis* of Clement of Alexandria," *JTS*, n.s., 10 (1959): 340 (cited by Smith). Cf. Shepherd, *LM*, 62, 63–64.

161 Shepherd, *LM*, 68.

162 John Ferguson, *Clement of Alexandria*, TWAS 289 (New York: Twayne, 1974), 113.

163 *Strom.* VII.18.110.4–111.3 These are the final comments of the *Stromateis*; the existing Book Eight was not originally part of the work. On Clement's use of disorder as a form of indirection, cf. Einar Molland, *The Conception of the Gospel in the Alexandrian Theology* (Oslo: 1 Kommisjon hos Jacob Dybwad, 1938), 5–14.

164 The word *Stromateis* means "miscellanies" or "patchwork."

165 E.L. Fortin, "Clement of Alexandria and the Esoteric Tradition," in *Studia Patristica* IX, part 3, ed. F.L. Cross, TU 94 (Berlin: Akademie-Verlag, 1966), 41–43, 43 n. 1.

166 Werner Jaeger, cited by Smith in *CA*, 38 (I quoted only a small portion of his comments).

167 E.g., John Kaye, *Some Account of the Writings and Opinions of Clement of Alexandria* (1835; reprint, London: Griffith, Farran, Okeden, and Welsh, n.d.), 214–15; F.J.A. Hort and J.B. Mayor, *Clement of Alexandria Miscellanies Book VII: The Greek Text with Introduction, Translation, Notes, Dissertations and Indices* (London: Macmillan, 1902), xxi; Eugène de Faye, *Clément d'Alexandrie: Étude sur les rapports du christianisme et de la philosophie grecque au IIe siècle*, 2d ed. (Paris: E. Leroux, 1906), 104; Lilla, *Christian Platonism*, 56, 144–50, 154–58, 162–63; Mortley, *Connaissance*, 56; James E. Davison, "Structural Similarities and Dissimilarities in the Thought of Clement of Alexandria and the Valentinians," *SecCent* 3 (1983): 209–12; Christoph Riedweg, *Mysterienterminologie bei Platon, Philon und Klemens von Alexandrien* (Berlin and New York: Walter de Gruyter, 1987), 139 n. 40 (cf. 141, 159); Guy G. Stroumsa, *Hidden Wisdom: Esoteric Traditions and the Roots of Christian Mysticism*, Studies in the History of Religions 70 (Leiden: E.J. Brill, 1996), 92–131.

168 Osborn, "1958–1982," 224; idem, "Teaching and Writing," 341.

169 Osborn, *The Philosophy of Clement of Alexandria* (Cambridge: Cambridge University Press, 1957), 168 (cf. 25, 120).

170 Citing Criddle, "On the Mar Saba Letter," 219–20. See also Ehrman, "Response to Charles Hedrick's Stalemate," 160–61. Osborn, "1958–1982," 224.

171 Osborn, "1958–1982," 224.

NOTES

172  Ferguson, *Clement of Alexandria*, 188–89. Werner Jaeger, *Early Christianity and Greek Paideia* (Cambridge, MA: Belknap Press of Harvard University Press, 1961), 57. Claude Mondésert, cited in Smith, *CA*, 37, 67. Cyril C. Richardson, review of *CA* and *SG*, *TS* 35 (1974): 571–72. William H.C. Frend, "A New Jesus?" *New York Review of Books* 20 (9 August 1973): 34. Robert M. Grant, "Morton Smith's Two Books," *AThR* 56 (1974): 58. R.P.C. Hanson, review of *CA*, *JTS*, n.s., 25 (1974): 515. André Méhat, review of *CA*, 196. Jean-Daniel Kaestli, "L'Évangile secret de Marc : Une version longue de l'Évangile de Marc réservée aux chrétiens avancés dans l'Église d'Alexandrie?" in *Le mystère apocryphe. Introduction à une littérature méconnue*, ed. J.-D. Kaestli and D. Marguerat (Genève: Labor et Fides, 1995), 88–93. Alain Le Boulluec, "La Lettre sur L'Évangile secret' de Marc et le *Quis dives salvetur?* de Clément d'Alexandrie," *Apocrypha* 7 (1996): 33. Guy G. Stroumsa, *Hidden Wisdom*, 112. Idem, "Comments on Charles Hedrick's Article," 153. Annewies van den Hoek, "Clement and Origen as Sources on 'Noncanonical' Scriptural Traditions during the Late Second and Earlier Third Centuries," in *Origeniana Sexta: Origène et la Bible/Origen and the Bible*, ed. Gilles Dorival and Alain Le Boulluec, Actes du Colloquium Origenianum Sextum Chantilly, 30 août–3 septembre 1993 (Leuven: Leuven University Press, 1995), 106. Kovacs, "Divine Pedagogy," 20 n. 76. Also important are the positive assessments of Frederick W. Danker, an expert in Greek philology and current editor of Walter Bauer's Greek-English Lexicon (review of *SG*, *Dialog* 13 [1974]: 316); G.W. Lampe, the editor of *A Patristic Greek Lexicon* (Smith, *CA*, 67); William M. Calder III, a classicist and colleague of Smith for eighteen years (private e-mail correspondence); and Birger A. Pearson, an expert on early Alexandrian Christianity ("Earliest Christianity in Egypt," 138).

173  Lilla, *Christian Platonism*, 56, 155. At the time he wrote this book, the *Letter to Theodore* was known to him only through a summary by Jaeger.

174  Noted by Smith in *CA*, 16–17.

175  For an argument that longer Mark influenced Clement's reading of Mark 10:17–31 in *Quis dives salvetur?* see Le Boulluec, "La Lettre."

176  Smith, *CA*, 284–85.

177  On Clement's role in the church and the catechetical school, see Annewies van den Hoek, "The 'Catechetical' School of Early Christian Alexandria and Its Philonic Heritage," *HTR* 90 (1997): 59–87; and Robert L. Wilken, "Alexandria: A School for Training in Virtue," in *Schools of Thought in the Christian Tradition*, ed. Patrick Henry (Philadelphia: Fortress, 1984), 15–19.

178  See Smith, *CA*, 283–84.

179  As translated in Black, *Apostolic Interpreter*, 138.

180  Black, *Apostolic Interpreter*, 12.

181  Grant, "Smith's Two Books," 62.

182  Van den Hoek, "Sources," 106 n. 80.

183  Black, *Apostolic Interpreter*, 154–55, 238; John A.T. Robinson, *Redating the New Testament* (London: SCM Press, 1976), 108–110.

184  Murgia, in *LM*, 58 (this is John M. Dillon's characterization of Murgia's position, which Murgia did nothing to correct); Musurillo, "Smith's Secret Gospel," 331.

185  Smith's negative opinion of Mark's competence as an author can be traced through Smith, "Comments," 21 and n. 3; 38 n. 23; idem, *CA*, 97–98; idem,

*The Aretalogy Used by Mark*, ed. Wilhelm H. Wuellner, Protocol of the Sixth Colloquy, 12 April 1973 (Berkeley: Center for Hermeneutical Studies in Hellenistic and Modern Culture, 1975), 30–33; idem, *Jesus the Magician*, 194 (note to p. 104); Dart, *Decoding Mark*, 133. Smith's inability to conceive of the gospels as literature is everywhere apparent in his own gospel scholarship and in the scholarship he preferred to consult.

# Chapter 3

1  The following discussion is based on the research presented in Werner Kelber, *The Oral and the Written Gospel: The Hermeneutics of Speaking and Writing in the Synoptic Tradition, Mark, Paul, and Q* (Philadelphia: Fortress, 1983), 1–34. Kelber's work is better informed by studies of oral tradition than any form-critical study that preceded it.

2  John C. Meagher, *Clumsy Construction in Mark's Gospel: A Critique of Form- and Redaktionsgeschichte*, Toronto Studies in Theology 3 (New York: Edwin Mellen, 1979), 3–15.

3  Kelber, *The Oral and the Written Gospel*, 46.

4  Smith, *CA*, 156–57; Wayne Shumaker and John S. Coolidge in *LM*, 61; John Dominic Crossan, *Four Other Gospels: Shadows on the Contours of Canon* (Minneapolis: Winston, 1985), 105; Lawrence M. Wills, *The Quest of the Historical Gospel: Mark, John, and the Origins of the Gospel Genre* (London and New York: Routledge, 1997), 242–43 n. 65.

5  Barnabas Lindars, "Rebuking the Spirit: A New Analysis of the Lazarus Story of John 11," *NTS* 38 (1992): 98.

6  Smith, *CA*, 104.

7  "Having become angry" is the reading found in D. The majority reading, "moved with pity," appears to be an attempt to change Jesus' anger into an emotion that makes better sense in this context, considering that the leper has done nothing that might reasonably anger Jesus. The lack of a parallel to this description of Jesus' emotion in Matthew and Luke is easier to explain if they depend on texts of Mark that referred to anger rather than pity. For a conclusive demonstration of the originality of the reading in D, see Mark Alan Proctor, "The Western Text of Mark 1:41: A Case for the Angry Jesus" (Ph.D. diss., Baylor University, 1999). More briefly: Bart D. Ehrman, "A Leper in the Hands of an Angry Jesus," in *New Testament Greek and Exegesis: Essays in Honor of Gerald F. Hawthorne*, ed. Amy M. Donaldson and Timothy B. Sailors (Grand Rapids: Eerdmans, 2003), 77–98.

8  E.g., James M. Robinson, *The Problem of History in Mark and Other Marcan Studies* (Philadelphia: Fortress, 1982), 88; Morna D. Hooker, *The Gospel According to St Mark*, BNTC (London: A and C Black, 1991), 79–81.

9  Proctor's attempt to read 1:43 as a rebuke and exorcism of a demon that remains after the man is cured of leprosy does not fit with the implication of v. 42 that the demon departed when the leprosy "went out from" the man (ἀπῆλθεν ἀπ' αὐτοῦ; cf. Luke 4:39) and with the fact that the word "him" in vv. 42 and 44 must refer to the man, not the demon. Proctor's position that Jesus is angered by the "half-flattering," "demonically inspired challenge" by the demon to cure

the leper also seems implausible, particularly since the demons in this story
know that the Son of God can destroy them. See Proctor, "Western Text of
Mark 1:41," 295–316 (citing pp. 295, 297).

10  Lindars, "Rebuking the Spirit," 92–97 (citing p. 95). See also Campbell Bonner, "Traces of Thaumaturgic Technique in the Miracles," *HTR* 20 (1927):
174–81; Howard Clark Kee, *Community of the New Age: Studies in Mark's Gospel*
(Philadelphia: Westminster, 1977), 35.

11  Lindars, "Rebuking the Spirit," 102.

12  On this subject, see Cullen I.K. Story, "The Mental Attitude of Jesus at Bethany:
John 11. 33, 38," *NTS* 37 (1991): 51–66, esp. 56–58. Story noted that he was
unable to find any parallels in Greek literature to John's use of ταράσσω in the
active voice with a reflexive pronoun for a direct object (p. 64 n. 70).

13  Edwyn Bevan, "Note on Mark i 41 and John xi 33, 38," *JTS* 33 (1932): 187–88.

14  Crossan, *Four Other Gospels*, 105. Cf. Smith, *CA*, 107.

15  Crossan, *Four Other Gospels*, 105. In a book exploring the origins of canonical
Mark and John, Lawrence M. Wills took the evidence from longer Mark as support for this conclusion (*Quest*, 99–102) and also noted the basic lines of this
argument, including the relevance of Lindars' article (pp. 242–43 n. 65).

16  Νεανίσκος (young man) occurs in LGM 1:7, 8, 9, 11 and 2:1. Θυγάτριον (little daughter) occurs in 5:23. Παιδίον (young child) is used in 5:39, 40 (2x), 41a
and 9:24. Κοράσιον (girl) appears in 5:41b, 42. And παιδιόθεν (childhood)
is found in 9:21.

17  On the subject of why John's gospel lacks exorcisms, see Graham H. Twelftree,
"Exorcisms in the Fourth Gospel and the Synoptics," in *Jesus in Johannine Tra-
dition*, ed. Robert T. Fortna and Tom Thatcher (Louisville: Westminster/John
Knox Press, 2001), 135–43.

18  E.g., Lindars, "Rebuking the Spirit," 100, 101, 104.

19  Reginald H. Fuller, "Longer Mark: Forgery, Interpolation, or Old Tradition?"
in *LM*, 7–8.

20  Kelber, *The Oral and the Written Gospel*, 49.

21  Fuller, *LM*, 8. Fuller's form-critical observations about the secondary character
of LGM 1b were accepted by Helmut Koester in his response to Reginald Fuller
in *LM*, 31; and by Hans-Martin Schenke in "The Mystery of the Gospel of
Mark," *SecCent* 4:2 (1984): 77; the latter offered a different reconstruction of
the original ending.

22  The phrase "the young man whom Jesus loved him" in LGM 2:1 has a parallel
in the Johannine expression "the disciple whom Jesus loved," which occurs in
later chapters of John. I believe that the Johannine expression is usually redactional but has its origin in the story of the raising of the dead man in Bethany
(cf. "he whom you love" in John 11:3). My arguments cannot be presented
here, but see Marvin Meyer, "The Youth in Secret Mark and the Beloved Disciple in John," in *Gospel Origins & Christian Beginnings: In Honor of James M.
Robinson*, ed. J.E. Goehring et al. (Sonoma: Polebridge Press, 1990), 94–105.

23  Smith, *SG*, 53.

24  Cf. Raymond E. Brown ("The Relation of 'The Secret Gospel of Mark' to the
Fourth Gospel," *CBQ* 36 [1974]: 480 n. 38), who conceded that "Critical
reconstructions have suggested that only one sister was involved in the original
pre-Johannine narrative."

25  Rudolf Bultmann (*The History of the Synoptic Tradition*, trans. John Marsh [New York: Harper and Row, 1963], 312–13) viewed the transformation of narrative material into direct speech as typical of later development. Apart from the plea of the bereaved sister, LGM 1 and 2 contain no direct discourse.

26  Cf. Bultmann, *History*, 309–10. Besides Jesus, the only named character in LGM 1 and 2 is Salome, who is not a participant in John's version.

27  Cf. Robert T. Fortna, *The Gospel of Signs: A Reconstruction of the Narrative Source Underlying the Fourth Gospel* (Cambridge: Cambridge University Press, 1970), 87. Fortna noted that none of the elements in John 11 that he would ascribe to John's redaction find parallels in LGM 1a. Longer Mark's parallels with John 11 are confined to elements found in Fortna's hypothetical Signs Source. In order to prevent confusion, I should point out that Fortna would ascribe to his Signs Source many of the elements in John 11 that I deem "Johannine" and secondary because he was trying to reconstruct a *written, Johannine* source that was based on oral traditions. LGM 1 is more "primitive" in form than the Signs Source. Raymond Brown was confused about this point ("Relation," 483–84). I should also point out that Fortna changed his mind about longer Mark's independence when he wrote *The Fourth Gospel and Its Predecessor* (Philadelphia: Fortress, 1988); see p. 94 n. 213.

28  E.g., F.F. Bruce, *The "Secret" Gospel of Mark* (London: Athlone Press, 1974), 11–12.

29  Kelber, *The Oral and the Written Gospel*, 49, 54.

30  For a convenient discussion of these differences, see Percival Gardner-Smith, *Saint John and the Synoptic Gospels* (Cambridge: Cambridge University Press, 1938).

31  Scott G. Brown, "Bethany beyond the Jordan: John 1:28 and the Longer Gospel of Mark," *RB* 110 (2003): 497–516.

32  James R. Edwards, "Appendix: The Secret Gospel of Mark," in his *The Gospel According to Mark* (Grand Rapids: Eerdmans, 2002), 511.

33  In 1997, Jordanian archaeologists began excavating the traditional site of Bethany beyond the Jordan, which is today called Wadi Kharrar (Tell el-Kharrar). It is located just over 1 km south of Jericho and 1.5 km east of the river. According to Mohammad Waheeb, they found "a 1st Century AD settlement with plastered pools and water systems that were used almost certainly for baptism, and a 5th–6th Century AD late Byzantine settlement with churches, a monastery, and other structures probably catering to religious pilgrims." The only thing missing is early evidence that this place was called Bethany. That evidence is supplied by longer Mark. See Waheeb, "Ancient Water System," *It's Time: Baptism 2000*. http://www.elmaghtas.com/ancient_water/ancient_water.html. Judith Sudilovsky, "Site of Jesus' Baptism Found—Again: Is It the Bible's 'Bethany beyond the Jordan'?" *BAR* 25:3 (1999): 14–15. Rami Khouri, "Where John Baptized: Bethany beyond the Jordan," *BAR* 31:1 (2005): 34–43.

34  See William H. Brownlee, "Whence the Gospel of John?" in *John and Qumran*, ed. James H. Charlesworth (London: Geoffrey Chapman, 1972), 166–73. Rainer Riesner, "Bethany beyond the Jordan (John 1:28): Topography, Theology and History in the Fourth Gospel," *Tyndale Bulletin* 38 (1987): 34–43. I am not convinced by their theory that John located Bethany in Batanaea but for theological reasons harmonized the spelling of *Batanaea* with *Bethany* (how could

John expect his readers to recognize that he meant Batanaea when he wrote *Bethany*?), but these scholars offered good evidence that John thought Bethany beyond the Jordan was nearer to Galilee than to Judea. Since the evidence in longer Mark better accords with the archaeological evidence, it would appear that John is a less reliable guide to the location.

35  *CBQ* 23 (1961): 143–60.

36  Bruce, *"Secret" Gospel*, 20, 11–12; Helmut Merkel, "Auf den Spuren des Urmarkus? Ein neuer Fund und seine Beurteilung," *ZTK* 71 (1974): 123–44; R.E. Brown, "Relation"; Robert M. Grant, "Morton Smith's Two Books," *AThR* 56 (1974): 60–61; Edward C. Hobbs, response to Reginald Fuller, in *LM*, 20–21, 66; Daryl Schmidt, ibid., 41–45; Frans Neirynck, "The Apocryphal Gospels and the Gospel of Mark," in *Evangelica II 1982–1991 Collected Essays by Frans Neirynck*, ed. Frans Van Segbroeck, BETL 99 (Leuven: Leuven University Press; Uitgeverij Peeters, 1991), 760–62; idem, "La fuite du jeune homme en Mc 14,51–52," in *Evangelica: Gospel Studies–Études d'évangile, Collected Essays*, ed. Frans Van Segbroeck, BETL 60 (Leuven: Leuven University Press; Uitgeverij Peeters, 1982), 223; Frans Neirynck et al., *Jean et les synoptiques: examen critique de l'exégèse de M.-É. Boismard*, BETL 49 (Leuven: Leuven University Press, 1979), 207 n. 493.

37  R.E. Brown, "Relation," 482–83.

38  B.W. Bacon, *The Fourth Gospel in Research and Debate*, 2d ed. (New Haven: Yale University Press, 1918), 321–22. This example is taken from D. Moody Smith, *John among the Gospels*, 2d ed. (Columbia, SC: University of South Carolina Press, 2001), 16–19.

39  Thomas L. Brodie, *The Quest for the Origin of John's Gospel* (New York: Oxford University Press, 1993).

40  Samuel Sandmel, "Parallelomania," *JBL* 81 (1962): 1.

41  Dennis R. MacDonald, *The Homeric Epics and the Gospel of Mark* (New Haven: Yale University Press, 2000); J. Edgar Bruns, *The Christian Buddhism of St. John: New Insights into the Fourth Gospel* (New York: Paulist Press, 1971).

42  R.E. Brown, "Relation," 478–79. Cf. Schmidt, *LM*, 42. Brown took it for granted that a non-canonical author would frequently become confused. See the postulated confusions in "Relation," 475 n. 19; 476 n. 20, which are actually projections of Brown's own confusion about which Bethany is the location of the miracle in LGM 1.

43  Hobbs, *LM*, 20–21.

44  Helmut Merkel, "Appendix: The 'Secret Gospel' of Mark," in *New Testament Apocrypha*, ed. Wilhelm Schneemelcher, 2d rev. ed. (Cambridge: James Clarke; Louisville: Westminster/John Knox Press, 1991), 107.

45  Schmidt, *LM*, 43.

46  Neirynck, "Apocryphal Gospels," 761. LGM 2:1 reads καὶ ἦσαν ἐκεῖ; Matt 27:55 has ἦσαν δὲ ἐκεῖ. Mark 15:40 omits ἐκεῖ.

47  Bruce, *"Secret" Gospel*, 13.

48  E.g., David Peabody, Allan J. McNicol, and Lamar Cope, eds., *One Gospel from Two: Mark's Use of Matthew and Luke* (Valley Forge, PA: Trinity Press International, 2002).

49  Raymond E. Brown, *The Gospel According to John*, 2d ed. (Garden City: Doubleday, 1980), 1:lxv, as cited in D. Moody Smith, *John among the Gospels*, 64.

50 That is true of nearly all of the canonical parallels offered by Helmut Merkel ("Auf den Spuren des Urmarkus?"; "Appendix"). These include "son of David, have mercy on me" (Mark 10:47, 48), "and there was there" (Mark 3:1), "but the disciples rebuked" (Mark 10:13), "and approaching" (Mark 1:31), "where...was" (Mark 2:4; 5:40), and "across the Jordan" (Mark 3:8; 10:1). Smith pointed this out in his article "Merkel on the Longer Text of Mark," *ZTK* 72 (1975): 136–45, but proponents of the pastiche theory continue to cite Merkel against Smith as if Smith had not refuted this facet of Merkel's argument.

51 The word *from* in Mark 16:3 is ἐκ in some manuscripts and ἀπό in others. The 26th edition of the Nestle-Aland Greek text offers ἐκ as the original reading. However, since longer Mark is usually closest to the Western D text, which has ἀπό, I have chosen the latter as the probable reading for 16:3 in longer Mark. See Smith, *CA*, 108.

52 Smith, "Merkel," 140–41.

53 Helmut Koester, "History and Development of Mark's Gospel (From Mark to *Secret Mark* and 'Canonical' Mark)," in *Colloquy on New Testament Studies: A Time for Reappraisal and Fresh Approaches*, ed. Bruce Corley (Macon, GA: Mercer University Press, 1983), 53; Crossan, *Four Other Gospels*, 115; idem, "Thoughts on Two Extracanonical Gospels," *Semeia* 49 (1990): 166–67.

54 E.g., Smith, *CA*, 107, 114, 145; idem, "Merkel," 143.

55 Smith, *CA*, 98, 135, 368–69.

56 C.H. Turner reasoned that the Western reading in D is the original reading because χρήματα rather than κτήματα occurs in the next verse ("those having wealth"). He thought χρήματα is a corruption from the Matthean parallel. See "Western Readings in the Second Half of St Mark's Gospel," *JTS* 29 (1927): 6.

57 E.g., Robert M. Grant, "Smith's Two Books," 60–61.

58 See Smith, *CA*, 146.

59 Werner Georg Kümmel, "Ein Jahrzehnt Jesusforschung (1965–1975)," *TRu*, n.s., 40 (1975): 303, as translated by Schenke in "Mystery," 70.

60 David Peabody, *Mark as Composer*, New Gospel Studies 1 (Macon, GA: Mercer University Press, 1986). Peabody used recurrent phraseology as a means of discriminating between the editorial work of the evangelist Mark and the content of his sources.

61 Smith, *CA*, 139.

62 Ernest Best, "Uncanonical Mark," review of *Redactional Style in the Marcan Gospel*, by E.J. Pryke, in Best's *Disciples and Discipleship: Studies in the Gospel According to Mark* (Edinburgh: T. and T. Clark, 1986), 197–205.

63 Best, "Uncanonical Mark," 199–201.

64 See, e.g., Kelber, *The Oral and the Written Gospel*, 30.

65 Peabody, *Mark as Composer*, 6–9. On the linguistic homogeneity of Mark's style, see William R. Telford, *Mark*, NTG (Sheffield: Sheffield Academic Press, 1995), 77.

66 Merkel, "Appendix," 107. He noted the opinions of Cyril C. Richardson and E. Best.

67 C.M. Tuckett, "Mark's Concerns in the Parables Chapter (Mark 4,1–34)," *Bib* 69 (1988): 5.

68 Smith, *CA*, 188–94.

69  Koester, "History and Development," 35–57. The 1983 book containing a revised version of this essay also includes a "Seminar Dialogue with Helmut Koester" in which he responded to the criticisms of his paper made by David Peabody and answered questions from other scholars. The quotation is from his second substantial paper on this topic, where longer Mark is addressed within a broader discussion of the textual histories of the synoptic gospels: "The Text of the Synoptic Gospels in the Second Century," in *Gospel Traditions in the Second Century: Origins, Recensions, Text, and Transmission*, ed. William L. Petersen (Notre Dame, IN: University of Notre Dame Press, 1989), 37.

70  Koester, "Text of the Synoptic Gospels," 21.

71  Koester, "Text of the Synoptic Gospels," 19.

72  Koester, "History and Development," 56; idem, *Ancient Christian Gospels: Their History and Development* (Philadelphia: SCM Press, 1990), 302. He was vague about why a public gospel could not include these stories.

73  Koester, "History and Development," 56; "Text of the Synoptic Gospels," 34 n. 49.

74  Koester, "History and Development," 55–56.

75  See Koester, "History and Development," 31.

76  Koester, "Seminar Dialogue with Helmut Koester," 74–75.

77  Koester, "History and Development," 49.

78  For Koester's arguments, see "History and Development," 43–54; "Text of the Synoptic Gospels," 21–25, 34–36; *Ancient Christian Gospels*, 276–84, 296–302.

79  David Peabody, "The Late Secondary Redaction of Mark's Gospel and the Griesbach Hypothesis: A Response to Helmut Koester," in *Colloquy on New Testament Studies*, ed. Bruce Corley, 87–132; Robert Lee Williams, "Helmut Koester on Mark," *PSTJ* 40 (1987): 28 (expressing his approval of Peabody's main criticisms); Frans Neirynck, "The Minor Agreements and Proto-Mark: A Response to H. Koester," in *Evangelica II 1982–1991 Collected Essays by Frans Neirynck*, ed. Frans Van Segbroeck, BETL 99 (Leuven: Leuven University Press; Uitgeverij Peeters, 1991), 59–73; Robert H. Gundry, "Excursus on the Secret Gospel of Mark," in his *Mark: A Commentary on His Apology for the Cross* (Grand Rapids: Eerdmans, 1993), 603–23; Philip Sellew, "*Secret Mark* and the History of Canonical Mark," in *The Future of Early Christianity: Essays in Honor of Helmut Koester*, ed. Birger A. Pearson (Minneapolis: Fortress, 1991), 242–57; Joel Marcus, *Mark 1–8: A New Translation with Introduction and Commentary*, AB 27 (New York: Doubleday, 2000), 47–51.

80  Koester, *Ancient Christian Gospels*, 12–14.

81  Koester, "From the Kerygma-Gospel to Written Gospels," *NTS* 35 (1989): 369.

82  Koester, "Kerygma-Gospel," 369 n. 1; *Ancient Christian Gospels*, 12 n. 2.

83  Koester, "History and Development," 43.

84  Helmut Koester, review of *SG* and *CA*, *AHR* 80 (1975): 620–21.

85  Koester, "History and Development," 48–49.

86  E.g., Peabody, "Late Secondary Redaction," 120–25; Sellew, "History," 250–51; Heikki Räisänen, *The "Messianic Secret" in Mark*, trans. Christopher Tuckett (Edinburgh: T. and T. Clark, 1990), 110 n. 116; Gundry, "Excursus," 607–10.

87  Scott G. Brown, "On the Composition History of the Longer ('Secret') Gospel of Mark," *JBL* 122 (2003): 89–110.

88   For discussion, see David C. Parker, *The Living Text of the Gospels* (Cambridge: Cambridge University Press, 1997), 132–37.

89   Frederik Wisse, "The Nature and Purpose of Redactional Changes in Early Christian Texts: The Canonical Gospels," in *Gospel Traditions in the Second Century: Origins, Recensions, Text, and Transmission*, ed. William L. Petersen, Christianity and Judaism in Antiquity 3 (Notre Dame, IN: University of Notre Dame Press, 1989), 45 and n. 26. For further criticisms along these lines, see Larry W. Hurtado, "Beyond the Interlude? Developments and Directions in New Testament Textual Criticism," in *Studies in the Early Text of the Gospels and Acts: The Papers of the First Birmingham Colloquium on the Textual Criticism of the New Testament*, ed. D.G.K. Taylor (Birmingham: University of Birmingham Press, 1999), 40–43.

90   Barbara Aland and Kurt Aland, *The Text of the New Testament*, trans. Erroll F. Rhoades (Grand Rapids: Eerdmans, 1987), 291, as cited in Wisse, "Redactional Changes," 46 n. 28.

# Chapter 4

1   For the history of the cognitive sense of *mystikon* in Christian writings, see Louis Bouyer, "'Mystique': Essai sur l'histoire d'un mot," *La vie spirituelle, ascétique, et mystique* supp. vol. 9 (1949): 3–23.

2   Wihelm Schneemelcher, ed., *New Testament Apocrypha*, trans. R. McL. Wilson, 2d rev. ed. (Cambridge: James Clarke; Louisville: Westminster/John Knox Press, 1991), 1:79–80. See also Martin Hengel, *Studies in the Gospel of Mark* (London: SCM Press, 1985), 65; Helmut Koester, "From the Kerygma-Gospel to Written Gospels," *NTS* 35 (1989): 380.

3   Translated into English, the phrase τοῦ Μάρκου εἶναι τὸ μυστικὸν εὐαγγέλιον (II.11–12) might sound like a title (the *mystikon* Gospel of Mark). But the same sense is not conveyed by the Greek. As I mentioned, "according to" (κατά), not a genitive phrase (τοῦ Μάρκου), is the regular construction found in the manuscripts for introducing the authors or communities named in gospel titles. Clement invariably used "according to" when naming the titles of gospels (*Strom.* I.21.145.2, 147.5; II.9.45.5; III.9.63.1; III.13.93.1; *Qds* 5.1; *Letter to Theodore* I.11–12). Moreover, in II.11–12 the words "of Mark" are separated from "the *mystikon* gospel" by a verb, "to be"—something that does not occur in other places where Clement related gospel titles.

4   E.g., Smith, *CA*, 447, which is the translation most often reproduced by others. He cannot be faulted for supplying a phrase here, for it is difficult to omit the subject of a sentence in English. In *SG* he decided to place these phrases in square brackets (16, 17).

5   The scholarly penchant to equate *logia* with "sayings" has a long history, which James Robinson traced as far back as Schleiermacher's influential argument (1832) that Papias's work *Exposition of the Lord's* Logia (Λογίων κυριακῶν ἐξήγησις) referred to a synoptic *sayings* source composed in Aramaic by Matthew. That argument led to Q being mislabelled a collection of *logia* rather than a collection of *logoi*. See James M. Robinson, Paul Hoffmann, and John S. Kloppenborg, eds., *The Critical Edition of Q* (Leuven: Peeters, 2000), xx–xxx.

6 Roger Gryson, "A propos du témoignage de Papias sur Matthieu: Le sens du mot λόγιον chez les Pères du second siècle," *ETL* 41 (1965): 530–47. See also Benjamin Warfield, "The Oracles of God," *Presbyterian and Reformed Review* 11 (1900): 217–60. In the twentieth century, the argument against translating *logia* as "sayings" began to be revived a few years after Smith discovered the letter, so it is not surprising that he translated *logia* as "sayings."

7 Gryson, "Témoignage," 546. See *Strom.* VI.15.123.1; VII.18.109.2, 3, 6; *Prot.* 10.107.1; and *Paed.* II.10.113.3.

8 Gryson, "Témoignage," 546 n. 77 (trans. mine).

9 F.F. Bruce, *The "Secret" Gospel of Mark* (London: Athlone Press, 1974), 7.

10 For a comprehensive discussion of the origins of the word *mystērion*, see Chrys C. Caragounis, *The Ephesian* Mysterion: *Meaning and Content*, Coniectanea Biblica New Testament Series 8 (Uppsala: CWK Gleerup, 1977), 3–19.

11 J.D.B. Hamilton, "The Church and the Language of Mystery: The First Four Centuries," *ETL* 53 (1977): 479–94. On the New Testament use of *mystērion*, see Raymond E. Brown, *The Semitic Background of the Term "Mystery" in the New Testament*, FBBS 21 (Philadelphia: Fortress, 1968).

12 Caragounis, *The Ephesian* Mysterion, 1–2.

13 This apologetic motive is evident, for instance, in A.D. Nock, "Hellenistic Mysteries and Christian Sacraments," *Mnemosyne*, 4th ser., vol. 5 (1952): 200, 204, 206; and Louis Bouyer, *"Mystērion," La vie spirituelle, ascétique et mystique* supp. vol. 23 (1952): 398–99.

14 A.E. Harvey, "The Use of Mystery Language in the Bible," *JTS*, n.s., 31 (1980): 329.

15 H.G. Marsh, "The Use of Μυστήριον in the Writings of Clement of Alexandria with Special Reference to His Sacramental Doctrine," *JTS* 37 (1936): 64–80. In the following discussion I will relate by way of summary a number of the points Marsh made on pp. 65–67. An independent assessment of Clement's use of *mystērion* can be found in H.A. Echle, "Sacramental Initiation as a Christian Mystery-Initiation According to Clement of Alexandria," in *Vom christlichen Mysterium: Gesammelte Arbeiten zum Gedächtnis von Odo Casel OSB*, ed. Anton Mayer, Johannes Quasten, and Burkhard Neunheuser (Düsseldorf: Patoms-Verlag, 1951), 54–65. Echle's conclusions basically corroborate those of Marsh, even though Echle sometimes categorized individual instances of the term differently. This concordance is important considering that Echle wished to push the case that, for Clement, baptism had aspects of a mystery rite. For criticisms of Echle's conclusion on this matter, see Hamilton, "Language of Mystery," 485. For a brief history of the discussion of Clement's use of *mystērion*, see Raoul Mortley, *Connaissance religieuse et herméneutique chez Clément d'Alexandrie* (Leiden: E.J. Brill, 1973), 174–77.

16 Marsh, "Μυστήριον," 65–66. See also Salvatore R.C. Lilla, *Clement of Alexandria: A Study in Christian Platonism and Gnosticism* (Oxford: Oxford University Press, 1971), 147 and n. 3.

17 Marsh, "Μυστήριον," 66; Lilla, *Christian Platonism*, 147–48; Mortley, *Connaissance*, 176.

18 Marsh, "Μυστήριον," 66–67. Also G. Bornkamm, "Μυστήριον, μυέω," *TDNT* 4 (1942; rpt. 1967): 825, who adds *type* (τύπος); and Echle, "Sacramental Initiation," 55. On Justin, see Markus N.A. Bockmuehl, *Revelation and Mystery in*

*Ancient Judaism and Pauline Christianity* (Tübingen: J.C.B. Mohr [Paul Siebeck], 1990), 218–19. Bockmuehl discussed the earliest second-century usages on pp. 214–20.

19  Marsh, "Μυστήριον," 67, 69–71, 78–79.

20  Marsh, "Μυστήριον," esp. 67–68, 70, 74.

21  Bornkamm, "Μυστήριον, μυέω," 808. Pp. 808–810 offer a very useful discussion of the figurative, philosophical appropriation of the cultic language of the mysteries and of the distinctive form this took in Alexandrian theology. The philosophical use of mystery-religion language is also discussed in Harvey, "Mystery Language," 321–25; A.J.M. Wedderburn, *Baptism and Resurrection: Studies in Pauline Theology against Its Graeco-Roman Background*, WUNT 44 (Tübingen: J.C.B. Mohr [Paul Siebeck], 1987), § 2 (esp. 113–139, 148–58); Édouard des Places, "Platon et la langue des mystères," in his *Études Platoniciennes: 1929–1979*, EPRO 90 (Leiden: E.J. Brill, 1981), 83–98; Bouyer, "Mystique," 9–13; and Hamilton, "Language of Mystery," 479–82. Hamilton also offered a broader and more systematic discussion of the Christian use of mystery language in the early centuries; see esp. pp. 482–87.

22  Massey Shepherd, response to Reginald Fuller, in *LM*, 50–51. See the similar discussion of the small and great mysteries in Lilla, *Christian Platonism*, 189–90; the whole of his chapter "Pistis, Gnosis, Cosmology, and Theology" (118–226) is relevant to this discussion.

23  Bornkamm, "Μυστήριον, μυέω," 808. This is the highest condition Clement believed could be realized in the body. In Clement's thought, the soul of the deceased gnostic (not the ordinary Christian) ascends through the heavens to become deified (θεοί—a dignity equal to the angels), so that, no longer constrained by materiality, it can contemplate God "face to face" and remain in his "rest" (e.g., *Strom.* VII.10.57.1; 11.68.5). See Lilla, *Christian Platonism*, 175–89.

24  The terminology of great and small mysteries comes from Eleusis, but was used by Plato in a metaphorical sense which became a standard figure for philosophy. Ἐποπτεία is the Eleusinian word for the highest grade of initiation, a state of divine vision. On this subject, see des Places, "Platon et la langue des mystères," 86–87; on this passage in Clement, see André Méhat, "Clément d'Alexandrie et les sens de l'Écriture: *Ier Stromate*, 176, I et 179, 3," in *Epektasis: Mélanges patristiques offerts au Cardinal Jean Daniélou*, ed. J. Fontaine and C. Kannengiesser (Paris: Beauchesne, 1972), 355–65.

25  On this passage and its connections with Philo, see Annewies van den Hoek, *Clement of Alexandria and His Use of Philo in the* Stromateis: *An Early Christian Reshaping of a Jewish Model* (Leiden: E.J. Brill, 1988), 188. On Philo's figurative use of the concepts of small and great mysteries, see Hamilton, "Language of Mystery," 481.

26  Lilla, *Christian Platonism*, 190 n. 1.

27  Walter Wagner, "Another Look at the Literary Problem in Clement of Alexandria's Major Writings," in *Studies in Early Christianity*, ed. Everett Ferguson et al. (New York and London: Garland, 1993), 2:170–71. If I understand him properly, Wagner would group φυσιολογία with the great mysteries rather than the lesser.

28  Massey Shepherd's remarks can be found in *LM*, 46–52 (esp. 49), 62, 67–68. Cf. Bruce, *"Secret" Gospel*, 18.

29  See, e.g., Smith, *SG*, 65 (citing Cyril C. Richardson's original opinion); John
    Crossan, *Four Other Gospels: Shadows on the Contours of Canon* (Minneapolis:
    Winston, 1985), 99; Walter Wink, "Jesus as Magician," *USQR* 30 (1974): 8;
    Karel Hanhart, *The Open Tomb: A New Approach, Mark's Passover Haggadah
    ([ca.] 72 C.E.)* (Collegeville, MN: Liturgical Press, 1995), 569.

30  See also the comments by Smith in *CA*, 40–41.

31  For a useful discussion of allegory and its use in ancient Alexandria, see David
    Dawson, *Allegorical Readers and Cultural Revision in Ancient Alexandria* (Berkley:
    University of California Press, 1992), 1–21. Clement's approach is the subject
    of chapter 4 (183–234). As Dawson pointed out, the term *allegory* is most prop-
    erly applied when either the literal level of the text or the literary level of the inter-
    pretation involves a narrative (pp. 3–7). I am using the word in its less technical
    sense, for its proper sense would not cover all types of this kind of reading in rela-
    tion to which Clement employed the word *mystikon*.

32  For further discussion of the topic with specific reference to μυστήριον, see
    Marsh, "Μυστήριον," 74–80; and Echle, "Sacramental Initiation," 56–65.

33  Marsh, "Μυστήριον," 72.

34  Bruce, *"Secret" Gospel*, 16. See also Birger A. Pearson, response to Reginald
    Fuller, in *LM*, 40; Robert M. Grant, "Morton Smith's Two Books," *AThR* 56
    (1974): 61–62. A useful discussion of Clement's words on John as a spiritual
    gospel can be found in G.H.C. Macgregor, *The Gospel of John*, MNTC (London:
    Hodder and Stoughton, 1928), xxv–xxvi.

35  John M. Dillon, in *LM*, 63.

36  The description is from H. von Campenhausen and was cited by W. Kümmel,
    "Ein Jahrzehnt Jesusforschung (1965–1975)," *TRu*, n.s., 40 (1975): 302, who
    in turn was cited by Helmut Merkel, "Appendix: The 'Secret Gospel' of Mark,"
    in *New Testament Apocrypha*, ed. Wilhelm Schneemelcher, 2d rev. ed. (Cam-
    bridge: James Clarke; Louisville: Westminster/John Knox Press, 1991), 108 n.
    5. These scholars deemed a church archive anachronistic for Clement's time.

37  Annewies van den Hoek, "How Alexandrian Was Clement of Alexandria? Reflec-
    tions on Clement and His Alexandrian Background," *HeyJ* 31 (1990): 179–194.

38  Smith, *CA*, 43. Cf. Mark 14:44 ("under guard").

39  Smith, *SG*, 142; *CA*, 283.

40  See Smith, *CA*, 36–37, 81, 194.

41  Other interpretations are possible, but this one seems most likely to me. See
    Scott G. Brown, "The More Spiritual Gospel: Markan Literary Techniques in the
    Longer Gospel of Mark" (Ph.D. diss., University of Toronto, 1999), 182–83.

42  Smith, *SG*, 40; *CA*, 90.

43  On this subject, see Lilla, *Christian Platonism*, 9–59. Clement's arguments about
    the origins of Greek philosophy are largely the same as those offered by Philo
    and Justin (pp. 19–27).

44  Hence Eric F. Osborn has little reason to suggest that Clement would not have
    depicted heretics stealing the truth in the literal sense of stealing a document. See
    "Clement of Alexandria: A Review of Research, 1958–1982," *SecCent* 3 (1983):
    224. His judgment was accepted by Andrew H. Criddle in "On the Mar Saba
    Letter Attributed to Clement of Alexandria," *JECS* 3 (1995): 216.

45  As reported by Sanka Knox in the article "A New Gospel Ascribed to Mark," *New
    York Times*, 30 December 1960, p. 17.

46 See, e.g., Barnabas Lindars, *The Gospel of John*, NCB (London: Oliphants, 1972), 50–51; Raymond E. Brown, *The Gospel According to John*, 2d ed. (Garden City: Doubleday, 1980), 1:xxxiv–xxxix; John Ashton, *Understanding the Fourth Gospel* (New York: Oxford University Press, 1993), 82–86, 199–204.

47 These similarities were noted by Smith in *CA*, 32, 81.

48 Cf. Bruce, *"Secret" Gospel*, 3–4.

49 See, for example, Thomas Talley, "Liturgical Time in the Ancient Church: The State of Research," *Studia Liturgica* 14 (1982): 45; C.S. Mann, *Mark: A New Translation and Commentary*, AB 27 (Garden City: Doubleday, 1986), 424; Robert M. Grant, "Smith's Two Books," 59, 61; Raymond E. Brown, *The Death of the Messiah: A Commentary on the Passion Narratives in the Four Gospels*, ABRL (New York: Doubleday, 1994), 1:297.

50 John Wenham, *Redating Matthew, Mark and Luke: A Fresh Assault on the Synoptic Problem* (London: Hodder and Stoughton, 1991), 144–45.

51 Hanhart, *Open Tomb*, 747 n. 106.

52 Marvin W. Meyer, "The Youth in the *Secret Gospel of Mark*," *Semeia* 49 (1990): 146. Compare the double transference that occurred in Pierson Parker's recollection ("An Early Christian Cover-up?" *New York Times Book Review* [22 July 1973]: 5): "After six days the lad came, clad only in a *white robe*, and spent the night with Jesus" (italics added). Raymond E. Brown ("The Relation of 'The Secret Gospel of Mark' to the Fourth Gospel," *CBQ* 36 [1974]: 477 n. 24) and Reginald Fuller ("Longer Mark: Forgery, Interpolation, or Old Tradition?" in *LM*, 3) also let the word *white* slip into their descriptions of a ritual presupposed by the gospel, as did Smith (*CA*, 165).

# Chapter 5

1 Over two dozen scholars have expressed this view. For the more important discussions, see Smith, *CA*, 167–88, 209–20; Robin Scroggs and Kent I. Groff, addendum to "Baptism in Mark: Dying and Rising with Christ," *JBL* 92 (1973): 547–48; Helmut Koester, "History and Development of Mark's Gospel (From Mark to *Secret Mark* and 'Canonical' Mark)," in *Colloquy on New Testament Studies: A Time for Reappraisal and Fresh Approaches*, ed. Bruce Corley (Macon, GA: Mercer University Press, 1983), 48–49; John Dominic Crossan, *Four Other Gospels: Shadows on the Contours of Canon* (Minneapolis: Winston, 1985), 114, 116–18, 119; idem, *The Historical Jesus: The Life of a Mediterranean Jewish Peasant* (San Francisco: Harper, 1991), 329–32; Thomas Talley, "Liturgical Time in the Ancient Church: The State of Research," *Studia Liturgica* 14 (1982): 45–47; Marvin W. Meyer, "The Youth in the *Secret Gospel of Mark*," *Semeia* 49 (1990): 145–46, 148; Brenda Deen Schildgen, *Power and Prejudice: The Reception of the Gospel of Mark* (Detroit: Wayne State University Press, 1999), 51.

2 Scott G. Brown, "Bethany beyond the Jordan: John 1:28 and the Longer Gospel of Mark," *RB* 110 (2003): 497–516.

3 See *Travels from Piacenza* 9, 11, as translated in John Wilkinson, *Jerusalem Pilgrims before the Crusades* (Warminster, Eng.: Aris and Phillips, 2002), 135–37.

4 For a first-hand account from 1984, see Glenn Bowman, "Christian Ideology and the Image of a Holy Land: The Place of Jerusalem Pilgrimage in the Various

Christianities," in *Contesting the Sacred: The Anthropology of Christian Pilgrimage*, ed. John Eade and Michael J. Sallnow (London: Routledge, 1991), 109. In Bowman's opinion, the baptism is "not truly a second baptism in theological terms but a replay of the first (and thus formally—but not in the minds of pilgrims—lacks sacerdotal quality)" (e-mail to author).

5 Robert H. Gundry, "Excursus on the Secret Gospel of Mark," in his *Mark: A Commentary on His Apology for the Cross* (Grand Rapids: Eerdmans, 1993), 622.

6 Gundry, "Excursus," 619.

7 Citing Thomas M. Finn, *Early Christian Baptism and the Catechumenate: Italy, North Africa, and Egypt*, Message of the Fathers of the Church 6 (Collegeville, MN: Liturgical Press, 1992), 5. See also Lawrence D. Folkemer, "A Study of the Catechumenate," in *Conversion, Catechumenate, and Baptism in the Early Church*, ed. Everett Ferguson et al., Studies in Early Christianity 11 (New York: Garland, 1993), 244–45. The ethical rather than intellectual focus of catechetical instruction is emphasized in the *Paedagogus*, where Clement explained that the role of "the Instructor" is *not* to impart knowledge to catechumens but to "cure" them of the "sickness" endemic to pagan living; only when they are "healthy" will they be ready to learn (*Paed.* I.1.1.4–2.1, 3.3; cf. the post-baptismal instruction in "To the Newly Baptized," which is attributed to Clement). Clement's successor, Origen, expressed very similar comments. See Annewies van den Hoek, "The 'Catechetical' School of Early Christian Alexandria and Its Philonic Heritage," *HTR* 90 (1997): 59–87, esp. 70.

8 Gundry, "Excursus," 619. This was a problem for the theory presented by Marvin Meyer in "The Youth in the *Secret Gospel of Mark*," 145–46, 148. Meyer has since refined his interpretation; see his "The Naked Youths in the Secret Gospel of Mark and the Villa of the Mysteries at Pompeii," in his *Secret Gospels: Essays on Thomas and the Secret Gospel of Mark* (Harrisburg: Trinity Press International, 2003), 163–64.

9 Contra Scroggs and Groff, "Baptism in Mark," 531–48; Steven R. Johnson, "The Identity and Significance of the *Neaniskos* in Mark," *FORUM* 8 (1992): 123–39, esp. 129, 133, 137.

10 Hans-Martin Schenke, "The Mystery of the Gospel of Mark," *SecCent* 4:2 (1984): 78–79.

11 Harry Fleddermann, "The Flight of the Young Man (Mark 14:51–52)," *CBQ* 41 (1979): 415. Michel Gourgues, "À propos du symbolisme christologique et baptismal de Marc 16.5," *NTS* 27 (1981): 675.

12 Morton Smith, "Clement of Alexandria and Secret Mark: The Score at the End of the First Decade," *HTR* 75 (1982): 457 n. 19; Meyer, "The Youth in the *Secret Gospel of Mark*," 145–46.

13 Smith, *CA*, 168; cf. 187. See George MacRae, "Yet Another Jesus," *Commonweal* 99 (25 January 1974): 418; Karel Hanhart, *The Open Tomb: A New Approach, Mark's Passover Haggadah ([ca.] 72 C.E.)* (Collegeville, MN: Liturgical Press, 1995), 749 n. 110.

14 See Crossan, *Historical Jesus*, 412; idem, *Four Other Gospels*, 114; Thomas Talley, *The Origins of the Liturgical Year* (New York: Pueblo, 1986), 207, 208–209; Philip Sellew, "*Secret Mark* and the History of Canonical Mark," in *The Future of Early Christianity: Essays in Honor of Helmut Koester*, ed. Birger A. Pearson (Minneapolis: Fortress, 1991), 256.

15 Smith, *CA*, 33–34.
16 Talley, "Liturgical Time," 44. For his documentation and the specifics of his theory, see 43–48. Smith and many others mistakenly assumed that baptism took place on Pascha in Alexandria.
17 Thomas J. Talley, "The Entry into Jerusalem in Liturgical Tradition," in *With Ever Joyful Hearts: Essays on Liturgy and Music Honoring Marion J. Hatchett*, ed. J. Neil Alexander (New York: Church, 1999), 221.
18 Talley, "Liturgical Time," 46.
19 Talley, "Liturgical Time," 46; see also his *Origins*, 210–11; John F. Baldovin, "A Lenten Sunday Lectionary in Fourth Century Jerusalem," in *Time and Community*, ed. J. Neil Alexander (Washington, DC: Pastoral Press, 1990), 117–18.
20 Talley, *Origins*, 208–209.
21 *Spiritual Meadow* (*Pratum spirituale*) V.176. The translation is from H.A. Echle, "The Baptism of the Apostles: A Fragment of Clement of Alexandria's Lost Work Ὑποτυπώσεις in the *Pratum Spirituale* of John Moschus," *Traditio* 3 (1945): 367. An English translation of the whole passage can be found in John Wortley, trans., *The Spiritual Meadow of John Moschos*, Cistercian Studies Series 139 (Kalamazoo, MI: Cistercian Publications, 1992), 144–46.
22 Smith, *CA*, 283.
23 Raymond E. Brown, "The Relation of 'The Secret Gospel of Mark' to the Fourth Gospel," *CBQ* 36 (1974): 477 and n. 24; see also 478 and n. 30; 480; 483; and his discussion of the young man in *The Death of the Messiah: A Commentary on the Passion Narratives in the Four Gospels*, ABRL (New York: Doubleday, 1994), 1:294–97 (mainly p. 297), 302.
24 Smith, *CA*, 33–34.
25 Smith, *CA*, 254; cf. 284.
26 Smith, *SG*, 66; *CA*, 94, 284.
27 Smith, *CA*, 283. See also *SG*, 65–66.
28 Smith, *SG*, 142.
29 Smith, *CA*, 186.
30 Richardson, review of *CA* and *SG*, 574–75.
31 For some discussion, see A.J.M. Wedderburn, *Baptism and Resurrection: Studies in Pauline Theology against Its Graeco-Roman Background*, WUNT 44 (Tübingen: J.C.B. Mohr [Paul Siebeck], 1987), 371–77, 300–10; and Morton Smith, "Transformation by Burial (I Cor 15.35–49; Rom 6.3–5 and 8.9–11)," *Eranos* 52 (1983): 87–112, esp. 107–12.
32 Richardson, review of *CA* and *SG*, 576.
33 E.g., Schenke, "Mystery," 75; idem, "The Function and Background of the Beloved Disciple in the Gospel of John," in *Nag Hammadi, Gnosticism, and Early Christianity*, ed. Charles W. Hedrick and Robert Hodgson, Jr. (Peabody, MA: Hendrickson, 1986), 121.
34 Smith, response to Reginald Fuller, in *LM*, 14.
35 E.g., Smith, *CA*, 121–22, 188–92; *SG*, 69–70; idem, "Merkel on the Longer Text of Mark," *ZTK* 72 (1975): 143; Walter Wink, "Jesus as Magician," *USQR* 30 (1974): 7; Koester, "History and Development," 42; Crossan, *Four Other Gospels*, 109–10; Ron Cameron, ed., *The Other Gospels: Non-Canonical Gospel Texts* (Philadelphia: Westminster, 1982), 68; Winsome Munro, "Women Disciples: Light from Secret Mark," *JFSR* 8 (1992): 54–61.

36  Cyril C. Richardson, review of *CA* and *SG*, 575. R.E. Brown, "Relation," 480.
37  See the discussion in Jouette M. Bassler, "The Parable of the Loaves," *JR* 66 (1986): 160.
38  Robert M. Fowler, *Let the Reader Understand: Reader-Response Criticism and the Gospel of Mark* (Minneapolis: Fortress, 1991), 135, 136. Fowler described this feature of Markan style with special reference to the chain of events in the prologue (pp. 14–24). Bassler ("Parable of the Loaves") discussed the use of gaps in Mark 6–8, esp. 8:14–21. Tom Shepherd offered a very useful discussion of gaps in "The Definition and Function of Markan Intercalation as Illustrated in a Narrative Analysis of Six Passages" (Ph.D. diss., Andrews University, 1991), 79–83.
39  Frank Kermode, *The Genesis of Secrecy: On the Interpretation of Narrative* (Cambridge: Harvard University Press, 1979), 64.
40  Andrew T. Lincoln, "The Promise and the Failure: Mark 16:7, 8," *JBL* 108 (1989): 288.
41  Mary Ann Tolbert, *Sowing the Gospel: Mark's World in Literary-Historical Perspective* (Minneapolis: Fortress, 1989), 28, 29.
42  Smith, *CA*, 90.
43  On the influence of Philo upon Clement, see Annewies van den Hoek, *Clement of Alexandria and His Use of Philo in the* Stromateis: *An Early Christian Reshaping of a Jewish Model* (Leiden: E.J. Brill, 1988).
44  Birger A. Pearson, "Earliest Christianity in Egypt: Some Observations," in *The Roots of Egyptian Christianity*, ed. Birger A. Pearson and James E. Goehring, SAC (Philadelphia: Fortress, 1986), 154. See also A.F.J. Klijn, "Jewish Christianity in Egypt," in ibid., 161–65; and David Dawson, *Allegorical Readers and Cultural Revision in Ancient Alexandria* (Berkley: University of California Press, 1992), 172 (and the scholars he cites on p. 285 nn. 55, 56).
45  Cf. James M. Robinson, *The Problem of History in Mark and Other Marcan Studies* (Philadelphia: Fortress, 1982), 125–26.
46  For the history of this conflict, see Dawson, *Allegorical Readers*, 172–74.
47  To use Kermode's language in *Genesis of Secrecy*, 18.

# Chapter 6

1  For an independent analysis of LGM 1 and 2 as an intercalation, see John Dart, *Decoding Mark* (Harrisburg: Trinity Press International, 2003), 34–43. Dart informed me that he first made this observation in "Why Secret Mark Was Part of the Original Gospel of Mark" (unpublished paper presented at the annual meeting of the SBL Pacific Coast Region, Long Beach, CA, 3 April 1987).
2  R.T. France, *The Gospel of Mark: A Commentary on the Greek Text*, The New Testament Greek Commentary (Grand Rapids: Eerdmans, 2002), 410.
3  This list was offered by Frans Neirynck in *Duality in Mark: Contributions to the Study of the Markan Redaction*, rev. ed. with Supplementary Notes, BETL 31 (Leuven: Leuven University Press, 1988), 133; Tom Shepherd in "Intercalation in Mark and the Synoptic Problem," in *Society of Biblical Literature 1991 Seminar Papers*, ed. Eugene H. Lovering, Jr., SBLSP 30 (Missoula: Scholars Press, 1991), 689; and G. van Oyen in "Intercalation and Irony in the Gospel of Mark," in *The Four Gospels 1992: Festschrift Frans Neirynck*, ed. Frans Van Seg-

broeck et al., BETL 100 (Leuven: Leuven University Press, 1992), 2:949. The verses in brackets represent disagreements over the boundaries of the literary units, as noted by Shepherd ("Intercalation in Mark," 689 n. 8).

4　See Tom Shepherd, "The Definition and Function of Markan Intercalation as Illustrated in a Narrative Analysis of Six Passages" (Ph.D. diss., Andrews University, 1991), 388–92.

5　E.g., Richard Schneck, *Isaiah in the Gospel of Mark, I–VIII*, Bibal Dissertation Series 1 (Vallejo, CA: Bibal Press, 1994), 199. On interpolations, see John R. Donahue, *Are You the Christ? The Trial Narrative in the Gospel of Mark*, SBLDS 10 (Missoula: Society of Biblical Literature, 1973), 77–84, 241–43.

6　James R. Edwards, "Markan Sandwiches: The Significance of Interpolations in Markan Narratives," *NovT* 31 (1989): 197.

7　LGM 1 is thirteen verses long, compared to two in 3:20–21, four in 5:21–24, seven in 6:7–13, three in 11:12–14, two in 14:1–2, and two in 14:53–54.

8　Shepherd, "Definition," 315. Cf. idem, "Intercalation in Mark," 689.

9　Shepherd, "Intercalation in Mark," 689.

10　Shepherd, "Definition," 317–18.

11　Shepherd, "Intercalation in Mark," 690.

12　Shepherd, "Intercalation in Mark," 689; "Definition," 320.

13　Joel F. Williams, *Other Followers of Jesus: Minor Characters as Major Figures in Mark's Gospel* (Sheffield: JSOT Press, 1994), 170, 171. His thesis is summarized in "Discipleship and Minor Characters in Mark's Gospel," *BSac* 153 (1996): 332–43.

14　Shepherd, "Intercalation in Mark," 690.

15　Shepherd, "Definition," 314, 316.

16　Shepherd, "Definition," 324 (italics removed).

17　Contra Robert M. Fowler, *Let the Reader Understand: Reader-Response Criticism and the Gospel of Mark* (Minneapolis: Fortress, 1991), 143–44.

18　Shepherd disagrees on this point ("Definition," 269–74), but see van Oyen, "Intercalation and Irony," 965–77.

19　As Schuyler Brown pointed out, the device of intercalation establishes that the people described in 3:21 as οἱ παρ' αὐτοῦ be the same characters who arrive in 3:31. See "Mk 3,21: A Forgotten Controversy?" in *Überlieferungsgeschichtliche Untersuchungen*, ed. Franz Paschke (Berlin: Akademie-Verlag, 1981), esp. 100–101.

20　The argument that follows is developed in Scott G. Brown, "Mark 11:1–12:12: A Triple Intercalation?" *CBQ* 64 (2002): 78–89, 720 (*erratum* for a typesetting error).

21　Edwards, "Markan Sandwiches," 196. The following represent influential discussions of intercalation from within this perspective: Ernest Best, *The Temptation and the Passion: The Markan Soteriology*, SNTSMS 2 (Cambridge: Cambridge University Press, 1965), *passim*; Robert H. Stein, *The Proper Methodology for Ascertaining a Marcan Redaktionsgeschichte* (Ann Arbor: University Microfilms, 1968), 184; Donahue, *Are You the Christ?* 60; Joanna Dewey, *Markan Public Debate: Literary Technique, Concentric Structure, and Theology in Mark 2:1–3:6*, SBLDS 48 (Chico, CA: Scholars Press, 1980), 21.

22　David Rhoads and Donald Michie, *Mark as Story* (Philadelphia: Fortress, 1982), 51. Cf. John Dominic Crossan, *Who Killed Jesus? Exposing the Roots of Anti-Semi-*

*tism in the Gospel Story of the Death of Jesus* (1995; reprint, San Francisco: Harper-SanFrancisco, 1996), 100–105.

23  Fowler, *Reader*, 143.

24  Shepherd, "Intercalation in Mark," 690. See, further, T.A. Burkill, *Mysterious Revelation: An Examination of the Philosophy of St. Mark's Gospel* (Ithaca, NY: Cornell University Press, 1963), 121 n. 10; Rhoads and Michie, *Mark as Story*, 51; Dewey, *Markan Public Debate*, 153–54, 241 n. 69.

25  The following survey of the history of interpretation of intercalation is dependent upon the determinations of relevant authors provided in previous studies of this history, specifically, the studies by Edwards, Shepherd, and van Oyen.

26  Dissertations: G.A. Wright, "Markan Intercalation: A Study in the Plot of the Gospel" (Ph.D. diss., The Southern Baptist Theological Seminary, 1985); Shepherd, "Definition" (1991). Articles: Ernst von Dobschütz, "Zur Erzählerkunst des Markus," *ZNW* 27 (1928): 193–98; Edwards, "Markan Sandwiches" (1989); Shepherd, "Intercalation in Mark" (1991); van Oyen, "Intercalation and Irony" (1992); Tom Shepherd, "The Narrative Function of Markan Intercalation," *NTS* 41 (1995): 522–40; Brown, "Triple Intercalation?" (2002).

27  Von Dobschütz, "Erzählerkunst," 193. Other scholars had already noted Mark's tendency to put one story inside another but did not consider it to have a narrative function. Hence they did not consider intercalation to be a literary technique. See van Oyen, "Intercalation and Irony," 958.

28  Von Dobschütz, "Erzählerkunst," 197–98.

29  Von Dobschütz, "Erzählerkunst," 196–97.

30  Von Dobschütz, "Erzählerkunst," 196.

31  This idea appears in Rudolf Bultmann, *The History of the Synoptic Tradition*, trans. John Marsh (New York: Harper and Row, 1963), 214, 301–302, having been added in the 2d ed. of 1931, as van Oyen noted ("Intercalation and Irony," 950); Erich Klostermann, *Das Markus-Evangelium* (Tübingen: J.C.B. Mohr [Paul Siebeck], 1950), 50; Sherman E. Johnson, *A Commentary on the Gospel According to St. Mark*, BNTC (London: A. and C. Black, 1960), 104, 123, 191; Dennis Eric Nineham, *The Gospel of St. Mark* (1963; reprint, Baltimore: Penguin Books, 1967), 112, 157, 172; Paul J. Achtemeier, "Toward the Isolation of Pre-Markan Miracle Catenae," *JBL* 89 (1970): 270; and Eduard Schweizer, *The Good News According to Mark*, trans. Donald H. Madvig (Richmond: John Knox Press, 1970), 116.

32  Klostermann, *Markus-Evangelium*, 36; Burkill, *Mysterious Revelation*, 121 and n. 10. Both are cited by Edwards in "Markan Sandwiches," 196 n. 14.

33  Burkill, *Mysterious Revelation*, 121–22. See his n. 11.

34  C.H. Bird, "Some Gar Clauses in St. Mark's Gospel," *JTS* 4 (1953): 171–87.

35  Bird, "Some Gar Clauses," 177.

36  Bird, "Some Gar Clauses," 180.

37  S.E. Johnson, *Mark*, 191.

38  Philip Carrington, *According to Mark: A Running Commentary on the Oldest Gospel* (Cambridge: Cambridge University Press, 1960), 301–302.

39  Paul S. Minear, *The Gospel According to Mark*, The Layman's Bible Commentary 17 (Richmond: John Knox Press, 1962), 108–109.

40  Minear, *Mark*, 121, 125–27.

41  Nineham, *Mark*, 112, 299, 300–301.

42  Etienne Trocmé, *The Formation of the Gospel According to Mark*, trans. Pamela Gaughan (1963; ET, Philadelphia: Westminster, 1975), 105–106 n. 1; cf. 135, 231.

43  Trocmé, *Formation*, 82 and n. 2.

44  See Frank Kermode, *The Genesis of Secrecy: On the Interpretation of Narrative* (Cambridge: Harvard University Press, 1979), 127–35; for citations of Kee, see, e.g., 128, 130.

45  Howard Clark Kee, *Community of the New Age: Studies in Mark's Gospel* (Philadelphia: Westminster, 1977), 54–56.

46  E.g., Edwin K. Broadhead, *Teaching with Authority: Miracles and Christology in the Gospel of Mark*, JSNT Sup 74 (Sheffield: JSOT Press, 1992), 201; Dennis C. Duling and Norman Perrin, *The New Testament: An Introduction. Proclamation and Parenesis, Myth and History*, 3d. ed. (Fort Worth: Harcourt Brace, 1994), 304.

47  Edwards, "Markan Sandwiches," 194–95.

48  Best, *Temptation*, 83, 76.

49  Stein, *Proper Methodology*, 214–15 (cited in van Oyen, "Intercalation and Irony," 951 and n. 10).

50  Neirynck, *Duality*, 36, 133; 244 (1988 Supplementary Notes).

51  Donahue, *Are You the Christ?* 42 (see 42–43, 58–63).

52  Vincent Taylor, *The Gospel According to St. Mark* (London: Macmillan, 1952); Willi Marxsen, *Mark the Evangelist: Studies on the Redaction History of the Gospel*, trans. James Boyce et al. (1956; ET, Nashville: Abingdon, 1969).

53  Paul J. Achtemeier, review of *CA* and *SG*, *JBL* 93 (1974): 626–27; William A. Beardslee, review of *SG*, *Int* 28 (1974): 236; Frederick W. Danker, review of *SG*, *Dialog* 13 (1974): 316; Joseph A. Gibbons, review of *SG*, *Sign* 53 (September 1973): 48; cf. Karl Paul Donfried, "New-Found Fragments of an Early Gospel," *ChrCent* 90 (18–25 July 1973): 760; John G. Gibbs, review of *SG*, *ThTo* 30 (1974): 424. In fairness to anyone who could entertain the thought that Smith was a closet literary critic, I should point out that Smith was aware of Bird's 1953 article, at least at some point before publishing *CA*. He cited it in connection with the γάρ clause in LGM 1:9 as support for his claim that "ἦν/ἦσαν γάρ, as introduction of an appended explanation...is a Markan trait" (114). He did not comment on Bird's argument that these awkward clauses are clues to a literary meaning, though he cited approvingly Bird's assumption that repeated patterns in the composition of Mark's story might have been identified and explained by teachers (166). When reading a sixty-page overview of John Dart's research on longer Mark in 1989, Smith did not comment on Dart's observation that LGM 1 and 2 formed a Markan sandwich, although Smith made many comments throughout. Narrative criticism did not interest him.

# Chapter 7

1  This *inclusio* around the passion narrative had already been pointed out in Pheme Perkins, *Resurrection: New Testament Witness and Contemporary Reflection* (Garden City: Doubleday, 1984), 122; Edward Lynn Bode, *The First Easter Morning: The Gospel Accounts of the Women's Visit to the Tomb of Jesus* (Rome: Biblical Institute Press, 1970), 48; John Dominic Crossan, *Who Killed Jesus? Exposing the*

*Roots of Anti-Semitism in the Gospel Story of the Death of Jesus* (1995; reprint, San Francisco: HarperSanFrancisco, 1996), 183–84.

2  Joanna Dewey, *Markan Public Debate: Literary Technique, Concentric Structure, and Theology in Mark 2:1–3:6*, SBLDS 48 (Chico, CA: Scholars Press, 1980), 31.

3  On this instance of framing stories, see Frank J. Matera, "The Incomprehension of the Disciples and Peter's Confession (Mark 6,14–8,30)," *Bib* 70 (1989): 153–72.

4  On the naturalness of reading a distinction here between the twelve and the followers, see Heikki Räisänen, *The "Messianic Secret" in Mark*, trans. Christopher Tuckett (Edinburgh: T. and T. Clark, 1990), 99 n. 80.

5  Mary Ann Tolbert, *Sowing the Gospel: Mark's World in Literary-Historical Perspective* (Minneapolis: Fortress, 1989), 109. The phenomenon of overlapping structures in Mark is documented in Joanna Dewey, "Mark as Interwoven Tapestry: Forecasts and Echoes for a Listening Audience," *CBQ* 53 (1991): 221–36.

6  Tolbert, *Sowing the Gospel*, 118. In Tolbert's opinion, Mark 11:1–11 introduces the second major division of the gospel. I have a different conception of Mark's structure.

7  This pattern is discussed in detail in Scott G. Brown, "On the Composition History of the Longer ('Secret') Gospel of Mark," *JBL* 122 (2003): 102–103, 105–106.

8  The Roman belief that people who die courageously for a noble cause will be vindicated by entering a better life is exemplified in the movie *Gladiator* directed by Ridley Scott.

9  For similar analyses see Quentin Quesnell, *The Mind of Mark: Interpretation and Method through the Exegesis of Mark 6,52* (Rome: Pontifical Biblical Institute, 1969), 146–50; Vernon K. Robbins, "Mark as a Jewish Document," in his *New Boundaries in Old Territory: Form and Social Rhetoric in Mark*, Emory Studies in Early Christianity 3 (New York: Peter Lang, 1994), 231–41.

10  Here I am following Robert M. Fowler's interpretation in *Let the Reader Understand: Reader-Response Criticism and the Gospel of Mark* (Minneapolis: Fortress, 1991), 172–73. The grammar of the sentence favours an interpretation that likens the kingdom, not the receiver, to a child: ὃς ἂν μὴ δέξηται τὴν βασιλείαν τοῦ θεοῦ ὡς παιδίον, οὐ μὴ εἰσέλθῃ εἰς αὐτήν.

11  A phrase used by Dan O. Via, Jr., in "Mark 10:32–52—A Structural, Literary and Theological Interpretation," in *Society of Biblical Literature 1979 Seminar Papers*, ed. Paul J. Achtemeier, SBLSP 17 (Missoula: Scholars Press, 1979), 2:194.

12  Burton L. Mack, *A Myth of Innocence: Mark and Christian Origins* (Philadelphia: Fortress, 1988), 302.

13  Robin Scroggs and Kent I. Groff, "Baptism in Mark: Dying and Rising with Christ," *JBL* 92 (1973): 536–37. Contrary to the position advanced in this article, the baptism referred to in Mark 10:38–39 is neither sacramental, vicarious, nor distinctively Pauline, since it denotes actual martyrdom.

14  Perkins, *Resurrection*, 298.

15  As noted in Christopher Francis Evans, *Resurrection and the New Testament*, SBT 2/12 (London: SCM Press, 1970), 81.

16  See Elizabeth Struthers Malbon's similar conclusions in *Narrative Space and Mythic Meaning in Mark* (San Francisco: Harper and Row, 1986), 54–56.

17 Fowler, *Reader*, 246.

18 Ernest Best, *Disciples and Discipleship: Studies in the Gospel According to Mark* (Edinburgh: T. and T. Clark, 1986), 170 n. 42.

19 C.F. Evans, *Resurrection*, 78–79.

20 On the significance of the white robe, see Wilhelm Michaelis, "Λευκός, λευκαίνω," *TDNT* 4 (1967): 241–50; and A.K. Jenkins, "Young Man or Angel?" *ExpTim* 94 (1983): 238–39.

21 Andrew T. Lincoln, "The Promise and the Failure: Mark 16:7, 8," *JBL* 108 (1989): 293.

22 Very similar views on the relation of Mark 16:7 to the discipleship motif of following "in the way" can be found in the following studies: Malbon, *Narrative Space*; Robert P. Meye, *Jesus and the Twelve: Discipleship and Revelation in Mark's Gospel* (Grand Rapids: Eerdmans, 1968), esp. 80–87; and Ched Myers, *Binding the Strong Man: A Political Reading of Mark's Story of Jesus* (Maryknoll, NY: Orbis Books, 1988), 397–404. The position presented in this chapter is probably closest to Raymond E. Brown's in *The Death of the Messiah: A Commentary on the Passion Narratives in the Four Gospels*, ABRL (New York: Doubleday, 1994), 1:130–33, 140–41. For a critique of the traditional reading of Mark 16:7 as a reference to Jesus physically going ahead of his disciples to Galilee in order to appear to them in bodily form, the symbolic reading of 16:7 as a reference to Jesus' leadership in the Gentile mission, and the redaction-critical reading of 16:7 as a reference to the parousia, see Scott G. Brown, "The More Spiritual Gospel: Markan Literary Techniques in the Longer Gospel of Mark" (Ph.D. diss., University of Toronto, 1999), 327–34.

23 C.F. Evans, *Resurrection*, 79.

24 Herman C. Waetjen, "The Ending of Mark and the Gospel's Shift in Eschatology," *ASTI* 4 (1965): 121.

25 Morna D. Hooker, *The Gospel According to St Mark*, BNTC (London: A. and C. Black, 1991), 385–86.

26 See Reginald H. Fuller, *The Formation of the Resurrection Narratives* (New York: Macmillan, 1971), chapter 2. Neill Q. Hamilton, "Resurrection Tradition and the Composition of Mark," *JBL* 84 (1965): 415–18.

27 See Gen 5:24 (Enoch); 2 Kings 2:1–12 (Elijah); Philo, *Questions on Genesis* 1.86; Josephus, *Antiquities* 4.8.48; *Assumption of Moses* (Moses).

28 Theodore J. Weeden, *Mark—Traditions in Conflict* (Philadelphia: Fortress, 1971), 106.

29 This interpretation of the empty tomb is offered by, among others, Elias Bickermann, "Das leere Grab," *ZNW* 23 (1924): 281–92; Philip Carrington, *According to Mark: A Running Commentary on the Oldest Gospel* (Cambridge: Cambridge University Press, 1960), 192–95; N.Q. Hamilton, "Resurrection Tradition," 415–21; John Anthony McGuckin, *The Transfiguration of Christ in Scripture and Tradition*, Studies in the Bible and Early Christianity 9 (Lewiston and Queenston: Edwin Mellen, 1986), 15–17; Joel Marcus, *The Way of the Lord: Christological Exegesis of the Old Testament in the Gospel of Mark* (Louisville: Westminster/John Knox Press, 1992), 87–90; A.Y. Collins, *The Beginning of the Gospel: Probings of Mark in Context* (Minneapolis: Fortress, 1992), 138–43.

30 On the transfiguration as a vision of Jesus' exaltation, see T.A. Burkill, *Mysterious Revelation: An Examination of the Philosophy of St. Mark's Gospel* (Ithaca, NY: Cornell University Press, 1963), 160–64.

31 B.M.F. van Iersel, "'To Galilee' or 'in Galilee' in Mark 14,28 and 16,7?" *ETL* 58 (1982): 369–70. On Mark's use of verbs of seeing to connote spiritual perception or misunderstanding, see Meye, *Jesus and the Twelve*, 78.

32 The same verb is also commonly used in relation to the theme of apprehending an extraordinary sight (1:10; 2:12; 5:16; 6:49, 50; 9:4, 8, 9, 15; 11:20; 13:26; 14:62; 16:5) and as a prelude to an action by a character (1:16, 19; 2:14, 16; 5:14; 6:33, 34, 48; 7:2; 9:14; 12:28; 14:67, 69).

33 I am developing insights drawn from van Iersel, "'To Galilee' or 'in Galilee,'" 369–70. A similar view was put forward by Ernest Best in *Following Jesus: Discipleship in the Gospel of Mark*, JSNT Sup 4 (Sheffield: JSOT Press, 1981), 201.

34 Christopher M. Tuckett, "Mark's Concerns in the Parables Chapter (Mark 4,1–34)," *Bib* 69 (1988): 17–18.

35 Elizabeth Struthers Malbon, "How Does the Story Mean?" in *Mark and Method: New Approaches in Biblical Studies*, ed. Janice Capel Anderson and Stephen D. Moore (Minneapolis: Fortress, 1992), 47.

36 On these topics, see Earl S. Johnson, "Mark VIII. 22–26: The Blind Man from Bethsaida," *NTS* 25 (1979): 380–83; and Matera, "Incomprehension," esp. 154, 163–65, 169–72. Johnson argued that the disciples see imperfectly throughout the story, which overlooks Jesus' assertion of the disciples' *blindness* in 8:18. Matera argued that they see imperfectly up to Peter's confession, but suggested that they see clearly after that. However, the immediate tiff between Jesus and Peter (8:31–33) seems to indicate that Peter did not comprehend the true significance of his insight that Jesus is the Christ. It makes more sense to suppose that the disciples are functionally blind before Peter's confession, see imperfectly from that point until the end, and will see clearly only after the story is over.

37 Elizabeth Struthers Malbon, "Mark: Myth and Parable," *BTB* 14 (1986): 11.

38 E.g., David Catchpole, "The Fearful Silence of the Women at the Tomb: A Study in Markan Theology," *JTSA* 18 (1977): 6; Elisabeth Schüssler Fiorenza, *In Memory of Her: A Feminist Theological Reconstruction of Christian Origins*, 10th anniversary ed. (New York: Crossroad, 1994), 322; Robert H. Gundry, *Mark: A Commentary on His Apology for the Cross* (Grand Rapids: Eerdmans, 1993), 1009.

39 Werner Kelber, *Mark's Story of Jesus* (Philadelphia: Fortress, 1979), 86. This position was first argued by Weeden in *Traditions in Conflict*. Weeden inconsistently interpreted the seeing of Jesus in 16:7b as referring to the parousia rather than to a resurrection appearance (p. 110) and 16:8 as implying a missed resurrection appearance (p. 50). This flaw was noticed by Catchpole in "Fearful Silence," 4 n. 4.

40 C.F. Evans, *Resurrection*, 80; cf. Malbon, *Narrative Space*, 37, 180 nn. 48, 49.

41 See chapter 5 n. 11.

42 I am elaborating the argument in Tolbert, *Sowing the Gospel*, 145–46, 195–218.

43 Benoît Standaert, *L'Évangile selon Marc: Composition et genre littéraire* (Nijmegen: Studentenpers, 1978), 157, as cited in F. Neirynck, "La fuite du jeune homme en Mc 14,51–52," in *Evangelica: Gospel Studies–Études d'évangile, Collected Essays*, ed. Frans Van Segbroeck, BETL 60 (Leuven: Leuven University Press; Uitgeverij Peeters, 1982), 237–38 (trans. mine).

44 Myers, *Binding*, 390–91. See also Ben Witherington III, *The Gospel of Mark: A Socio-Rhetorical Commentary* (Grand Rapids: Eerdmans, 2001), 39.

45 David Ulansey, "The Heavenly Veil Torn: Mark's Cosmic *Inclusio*," *JBL* 110:1 (1991): 123–25. S. Motyer, "The Rending of the Veil: A Markan Pentecost?" *NTS* 33 (1987): 155–57. See also Donald H. Juel, *A Master of Surprise: Mark Interpreted* (Minneapolis: Fortress, 1994), 33–43.

46 I have adapted and modified the chart in Myers, *Binding*, 390–91.

# Chapter 8

1 David Rhoads and Donald Michie, *Mark as Story* (Philadelphia: Fortress, 1982), 46–47. See also Werner H. Kelber, *The Oral and the Written Gospel: The Hermeneutics of Speaking and Writing in the Synoptic Tradition, Mark, Paul, and Q* (Philadelphia: Fortress, 1983), 67; Christopher D. Marshall, *Faith as a Theme in Mark's Narrative*, SNTSMS 64 (Cambridge: Cambridge University Press, 1989), 1, 23–24; John R. Donahue and Daniel J. Harrington, *The Gospel of Mark*, SPS 2 (Collegeville, MN: Liturgical Press, 2002), 19. Verbal echoes have been examined as a Markan literary technique by Joanna Dewey ("Mark as Interwoven Tapestry: Forecasts and Echoes for a Listening Audience," *CBQ* 53 [1991]: 221–36) and Elizabeth Struthers Malbon ("Echoes and Foreshadowings in Mark 4–8: Reading and Rereading," *JBL* 11 [1993]: 211–30). Relevant instances are noted in Smith, *CA*, 135–38.

2 By "prominent parallel" I usually mean parallels of four or more consecutive words, though other features can make a parallel prominent. In the case of "for he was rich" (ἦν γὰρ πλούσιος), the similarity to "for he had many possessions" (ἦν γὰρ ἔχων κτήματα πολλά) consists in the fact that both clauses form abrupt explanatory conclusions to sections of a narrative, and the variant words have a similar meaning. The "great cry" in LGM 1:5 has four parallels in Mark but is prominent mainly because it stands out in LGM 1 as a very strange detail.

3 C.H. Bird, "Some Gar Clauses in St. Mark's Gospel," *JTS* 4 (1953): 171–87. I am drawing especially on pp. 178–79.

4 See Temma F. Berg, "Reading in/to Mark," *Semeia* 48 (1989): 199–200.

5 That this particular *gar* clause has a symbolic function was argued by William R. Telford, *The Barren Temple and the Withered Tree*, JSNT Sup 1 (Sheffield: JSOT Press, 1980), 91 n. 84; Robert H. Stein, "The Cleansing of the Temple in Mark (11:15–19)," in his *Gospels and Tradition: Studies on Redaction Criticism of the Synoptic Gospels* (Grand Rapids: Baker Book House, 1991), 129; James G. Williams, *Gospel against Parable: Mark's Language of Mystery* (Sheffield: Almond Press, 1985), 73–74; and Morna D. Hooker, *The Gospel According to St Mark*, BNTC (London: A. and C. Black, 1991), 262.

6 Robert M. Fowler, *Let the Reader Understand: Reader-Response Criticism and the Gospel of Mark* (Minneapolis: Fortress, 1991), 96–97. His discussion is situated within the broader category of "*gar* clauses that offer strategically withheld information."

7 Robert H. Gundry, "Excursus on the Secret Gospel of Mark," in his *Mark: A Commentary on His Apology for the Cross* (Grand Rapids: Eerdmans, 1993), 622.

8  I am presupposing my discussion in chapter 7 of the resurrection/exaltation symbolism of the transfiguration.

9  Cf. Smith, *CA*, 136–37; Hans-Martin Schenke, "The Mystery of the Gospel of Mark," *SecCent* 4:2 (1984): 79–80.

10  Andrew T. Lincoln, "The Promise and the Failure: Mark 16:7, 8," *JBL* 108 (1989): 294. This point was argued by John Anthony McGuckin in *The Transfiguration of Christ in Scripture and Tradition*, Studies in the Bible and Early Christianity 9 (Lewiston and Queenston: Edwin Mellen, 1986), esp. 26–27, 79–80. See also Mary Ann Tolbert, *Sowing the Gospel: Mark's World in Literary-Historical Perspective* (Minneapolis: Fortress, 1989), 205–207.

11  Cf. Leif Vaage, "Bird-watching at the Baptism of Jesus: Early Christian Mythmaking in Mark 1:9–11," in *Reimagining Christian Origins: A Colloquium Honoring Burton L. Mack*, ed. Elizabeth A. Castelli and Hal Taussig (Valley Forge: Trinity Press International, 1996), 283–86.

12  McGuckin, *Transfiguration of Christ*, 78.

13  Sherman E. Johnson, response to Reginald Fuller, in *LM*, 26.

14  Pierson Parker, "An Early Christian Cover-up?" *New York Times Book Review* (22 July 1973): 5; Saul Levin, "The Early History of Christianity, in Light of the 'Secret Gospel' of Mark," *ANRW* II 25:6 (1988): 4281.

15  More primitive: Smith, *CA*, 157; Reginald Fuller, "Longer Mark: Forgery, Interpolation, or Old Tradition?" in *LM*, 3. More developed: Walter Wink, "Jesus as Magician," *USQR* 30 (1974): 5; Raymond E. Brown, "The Relation of 'The Secret Gospel of Mark' to the Fourth Gospel," *CBQ* 36 (1974): 482.

16  John Dominic Crossan, *Four Other Gospels: Shadows on the Contours of Canon* (Minneapolis: Winston, 1985), 105. Cf. Smith, *CA*, 107.

17  See James M. Robinson, *The Problem of History in Mark and Other Marcan Studies* (Philadelphia: Fortress, 1982), 87.

18  Frederick W. Danker, "The Demonic Secret in Mark: A Reexamination of the Cry of Dereliction (15:34)," *ZNW* 61 (1970): 52.

19  Gundry, *Mark*, 241 (the authors he cited summarize the evidence). See also Howard Clark Kee, "The Terminology of Mark's Exorcism Stories," *NTS* 14 (1968): 236–37.

20  Robert A. Guelich, *Mark 1–8:26*, WBC 34 (Dallas: Word Books, 1989), 282, as cited in Richard Schneck, *Isaiah in the Gospel of Mark, I–VIII*, Bibal Dissertation Series 1 (Vallejo, CA: Bibal Press, 1994), 136.

21  Apart from the description of the large upper room which Jesus reserved for the last supper (14:15) and the reference to "those who wish to be great" in 10:43, the remaining occurences of the adjective *great* describe reactions to events involving the defeat of death. The disciples respond to the rebuking of the sea with "a great fear" (4:41), and observers of the raising of Jairus's daughter were overcome with "great amazement" (5:42). The substantive "great [men]" occurs in Mark 10:42, and the superlative in 9:34 ("for on the way they had discussed with one another who was the greatest").

22  David Winston, in *LM*, 61.

23  Robinson, *Problem of History*, 87.

24  On the matter of how "*over*precision" in narration can create blanks, see Jouette M. Bassler, "The Parable of the Loaves," *JR* 66 (1986): 164 n. 18, who cited Wolfgang Iser.

25  McGuckin, *Transfiguration of Christ*, 78.

26  Winsome Munro, "Women Disciples: Light from Secret Mark," *JFSR* 8 (1992): 54; cf. Schenke, "Mystery," 77–78.

27  Charles E. Carlston, *The Parables of the Triple Tradition* (Philadelphia: Fortress, 1975), 98, as cited in Priscilla C. Patten, "The Form and Function of Parables in Select Apocalyptic Literature and Their Significance for Parables in the Gospel of Mark," *NTS* 29 (1983): 254.

28  On this topic, see G.H. Boobyer, "The Redaction of Mark IV.1–34," *NTS* 8 (1961–1962): 61, 63–64; Patten, "Form and Function," 253; Madeleine Boucher, *The Mysterious Parable: A Literary Study*, CBQMS 6 (Washington: The Catholic Biblical Association of America, 1977), 69; Mary Ann Beavis, *Mark's Audience: The Literary and Social Setting of Mark 4.11–12*, JSNT Sup 33 (Sheffield: JSOT Press, 1989), 111–14; Marshall, *Faith*, 60–74; Frank J. Matera, "'He Saved Others; He Cannot Save Himself': A Literary-Critical Perspective on the Markan Miracles," *Int* 47 (1993): 18–19, 24. For a detailed study of the Markan miracles as parabolic demonstrations of the eschatological power of God's kingdom, see chapter 3 of Marshall's book.

29  Eduard Schweizer, "Mark's Theological Achievement," in *The Interpretation of Mark*, ed. William R. Telford, Studies in New Testament Interpretation, 2d ed. (Edinburgh: T. and T. Clark, 1995), 71; idem, "The Question of the Messianic Secret in Mark," in *The Messianic Secret*, ed. and trans. Christopher M. Tuckett, IRT 1 (Philadelphia: Fortress; London: SPCK, 1983), 69–70.

30  Boucher, *Mysterious Parable*, 81–83.

31  Priscilla C. Patten, "Parable and Secret in the Gospel of Mark in the Light of Select Apocalyptic Literature," *The Drew Gateway* 47:2–3 (1976–1977): 136. Idem, "Form and Function," 257.

32  J.G. Williams, *Gospel against Parable*, 44, 98.

33  John R. Donahue, *The Gospel in Parable: Metaphor, Narrative, and Theology in the Synoptic Gospels* (Philadelphia: Fortress, 1988), 44–46 (44, 46); Donahue and Harrington, *Mark*, 141, 146.

34  See John C. Meagher, *Clumsy Construction in Mark's Gospel: A Critique of Form- and Redaktionsgeschichte*, Toronto Studies in Theology 3 (New York: Edwin Mellen, 1979), 85–92, 99–138.

35  On the meaning of γίνεται, see Meagher, *Clumsy Construction*, 114; Werner H. Kelber, *The Kingdom in Mark: A New Place and a New Time* (Philadelphia: Fortress, 1974), 32–33; Beavis, *Mark's Audience*, 147. On ἐν παραβολαῖς as "in riddles," see Elian Cuvillier, *Le concept de ΠΑΡΑΒΟΛΗ dans le second évangile*, Études Bibliques, n.s., 19 (Paris: J. Gabalda, 1993), 195.

36  Schweizer, "Messianic Secret," 68; Quentin Quesnell, *The Mind of Mark: Interpretation and Method through the Exegesis of Mark 6,52* (Rome: Pontifical Biblical Institute, 1969), 213; Boucher, *Mysterious Parable*, 81–82; Jonathan Bishop, "*Parabole* and *Parrhesia* in Mark," *Int* 40 (1986): 39–40; Cuvillier, *Le concept de ΠΑΡΑΒΟΛΗ*, 110.

37  On viewing Mark 4:1–8:26 as a discrete section of narrative dominated by the motif of the sea voyage and the development of the motif that the disciples are as uncomprehending as "those outside," see Norman R. Petersen, "The Composition of Mark 4:1–8:26," *HTR* 73 (1980): 185–217. For the development of the incomprehension theme within 6:14–8:30, see Frank J. Matera, "The

Incomprehension of the Disciples and Peter's Confession (Mark 6,14–8,30)," *Bib* 70 (1989): 153–72.

38  Cf. J.G. Williams, *Gospel against Parable*, 43. Hooker (*St Mark*, 120, 130–31) drew attention to the fact that the words about the mystery (4:11–12) are enclosed within (i.e., framed by) the Sower parable and its interpretation.

39  This felicitous phrase is taken from Rikki E. Watts, *Isaiah's New Exodus and Mark*, WUNT, 2d ser., 88 (Tübingen: Mohr Siebeck, 1997), 230.

40  Cf. Bishop, "*Parabole* and *Parrhesia* in Mark," 39–40.

41  Robinson, *Problem of History*, 125. Cf. Boucher, *Mysterious Parable*, 45–46.

42  Joel Marcus, *The Mystery of the Kingdom of God*, SBLDS 90 (Atlanta: Scholars Press, 1986), 142. On p. 131 he pointed out that since this is a personified lamp that "comes" with a purpose, it may also symbolize Jesus (cf. the use of ἔρχομαι of Jesus in 1:24, 38; 2:17c; 10:45).

43  B.M.F. van Iersel, "The Reader of Mark as Operator of a System of Connotations," *Semeia* 48 (1989): 94.

44  Bassler, "Parable of the Loaves," 163; he cited Quesnell, *Mind of Mark*, 66.

45  Bassler, "Parable of the Loaves," 164–65.

46  Frank Kermode, *The Genesis of Secrecy: On the Interpretation of Narrative* (Cambridge: Harvard University Press, 1979), 46, 47.

47  Bassler, "Parable of the Loaves," 165 (italics original). See also van Iersel, "Operator," 97; W. Randolph Tate, *Reading Mark from the Outside: Eco and Iser Leave Their Marks* (San Francisco: International Scholars Publications, 1994), 120–22.

48  Meagher, *Clumsy Construction*, 77. Meagher supposed that Mark thought there must be a deeper truth here yet could not manage to fathom it himself. It is worth noting that some scholars view this whole passage, with the exception of the saying about the leaven, as a Markan creation: Quesnell, *Mind of Mark*, 103–25; Beavis, *Mark's Audience*, 106–13; Heikki Räisänen, *The "Messianic Secret" in Mark*, trans. Christopher Tuckett (Edinburgh: T. and T. Clark, 1990), 200–201.

49  Bassler, "Parable of the Loaves," 166–69 (Bassler was not specifically interested in the mystery of the kingdom of God). See also Boucher, *Mysterious Parable*, 72–75; and Watts, *Isaiah's New Exodus and Mark*, 228–36.

# Chapter 9

1  It is interesting to note that some scholars interpret the mystery theme in the canonical gospel as having a philosophical dimension. See A.E. Harvey, "The Use of Mystery Language in the Bible," *JTS*, n.s., 31 (1980): 332–36, esp. 335–36; Mary Ann Beavis, *Mark's Audience: The Literary and Social Setting of Mark 4.11–12*, JSNT Sup 33 (Sheffield: JSOT Press, 1989), 143–46.

2  Smith, *CA*, 76.

3  James R. Edwards, "Appendix: The Secret Gospel of Mark," in his *The Gospel According to Mark* (Grand Rapids: Eerdmans, 2002), 512. Similar comments appear in R.T. France, *The Gospel of Mark: A Commentary on the Greek Text*, The New Testament Greek Commentary (Grand Rapids: Eerdmans, 2002), 410–11.

4  Various scholars have argued that the procession to Jerusalem (Mark 11:1–10) originally concluded in a much more dramatic fashion with the clearing of the temple, the way it does in Matt 21:1–13, and that Mark's anticlimactic reference

to Jesus' inspection of the temple and return to Bethany (11:11) was devised to make room for the first part of the cursing of the fig tree (11:12–14). Likewise the second part of that nature miracle (11:20–25) disrupts the connection between the demonstration in the temple and the questioning of Jesus' authority to do these things (11:15–18, 27–33), which remain joined in John 2:13–22. For a fuller demonstration of this point, see William R. Telford, *The Barren Temple and the Withered Tree*, JSNT Sup 1 (Sheffield: JSOT Press, 1980), 42–49.

5 Tom Shepherd, "Intercalation in Mark and the Synoptic Problem," in *Society of Biblical Literature 1991 Seminar Papers*, ed. Eugene H. Lovering, Jr., SBLSP 30 (Missoula: Scholars Press, 1991), 689.

6 James R. Edwards, "Markan Sandwiches: The Significance of Interpolations in Markan Narratives," *NovT* 31 (1989): 197.

7 Tom Shepherd, "Intercalation in Mark," 689.

8 The verbal parallels in these incidents are highlighted in David Peabody, *Mark as Composer*, New Gospel Studies 1 (Macon, GA: Mercer University Press, 1987), 80–81, 106.

9 Terence Y. Mullins, "Papias and Clement and Mark's Two Gospels," *VC* 30 (1976): 191–92.

10 Terence Y. Mullins, "Papias on Mark's Gospel," *VC* 14 (1960): 216–24.

11 Mullins, "Papias and Clement," 189–92.

12 Jean Carmignac, *The Birth of the Synoptic Gospels*, trans. Michael J. Wrenn (Chicago: Franciscan Herald Press, 1987), 57.

13 David Peabody, "The Late Secondary Redaction of Mark's Gospel and the Griesbach Hypothesis: A Response to Helmut Koester," in *Colloquy on New Testament Studies: A Time for Reappraisal and Fresh Approaches*, ed. Bruce Corley (Macon, GA: Mercer University Press, 1983), 130–32.

14 Pierson Parker, cited by Smith in *CA*, 133.

15 Carroll D. Osburn, "The Historical Present in Mark as a Text-Critical Criterion," *Bib* 64 (1983): 496, 498, 499.

16 See Bart D. Ehrman, *The Orthodox Corruption of Scripture: The Effect of Early Christological Controversies on the Text of the New Testament* (New York: Oxford University Press, 1993).

17 Brenda Deen Schildgen, *Power and Prejudice: The Reception of the Gospel of Mark* (Detroit: Wayne State University Press, 1999), 38, 56; see also p. 62.

18 See Mary Ann Tolbert, *Sowing the Gospel: Mark's World in Literary-Historical Perspective* (Minneapolis: Fortress, 1989).

19 Note Edwards, "Markan Sandwiches," 202–203: "By way of summary on the sandwich technique prior to Mark, we might say that although the suspension of a narrative for one reason or another was not uncommon in ancient literature, the use of an inserted middle to give new meaning or to resolve a tension in a host passage can be seen, to the best of my knowledge, only in the Hebrew Scriptures, and there seldomly."

20 Papias, *Exposition of the Lord's Logia*, as cited in Eusebius, *Church History* III.39.15 and translated in Ben Witherington III, *The Gospel of Mark: A Socio-Rhetorical Commentary* (Grand Rapids: Eerdmans, 2001), 22.

21 Witherington III, *Mark*, 22. See also Josef Kürzinger, "Das Papiaszeugnis und die Erstgestalt des Matthäusevangeliums," *BZ* 4 (1960): 19–38; idem, "Die Aussage des Papias von Hierapolis zur literarischen Form des Markusevangeli-

ums," *BZ* 21 (1977): 245–64; C. Clifton Black, *Mark: Images of an Apostolic Interpreter* (Columbia: University of South Carolina Press, 1994), 91 (86–94).

22 Black, *Apostolic Interpreter*, 91.

23 Augustine, *Harmony of the Evangelists* (*De Consensu Evangelistarum*) I.2.4, as cited in William R. Telford, ed., *The Interpretation of Mark*, Studies in New Testament Interpretation, 2d ed. (Edinburgh: T. and T. Clark, 1995), 3, who is citing Vincent Taylor, *The Gospel According to St. Mark*, 2d ed. (London: Macmillan, 1966), 9.

24 For a good overview of the evolution of the study of Mark from the late nineteenth century until the mid-1970s, see Norman Perrin, "The Interpretation of the Gospel of Mark," *Int* 30 (1976): 115–24.

25 See Dwight N. Petersen, *The Origins of Mark: The Markan Community in Current Debate*, Biblical Interpretation Series 48 (Leiden: E.J. Brill, 2000).

26 For a critique of the assumption that the evangelists wrote for specific communities, see Richard Bauckham, ed., *The Gospel for All Christians: Rethinking the Gospel Audiences* (Grand Rapids: Eerdmans, 1998). I agree that it makes little sense to talk about a Markan or a Lukan community, but I think Bauckham pushed his case too far by arguing that *all* the canonical gospels were written for *all* Christians. For arguments supporting the origin of canonical Mark in Rome, see C. Clifton Black, "Was Mark a Roman Gospel?" *ExpTim* 105 (1993): 36–40; B.M.F. van Iersel, *Mark: A Reader-Response Commentary*, trans. W.H. Bisscheroux, JSNT Sup 164 (Sheffield: Sheffield Academic Press, 1998), 30–57; Witherington III, *Mark*, 20–21.

27 C. Wilfred Griggs, *Early Egyptian Christianity: From Its Origins to 451 C.E.*, Coptic Studies 2, 2d ed. (Leiden: E.J. Brill, 1991), 21.

28 On the date of Papias, see Robert H. Gundry, *Mark: A Commentary on His Apology for the Cross* (Grand Rapids: Eerdmans, 1993), 1027–31.

29 Lucian of Samosata, *How to Write History* 47–48, as cited in Black, *Apostolic Interpreter*, 142.

30 See Scott G. Brown, "On the Composition History of the Longer ('Secret') Gospel of Mark," *JBL* 122 (2003): 101–106.

31 See Philip Sellew, "*Secret Mark* and the History of Canonical Mark," in *The Future of Early Christianity: Essays in Honor of Helmut Koester*, ed. Birger A. Pearson (Minneapolis: Fortress, 1991), 251–52.

32 Heikki Räisänen, *The "Messianic Secret" in Mark*, trans. Christopher M. Tuckett (Edinburgh: T. and T. Clark, 1990), 93, 104–105; cf. Christopher M. Tuckett, "Mark's Concerns in the Parables Chapter (Mark 4,1–34)," *Bib* 69 (1988): 5–6.

33 The abundant evidence of Markan redaction in 4:1–2; 4:10–11; and 4:33–34 is discussed in J. Lambrecht, "Redaction and Theology in Mk., IV," in *L'Évangile selon Marc: Tradition et rédaction*, ed. M. Sabbe, BETL 34, 2d ed. (Leuven: Leuven University Press, 1988), 269–308.

34 David Peabody, Allan J. McNicol, and Lamar Cope, eds., *One Gospel from Two: Mark's Use of Matthew and Luke* (Harrisburg: Trinity Press International, 2002), 55.

35 Charles W. Hedrick, "The Secret Gospel of Mark: Stalemate in the Academy," *JECS* 11 (2003): 133–45.

36  Marie-Émile Boismard, A. Lamouille, and G. Rochais, *Synopse des quatre évangiles en français, vol. III, L'évangile de Jean* (Paris: Cerf, 1977), 279. Robert T. Fortna, *The Fourth Gospel and Its Predecessor* (Philadelphia: Fortress, 1988), 94 and n. 213.

37  Raymond E. Brown, *The Gospel According to John*, 2d ed. (Garden City: Doubleday, 1980), 1:xxxvii, 414, 428; Barnabas Lindars, *The Gospel of John*, NCB (London: Oliphants, 1972), 50, 379–82; Alexander J. Burke, Jr., "The Raising of Lazarus and the Passion of Jesus in John 11 and 12: A Study of John's Literary Structure and His Narrative Theology" (Ph.D. diss., Fordham University, 2002), 30–34.

38  The quoted words are from Cyril C. Richardson, review of *CA* and *SG*, *TS* 35 (1974): 575. The "sobriety fellowship" interpretation is offered in John C. Mellon, *Mark as Recovery Story: Alcoholism and the Rhetoric of Gospel Mystery* (Urbana and Chicago: University of Illinois Press, 1995), 234–35.

39  See, e.g., James F. McCue, "Orthodoxy and Heresy: Walter Bauer and the Valentinians," *VC* 33 (1979): 118–30; Colin H. Roberts, *Manuscript, Society and Belief in Early Christian Egypt*, The Schweich Lectures of the British Academy, 1977 (London: Oxford University Press, 1979), esp. 49–73; Birger A. Pearson, "Earliest Christianity in Egypt: Some Observations," in *The Roots of Egyptian Christianity*, ed. Birger A. Pearson and James E. Goehring, SAC (Philadelphia: Fortress, 1986), 132–56; and Griggs, *Early Egyptian Christianity*, 16–34.

40  Helmut Koester, "The Text of the Synoptic Gospels in the Second Century," in *Gospel Traditions in the Second Century: Origins, Recensions, Text, and Transmission*, ed. William L. Petersen (Notre Dame, IN: University of Notre Dame Press, 1989), 19–37. For a summary of some of the discussions of Koester's theory by textual critics, see Eldon Jay Epp, "The Multivalence of the Term 'Original Text' in New Testament Textual Criticism," *HTR* 92 (1999): 245–81.

41  For additional discussion, see Hedrick, "Stalemate," 139–40.

42  David C. Parker stressed this point in his book *The Living Text of the Gospels* (New York: Cambridge University Press, 1997).

# ⊰ Bibliography ⊱

## Reviews of Morton Smith's Books on Longer Mark

Achtemeier, Paul J. *JBL* 93 (1974): 625–28.

Alexander, P.S. *JJS* 27:2 (1976): 217–18.

Beardslee, William A. *Int* 28 (1974): 234–36.

Danker, Frederick W. *Dialog* 13 (1974): 316.

Donfried, Karl Paul. "New-Found Fragments of an Early Gospel." *ChrCent* 90 (18–25 July 1973): 759–60.

Fitzmyer, Joseph A. "How to Exploit a Secret Gospel." *America* 128 (23 June 1973): 570–72.

Frend, William H.C. "A New Jesus?" *New York Review of Books* 20 (9 August 1973): 34–35.

Gibbons, Joseph A. *Sign* 53 (September 1973): 48.

Gibbs, John G. *ThTo* 30 (1974): 423–26.

Grant, Robert M. "Morton Smith's Two Books." *AThR* 56 (1974): 58–64.

Hanson, R.P.C. *JTS*, n.s., 25 (1974): 513–21.

Jewett, Robert. *The Christian Advocate* 14 (6 December 1973): 15–16.

Johnson, Marshall D. *LQ* 25 (1973): 426–27.

Kee, Howard Clark. *JAAR* 43 (1975): 326–29.

Koester, Helmut. *AHR* 80 (1975): 620–22.

MacRae, George. "Yet Another Jesus." *Commonweal* 99 (25 January 1974): 417–420.

Méhat, André. *Revue de l'histoire des religions* 190 (1976): 196–97.

Mitton, C. Leslie. *ExpTim* 86 (1974–1975): 130–32.

Nineham, Dennis. *JTS* 27 (April 1976): 195–97.

Parker, Pierson. "An Early Christian Cover-up?" *New York Times Book Review* (22 July 1973): 5.

Petersen, Norman R. *Southern Humanities Review* 8 (1974): 525–31.

Quesnell, Quentin. "'Secret Gospel': Improbable Puzzle." *National Catholic Reporter* (30 November 1973): 12.

Reese, James M. *CBQ* 36 (1974): 434–35.

Richardson, Cyril C. *TS* 35 (1974): 571–77.

Scroggs, Robin. *CTSR* 64:1 (November 1973): 58–60.

Sider, Ronald J. "Unfounded 'Secret.'" *CT* 18:3 (9 November 1973): 26 (160).

Skehan, Patrick W. *CHR* 60 (1974–1975): 451–53.

Stagg, Frank. *RevExp* 71 (1974): 108–10.

Talbert, Charles H. *ANQ* 14 (1974): 283–85.

Trevor-Roper, Huge. "Gospel of Liberty." *Sunday Times* (London, 30 June 1974): 15.

Trocmé, Etienne. "Trois critiques au miroir de l'Évangile selon Marc." *RHPR* 55 (1975): 289–95.

Yamauchi, Edwin M. "A Secret Gospel of Jesus as 'Magus'? A Review of the Recent Works of Morton Smith." *CSR* 4:3 (1975): 238–51.

## Works That Discuss Longer Mark

Akenson, Donald Harman. *Saint Saul: A Skeleton Key to the Historical Jesus*. Oxford and New York: Oxford University Press, 2000. Akenson argues that LGM is a "gay joke."

———. *Surpassing Wonder: The Invention of the Bible and Talmuds*. Montreal: McGill-Queen's University Press, 1998. Pp. 595–97 contain an earlier version of the discussion of LGM in *Saint Saul*.

Baldovin, John F. "A Lenten Sunday Lectionary in Fourth Century Jerusalem." In *Time and Community*. Festschrift Thomas Julian Talley, ed. J. Neil Alexander, 115–22. Washington, DC: Pastoral Press, 1990. On p. 117 (and 122 n. 17) Baldovin gives a helpful summary of Thomas Talley's theory about the relationship between LGM and Lazarus Saturday.

Baltz, Frederick W. *Lazarus and the Fourth Gospel Community*. Mellen Biblical Press Series 37. Lewiston: Edwin Mellen, 1996. On p. 104 Baltz uses LGM as evidence that some early Christians did not think the beloved disciple was John son of Zebedee.

Bauckham, Richard. "Salome the Sister of Jesus, Salome the Disciple of Jesus, and the Secret Gospel of Mark." *NovT* 33 (1991): 245–75.

———. "The Two Salomes and the *Secret Gospel of Mark*." Chap. 7 in his *Gospel Women: Studies in the Named Women in the Gospels*. Grand Rapids: Eerdmans, 2002.

Beskow, Per. *Strange Tales about Jesus: A Survey of Unfamiliar Gospels*. Philadelphia: Fortress, 1983. The discussion of longer Mark in this book was revised in the 1985 reprint of this edition. The 1983 edition is a revised English translation of *Fynd och fusk i Bibelns värld*. Stockholm: Proprius förlag, 1979.

Best, Ernest. "Mark 10:13–16: The Child as Model Recipient." Chap. 6 in his *Disciples and Discipleship: Studies in the Gospel According to Mark*. Edinburgh: T. and T. Clark, 1986. Best critiques Morton Smith's theory that Mark 10:13–45 is related to baptism.

———. "Uncanonical Mark." Review of *Redactional Style in the Marcan Gospel*, by E.J. Pryke. Chap. 11 in Best's *Disciples and Discipleship: Studies in the Gospel According to Mark*. Edinburgh: T. and T. Clark, 1986. Originally published in *JSNT* 4 (1979): 69–76. Best argues that LGM is too Markan to be by Mark.

Black, C. Clifton. *Mark: Images of an Apostolic Interpreter*. Columbia: University of South Carolina Press, 1994. In chap. 5, Black discusses the *Letter to Theodore* in relation to Clement's other traditions about Mark the evangelist.

Boismard, Marie-Émile, with A. Lamouille and G. Rochais. *Synopse des quatre évangiles en français, vol. III, L'évangile de Jean*. Paris: Cerf, 1977. On p. 279 Boismard uses LGM 1:1 to reconstruct the opening of John's source for the raising of Lazarus.

Brown, Raymond E. *The Death of the Messiah: A Commentary on the Passion Narratives in the Four Gospels*. Vol. 1. ABRL. New York: Doubleday, 1994. Pp. 294–304 offer a discussion of the young man from Mark 14:51–52 and LGM.

———. "The *Gospel of Peter* and Canonical Gospel Priority." *NTS* 33 (1987): 321–43. On pp. 322–23, 327 Brown registers his theological objection to the theory of longer Markan priority.

———. "The Relation of 'The Secret Gospel of Mark' to the Fourth Gospel." *CBQ* 36 (1974): 466–85.

Brown, Scott G. "Bethany beyond the Jordan: John 1:28 and the Longer Gospel of Mark." *RB* 110 (2003): 497–516.

———. "The More Spiritual Gospel: Markan Literary Techniques in the Longer Gospel of Mark." Ph.D. diss., University of Toronto, 1999.

———. "On the Composition History of the Longer ('Secret') Gospel of Mark." *JBL* 122 (2003): 89–110.

———. "The Secret Gospel of Mark: Is It Real? And Does It Identify 'Bethany beyond the Jordan'?" *BAR* 31:1 (2005): 44–49, 60–61.

Bruce, F.F. *Jesus and Christian Origins outside the New Testament*. London: Hodder and Stoughton, 1974. Bruce's first impressions about the LGM are recorded on pp. 164–66.

———. *The "Secret" Gospel of Mark*. Ethel M. Wood Lecture, University of London, 11 February 1974. London: Athlone Press, 1974. This is reprinted with slight revision in Appendix I of his *The Canon of Scripture* (Downers Grove: InterVarsity Press, 1988).

Calder, William M., III. "Morton Smith." *Gnomon* 64 (1992): 382–84. Reprinted in his *Men in Their Books: Studies in the Modern History of Classical Scholarship*, ed. John P. Harris and R. Scott Smith, 2d ed., Spudasmata 67 (Zurich: Georg Olms Verlag Hildesheim, 2002), 229–31.

Cameron, Ron, ed. *The Other Gospels: Non-Canonical Gospel Texts*. Philadelphia: Westminster, 1982. Cameron's discussion of longer Mark is reprinted in *The Other Bible*, ed. Willis Barnstone (San Francisco: Harper and Row, 1984).

Carmignac, Jean. *The Birth of the Synoptic Gospels*. Trans. Michael J. Wrenn. Chicago: Franciscan Herald Press, 1987. On pp. 56–57 Carmignac discusses the *Letter to Theodore* in relation to Papias's tradition about Mark (pp. 52–54). Originally published as *La naissance des évangiles synoptiques*, 3d ed. avec réponse aux critiques (Paris: O.E.I.L., 1984). The corresponding discussion is on pp. 61–63, 65–66.

Charlesworth, James H. *Authentic Apocrypha: False and Genuine Christian Apocrypha*. North Richland Hills, TX: Bibal Press, 1998. A photographic memento of his attempt to find the letter is contained on p. 32.

Charlesworth, James H., and Craig A. Evans. "Jesus in the Agrapha and Apocryphal Gospels." In *Studying the Historical Jesus: Evaluations of the State of Current Research*, ed. Bruce Chilton and Craig A. Evans, 479–533. NTTS 19. Leiden: E.J. Brill, 1994. The discussion of LGM (pp. 526–32) was written by Evans.

Choufrine, Arkadi. *Gnosis, Theophany, Theosis: Studies in Clement of Alexandria's Appropriation of His Background*. Patristic Studies 5. New York: Peter Lang, 2002. Choufrine attempts to relate LGM 1 to Clement's baptismal theology on pp. 30–31.

Cohen, Shaye J.D. "In Memoriam Morton Smith: Morton Smith and His Scholarly Achievement." In *Josephus and the History of the Greco-Roman Period: Essays in Memory of Morton Smith*, ed. Fausto Parente and Joseph Sievers, 1–8. Leiden and New York: E.J. Brill, 1994.

Consoli, Massimo. *Ecce Homo: L'omosessualità nella Bibbia*. Milano: Kaos, 1998. See pp. 131–35.

Conzelmann, Hans. "Literaturbericht zu den Synoptischen Evangelien (Fortsetzung)." *TRu* 43 (1978): 3–51. Smith's work is reviled on p. 23. An English translation of Conzelmann's remarks can be found in the article "The Mystery of the Gospel of Mark," by Hans-Martin Schenke.

Criddle, Andrew H. "On the Mar Saba Letter Attributed to Clement of Alexandria." *JECS* 3 (1995): 215–20.

———. "Secret Mark—Further Comments." <http://www-user.uni-bremen.de/~wie/Secret/Criddle-Feb99.html>.

Crossan, John Dominic. *The Cross That Spoke: The Origins of the Passion Narrative*. San Francisco: Harper and Row, 1988. LGM is discussed on pp. 283–84.

———. *Four Other Gospels: Shadows on the Contours of Canon*. Minneapolis: Winston, 1985.

———. *The Historical Jesus: The Life of a Mediterranean Jewish Peasant*. San Francisco: Harper, 1991. LGM is discussed on pp. 328–32, 411–16, 429–30.

———. "Thoughts on Two Extracanonical Gospels." *Semeia* 49 (1990): 155–68.

Dart, John. *Decoding Mark*. Harrisburg: Trinity Press International, 2003. Dart argues on the basis of chiastic patterns that LGM 1 and 2 were originally part of Mark's gospel.

———. "Why Secret Mark Was Part of the Original Gospel of Mark." Unpublished paper presented at the annual meeting of the SBL Pacific Coast Region, Long Beach, CA, 3 April 1987.

Davies, Stevan L. <miser17@epix.net>. "REPLY: Secret Mark." In IOUDAIOS-L. <ioudaios-l@lehigh.edu>. 30 June 1995. Archived at: <ftp://ftp.lehigh.edu/pub/listserv/ioudaios-l/archives/9506e.Z>.

Davila, James R. <jrd4@st-andrews.ac.uk>. "REPLY: Secret Mark." In IOUDAIOS-L. <ioudaios-l@lehigh.edu>. 1 July 1995. Archived at: <ftp://ftp.lehigh.edu/pub/listserv/ioudaios-l/archives/9507a.Z>.

Dunn, James D.G. *Christianity in the Making*. Vol. 1, *Jesus Remembered*. Grand Rapids: Eerdmans, 2003. Dunn believes longer Mark is "an allusive echo" of John 11 (pp. 169–70).

———. *The Evidence for Jesus*. Philadelphia: Westminster, 1985. Smith's views about Jesus based on longer Mark are dismissed on pp. 51–52.

Edwards, James R. "Appendix: The Secret Gospel of Mark." In his *The Gospel According to Mark*, 509–12. Grand Rapids: Eerdmans, 2002.

Ehrman, Bart D. "The Forgery of an Ancient Discovery? Morton Smith and the Secret Gospel of Mark." In his *Lost Christianities: The Battles for Scripture and the Faiths We Never Knew*, 67–89. New York: Oxford University Press, 2003.

———. "Response to Charles Hedrick's Stalemate." *JECS* 11 (2003): 155–63.

———. "Too Good to Be False? A Text Critic Looks at the Secret Gospel of Mark." Paper presented at the annual meeting of the SBL, Toronto, ON, Canada, November 2002. Ehrman argues that there is a suspicious congruence between the contents of the *Letter to Theodore* and the contents of the book into which the letter was copied.

Elliott, J.K. *The Apocryphal New Testament: A Collection of Apocryphal Christian Literature in an English Translation*. Oxford: Clarendon Press, 1993. LGM 1 and 2 are quoted on pp. 148–49.

Epp, Eldon Jay. "The Multivalence of the Term 'Original Text' in New Testament Textual Criticism." *HTR* 92 (1999): 245–81. This essay includes a discussion of how textual critics have responded to Helmut Koester's theory that there were multiple versions of Mark in the second century.

Evans, Craig A. *Jesus and His Contemporaries: Comparative Studies*. Leiden: E.J. Brill, 1995. Evans uses "secret" Mark to debunk liberal Jesus scholarship on pp. 32–33.

———. "The Need for the 'Historical Jesus': A Response to Jacob Neusner's Review of Crossan and Meier." *BBR* 4 (1994): 127–34. Evans objects to Neusner's claim that the *Letter to Theodore* is a modern forgery and an embarrassment to Jesus scholarship. He also declares that the gospel quotations "are spurious and therefore of no value for serious Jesus research" (p. 129).

Eyer, Shawn. "The Strange Case of the Secret Gospel According to Mark: How Morton Smith's Discovery of a Lost Letter of Clement of Alexandria Scandalized Biblical Scholarship." *Alexandria* 3 (1995): 103–29. Online at: <http://www-user.uni-bremen.de/~wie/Secret/secmark-engl.html>. Eyer exposes the theological underbelly of New Testament scholarship on the longer gospel.

Ferguson, John. *Clement of Alexandria*. TWAS 289. New York: Twayne, 1974. The letter is discussed on pp. 188–89.

Fitzmyer, Joseph A. "Mark's 'Secret Gospel'?" *America* 129 (4 August 1973): 65.

Fortna, Robert T. *The Fourth Gospel and Its Predecessor*. Philadelphia: Fortress, 1988. In this book Fortna adopted Boismard's reconstruction of the opening of John's source for the raising of Lazarus, which Boismard based on LGM 1:1 (p. 94 n. 213). Yet Fortna also reversed the opinion he stated in *The Gospel of Signs* (p. 87) that LGM is an independent and more primitive version of the tradition behind John 11.

———. *The Gospel of Signs: A Reconstruction of the Narrative Source Underlying the Fourth Gospel*. Cambridge: Cambridge University Press, 1970.

Fowler, Miles. "Identification of the Bethany Youth in the Secret Gospel of Mark with Other Figures Found in Mark and John." *JHC* 5:1 (1998): 3–22.

France, R.T. *The Evidence for Jesus*. London: Hodder, 1986. LGM is discussed on pp. 80–83.

———. *The Gospel of Mark: A Commentary on the Greek Text*. The New Testament Greek Commentary. Grand Rapids: Eerdmans, 2002. LGM is discussed on pp. 410–11.

Fuller, Reginald H. "Longer Mark: Forgery, Interpolation, or Old Tradition?" In *Longer Mark: Forgery, Interpolation, or Old Tradition?* ed. Wilhelm H. Wuellner, 1–11. Protocol of the Eighteenth Colloquy: 7 December 1975. Berkeley: Center for Hermeneutical Studies in Hellenistic and Modern Culture, 1976. Fuller subjects LGM 1 to the methods of tradition analysis.

Funk, Robert W. *Honest to Jesus: Jesus for a New Millennium*. San Francisco: HarperSanFrancisco, 1996. Funk's comments about longer Mark appear on p. 73.

Funk, Robert W., and the Jesus Seminar. *The Acts of Jesus: The Search for the Authentic Deeds of Jesus*. San Francisco: HarperSanFrancisco, 1998.

Funk, Robert W., Roy W. Hoover, and the Jesus Seminar, eds. *The Five Gospels: The Search for the Authentic Words of Jesus*. New York: Macmillan, 1993.

Furnish, Victor Paul. "Mark, Secret Gospel of." In *The Interpreter's Dictionary of the Bible. Supplementary Volume*, ed. Keith Crim et al. Nashville: Abingdon, 1976.

Gero, Stephen. "Apocryphal Gospels: A Survey of Textual and Literary Problems." *ANRW* II 25:5 (1988): 3969–96. LGM 1 and 2 are translated and discussed on pp. 3976–78.

Green, Julien. *L'avenir n'est à personne: Journal 1990–1992*. Paris: Fayard, 1993. Green reproduces a letter by Joseph Paramelle recounting the latter's thoughts on the contents of the *Letter to Theodore* and Morton Smith's theories (p. 222).

Grelot, Pierre. *L'origine des évangiles: Controverse avec J. Carmignac*. Apologique. Paris: Cerf, 1986. Grelot rebuts Carmignac's use of the *Letter to Theodore* to illuminate Papias's tradition about Mark (pp. 84–88).

Griggs, C. Wilfred. *Early Egyptian Christianity: From Its Origins to 451 C.E.* Coptic Studies 2. 2d ed. Leiden: E.J. Brill, 1991. Griggs integrates the *Letter to Theodore* into his discussion of the origins of Egyptian Christianity (pp. 20–21).

Gundry, Robert H. "Excursus on the Secret Gospel of Mark." In his *Mark: A Commentary on His Apology for the Cross*, 603–23. Grand Rapids: Eerdmans, 1993. Gundry disputes arguments advanced in support of longer Markan priority.

Gunther, John J. "The Association of Mark and Barnabas with Egyptian Christianity (Part I)." *EvQ* 54 (1982): 219–33. Gunther views the letter as evidence that "non-Gnostic Christianity had taken root in Egypt during apostolic times" (p. 223; cf. 230–31).

Hanhart, Karel. *The Open Tomb: A New Approach, Mark's Passover Haggadah ([ca.] 72 C.E.)*. Collegeville, MN: Liturgical Press, 1995. This is an ambitious attempt to integrate LGM into the composition history of canonical Mark. Hanhart's descriptions of the longer gospel and the relevant scholarship are often erroneous and contradictory.

Harvey, Bob. "Mark's Secret Gay Gospel a Hoax, Scholar Argues." *The Ottawa Citizen*, 6 August 2000. The scholar in question is Donald Akenson.

Hedrick, Charles W. "The Secret Gospel of Mark: Stalemate in the Academy." *JECS* 11 (2003): 133–45. Hedrick draws attention to the pervasive tendency among New Testament scholars to discredit longer Mark rather than investigate it. See also the responses by Guy Stroumsa and Bart Ehrman in the same issue.

Hedrick, Charles W., and Nikolaos Olympiou. "Secret Mark: New Photographs, New Witnesses." *The Fourth R* 13:5 (2000): 3–16.

Hobbs, Edward C. Response to Reginald Fuller. In *Longer Mark: Forgery, Interpolation, or Old Tradition?* ed. Wilhelm H. Wuellner, 19–25. Protocol of the Eighteenth Colloquy: 7 December 1975. Berkeley: Center for Hermeneutical Studies in Hellenistic and Modern Culture, 1976.

Hoek, Annewies van den. "Clement and Origen as Sources on 'Noncanonical' Scriptural Traditions during the Late Second and Earlier Third Centuries." In *Origeniana Sexta: Origène et la Bible/Origen and the Bible*, ed. Gilles Dorival and Alain Le Boulluec, 93–113. Actes du Colloquium Origenianum Sextum Chantilly, 30 août – 3 septembre 1993. Leuven: Leuven University

Press, 1995. This paper situates longer Mark and other non-canonical texts within the range of gospel traditions that were considered acceptable in Alexandria at the end of the second century.

Horst, Pieter W. van der. "Het 'Geheime Markusevangelie.' Over een nieuwe vondst." In his *De onbekende god: Essays over de joodse en hellenistische achtergrond van het vroege christendom*, 37–64. Utrechtse Theologische Reeks 2. Utrecht: Universiteitsdrukkerij, 1988. Originally published in *NedTT* 33 (1979): 27–51. This paper introduces the scholarship on longer Mark to scholars in the Netherlands. It includes a Dutch translation of the letter and the author's own thoughts.

Hurtado, Larry W. "Beyond the Interlude? Developments and Directions in New Testament Textual Criticism." In *Studies in the Early Text of the Gospels and Acts: The Papers of the First Birmingham Colloquium on the Textual Criticism of the New Testament*, ed. D.G.K. Taylor, 26–48. Birmingham: University of Birmingham Press, 1999. Hurtado addresses Helmut Koester's theory of the composition of the Gospel of Mark (pp. 40–43).

———. *Lord Jesus Christ: Devotion to Jesus in Earliest Christianity*. Grand Rapids: Eerdmans, 2003. LGM is discussed on pp. 314–15, 433–37.

Jackson, Howard M. "Why the Youth Shed His Cloak and Fled Naked: The Meaning and Purpose of Mark 14:51–52." *JBL* 116 (1997): 273–89. LGM is discussed on pp. 274–76.

Jaeger, Werner. *Early Christianity and Greek Paideia*. Cambridge, MA: Harvard University Press, Belknap Press, 1961. Jaeger offers longer Mark as an example of the Alexandrian fascination with esoteric writings (pp. 56–57).

Jakab, Attila. "Une lettre 'perdue' de Clément d'Alexandrie? Morton Smith et l'Évangile secret' de Marc." *Apocrypha* 10 (1999): 7–15. Jakab offers some uncommon (to my mind, peculiar) arguments against the authenticity of the letter.

Jenkins, Philip. *Hidden Gospels: How the Search for Jesus Lost Its Way*. New York: Oxford University Press, 2001. Jenkins draws attention to the 1940 evangelical novel *The Mystery of Mar Saba*, which describes the discovery of a forged ancient Christian document at Mar Saba (pp. 101–102).

Jennings, Theodore W., Jr. *The Man Jesus Loved: Homoerotic Narratives from the New Testament*. Cleveland: Pilgrim Press, 2003. Chap. 7 uses longer Mark as evidence that Jesus was gay.

Johnson, Sherman E. "The Mystery of St Mark." *History Today* 25 (1975): 89–97.

———. Response to Reginald Fuller. In *Longer Mark: Forgery, Interpolation, or Old Tradition?* ed. Wilhelm H. Wuellner, 26–28. Protocol of the Eighteenth Colloquy: 7 December 1975. Berkeley: Center for Hermeneutical Studies in Hellenistic and Modern Culture, 1976.

Johnson, Steven R. "The Identity and Significance of the *Neaniskos* in Mark." *FORUM* 8 (1992): 123–39.

Kaestli, Jean-Daniel. "L'Évangile secret de Marc. Une version longue de l'Évangile de Marc réservée aux chrétiens avancés dans l'Église d'Alexandrie?" and "Fragment d'une lettre de Clément d'Alexandrie au sujet de l'Évangile secret de Marc" (Kaestli's translation). In *Le Mystère apocryphe. Introduction à une littérature méconnue*, ed. J.-D. Kaestli and D. Marguerat, 85–106. Genève: Labor et Fides, 1995.

———. "Introduction de l'Évangile secret de Marc" and "L'Évangile secret de Marc." In *Écrits apocryphes chrétiens*. Vol. 1, ed. François Bovon and Pierre Geoltrain, 55–69. 2d ed. Paris: Gallimard, 1997.

Keenan, John P. *The Gospel of Mark: A Mahāyāna Reading*. Maryknoll, NY: Orbis Books, 1995. Keenan accepts Crossan's theory about longer Mark (pp. 359–61).

Kermode, Frank. *The Genesis of Secrecy: On the Interpretation of Narrative*. Cambridge: Harvard University Press, 1979. Chap. 3 presents the first literary-critical interpretation of LGM 1 and 2 within the context of Mark's gospel.

———. "The Quest for the Magical Jesus." Review of *Jesus the Magician*, by Morton Smith. *The New York Review of Books*. 26 October 1978.

Kirkland, J.R. "The Earliest Understanding of Jesus' Use of Parables: Mark IV 10–12 in Context." *NovT* 19 (1977): 1–21. Kirkland critiques Smith's interpretation of "the mystery of the kingdom of God" on p. 11 n. 50; see also p. 9 n. 43.

Klauck, Hans-Josef. *Apocryphal Gospels: An Introduction*. Trans. Brian McNeil. London and New York: T. and T. Clark, 2003. See pp. 32–35.

Klijn, A.F.J. "Jewish Christianity in Egypt." In *The Roots of Egyptian Christianity*, ed. Birger A. Pearson and James E. Goehring, 161–75. SAC. Philadelphia: Fortress, 1986. Klijn notes in passing how LGM accords with the literature of second-century Alexandrian Christianity.

———. *Jezus in de apocriefe evangeliën: buitenbijbelse beelden van Jezus*. Kampen: Uitgeverij Kok, 1999. A Dutch translation of the gospel excerpts is offered on pp. 96–98.

Knox, Sanka. "Expert Disputes 'Secret Gospel.'" *New York Times*. 31 December 1960, p. 7. This article briefly summarizes the report Pierson Parker gave on the stylistic traits of the letter's gospel quotations at the 1960 AAR-SBL meeting.

———. "A New Gospel Ascribed to Mark." *New York Times*. 30 December 1960, pp. 1, 17. This is a report on Morton Smith's formal announcement of his discovery.

Koester, Helmut. *Ancient Christian Gospels: Their History and Development*. Philadelphia: SCM Press, 1990.

———. "Apocryphal and Canonical Gospels." *HTR* 73 (1980): 105–30. A glimpse of Koester's thinking before he worked out his theory of longer Markan priority can be seen on p. 112 n. 24. See also Koester's review of Smith's two books on longer Mark and his response to Reginald Fuller.

———. "History and Development of Mark's Gospel (From Mark to *Secret Mark* and 'Canonical' Mark)." In *Colloquy on New Testament Studies: A Time for Reappraisal and Fresh Approaches*, ed. Bruce Corley, 35–57. Macon, GA: Mercer University Press, 1983. This essay rescued longer Mark from oblivion.

———. *Introduction to the New Testament.* Vol. 2, *History and Literature of Early Christianity.* Hermeneia—Foundations and Facets. Philadelphia: Fortress, 1982. LGM is discussed on pp. 168–69, 222–23.

———. Response to Reginald Fuller. In *Longer Mark: Forgery, Interpolation, or Old Tradition?* ed. Wilhelm H. Wuellner, 29–32. Protocol of the Eighteenth Colloquy: 7 December 1975. Berkeley: Center for Hermeneutical Studies in Hellenistic and Modern Culture, 1976.

———. "Seminar Dialogue with Helmut Koester." In *Colloquy on New Testament Studies: A Time for Reappraisal and Fresh Approaches*, ed. Bruce Corley, 59–85. Macon, GA: Mercer University Press, 1983. The missing text between pp. 77 and 78 is supplied in Robert Lee Williams, "Helmut Koester on Mark," *PSTJ* 40 (1987): 29–30.

———. "The Text of the Synoptic Gospels in the Second Century." In *Gospel Traditions in the Second Century: Origins, Recensions, Text, and Transmission*, ed. William L. Petersen, 19–37. Notre Dame, IN: University of Notre Dame Press, 1989.

Koester, Helmut, and Stephen J. Patterson. "The Secret Gospel of Mark" (draft translation, introduction and notes). In *The Complete Gospels: Annotated Scholars Version*, ed. Robert J. Miller, 402–405. Sonoma: Polebridge Press, 1992. Also published as "Secret Mark," *The Fourth R* 4:3 (1991): 14–16.

Kovacs, Judith L. "Divine Pedagogy and the Gnostic Teacher According to Clement of Alexandria." *JECS* 9 (2001): 3–25. On pp. 20–21 Kovacs uses the letter to illustrate Clement's use of "a pedagogical lie."

Kremer, Jacob. *Lazarus. Die Geschichte einer Auferstehung. Text, Wirkungsgeschichte und Botschaft von Joh 11, 1–46.* Stuttgart: Verlag Katholisches Bibelwerk, 1985. Kremer discusses LGM on pp. 116–17.

Kümmel, Werner Georg. "Ein Jahrzehnt Jesusforschung (1965–1975)." *TRu*, n.s., 40 (1975): 289–336. Kümmel discusses then dismisses longer Mark on pp. 299–303. An English translation of Kümmel's dismissive comments is provided by Hans-Martin Schenke in "The Mystery of the Gospel of Mark."

Le Boulluec, Alain. "La Lettre sur L'Évangile secret' de Marc et le *Quis dives salvetur?* de Clément d'Alexandrie." *Apocrypha* 7 (1996): 27–41. This paper suggests that longer Mark might have influenced Clement's reading of Mark 10:17–31.

Levin, Saul. "The Early History of Christianity, in Light of the 'Secret Gospel' of Mark." *ANRW* II 25:6 (1988): 4270–92.

Lilla, Salvatore R.C. *Clement of Alexandria: A Study in Christian Platonism and Gnosticism.* Oxford: Oxford University Press, 1971. Longer Mark is discussed on p. 56.

Lührmann, Dieter. "Das 'geheime Markusevangelium' bei Pseudo-Clemens." In his *Fragmente apokryph gewordener Evangelien in griechischer und lateinischer Sprache*, 182–85. Münchener theologische Studien 59. Marburg: N.G. Elwert, 2000. Lührmann offers a German translation and argues that the letter is by an imitator of Clement.

MacDonald, Dennis R. *The Homeric Epics and the Gospel of Mark*. New Haven: Yale University Press, 2000. MacDonald critiques the theory of longer Markan priority on p. 128.

Mack, Burton L. *A Myth of Innocence: Mark and Christian Origins*. Philadelphia: Fortress, 1988. Mack queries Helmut Koester's premise that the singular form of *mystērion* in Mark 4:11 would have a baptismal reference in the context of the parable chapter (p. 157 n. 16). Cf. the comments by Kirkland.

Mann, C.S. *Mark: A New Translation and Commentary*. AB 27. Garden City: Doubleday, 1986. Longer Mark is discussed in an appendix on pp. 423–30.

Marchadour, Alain. *Lazare: Histoire d'un récit, récits d'une histoire*. LD 132. Paris: Cerf, 1988. Marchadour is of the opinion that LGM 1 is a pastiche. See pp. 40, 58–60.

Marcus, Joel. *Mark 1–8: A New Translation with Introduction and Commentary*. AB 27. New York: Doubleday, 2000. See pp. 47–51.

Martin, Raymond A. "Syntax Criticism of Morton Smith's Letter of Clement and Secret Mark." Appendix 6 in his *Syntax Criticism of the Synoptic Gospels*. Studies in the Bible and Early Christianity 10. Lewiston: Edwin Mellen, 1987. Martin addresses the question of whether the letter and the gospel quotations display the characteristics of translation Greek.

Meeks, Wayne A. "*Hypomnēmata* from an Untamed Sceptic: A Response to George Kennedy." In *The Relationships among the Gospels: An Interdisciplinary Dialogue*, ed. William O. Walker, Jr., 157–72. Trinity University Monograph Series in Religion 5. San Antonio: Trinity University Press, 1978. Meeks notes that the tradition about Mark in the *Letter to Theodore* supports Kennedy's theory that Papias was referring, not to the creation of Mark's gospel, but to the note-taking that preceded it (pp. 167–68).

Meier, John P. *A Marginal Jew: Rethinking the Historical Jesus*. Vol. 1, *The Roots of the Problem and the Person*. New York: Doubleday, 1991. Longer Mark's irrelevance to historical Jesus research is argued on pp. 120–22, 151–52.

Mellon, John C. *Mark as Recovery Story: Alcoholism and the Rhetoric of Gospel Mystery*. Urbana and Chicago: University of Illinois Press, 1995. Mellon suggests that LGM 1b depicts the ancient equivalent of an Alcoholics Anonymous meeting (pp. 234–35).

Merkel, Helmut. "Appendix: The 'Secret Gospel' of Mark." In *New Testament Apocrypha*. Vol. 1, *Gospels and Related Writings*. 2d rev. ed. Ed. Wilhelm Schneemelcher. English translation ed. R. McL. Wilson, 106–109. Cambridge: James Clarke; Louisville: Westminster/John Knox Press, 1991.

———. "Auf den Spuren des Urmarkus? Ein neuer Fund und seine Beurteilung."
    *ZTK* 71 (1974): 123–44.

Metzger, Bruce M. *Reminiscences of an Octogenarian*. Peabody, MA: Hendrickson,
    1997. Metzger summarizes various scholars' reasons for doubting longer
    Mark's authenticity, without drawing a definite conclusion (pp. 128–32).

Meyer, Marvin W. "Clement of Alexandria, 'To Theodore.'" In *The Ancient Mys-
    teries: A Sourcebook. Sacred Texts of the Mystery Religions of the Ancient Mediter-
    ranean World*. Introduction by Marvin Meyer and English trans. Morton
    Smith, 231–34. San Francisco: Harper and Row, 1987.

———. "Mark, Secret Gospel of." In *The Anchor Bible Dictionary*. Vol. 4. Ed.
    David Noel Freedman et al., 558–59. New York: Doubleday, 1992.

———. "The Naked Youths in the Secret Gospel of Mark and the Villa of the Mys-
    teries at Pompeii." Paper presented at the SBL Pacific Coast Regional Meet-
    ing, Claremont, CA, March 2001.

———. *Secret Gospels: Essays on Thomas and the Secret Gospel of Mark*. Harrisburg:
    Trinity Press International, 2003. This book contains Meyer's four essays
    on longer Mark, which he revised slightly and updated.

———. "Taking Up the Cross and Following Jesus: Discipleship in the Gospel
    of Mark." *CTJ* 37 (2002): 230–38.

———. "The Youth in Secret Mark and the Beloved Disciple in John." In *Gospel
    Origins & Christian Beginnings: In Honor of James M. Robinson*, ed. J.E.
    Goehring et al., 94–105. Sonoma: Polebridge Press, 1990.

———. "The Youth in the *Secret Gospel of Mark*." *Semeia* 49 (1990): 129–53.

Miller, Robert J., ed. *The Complete Gospels: Annotated Scholars Version*. Sonoma:
    Polebridge Press, 1992.

Mullins, Terence Y. "Papias and Clement and Mark's Two Gospels." *VC* 30 (1976):
    189–92.

Munro, Winsome. "Women Disciples: Light from Secret Mark." *JFSR* 8 (1992):
    47–64.

Murgia, Charles E. "Secret Mark: Real or Fake?" In *Longer Mark: Forgery, Inter-
    polation, or Old Tradition?* ed. Wilhelm H. Wuellner, 35–40. Protocol of the
    Eighteenth Colloquy: 7 December 1975. Berkeley: Center for Hermeneut-
    ical Studies in Hellenistic and Modern Culture, 1976.

Musurillo, Herbert. "Morton Smith's Secret Gospel." *Thought* 48 (1973): 327–31.

Neirynck, Frans. "The Apocryphal Gospels and the Gospel of Mark." In *Evan-
    gelica II 1982–1991 Collected Essays by Frans Neirynck*, ed. Frans Van Seg-
    broeck, 715–72. BETL 99. Leuven: Leuven University Press; Uitgeverij
    Peeters, 1991. Originally published in *The New Testament in Early Christian-
    ity*, ed. Jean-Marie Sevrin, BETL 86 (Leuven: Leuven University Press,
    1989), 123–75.

———. "La fuite du jeune homme en Mc 14,51–52." In *Evangelica: Gospel Stud-
    ies–Études d'évangile. Collected Essays*, ed. Frans Van Segbroeck, 215–38.
    BETL 60. Leuven: Leuven University Press; Uitgeverij Peeters, 1982.

Neirynck argues that LGM is a pastiche (pp. 223–24). Originally published in *ETL* 55 (1979): 43–66.

———. "The Minor Agreements and Proto-Mark: A Response to H. Koester." In *Evangelica II 1982–1991 Collected Essays by Frans Neirynck*, ed. Frans Van Segbroeck, 59–73. BETL 99. Leuven: Leuven University Press; Uitgeverij Peeters, 1991. Originally published in *ETL* 67 (1991): 82–94.

Neirynck, Frans, et al. *Jean et les synoptiques: Examen critique de l'exégèse de M.-É. Boismard*. BETL 49. Leuven: Leuven University Press, 1979. Neirynck disputes Boismard's use of LGM 1:1 to reconstruct the opening of John's source for the raising of Lazarus (p. 207 n. 493).

Neusner, Jacob. *Are There Really Tannaitic Parallels to the Gospels? A Refutation of Morton Smith*. SFSHJ 80. Atlanta: Scholars Press, 1993.

———. Forward to *Memory and Manuscript: Oral Tradition and Written Transmission in Rabbinic Judaism and Early Christianity* with *Tradition and Transmission in Early Christianity*, by Birger Gerhardsson. 1961 and 1964. Reprint, Grand Rapids: Eerdmans, 1998.

———. *Rabbinic Literature and the New Testament: What We Cannot Show, We Do Not Know*. Valley Forge: Trinity Press International, 1994.

———. "Who Needs 'the Historical Jesus'? Two Elegant Works Rehabilitate a Field Disgraced by Fraud." In his *Ancient Judaism: Debates and Disputes: Third Series*, 171–84. SFSHJ 83. Atlanta: Scholars Press, 1993. Also published as "Who Needs 'the Historical Jesus'? An Essay-Review," *BBR* 4 (1994): 113–26.

Neusner, Jacob, and Noam M.M. Neusner. *The Price of Excellence: Universities in Conflict during the Cold War Era*. New York: Continuum, 1995.

Osborn, Eric F. "Clement of Alexandria: A Review of Research, 1958–1982." *SecCent* 3 (1983): 219–44. The *Letter to Theodore* is labelled a "pious forgery" on pp. 223–25.

Pagels, Elaine. Forward to *The Secret Gospel: The Discovery and Interpretation of the Secret Gospel According to Mark*, by Morton Smith. 1973. Reprint, Clearlake, CA: Dawn Horse Press, 1982.

Parker, David C. *The Living Text of the Gospels*. Cambridge: Cambridge University Press, 1997. Parker examines Helmut Koester's theory on pp. 103–10.

Parker, Pierson. "On Professor Morton Smith's Find at Mar-Saba." *AThR* 56 (1974): 53–57. This is the report Parker gave when Smith announced the discovery of the *Letter to Theodore*. See also Sanka Knox, "Expert Disputes 'Secret Gospel.'"

Peabody, David. "The Late Secondary Redaction of Mark's Gospel and the Griesbach Hypothesis: A Response to Helmut Koester." In *Colloquy on New Testament Studies: A Time for Reappraisal and Fresh Approaches*, ed. Bruce Corley, 87–132. Macon, GA: Mercer University Press, 1983.

Pearson, Birger A. "Earliest Christianity in Egypt: Some Observations." In *The Roots of Egyptian Christianity*, ed. Birger A. Pearson and James E. Goehring, 132–56. SAC. Philadelphia: Fortress, 1986.

————. Response to Reginald Fuller. In *Longer Mark: Forgery, Interpolation, or Old Tradition?* ed. Wilhelm H. Wuellner, 40. Protocol of the Eighteenth Colloquy: 7 December 1975. Berkeley: Center for Hermeneutical Studies in Hellenistic and Modern Culture, 1976.

Penna, Romano. "Homosexuality and the New Testament." In *Christian Anthropology and Homosexuality*, ed. Mario Agnes. L'Osservatore Romano Reprints 38. Vatican City: L'Osservatore Romano, 1997.

Pokorný, Petr. "Das Markusevangelium: Literarische und theologische Einleitung mit Forschungsbericht." *ANRW* II 25:3 (1985): 1969–2035. Longer Mark is discussed on pp. 2000–2001.

Price, Robert M. "Second Thoughts on the Secret Gospel." *BBR* 14 (2004): 127–32. Price offers baseless conjectures and distorted facts in order to cast suspicion on Smith.

Quesnell, Quentin. "The Mar Saba Clementine: A Question of Evidence." *CBQ* 37 (1975): 48–67.

————. "A Reply to Morton Smith." *CBQ* 38 (1976): 200–203.

Räisänen, Heikki. *The "Messianic Secret" in Mark*. Trans. Christopher Tuckett. Edinburgh: T. and T. Clark, 1990. Koester's theory is discussed on pp. 110–11 n. 116.

Rau, Eckhard. *Das geheime Markusevangelium: Ein Schriftfund voller Rätsel*. Neukirchen-Vluyn: Neukirchener Verl., 2003.

Rebell, Walter. *Neutestamentliche Apokryphen und Apostolische Väter*. München: Chr. Kaiser, 1992. For longer Mark, see pp. 120–24.

Riedweg, Christoph. *Mysterienterminologie bei Platon, Philon und Klemens von Alexandrien*. Berlin and New York: Walter de Gruyter, 1987. Longer Mark is discussed on p. 140 n. 43.

Robinson, John A.T. *Redating the New Testament*. London: SCM Press, 1976. Robinson considers the letter's tradition about Mark the evangelist on pp. 108–10.

Schenke, Hans-Martin. "The Function and Background of the Beloved Disciple in the Gospel of John." In *Nag Hammadi, Gnosticism, and Early Christianity*, ed. Charles W. Hedrick and Robert Hodgson, Jr., 111–25. Peabody, MA: Hendrickson, 1986. Schenke examines the similarities and differences between the young man in longer Mark and the beloved disciple in John (pp. 120–21).

————. "The Mystery of the Gospel of Mark." *SecCent* 4:2 (1984): 65–82.

Schildgen, Brenda Deen. *Power and Prejudice: The Reception of the Gospel of Mark*. Detroit: Wayne State University Press, 1999. Schildgen adopts Smith's position that longer Mark functioned as a baptismal lection (pp. 50–52).

Schmidt, Daryl. Response to Reginald Fuller. In *Longer Mark: Forgery, Interpolation, or Old Tradition?* ed. Wilhelm H. Wuellner, 41–45. Protocol of the Eighteenth Colloquy: 7 December 1975. Berkeley: Center for Hermeneutical Studies in Hellenistic and Modern Culture, 1976.

Scroggs, Robin, and Kent I. Groff. Addendum to "Baptism in Mark: Dying and Rising with Christ." *JBL* 92 (1973): 547–48. The authors note that their baptismal interpretation of Mark 14:51–52 finds support in LGM 1b.

Sellew, Philip. "*Secret Mark* and the History of Canonical Mark." In *The Future of Early Christianity: Essays in Honor of Helmut Koester*, ed. Birger A. Pearson, 242–57. Minneapolis: Fortress, 1991.

Shenker, Israel. "Jesus: New Ideas about His Powers." *The New York Times*. 3 June 1973, IV, p. 12. This article includes extremely brief excerpts from interviews with Morton Smith, James M. Robinson, and Hans Dieter Betz.

Shepherd, Massey H. Response to Reginald Fuller. In *Longer Mark: Forgery, Interpolation, or Old Tradition?* ed. Wilhelm H. Wuellner, 46–52. Protocol of the Eighteenth Colloquy: 7 December 1975. Berkeley: Center for Hermeneutical Studies in Hellenistic and Modern Culture, 1976.

Smith, D. Moody. *John*. ANTC. Nashville: Abingdon, 1999. Smith offers a few tentative remarks about longer Mark's relationship to the Gospel of John on pp. 216–17.

Smith, Mahlon H. <mahlonh.smith@worldnet.att.net>. REPLY: [XTalk] Secret Mark." In SYNOPTIC-L. <synoptic-l@bham.ac.uk>. 9 October 2000. Archived at: <http://groups.yahoo.com/group/synoptic-l/message/4935>.

Smith, Morton. *Clement of Alexandria and a Secret Gospel of Mark*. Cambridge: Harvard University Press, 1973.

———. "Clement of Alexandria and Secret Mark: The Score at the End of the First Decade." *HTR* 75 (1982): 449–61.

———. "Ἑλληνικὰ χειρόγραφα ἐν τῇ Μονῇ τοῦ ἁγίου Σάββα." Trans. Archimandrite Constantine Michaelides. *NEA ΣΙΟΝ* 52 (1960): 110–25, 245–56. This is Smith's report of the manuscripts he catalogued at Mar Saba.

———. "In Quest of Jesus." A Reply to "The Quest for the Magical Jesus," by Frank Kermode. *The New York Review of Books*. 21 December 1978. This is Smith's first rejoinder to Kermode in a debate over the significance of the linen sheet worn by the young man in Gethsemane. Smith's second reply is titled "Under the Sheet." The debate was sparked by Kermode's review of *Jesus the Magician*.

———. *Jesus the Magician*. San Francisco: Harper and Row, 1978. Longer Mark is referred to on pp. 133–35, 138, 203, 207, 210.

———. "Mark's 'Secret Gospel'?" *America* 129 (4 August 1973): 64–65.

———. "Merkel on the Longer Text of Mark." *ZTK* 72 (1975): 133–50.

———. "Monasteries and Their Manuscripts." *Archaeology* 13 (1960): 172–77.

———. "On the Authenticity of the Mar Saba Letter of Clement." *CBQ* 38 (1976): 196–99. This is Smith's reply to Quesnell's article in the same journal.

———. "On the Secret Gospel." Interview by Saniel Bonder. *The Laughing Man* 2:2 (1981).

————. Postscript to his *The Secret Gospel: The Discovery and Interpretation of the Secret Gospel According to Mark*. 1973. Reprint, Clearlake, CA: Dawn Horse Press, 1982.

————. "A Rare Sense of Προκόπτω and the Authenticity of the Letter of Clement of Alexandria." In *God's Christ and His People: Studies in Honour of Nils Alstrup Dahl*, ed. Jacob Jervell and Wayne A. Meeks, 261–64. Oslo: Universitetsforl, 1977.

————. "Regarding *Secret Mark*: A Response by Morton Smith to the Account by Per Beskow." *JBL* 103 (1984): 624. Fortress Press paid for advertising space in *JBL* in order to allow Smith to correct some of the misrepresentations of his scholarship on longer Mark contained in Per Beskow's book *Strange Tales about Jesus* (1983). The revised version of this book published in 1985 takes Smith's response into account.

————. Response to Reginald Fuller. In *Longer Mark: Forgery, Interpolation, or Old Tradition?* ed. Wilhelm H. Wuellner, 12–15. Protocol of the Eighteenth Colloquy: 7 December 1975. Berkeley: Center for Hermeneutical Studies in Hellenistic and Modern Culture, 1976.

————. *The Secret Gospel: The Discovery and Interpretation of the Secret Gospel According to Mark*. New York: Harper and Row, 1973.

————. "Two Ascended to Heaven—Jesus and the Author of 4Q491." In *Studies in the Cult of Yahweh*. Vol. 2, *New Testament, Early Christianity, and Magic*, ed. Shaye J.D. Cohen, 68–78. Leiden: E.J. Brill, 1996. Originally published in *Jesus and the Dead Sea Scrolls*, ed. J.H. Charlesworth (New York: Doubleday, 1992), 290–301.

————. "Under the Sheet." A Reply to Frank Kermode. *The New York Review of Books*. 8 February 1979.

Stählin, Otto, ed. *Clemens Alexandrinus*. Re-edited by Ludwig Früchtel. 4 vols. GCS. Berlin: Akademie-Verlag, 1972. The *Letter to Theodore* was added to Vol. 4, Part 1, *Literatur und Addenda zu Band III*, re-edited by Ursula Treu, xvii–xviii. 1980.

Stanton, Graham. *Gospel Truth? New Light on Jesus and the Gospels*. Valley Forge: Trinity Press International, 1995. Longer Mark is discussed on pp. 93–95.

Stewart, Desmond. *The Foreigner: A Search for the First-Century Jesus*. London: Hamish Hamilton, 1981. Stewart views LGM 1a as evidence that Lazarus was the beloved disciple and a man who practised mystery initiations; his raising is a misunderstanding of a ritual of simulated death whereby Lazarus spent "a certain period of time in the condition of a corpse" (pp. 108–12). Cf. Cyril C. Richardson's review of *CA* and *SG*.

Stroumsa, Guy G. "Comments on Charles Hedrick's Article: A Testimony." *JECS* 11 (2003): 147–53. Stroumsa recounts seeing the manuscript at Mar Saba in 1976 and quotes from an extensive letter correspondence between Morton Smith and Gershom Scholem. These letters reveal how Smith's thought and work progressed in the years following his discovery of the manuscript.

———. *Hidden Wisdom: Esoteric Traditions and the Roots of Christian Mysticism*. Studies in the History of Religions 70. Leiden: E.J. Brill, 1996. Stroumsa discusses LGM as a facet of the broader phenomenon of esoteric traditions in early Christianity (pp. 40–41, 71, 87, 112).

Talley, Thomas J. "The Entry into Jerusalem in Liturgical Tradition." In *With Ever Joyful Hearts: Essays on Liturgy and Music Honoring Marion J. Hatchett*, ed. J. Neil Alexander, 211–26. New York: Church, 1999. In this and the following items, Talley connects LGM 1 with the liturgical tradition and the origin of Lent.

———. "Liturgical Time in the Ancient Church: The State of Research." *Studia Liturgica* 14 (1982): 34–51. Also published in *Liturgisches Jahrbuch* 32 (1982): 25–45. This article is an English Translation of "Le Temps Liturgique dans l'Église ancienne," *La Maison-Dieu* 147 (1981): 29–60.

———. "The Origin of Lent at Alexandria." *Studia Patristica* 17 (1982): 594–612. Reprinted in *Between Memory and Hope: Readings on the Liturgical Year*, ed. Maxwell Johnson (Collegeville, MN: Liturgical Press, 2000), 183–206.

———. *The Origins of the Liturgical Year*. New York: Pueblo, 1986.

Wenham, John. *Redating Matthew, Mark and Luke: A Fresh Assault on the Synoptic Problem*. London: Hodder and Stoughton, 1991. Wenham discusses Clement's traditions about Mark on pp. 140–45.

Williams, Robert Lee. "Helmut Koester on Mark." *PSTJ* 40 (1987): 26–30.

Wills, Lawrence M. *The Quest of the Historical Gospel: Mark, John, and the Origins of the Gospel Genre*. London and New York: Routledge, 1997. Wills is interested in the way LGM 1 augments the sequence of parallel features in John and Mark. See pp. 98–102.

Wink, Walter. "Jesus as Magician." *USQR* 30 (1974): 3–14.

Wisse, Frederik. "The Nature and Purpose of Redactional Changes in Early Christian Texts: The Canonical Gospels." In *Gospel Traditions in the Second Century: Origins, Recensions, Text, and Transmission*, ed. William L. Petersen, 39–53. Christianity and Judaism in Antiquity 3. Notre Dame, IN: University of Notre Dame Press, 1989. This paper indirectly raises important challenges to the theory that canonical Mark emerged through the redaction of longer Mark in the mid-second century. See esp. pp. 43 n. 17; 52 n. 51.

Witherington, Ben, III. *The Jesus Quest: The Third Search for the Jew of Nazareth*. Downers Grove: InterVarsity Press, 1995. Longer Mark is summarily dismissed on pp. 80–81.

Wojciechowski, Michał. "Tajemna ewangelia Marka: Z Listu Klemensa z Aleksandrii do Teodora." *Studia Theologica Varsaviensia* 37(1999) nr 1, 41–52. An introduction to the *Letter to Theodore* with a Polish translation. Online at: <http://www.opoka.org.pl/biblioteka/T/TB/ew_marka_taj.html>

Wuellner, Wilhelm H., ed. *Longer Mark: Forgery, Interpolation, or Old Tradition?* Protocol of the Eighteenth Colloquy: 7 December 1975. Berkeley: Center for Hermeneutical Studies in Hellenistic and Modern Culture, 1976. This book contains numerous responses to Reginald Fuller's form-critical essay on longer Mark.

## Other Works

Achtemeier, Paul J. "Toward the Isolation of Pre-Markan Miracle Catenae." *JBL* 89 (1970): 265–91.

Aichele, George. *Jesus Framed*. Biblical Limits. London and New York: Routledge, 1996.

Aland, Kurt et al., eds. *The Greek New Testament*. 3d ed. corrected. Stuttgart: United Bible Societies, 1984.

Alexander, Patrick H. et al., eds. *The SBL Handbook of Style: For Ancient Near Eastern, Biblical, and Early Christian Studies*. Peabody, MA: Hendrickson, 1999.

Ashton, John. *Understanding the Fourth Gospel*. New York: Oxford University Press, 1993.

Bacon, B.W. *The Fourth Gospel in Research and Debate*. 2d ed. New Haven: Yale University Press, 1918.

Barnard, L.W. "St. Mark and Alexandria." *HTR* 57 (1964): 145–50.

Barrow, W.J. *Manuscripts and Documents: Their Deterioration and Restoration*. Charlottesville: University of Virginia Press, 1955.

Bassler, Jouette M. "The Parable of the Loaves." *JR* 66 (1986): 157–72.

Bauckham, Richard, ed. *The Gospel for All Christians: Rethinking the Gospel Audiences*. Grand Rapids: Eerdmans, 1998.

Beavis, Mary Ann. *Mark's Audience: The Literary and Social Setting of Mark 4.11–12*. JSNT Sup 33. Sheffield: JSOT Press, 1989.

Berg, Temma F. "Reading In/to Mark." *Semeia* 48 (1989): 187–206.

Best, Ernest. *Disciples and Discipleship: Studies in the Gospel According to Mark*. Edinburgh: T. and T. Clark, 1986.

———. *Following Jesus: Discipleship in the Gospel of Mark*. JSNT Sup 4. Sheffield: JSOT Press, 1981.

———. *The Temptation and the Passion: The Markan Soteriology*. SNTSMS 2. Cambridge: Cambridge University Press, 1965.

Bevan, Edwyn. "Note on Mark i 41 and John xi 33, 38." *JTS* 33 (1932): 186–88.

Bickermann, Elias. "Das leere Grab." *ZNW* 23 (1924): 281–92.

Bird, C.H. "Some Gar Clauses in St. Mark's Gospel." *JTS* 4 (1953): 171–87.

Bishop, Jonathan. "*Parabole* and *Parrhesia* in Mark." *Int* 40 (1986): 39–52.

Black, C. Clifton. "Was Mark a Roman Gospel?" *ExpTim* 105 (1993): 36–40.

Bockmuehl, Markus N.A. *Revelation and Mystery in Ancient Judaism and Pauline Christianity*. Tübingen: J.C.B. Mohr (Paul Siebeck), 1990.

Bode, Edward Lynn. *The First Easter Morning: The Gospel Accounts of the Women's Visit to the Tomb of Jesus*. Rome: Biblical Institute Press, 1970.

Bonner, Campbell. "Traces of Thaumaturgic Technique in the Miracles." *HTR* 20 (1927): 171–81.

Boobyer, G.H. "The Redaction of Mark IV.1–34." *NTS* 8 (1961–1962): 59–70.

Bornkamm, Günther. "Μυστήριον, μυέω." *TDNT* 4 (1942; reprint, 1967): 802–28.

Boucher, Madeleine. *The Mysterious Parable: A Literary Study*. CBQMS 6. Washington: Catholic Biblical Association of America, 1977.

Bouyer, Louis. "*Mystērion*." *La vie spirituelle, ascétique et mystique* supp. vol. 23 (1952): 397–412.

———. "'Mystique': Essai sur l'histoire d'un mot." *La vie spirituelle, ascétique et mystique* supp. vol. 9 (1949): 3–23.

Bowman, Glenn. "Christian Ideology and the Image of a Holy Land: The Place of Jerusalem Pilgrimage in the Various Christianities." In *Contesting the Sacred: The Anthropology of Christian Pilgrimage*, ed. John Eade and Michael J. Sallnow, 98–121. London: Routledge, 1991.

Broadhead, Edwin K. *Teaching with Authority: Miracles and Christology in the Gospel of Mark*. JSNT Sup 74. Sheffield: JSOT Press, 1992.

Brodie, Thomas L. *The Quest for the Origin of John's Gospel*. New York: Oxford University Press, 1993.

Brown, Raymond E. *The Gospel According to John*. 2 vols. 2d ed. Garden City: Doubleday, 1980.

———. "Incidents That Are Units in the Synoptic Gospels but Dispersed in St. John." *CBQ* 23 (1961): 143–60.

———. *The Semitic Background of the Term "Mystery" in the New Testament*. FBBS 21. Philadelphia: Fortress, 1968.

Brown, Schuyler. "Mk 3,21: A Forgotten Controversy?" In *Überlieferungsgeschichtliche Untersuchungen*, ed. Franz Paschke, 99–108. Berlin: Akademie-Verlag, 1981.

Brown, Scott G. "Mark 11:1–12:12: A Triple Intercalation?" *CBQ* 64 (2002): 78–89. Note the *erratum* in *CBQ* 64 (2002): 720, which rectifies a significant typesetting error.

Brownlee, William H. "Whence the Gospel of John?" In *John and Qumran*, ed. James H. Charlesworth, 166–94. London: Geoffrey Chapman, 1972.

Bruns, J. Edgar. *The Christian Buddhism of St. John: New Insights into the Fourth Gospel*. New York: Paulist Press, 1971.

Bultmann, Rudolf. *The History of the Synoptic Tradition*. Trans. John Marsh. New York: Harper and Row, 1963.

Burke, Alexander J., Jr. "The Raising of Lazarus and the Passion of Jesus in John 11 and 12: A Study of John's Literary Structure and His Narrative Theology." Ph.D. diss., Fordham University, 2002.

Burkett, Delbert. "Two Accounts of Lazarus' Resurrection in John 11." *NovT* 36 (1994): 209–32.

Burkill, T.A. *Mysterious Revelation: An Examination of the Philosophy of St. Mark's Gospel*. Ithaca, NY: Cornell University Press, 1963.

Butterworth, G.W. *Clement of Alexandria: "The Exhortation to the Greeks," "The Rich Man's Salvation," and the Fragment of an Address Entitled "To the Newly Baptized."* London: William Heinemann, 1919.

Caragounis, Chrys C. *The Ephesian* Mysterion: *Meaning and Content*. ConBNT 8. Uppsala: CWK Gleerup, 1977.

Carlston, Charles E. *The Parables of the Triple Tradition*. Philadelphia: Fortress, 1975.

Carrington, Philip. *According to Mark: A Running Commentary on the Oldest Gospel*. Cambridge: Cambridge University Press, 1960.

Catchpole, David. "The Fearful Silence of the Women at the Tomb: A Study in Markan Theology." *JTSA* 18 (1977): 3–10.

Cohen, Shaye J.D. Review of *Are There Really Tannaitic Parallels to the Gospels?* by Jacob Neusner. *JAOS* 116:1 (1996): 85–89.

Collins, A.Y. *The Beginning of the Gospel: Probings of Mark in Context*. Minneapolis: Fortress, 1992.

Crossan, John Dominic. "Empty Tomb and Absent Lord (Mark 16:1–8)." In *The Passion in Mark: Studies on Mark 14–16*, ed. Werner H. Kelber, 135–52. Philadelphia: Fortress, 1976.

———. "Historical Jesus as Risen Lord." In *The Jesus Controversy: Perspectives in Conflict*, ed. John Dominic Crossan, Luke Timothy Johnson, and Werner Kelber, 1–47. Harrisburg: Trinity Press International, 1999.

———. *Who Killed Jesus? Exposing the Roots of Anti-Semitism in the Gospel Story of the Death of Jesus*. 1995. Reprint, San Francisco: HarperSanFrancisco, 1996.

Cuvillier, Elian. *Le concept de ΠΑΡΑΒΟΛΗ dans le second évangile: Son arrière-plan littéraire, sa signification dans le cadre de la rédaction marcienne, son utilisation dans la tradition de Jésus*. Études Bibliques, n.s., 19. Paris: J. Gabalda, 1993.

Danker, Frederick W. "The Demonic Secret in Mark: A Reexamination of the Cry of Dereliction (15:34)." *ZNW* 61 (1970): 48–69.

Davison, James E. "Structural Similarities and Dissimilarities in the Thought of Clement of Alexandria and the Valentinians." *SecCent* 3 (1983): 201–17.

Dawson, David. *Allegorical Readers and Cultural Revision in Ancient Alexandria*. Berkley: University of California Press, 1992.

De Faye, Eugène. *Clément d'Alexandrie: Étude sur les rapports du christianisme et de la philosophie grecque au IIe siècle*. 2d ed. Paris: E. Leroux, 1906.

Des Places, Édouard. "Platon et la langue des mystères." In *Études Platoniciennes: 1929–1979*. EPRO 90. Leiden: E.J. Brill, 1981.

Dewey, Joanna. *Markan Public Debate: Literary Technique, Concentric Structure, and Theology in Mark 2:1–3:6*. SBLDS 48. Chico, CA: Scholars Press, 1980.

———. "Mark as Interwoven Tapestry: Forecasts and Echoes for a Listening Audience." *CBQ* 53 (1991): 221–36.

Dobschütz, Ernst von. "Zur Erzählerkunst des Markus." *ZNW* 27 (1928): 193–98.

Donahue, John R. *Are You the Christ? The Trial Narrative in the Gospel of Mark.* SBLDS 10. Missoula: Society of Biblical Literature, 1973.

———. *The Gospel in Parable: Metaphor, Narrative, and Theology in the Synoptic Gospels.* Philadelphia: Fortress, 1988.

Donahue, John R., and Daniel J. Harrington. *The Gospel of Mark.* SPS 2. Collegeville, MN: Liturgical Press, 2002.

Duling, Dennis C., and Norman Perrin. *The New Testament: An Introduction. Proclamation and Parenesis, Myth and History.* 3d. ed. Fort Worth: Harcourt Brace, 1994.

Echle, Harry A. "The Baptism of the Apostles: A Fragment of Clement of Alexandria's Lost Work Ὑποτυπώσεις in the *Pratum Spirituale* of John Moschus." *Traditio* 3 (1945): 365–68.

———. "Sacramental Initiation as a Christian Mystery-Initiation According to Clement of Alexandria." In *Vom christlichen Mysterium: Gesammelte Arbeiten zum Gedächtnis von Odo Casel OSB,* ed. Anton Mayer, Johannes Quasten, and Burkhard Neunheuser, 54–65. Düsseldorf: Patoms-Verlag, 1951.

Edwards, James R. "Markan Sandwiches: The Significance of Interpolations in Markan Narratives." *NovT* 31 (1989): 193–216.

Ehrman, Bart D. "A Leper in the Hands of an Angry Jesus." In *New Testament Greek and Exegesis: Essays in Honor of Gerald F. Hawthorne,* ed. Amy M. Donaldson and Timothy B. Sailors, 77–98. Grand Rapids: Eerdmans, 2003.

———. *The Orthodox Corruption of Scripture: The Effect of Early Christological Controversies on the Text of the New Testament.* New York: Oxford University Press, 1993.

Evans, Christopher Francis. *Resurrection and the New Testament.* SBT 2/12. London: SCM Press, 1970.

Ferguson, John. *Clement of Alexandria.* TWAS 289. New York: Twayne, 1974.

———, trans. *Clement of Alexandria: Stromateis, Books One to Three.* Washington: Catholic University of America Press, 1991.

Finn, Thomas M. *Early Christian Baptism and the Catechumenate: Italy, North Africa, and Egypt.* Message of the Fathers of the Church 6. Collegeville, MN: Liturgical Press, 1992.

Fleddermann, Harry. "The Flight of a Naked Young Man (Mark 14:51–52)." *CBQ* 41 (1979): 412–18.

Folkemer, Lawrence D. "A Study of the Catechumenate." In *Conversion, Catechumenate, and Baptism in the Early Church,* ed. Everett Ferguson et al., 244–65. Studies in Early Christianity 11. New York: Garland, 1993.

Fortin, E.L. "Clement of Alexandria and the Esoteric Tradition." In *Studia Patristica.* Vol. 9, part 3, ed. F.L. Cross, 41–56. TU 94. Berlin: Akademie-Verlag, 1966.

Fowler, Robert M. *Let the Reader Understand: Reader-Response Criticism and the Gospel of Mark*. Minneapolis: Fortress, 1991.

———. "Reader-Response Criticism: Figuring Mark's Reader." In *Mark and Method: New Approaches in Biblical Studies*, ed. Janice Capel Anderson and Stephen D. Moore, 50–83. Minneapolis: Fortress, 1992.

Fuller, Reginald H. *The Formation of the Resurrection Narratives*. New York: Macmillan, 1971.

Gardner-Smith, Percival. *Saint John and the Synoptic Gospels*. Cambridge: Cambridge University Press, 1938.

Gilliard, Frank D. "More Silent Reading in Antiquity: *NON OMNE VERBUM SONABAT*." *JBL* 112 (1993): 689–96.

Goodspeed, Edgar J. *Strange New Gospels*. Chicago: University of Chicago Press, 1931.

Gourgues, Michel. "À propos du symbolisme christologique et baptismal de Marc 16.5." *NTS* 27 (1981): 672–78.

Green, Joel B. *The Death of Jesus: Tradition and Interpretation in the Passion Narrative*. Tübingen: J.C.B. Mohr (Paul Siebeck), 1988.

Gryson, Roger. "À propos du témoignage de Papias sur Matthieu: Le sens du mot λόγιον chez les Pères du second siècle." *ETL* 41 (1965): 530–47.

Guelich, Robert A. *Mark 1–8:26*. WBC 34. Dallas: Word Books, 1989.

Gundry, Robert H. *Mark: A Commentary on His Apology for the Cross*. Grand Rapids: Eerdmans, 1993.

Hamilton, J.D.B. "The Church and the Language of Mystery: The First Four Centuries." *ETL* 53 (1977): 479–94.

Hamilton, Neill Q. "Resurrection Tradition and the Composition of Mark." *JBL* 84 (1965): 415–21.

Harvey, A.E. "The Use of Mystery Language in the Bible." *JTS*, n.s., 31 (1980): 320–36.

Hedrick, Charles W., and Paul A. Mirecki. *Gospel of the Savior: A New Ancient Gospel*. Santa Rosa, CA: Polebridge Press, 1999.

Hengel, Martin. *Studies in the Gospel of Mark*. London: SCM Press, 1985.

Hoek, Annewies van den. "The 'Catechetical' School of Early Christian Alexandria and Its Philonic Heritage." *HTR* 90 (1997): 59–87.

———. *Clement of Alexandria and His Use of Philo in the* Stromateis: *An Early Christian Reshaping of a Jewish Model*. Leiden: E.J. Brill, 1988.

———. "How Alexandrian Was Clement of Alexandria? Reflections on Clement and His Alexandrian Background." *HeyJ* 31 (1990): 179–94.

Hooker, Morna D. *The Gospel According to St Mark*. BNTC. London: A. and C. Black, 1991.

Hort, F.J.A., and J.B. Mayor. *Clement of Alexandria* Miscellanies *Book VII: The Greek Text with Introduction, Translation, Notes, Dissertations and Indices*. London: Macmillan, 1902.

Hunter, James Hogg. *The Mystery of Mar Saba*. New York: Evangelical, 1940.

Jenkins, A.K. "Young Man or Angel?" *ExpTim* 94 (1983): 237–40.

Johnson, Earl S. "Mark VIII. 22–26: The Blind Man from Bethsaida." *NTS* 25 (1979): 370–83.

Johnson, Sherman E. *A Commentary on the Gospel According to St. Mark.* BNTC. London: A. and C. Black, 1960.

Juel, Donald H. *A Master of Surprise: Mark Interpreted.* Minneapolis: Fortress, 1994.

Kaye, John. *Some Account of the Writings and Opinions of Clement of Alexandria.* 1835. Reprint, London: Griffith, Farran, Okeden, and Welsh, n.d.

Kee, Howard Clark. *Community of the New Age: Studies in Mark's Gospel.* Philadelphia: Westminster, 1977.

———. "The Terminology of Mark's Exorcism Stories." *NTS* 14 (1968): 232–46.

Kelber, Werner H. *The Kingdom in Mark: A New Place and a New Time.* Philadelphia: Fortress, 1974.

———. *Mark's Story of Jesus.* Philadelphia: Fortress, 1979.

———. *The Oral and the Written Gospel: The Hermeneutics of Speaking and Writing in the Synoptic Tradition, Mark, Paul, and Q.* Philadelphia: Fortress, 1983.

Khouri, Rami. "Where John Baptized: Bethany beyond the Jordon." *BAR* 31:1 (2005): 34–43.

Klostermann, Erich. *Das Markus-Evangelium.* Tübingen: J.C.B. Mohr (Paul Siebeck), 1950.

Koester, Helmut. "From the Kerygma-Gospel to Written Gospels." *NTS* 35 (1989): 361–81.

Kürzinger, Josef. "Die Aussage des Papias von Hierapolis zur literarischen Form des Markusevangeliums." *BZ* 21 (1977): 245–64.

———. "Das Papiaszeugnis und die Erstgestalt des Matthäusevangeliums." *BZ* 4 (1960): 19–38.

Lambrecht, J. "Redaction and Theology in Mk., IV." In *L'Évangile selon Marc: Tradition et rédaction,* ed. M. Sabbe, 269–308. BETL 34. 2d ed. Leuven: Leuven University Press, 1988.

Lee, G.M. "Eusebius on St. Mark and the Beginnings of Christianity in Egypt." In *Studia Patristica XII,* ed. Elizabeth A. Livingston, 422–31. TU 115. Berlin: Akademie-Verlag, 1975.

Lieberman, Saul. "A Tragedy or a Comedy?" *JAOS* 104 (1984): 315–19.

Lincoln, Andrew T. "The Promise and the Failure: Mark 16:7, 8." *JBL* 108 (1989): 283–300.

Lindars, Barnabas. *The Gospel of John.* NCB. London: Oliphants, 1972.

———. "Rebuking the Spirit: A New Analysis of the Lazarus Story of John 11." *NTS* 38 (1992): 89–104.

Macgregor, G.H.C. *The Gospel of John.* MNTC. London: Hodder and Stoughton, 1928.

Malbon, Elizabeth Struthers. "Echoes and Foreshadowings in Mark 4–8: Reading and Rereading." *JBL* 11 (1993): 211–30.

————. "How Does the Story Mean?" In *Mark and Method: New Approaches in Biblical Studies*, ed. Janice Capel Anderson and Stephen D. Moore, 23–49. Minneapolis: Fortress, 1992.

————. "Mark: Myth and Parable." *BTB* 14 (1986): 8–17.

————. *Narrative Space and Mythic Meaning in Mark*. San Francisco: Harper and Row, 1986.

Marcus, Joel. *The Mystery of the Kingdom of God*. SBLDS 90. Atlanta: Scholars Press, 1986.

————. *The Way of the Lord: Christological Exegesis of the Old Testament in the Gospel of Mark*. Louisville: Westminster/John Knox Press, 1992.

Marsh, H.G. "The Use of Μυστήριον in the Writings of Clement of Alexandria with Special Reference to His Sacramental Doctrine." *JTS* 37 (1936): 64–80.

Marshall, Christopher D. *Faith as a Theme in Mark's Narrative*. SNTSMS 64. Cambridge: Cambridge University Press, 1989.

Marxsen, Willi. *Mark the Evangelist: Studies on the Redaction History of the Gospel*. Trans. James Boyce et al. Nashville: Abingdon, 1969. Originally published in German in 1956.

Matera, Frank J. "'He Saved Others; He Cannot Save Himself': A Literary-Critical Perspective on the Markan Miracles." *Int* 47 (1993): 15–26.

————. "The Incomprehension of the Disciples and Peter's Confession (Mark 6,14–8,30)." *Bib* 70 (1989): 153–72.

————. "The Prologue as the Interpretative Key to Mark's Gospel." *JSNT* 34 (1988): 3–20.

McCue, James F. "Orthodoxy and Heresy: Walter Bauer and the Valentinians." *VC* 33 (1979): 118–30.

McGuckin, John Anthony. *The Transfiguration of Christ in Scripture and Tradition*. Studies in the Bible and Early Christianity 9. Lewiston and Queenston: Edwin Mellen, 1986.

Meacham, Tirzah. "Neusner's *Talmud of the Land of Israel*." *JQR* 77 (1986): 74–81.

Meagher, John C. *Clumsy Construction in Mark's Gospel: A Critique of Form- and Redaktionsgeschichte*. Toronto Studies in Theology 3. New York: Edwin Mellen, 1979.

Méhat, André. "Clément d'Alexandrie et les sens de l'Écriture: *Ier Stromate*, 176, I et 179, 3." In *Epektasis: Mélanges patristiques offerts au Cardinal Jean Daniélou*, ed. J. Fontaine and C. Kannengiesser, 355–65. Paris: Beauchesne, 1972.

Meye, Robert P. *Jesus and the Twelve: Discipleship and Revelation in Mark's Gospel*. Grand Rapids: Eerdmans, 1968.

Michaelis, Wilhelm. "Λευκός, λευκαίνω." *TDNT* 4 (1967): 241–50.

Minear, Paul S. *The Gospel According to Mark*. The Layman's Bible Commentary 17. Richmond: John Knox Press, 1962.

Molland, Einar. *The Conception of the Gospel in the Alexandrian Theology*. Oslo: 1 Kommisjon hos Jacob Dybwad, 1938.

Mortley, Raoul. *Connaissance religieuse et herméneutique chez Clément d'Alexandrie*. Leiden: E.J. Brill, 1973.

Motyer, S. "The Rending of the Veil: A Markan Pentecost?" *NTS* 33 (1987): 155–57.

Mullins, Terence Y. "Papias on Mark's Gospel." *VC* 14 (1960): 216–24.

Myers, Ched. *Binding the Strong Man: A Political Reading of Mark's Story of Jesus*. Maryknoll, NY: Orbis Books, 1988.

Neirynck, Frans. *Duality in Mark: Contributions to the Study of the Markan Redaction*. Revised Edition with Supplementary Notes. BETL 31. Leuven: Leuven University Press, 1988.

Neusner, Jacob. "New Problems, New Solutions. Current Events in Rabbinic Studies." In his *The Academic Study of Judaism: Essays and Reflections, Third Series: Three Contexts of Jewish Learning*, 82–105. New York: Ktav, 1980.

———, ed. *The Talmud of the Land of Israel: A Preliminary Translation and Explanation*. 35 vols. Chicago: University of Chicago Press, 1982.

Nickel, Joel. *Pen, Ink, and Evidence: A Study of Writing and Writing Materials for the Penman, Collector, and Document Detective*. Lexington: University Press of Kentucky, 1990.

Nineham, Dennis Eric. *The Gospel of St. Mark*. 1963. Reprint, Baltimore: Penguin Books, 1967.

Nock, A.D. "Hellenistic Mysteries and Christian Sacraments." *Mnemosyne*, 4th ser., vol. 5 (1952): 177–213.

Orchard, B. "Mark and the Fusion of Traditions." In *The Four Gospels 1992: Festschrift Frans Neirynck*. Vol. 2, ed. Frans Van Segbroeck et al., 779–800. BETL 100. Leuven: Leuven University Press, 1992.

Osborn, Eric F. *The Philosophy of Clement of Alexandria*. Cambridge: Cambridge University Press, 1957.

———. "Teaching and Writing in the First Chapter of the *Stromateis* of Clement of Alexandria." *JTS*, n.s., 10 (1959): 335–44.

Osburn, Carroll D. "The Historical Present in Mark as a Text-Critical Criterion." *Bib* 64 (1983): 486–500.

Patten, Priscilla C. "The Form and Function of Parables in Select Apocalyptic Literature and Their Significance for Parables in the Gospel of Mark." *NTS* 29 (1983): 246–58.

———. "Parable and Secret in the Gospel of Mark in the Light of Select Apocalyptic Literature." *The Drew Gateway* 47:2–3 (1976–1977): 135–36.

Peabody, David. *Mark as Composer*. New Gospel Studies 1. Macon, GA: Mercer University Press, 1987.

Peabody, David, Allan J. McNicol, and Lamar Cope, eds. *One Gospel from Two: Mark's Use of Matthew and Luke*. Harrisburg: Trinity Press International, 2002.

Perkins, Pheme. *Resurrection: New Testament Witness and Contemporary Reflection*. Garden City: Doubleday, 1984.

Perrin, Norman. "The Interpretation of the Gospel of Mark." *Int* 30 (1976): 115–24.

Petersen, Dwight N. *The Origins of Mark: The Markan Community in Current Debate*. Biblical Interpretation Series 48. Leiden: E.J. Brill, 2000.

Petersen, Norman R. "The Composition of Mark 4:1–8:26." *HTR* 73 (1980): 185–217.

Proctor, Mark Alan. "The Western Text of Mark 1:41: A Case for the Angry Jesus." Ph.D. diss., Baylor University, 1999.

Pryke, E.J. *Redactional Style in the Marcan Gospel: A Study of Syntax and Vocabulary as Guides to Redaction in Mark*. Cambridge: Cambridge University Press, 1978.

Quesnell, Quentin. *The Mind of Mark: Interpretation and Method through the Exegesis of Mark 6,52*. Rome: Pontifical Biblical Institute, 1969.

Rhoads, David, and Donald Michie. *Mark as Story*. Philadelphia: Fortress, 1982.

Riesner, Rainer. "Bethany beyond the Jordan (John 1:28): Topography, Theology and History in the Fourth Gospel." *Tyndale Bulletin* 38 (1987): 34–43.

Robbins, Vernon K. "Mark as a Jewish Document." In his *New Boundaries in Old Territory: Form and Social Rhetoric in Mark*. Emory Studies in Early Christianity 3. New York: Peter Lang, 1994.

Roberts, Colin H. *Manuscript, Society and Belief in Early Christian Egypt*. The Schweich Lectures of the British Academy, 1977. London: Oxford University Press, 1979.

Robinson, James M. *The Problem of History in Mark and Other Marcan Studies*. Philadelphia: Fortress, 1982.

Robinson, James M., Paul Hoffmann, and John S. Kloppenborg, eds. *The Critical Edition of Q*. Leuven: Peeters, 2000.

Rosenblum, Joseph. *Practice to Deceive: The Amazing Stories of Literary Forgery's Most Notorious Practitioners*. New Castle, DE: Oak Knoll Press, 2000.

Sandmel, Samuel. "Parallelomania." *JBL* 81 (1962): 1–13.

Satran, David. "Pedagogy and Deceit in the Alexandrian Theological Tradition." In *Origeniana Quinta*, ed. Robert J. Daly, 119–24. Leuven: Leuven University Press, 1992.

Schneck, Richard. *Isaiah in the Gospel of Mark, I–VIII*. Bibal Dissertation Series 1. Vallejo, CA: Bibal Press, 1994.

Schneemelcher, Wilhelm, ed. *New Testament Apocrypha*. Vol. 1, *Gospels and Related Writings*. 2d rev. ed. English translation ed. R. McL. Wilson. Cambridge: James Clarke; Louisville: Westminster/John Knox Press, 1991.

Schüssler Fiorenza, Elisabeth. *In Memory of Her: A Feminist Theological Reconstruction of Christian Origins*. Tenth Anniversary Edition. New York: Crossroad, 1994.

Schweizer, Eduard. *The Good News According to Mark*. Translated by Donald H. Madvig. Richmond: John Knox Press, 1970.

———. "Mark's Theological Achievement." In *The Interpretation of Mark*, ed. William R. Telford, 63–87. Studies in New Testament Interpretation. 2d ed. Edinburgh: T. and T. Clark, 1995.

———. "The Question of the Messianic Secret in Mark." In *The Messianic Secret*, ed. and trans. Christopher M. Tuckett, 65–74. IRT 1. Philadelphia: Fortress; London: SPCK, 1983.

Scroggs, Robin, and Kent I. Groff. "Baptism in Mark: Dying and Rising with Christ." *JBL* 92 (1973): 531–48.

Shanks, Hershel. "Annual Meetings Offer Intellectual Bazaar and Moments of High Drama." *BAR* 11:2 (1985): 14–16.

———. "Neusner Decides Not to Sue." *BAR* 11:4 (1985): 8.

———. "Neusner Joins Ranks of Superman." *BAR* 11:3 (1985): 8.

———. "The Neusner Phenomenon—Personality and Substance." *BAR* 11:6 (1985): 60–69.

Shepherd, Tom. "The Definition and Function of Markan Intercalation as Illustrated in a Narrative Analysis of Six Passages." Ph.D. diss., Andrews University, 1991.

———. "Intercalation in Mark and the Synoptic Problem." In *Society of Biblical Literature 1991 Seminar Papers*, ed. Eugene H. Lovering, Jr., 687–97. SBLSP 30. Missoula: Scholars Press, 1991.

———. "The Narrative Function of Markan Intercalation." *NTS* 41 (1995): 522–40.

Smith, D. Moody. *John among the Gospels*. 2d ed. Columbia, SC: University of South Carolina Press, 2001.

Smith, Morton. *The Aretalogy Used by Mark*. Protocol of the Sixth Colloquy, 12 April 1973. Ed. Wilhelm H. Wuellner. Berkeley: Center for Hermeneutical Studies in Hellenistic and Modern Culture, 1975.

———. "Ascent to the Heavens and the Beginning of Christianity." In *Studies in the Cult of Yahweh*. Vol. 2, *New Testament, Early Christianity, and Magic*, ed. Shaye J.D. Cohen, 47–67. Leiden: E.J. Brill, 1996. Originally published in *Eranos* 50 (1981): 403–29.

———. "Comments on Taylor's Commentary on Mark." *HTR* 48 (1955): 21–64.

———. "Jesus' Attitude towards the Law." In *Papers of the Fourth World Congress of Jewish Studies*. Vol. 1, ed. World Congress of Jewish Studies, 241–44. Jerusalem: World Union of Jewish Studies, 1967.

———. "The Jewish Elements in the Gospels." *JBR* 24 (1956): 90–96.

———. Letter to editor. *BAR* 11:3 (1985): 18.

———. "Mark 6:32–15:47 and John 6:1–19:42." In *Society of Biblical Literature 1978 Seminar Papers*. Vol. 2, ed. Paul J. Achtemeier, 281–87. Missoula: Scholars Press, 1978.

———. "The Origin and History of the Transfiguration Story." *USQR* 36 (1980): 39–44.

———. "Palestinian Judaism in the First Century." In *Studies in the Cult of Yahweh*. Vol. 1, *Studies in Historical Method, Ancient Israel, Ancient Judaism*, ed. Shaye J.D. Cohen, 104–15. Leiden: E.J. Brill, 1996. Originally published in *Israel: Its Role in Civilization*, ed. M. Davis (New York: Harper and Brothers, 1956), 67–81.

———. "Pauline Worship as Seen by Pagans." *HTR* 73 (1980): 241–50.

———. "Paul's Arguments as Evidence of the Christianity from Which He Diverged." *HTR* 79 (1986): 254–60.

———. "The Reason for the Persecution of Paul and the Obscurity of Acts." In *Studies in the Cult of Yahweh*. Vol. 2, *New Testament, Early Christianity, and Magic*, ed. Shaye J.D. Cohen, 87–94. Leiden: E.J. Brill, 1996. Originally published in *Studies in Mysticism and Religion Presented to G.G. Scholem on His Seventieth Birthday*, ed. E.E. Urbach, R.J. Zwi Werblowsky, and C. Wirszubski (Jerusalem: Magnes Press, 1967), 261–68.

———. Review of *Development of a Legend*, by Jacob Neusner. *Conservative Judaism* 26:4 (1970): 76–77.

———. Review of *A History of the Jews in Babylonia I*, by Jacob Neusner. *JAAR* 35 (1967): 180–82.

———. Review of *A History of the Jews in Babylonia III, IV, V*, by Jacob Neusner. *JBL* 89 (1970): 491–92.

———. "Salvation in the Gospels, Paul, and the Magical Papyri." In *Studies in the Cult of Yahweh*. Vol. 2, *New Testament, Early Christianity, and Magic*, ed. Shaye J.D. Cohen, 130–39. Leiden: E.J. Brill, 1996. Originally published in *Helios* 13 (1986): 63–74.

———. "Transformation by Burial (I Cor 15.35–49; Rom 6.3–5 and 8.9–11)." *Eranos* 52 (1983): 87–112.

Standaert, Benoît. *L'Évangile selon Marc: Composition et genre littéraire*. Nijmegen: Studentenpers, 1978.

Steely, John E. *Gnosis: The Doctrine of Christian Perfection in the Writings of Clement of Alexandria*. Louisville: The Microcard Foundation for the American Theological Library Association, 1954.

Stein, Robert H. "The Cleansing of the Temple in Mark (11:15–19)." In his *Gospels and Tradition: Studies on Redaction Criticism of the Synoptic Gospels*, 121–33. Grand Rapids: Baker Book House, 1991.

———. *The Proper Methodology for Ascertaining a Marcan Redaktionsgeschichte*. Ann Arbor: University Microfilms, 1968.

Story, Cullen I.K. "The Mental Attitude of Jesus at Bethany: John 11. 33, 38." *NTS* 37 (1991): 51–66.

Sudilovsky, Judith. "Site of Jesus' Baptism Found—Again: Is It the Bible's 'Bethany beyond the Jordan'?" *BAR* 25:3 (1999): 14–15.

Tate, W. Randolph. *Reading Mark from the Outside: Eco and Iser Leave Their Marks*. San Francisco: International Scholars Publications, 1994.

Taylor, Vincent. *The Gospel According to St. Mark*. 2d ed. London: Macmillan, 1966. Originally published in 1952.

Telford, William R. *The Barren Temple and the Withered Tree: A Redaction-Critical Analysis of the Cursing of the Fig-Tree Pericope in Mark's Gospel and Its Relation to the Clearing of the Temple Tradition*. JSNT Sup 1. Sheffield: JSOT Press, 1980.

———, ed. *The Interpretation of Mark*. Studies in New Testament Interpretation. 2d ed. Edinburgh: T. and T. Clark, 1995.

———. *Mark*. NTG. Sheffield: Sheffield Academic Press, 1995.

Tolbert, Mary Ann. *Sowing the Gospel: Mark's World in Literary-Historical Perspective*. Minneapolis: Fortress, 1989.

Trocmé, Etienne. *The Formation of the Gospel According to Mark*. Trans. Pamela Gaughan. Philadelphia: Westminster, 1975. Originally published as *La formation de l'Évangile selon Marc* (Paris: PUF, 1963).

Tuckett, Christopher M. "Mark's Concerns in the Parables Chapter (Mark 4,1–34)." *Bib* 69 (1988): 1–26.

Turner, C.H. "Western Readings in the Second Half of St Mark's Gospel." *JTS* 29 (1927): 1–16.

Twelftree, Graham H. "Exorcisms in the Fourth Gospel and the Synoptics." In *Jesus in Johannine Tradition*, ed. Robert T. Fortna and Tom Thatcher, 135–43. Louisville: Westminster/John Knox Press, 2001.

Ulansey, David. "The Heavenly Veil Torn: Mark's Cosmic *Inclusio*." *JBL* 110 (1991): 123–25.

Vaage, Leif. "Bird-watching at the Baptism of Jesus: Early Christian Mythmaking in Mark 1:9–11." In *Reimagining Christian Origins: A Colloquium Honoring Burton L. Mack*, ed. Elizabeth A. Castelli and Hal Taussig, 280–94. Valley Forge: Trinity Press International, 1996.

Van Iersel, B.M.F. *Mark: A Reader-Response Commentary*. Trans. W.H. Bisscheroux. JSNT Sup 164. Sheffield: Sheffield Academic Press, 1998.

———. "The Reader of Mark as Operator of a System of Connotations." *Semeia* 48 (1989): 83–114.

———. "'To Galilee' or 'in Galilee' in Mark 14,28 and 16,7?" *ETL* 58 (1982): 365–70.

Van Oyen, G. "Intercalation and Irony in the Gospel of Mark." In *The Four Gospels 1992: Festschrift Frans Neirynck*. Vol. 2, ed. Frans Van Segbroeck et al., 949–74. BETL 100. Leuven: Leuven University Press, 1992.

Via, Dan O., Jr. "Mark 10:32–52—A Structural, Literary and Theological Interpretation." *Society of Biblical Literature 1979 Seminar Papers*. Vol. 2, ed. Paul J. Achtemeier, 187–203. SBLSP 17. Missoula: Scholars Press, 1979.

Vorster, Willem S. "Meaning and Reference: The Parables of Jesus in Mark 4." In Bernard C. Lategan and Willem S. Vorster, *Text and Reality: Aspects of Reference in Biblical Texts*. 27–65. Philadelphia: Fortress; Atlanta: Scholars Press, 1985.

Waetjen, Herman C. "The Ending of Mark and the Gospel's Shift in Eschatology." *ASTI* 4 (1965): 114–31.

———. *A Reordering of Power: A Socio-Political Reading of Mark's Gospel*. Minneapolis: Fortress, 1989.

Wagner, Walter. "Another Look at the Literary Problem in Clement of Alexandria's Major Writings." In *Studies in Early Christianity*. Vol. 2, *Literature of the Early Church*, ed. Everett Ferguson et al., 165–74. New York and London: Garland, 1993. Originally published in *Church History* 37 (1968): 251–60.

Waheeb, Mohammad. "Ancient Water System." *It's Time: Baptism 2000*. <http://www.elmaghtas.com/ancient_water/ancient_water.html>.

Warfield, Benjamin. "The Oracles of God." *Presbyterian and Reformed Review* 11 (1900): 217–60.

Watts, Rikki E. *Isaiah's New Exodus and Mark*. WUNT, 2d ser., 88. Tübingen: Mohr Siebeck, 1997.

Wedderburn, A.J.M. *Baptism and Resurrection: Studies in Pauline Theology against Its Graeco-Roman Background*. WUNT 44. Tübingen: J.C.B. Mohr (Paul Siebeck), 1987.

Weeden, Theodore J. *Mark—Traditions in Conflict*. Philadelphia: Fortress, 1971.

Wilken, Robert L. "Alexandria: A School for Training in Virtue." In *Schools of Thought in the Christian Tradition*, ed. Patrick Henry, 15–30. Philadelphia: Fortress, 1984.

Wilkinson, John. *Jerusalem Pilgrims before the Crusades*. Warminster, UK: Aris and Phillips, 2002.

Williams, James G. *Gospel against Parable: Mark's Language of Mystery*. Sheffield: Almond Press, 1985.

Williams, Joel F. "Discipleship and Minor Characters in Mark's Gospel." *BSac* 153 (1996): 332–43.

———. *Other Followers of Jesus: Minor Characters as Major Figures in Mark's Gospel*. JSNT Sup 102. Sheffield: JSOT Press, 1994.

Wilson, William. *Clement of Alexandria*. ANCL 4, 12, 22, 24. Edinburgh: T. and T. Clark, 1867–1872. Reprinted in ANF 2. Buffalo: Christian Literature Publishing, 1887.

Witherington, Ben, III. *The Gospel of Mark: A Socio-Rhetorical Commentary*. Grand Rapids: Eerdmans, 2001.

Wortley, John, trans. *The Spiritual Meadow of John Moschos*. Cistercian Studies Series 139. Kalamazoo, MI: Cistercian Publications, 1992.

Wright, G.A. "Markan Intercalation: A Study in the Plot of the Gospel." Ph.D. diss., Southern Baptist Theological Seminary, 1985.

# ⇥ Modern Authors Index ⇤

# ≈ Ancient Sources Index ≈

# ⊰ Subject Index ⊱

# Series Published by Wilfrid Laurier University Press for the Canadian Corporation for Studies in Religion/Corporation Canadienne des Sciences Religieuses

Series numbers not mentioned are out of print.

## <sup>Series</sup><sub>no.</sub> Editions SR

2 *The Conception of Punishment in Early Indian Literature*
Terence P. Day / 1982 / iv + 328 pp.

4 *Le messianisme de Louis Riel*
Gilles Martel / 1984 / xviii + 483 p.

7 *L'étude des religions dans les écoles : l'expérience américaine, anglaise et canadienne*
Fernand Ouellet / 1985 / xvi + 666 p.

8 *Of God and Maxim Guns: Presbyterianism in Nigeria, 1846-1966*
Geoffrey Johnston / 1988 / iv + 322 pp.

10 *Prometheus Rebound: The Irony of Atheism*
Joseph C. McLelland / 1988 / xvi + 366 pp.

11 *Competition in Religious Life*
Jay Newman / 1989 / viii + 237 pp.

12 *The Huguenots and French Opinion, 1685-1787: The Enlightenment Debate on Toleration*
Geoffrey Adams / 1991 / xiv + 335 pp.

13 *Religion in History: The Word, the Idea, the Reality / La religion dans l'histoire : le mot, l'idée, la réalité*
Edited by/Sous la direction de Michel Despland and/et Gérard Vallée
1992 / x + 252 pp.

14 *Sharing Without Reckoning: Imperfect Right and the Norms of Reciprocity*
Millard Schumaker / 1992 / xiv + 112 pp.

15 *Love and the Soul: Psychological Interpretations of the Eros and Psyche Myth*
James Gollnick / 1992 / viii + 174 pp.

16 *The Promise of Critical Theology: Essays in Honour of Charles Davis*
Edited by Marc P. Lalonde / 1995 / xii + 146 pp.

17 *The Five Aggregates: Understanding Theravāda Psychology and Soteriology*
Mathieu Boisvert / 1995 / xii + 166 pp.

18 *Mysticism and Vocation*
James R. Horne / 1996 / vi + 110 pp.

19 *Memory and Hope: Strands of Canadian Baptist History*
Edited by David T. Priestley / 1996 / viii + 211 pp.

20 *The Concept of Equity in Calvin's Ethics* *
Guenther H. Haas / 1997 / xii + 205 pp.
**\*Available in the United Kingdom and Europe from Paternoster Press.**

21 *The Call of Conscience: French Protestant Responses to the Algerian War, 1954-1962*
Geoffrey Adams / 1998 / xxii + 270 pp.

22 *Clinical Pastoral Supervision and the Theology of Charles Gerkin*
Thomas St. James O'Connor / 1998 / x + 152 pp.

23 *Faith and Fiction: A Theological Critique of the Narrative Strategies of Hugh MacLennan and Morley Callaghan*
Barbara Pell / 1998 / v + 141 pp.

24 *God and the Chip: Religion and the Culture of Technology*
William A. Stahl / 1999 / vi + 186 pp.

# Comparative Ethics Series / Collection d'Éthique Comparée

# Studies in Christianity and Judaism / Études sur le christianisme et le judaïsme

11  *Mishnah and the Social Formation of the Early Rabbinic Guild:*
    *A Socio-Rhetorical Approach*
    Jack N. Lightstone / 2002 / xii + 240 pp.

12  *The Social Setting of the Ministry as Reflected in the Writings of Hermas,*
    *Clement and Ignatius*
    Harry O. Maier / 1991, second impression 2002 / x + 234 pp.

13  *Playing a Jewish Game: Gentile Christian Judaizing in the First and*
    *Second Centuries CE*
    Michele Murray / 2004 / xii + 228 pp.

14  *Religious Rivalries and the Struggle for Success in Sardis and Smyrna*
    Edited by Richard S. Ascough / 2005 / xvi + 360 pp.

15  *Mark's Other Gospel: Rethinking Morton Smith's Controversial Discovery*
    Scott G. Brown / 2005 / xxiv + 336 pp.

## The Study of Religion in Canada / Sciences Religieuses au Canada

Series no.

1  *Religious Studies in Alberta: A State-of-the-Art Review*
   Ronald W. Neufeldt / 1983 / xiv + 145 pp.

2  *Les sciences religieuses au Québec depuis 1972*
   Louis Rousseau et Michel Despland / 1988 / 158 pp.

3  *Religious Studies in Ontario: A State-of-the-Art Review*
   Harold Remus, William Closson James and Daniel Fraikin / 1992 / xviii + 422 pp.

4  *Religious Studies in Manitoba and Saskatchewan: A State-of-the-Art Review*
   John M. Badertscher, Gordon Harland and Roland E. Miller / 1993 / vi + 166 pp.

5  *The Study of Religion in British Columbia: A State-of-the-Art Review*
   Brian J. Fraser / 1995 / x + 127 pp.

6  *Religious Studies in Atlantic Canada: A State-of-the-Art Review*
   Paul W. R. Bowlby with Tom Faulkner / 2001 / xii + 208 pp.

## Studies in Women and Religion / Études sur les femmes et la religion

Series no.

1  *Femmes et religions* *
   Sous la direction de Denise Veillette / 1995 / xviii + 466 p.

2  *The Work of Their Hands: Mennonite Women's Societies in Canada*
   Gloria Neufeld Redekop / 1996 / xvi + 172 pp.

3  *Profiles of Anabaptist Women: Sixteenth-Century Reforming Pioneers*
   Edited by C. Arnold Snyder and Linda A. Huebert Hecht / 1996 / xxii + 438 pp.

4  *Voices and Echoes: Canadian Women's Spirituality*
   Edited by Jo-Anne Elder and Colin O'Connell / 1997 / xxviii + 237 pp.

5  *Obedience, Suspicion and the Gospel of Mark: A Mennonite-Feminist*
   *Exploration of Biblical Authority*
   Lydia Neufeld Harder / 1998 / xiv + 168 pp.

6  *Clothed in Integrity: Weaving Just Cultural Relations and the Garment Industry*
   Barbara Paleczny / 2000 / xxxiv + 352 pp.

7  *Women in God's Army: Gender and Equality in the Early Salvation Army*
   Andrew Mark Eason / 2003 / xiv + 246 pp.

8  *Pour libérer la théologie. Variations autour de la pensée féministe d'Ivone*
   Gebara Pierrette Daviau, dir. / 2002 / 212 pp.

9  *Linking Sexuality & Gender: Naming Violence against Women in The United*
   *Church of Canada*
   Tracy J. Trothen / 2003 / x + 166 pp.

10 *Canadian Methodist Women, 1766–1925: Marys, Marthas, Mothers in Israel*
   Marilyn Färdig Whiteley / 2005 / xii + 312 pp.

**\*Only available from Les Presses de l'Université Laval**

Series
no. **SR Supplements**

9 *Developments in Buddhist Thought: Canadian Contributions to Buddhist Studies*
Edited by Roy C. Amore / 1979 / iv + 196 pp.
11 *Political Theology in the Canadian Context*
Edited by Benjamin G. Smillie / 1982 / xii + 260 pp.
14 *The Moral Mystic*
James R. Horne / 1983 / x + 134 pp.
16 *Studies in the Book of Job*
Edited by Walter E. Aufrecht / 1985 / xii + 76 pp.
17 *Christ and Modernity: Christian Self-Understanding in a Technological Age*
David J. Hawkin / 1985 / x + 181 pp.
19 *Modernity and Religion*
Edited by William Nicholls / 1987 / vi + 191 pp.

**Series discontinued**

Available from:

**Wilfrid Laurier University Press**
Waterloo, Ontario, Canada N2L 3C5
Telephone: (519) 884-0710, ext. 6124
Fax: (519) 725-1399
E-mail: press@wlu.ca
Website: http://www.wlupress.wlu.ca